A "JEWISH MARSHALL PLAN"

THE MODERN JEWISH EXPERIENCE
Deborah Dash Moore and Marsha L. Rozenblit, editors
Paula Hyman, founding coeditor

A "JEWISH MARSHALL PLAN"

The American Jewish Presence in Post-Holocaust France

LAURA HOBSON FAURE

INDIANA UNIVERSITY PRESS

This book is a publication of

Indiana University Press
Office of Scholarly Publishing
Herman B Wells Library 350
1320 East 10th Street
Bloomington, Indiana 47405 USA

iupress.org

© 2022 by Laura Hobson Faure

All rights reserved
No part of this book may be reproduced or utilized in any form or by any means, electronic or mechanical, including photocopying and recording, or by any information storage and retrieval system, without permission in writing from the publisher. The paper used in this publication meets the minimum requirements of the American National Standard for Information Sciences—Permanence of Paper for Printed Library Materials, ANSI Z39.48–1992.

Manufactured in the United States of America
First printing 2022
Cataloging is available from the Library of Congress.
ISBN 978-0-253-05966-6 (hardcover)
ISBN 978-0-253-05968-0 (paperback)
ISBN 978-0-253-05967-3 (ebook)

*To my parents,
Sherry and Jim Hobson*

CONTENTS

List of Images ix

List of Tables xi

Acknowledgments xiii

List of Abbreviations xvii

Introduction 1

1. Before the "Jewish Marshall Plan": Considering the Diaspora 15
2. Jewish Encounters in Liberation France: Chaplains, Soldiers, Survivors 40
3. Emerging from Catastrophe: American and French Jewish Welfare in the Immediate Postwar Period 76
4. Long-Term Reconstruction: The End of French Dependence? 113
5. American Jewish Organizations and the Postwar World: A Political Presence 142
6. "From Charity to Social Work": American Jewish Aid and the Reform of French Social Work 178

Conclusion 212

Notes 223

Bibliography 303

Index 335

IMAGES

FIGURE 1.1. Nina and Jules (Dika) Jefroykin in Spain in 1944 after having crossed the Pyrenees. Mémorial de la Shoah, Collection ARJF.

FIGURE 1.2. Maurice Brener, Mémorial de la Shoah.

FIGURE 2.1. A group of friends, American Jewish GIs and Polish Jewish Women, Place de la République, Paris, circa 1945. The group of friends spoke Yiddish together. The child, René Lichtman (*first row*), was recently reunited with his mother, both had survived the war in hiding. Private collection of René Lichtman.

FIGURE 2.2. The same group of friends posing together in a private studio, circa 1945. Private collection of René Lichtman.

FIGURE 2.3. Army Signal Corps wire chief Hyman Fox, circa 1945. Private collection of Hyman Fox.

FIGURE 2.4. Passover in 1945 in Nancy drew American troops from throughout the region and was held in the local synagogue. Private collection of Hyman Fox.

FIGURE 2.5. Chaplain Isaac Klein (*left*) and his assistant (*right*) with the members of the Reims Religious School, December 1945. Private collection of Denyse Marx.

FIGURE 2.6. Young Denyse Marx and soldiers Harry Stein and David Schoem, Reims, January 13, 1946. The inscription reads, "As a souvenir of our friendship, [hoping] to see you again soon." Private collection of Denyse Marx.

FIGURE 3.1. The employees of the JDC in Lisbon celebrating the end of the war, May 8, 1945. Lolita Goldstein is holding the flag of her new country. Private collection of Lolita Goldstein.

FIGURE 3.2. Contribution to French Jewish welfare by organization, 1946. JDC-I, Laura Margolis Jarblum Archives, uncatalogued, Statistical Report, France, Country Directors Conference, October 1952.

FIGURE 4.1. Laura Margolis (*left*) with Eleanor Roosevelt visiting an OSE children's home (most likely after 1946). OSE collection of the Mémorial de la Shoah.

FIGURE 6.1. Children in an OSE home receiving packages sent by the National Council of Jewish Women in 1946. OSE collection of the Mémorial de la Shoah.

FIGURE 6.2. The Château de la Maye, Versailles, December 1950. Private collection of Jacqueline Houri-Vignon.

FIGURE 6.3. The faculty of the PBS, 1950–1951, including Shirley Hellenbrand (*back row, second from left*). Private collection of Jacqueline Houri-Vignon.

FIGURE 6.4. Freda Goldsmith at the PBS, Versailles, August 1951. Private collection of Jacqueline Houri-Vignon.

FIGURE 6.5. Celebrating Purim at the PBS, April 9, 1951. Private collection of Jacqueline Houri-Vignon.

FIGURE 6.6. Students from the class of 1950–1951 with Shirley Hellenbrand (*second from left*). Private collection of Jacqueline Houri-Vignon.

TABLES

TABLE 1.1. JDC Aid to France, 1933–1939 (in US Dollars of the 1930s)
TABLE 1.2. JDC Funding for France, 1941–1944, by Source and Year (in US Dollars of the 1940s)
TABLE 4.1. JDC Program in France Compared with Global JDC Expenditures and United Jewish Appeal Results, 1944–1948

ACKNOWLEDGMENTS

ONE OF THE JOYS OF writing a book in two languages is being able to say thank you twice. This book represents a fully revised second edition of its French version, which first appeared in 2013. My gratitude and admiration for Professor Nancy L. Green, who directed my PhD at the Ecole des hautes études en sciences sociales in Paris, continue to grow, years after first walking into her office on the Boulevard Raspail. Her intellectual integrity and human qualities have provided me with the best model for becoming an "American in Paris." Her mentorship and friendship have meant so very much.

I would also like to sincerely thank Professors Catherine Collomp, Maud Mandel, Catherine Nicault, Michel Prum, and Isabelle Richet. Their comments on my work have proven extremely helpful. Maud Mandel deserves a special note of thanks for helping me find a place in the Jewish studies community in the United States, as does Catherine Nicault for her generous advice on France. I also would like to thank my former colleagues in American studies at the Université Sorbonne Nouvelle, with whom I worked from 2010–2019, and my current colleagues in the history department at the Université Panthéon-Sorbonne-Paris 1 and the Centre d'histoire sociale for their advice and encouragement. I am especially grateful to Hélène Le Dantec-Lowry for her guidance and kindness.

I am indebted to the individuals, archives, and institutions that made this research possible. Archivists at the American Jewish Joint Distribution Committee Archive in New York and Jerusalem, including Sherry Hyman, Shelley Helfand, Misha Mistel, Sara Kadosh, and Linda Levi, as well as Gunnar Berg and his colleagues at the YIVO Institute for Jewish Research provided excellent advice and much appreciated enthusiasm. The American Jewish Historical

Society and the Dorot Collection at the New York Public Library also deserve thanks, as do Kevin Proffitt and Ina Remus at the American Jewish Archive. Access to the interviews from the Oral History Division of the Avram Harman Institute at the Hebrew University in Jerusalem has greatly enriched this book. Thank you to the generous researchers who shared their work, allowing future generations to study those who are no longer able to provide testimony. My research also greatly benefitted from the historical knowledge and archival skills of Pierre Boichu at the Departmental Archives of Seine Saint-Denis, as well as the archivists at the Archives Nationales and the Préfecture de Police de Paris. I especially thank Ariel Sion, Karen Taieb, and Lior Lalieu-Smadja at the Mémorial de la Shoah (CDJC) and their staff for their help and support over the years. Katy Hazan and Dominique Rotermund at the Oeuvre de secours aux enfants have enriched this project in multiple ways, as have Jean-Claude Kuperminc and his staff at the Alliance israélite universelle. Philippe Landau and Jean-Pierre Lévy at the Consistory archives were also extremely helpful. Laure Politis, Gabriel Vadnaï, and Karen Fredj of the Fondation CASIP-COJASOR have proven to be formidable advocates for Jewish studies in France, not only by making their archives available but also by creating an intellectual forum for scholars working on Jewish welfare. *Merci!* I would also like to thank Steven Feldman at the US Holocaust Memorial Museum for his advice on academic publishing in the United States. And thank you to Ted Comet, who provided continual encouragement.

Over fifty individuals extended their trust and hospitality by sharing their experiences of surviving the Holocaust in France and working to help survivors in its aftermath. The oral history interviews I conducted allowed me to develop a more intimate relationship with my subject, helping me rethink my assumptions and engage fully with its human dimension. I would especially like to thank Lolita Goldstein (z"l) and Gaby Wolff Cohen (z"l). Both women opened their homes and spoke frankly about their memories of the period. Their vivacious love of humanity gave me much more than I had initially sought in their presence. A special thank-you also goes out to my dear friend René Lichtman, who lives next-door to my parents. Visits home have always included moments with René, who has shared his experiences as a hidden child outside of Paris and his photo albums that document the complexities of postwar French Jewish life.

Researching Jewish life in France and the United States from a transnational perspective required travel. Support from the French Ministry of Research and New Technologies, the Doctoral School of the Ecole des hautes études en sciences sociales, the Fondation du Judaïsme français, the Rothschild Foundation Hanadiv Europe, and the American Jewish Archives facilitated this research, as did funding from the Centre Alberto Benveniste at the Ecole pratique des hautes études, the Alliance israélite universelle, and the Fondation CASIP-COJASOR. This book has also benefitted from my participation in international conferences, funded in large part by my former research group, the Center for Research on the English-Speaking World at the Université Sorbonne Nouvelle, as well as the Centre d'histoire social des mondes contemporains. My dear friends Nat Bender, Meagan MacDonald, Anjali Malhotra Roye, and Meera Malhotra Marti listened to my adventures in the archives and provided a home away from home on research trips.

This book has greatly benefitted from the comments of my two anonymous readers and the series editors, Deborah Dash Moore and Marsha Rozenblit. I thank them for their rigorous reviews. My gratitude also extends to Dee Mortensen, Ashante Thomas, and the members of the editorial staff at the Indiana University Press for their meticulous work. It has been a pleasure working with them.

This book has also been shaped by conversations with fellow scholars who have given me much appreciated insight, support, and feedback on this book, in particular Yann Scioldo-Zürcher, Veerle Vanden Daelen, Nadia Malinovich, Daniella Doron, Sarah Gensburger, Atina Grossmann, Lisa Moses Leff, Alexandra Garbarini, Constance Pâris de Bollardière, Martin Messika, Nick Underwood, Shaina Hammerman, Erin Corber, and Naomi Davidson. Ellen Hampton deserves a special note of thanks for having encouraged this book from its earliest stages. My sister Jenny Hobson Groot embodies the word *sisterhood*, having offered her concrete help and support at the most crucial moments. While many have helped bring this book to fruition, I alone remain responsible for any errors.

On a personal note, I would like to sincerely thank Madame Afifia Medjahed, who provided my children with loving care while I worked, allowing me to pursue my research with peace of mind. My mother-in-law, Brigitte Meudec-Mouhica, has been a constant support in my life, guiding my (continual) discovery of the French language. The loving, loud, and always late Hobson family, including my three sisters, Lisa, Nicole, and Jenny; my parents, Jim and Sherry; and now my nieces, nephews, and brothers-in-law, spread over three continents, has encouraged me in so many ways and taught me the multiple meanings of "home." It is hard to find the words to express my gratitude to my husband, Jérôme Faure, and our children, Léo and Talia. Their presence in my life has brought me joy, laughter, and needed interruptions. This book has benefitted tremendously from their insight and love.

I dedicate this book to Jim and Sherry Hobson, my parents.

ABBREVIATIONS

ARCHIVES

ACIC	Association consistoriale israélite centrale
ACIP	Association consistoriale israélite de Paris
ADSSD	Archives départementales de Seine Saint Denis
AIU	Alliance israélite universelle
AJA	American Jewish Archives
AJHS	American Jewish Historical Society
AN	Archives nationales
APP	Archives de la Préfecture de police de Paris
CASIP-COJASOR	Fondation CASIP-COJASOR
CDJC	Centre de documentation juive contemporaine Mémorial de la Shoah
JDC-I	American Jewish Joint Distribution Committee Archives, Israel
JDC-NY	American Jewish Joint Distribution Committee Archives, New York
NYPL	New York Public Library
OHD	Oral History Division of the Avram Hartman Institute of Contemporary Jewry, Hebrew University of Jerusalem
OSE	Oeuvre de secours aux enfants, Paris Headquarters
YIVO	YIVO Institute for Jewish Research

ABBREVIATIONS

ORGANIZATIONS

AIU	Universal Israelite Alliance (Alliance israélite universelle)
AJC	American Jewish Committee
AJRC	American Jewish Relief Committee
ANAS	National Association of Social Workers (Association nationale des assistantes sociales)
ARA	American Relief Administration
CANRA	Commission on Jewish Chaplaincy
CAR	Comité d'assistance aux réfugiés
CASIP	Israelite Social Action Fund of Paris (Caisse d'action sociale israélite de Paris)
CBIP	Committee for Israelite Charity of Paris (Comité de bienfaisance israélite de Paris)
CCE	Central Commission for Children (Commission centrale de l'enfance)
CCI	Paris Israelite Center for Information (Centre israélite d'information de Paris)
CCR	Central Committee for the Relief of Jews Suffering through the War
CGD	General Defense Committee (Comité général de défense)
Claims Conference	Conference on Jewish Material Claims against Germany
COJASOR	Jewish Committee for Social Action and Reconstruction (Comité juif d'action sociale et de reconstruction)
Consistory	Central Consistory (Consistoire central)
COSOR	Social Aid Committee for Resistance Organizations (Comité des oeuvres sociales des organisations de résistance)
CRIF	Representative Council of Israelites in France (Conseil représentatif des israélites de France)
CRJTF	Representative Council of Traditional Judaism of France (Conseil représentatif du judaïsme traditionaliste de France)
CUDJF	Committee for the Union and Defense of Jews of France (Comité d'union et de défense des juifs de France)
EIF	The Jewish Scouts of France (Éclaireurs Israélites de France)
FSJF	Federation of Jewish Societies of France (Fédération des sociétés juives de France)

FSJU	Unified Jewish Social Fund (Fonds social juif unifié)
HIAS	Hebrew Sheltering and Immigrant Aid Society
ICA	Jewish Colonization Association
IGCR	Intergovernmental Committee on Refugees
JDC	Joint Distribution Committee
JLC	Jewish Labor Committee
KKL	Jewish National Fund
LICA	International League against Antisemitism (Ligue internationale contre l'antisémitisme)
MPDR	Ministry of Prisoners of War, Deportees and Refugees (Ministère des prisonniers, déportés et réfugiés)
MRAP	Movement against Racism for Friendship among People (Mouvement contre le racisme et pour l'amitié des peuples)
National Committee	National Committee of Assistance to German Refugees Victims of Antisemitism (Comité national français de secours aux réfugiés allemands victimes de l'antisémitisme)
NCJW	National Council of Jewish Women
OPEJ	Program for the Protection of Jewish Children (Oeuvre de protection des enfants juifs)
OSE	Children's Relief Agency (Oeuvre de secours aux enfants)
PBS	Paul Baerwald School
SHAEF	Supreme Headquarters, Allied Expeditionary Forces
SSI	Special Service for Immigrants (Service spécial des immigrants)
SSJ	Social Service for Youth (Service social des jeunes)
UGIF	General Union of Israelites in France (Union générale des israélites de France)
UJA	United Jewish Appeal
UJRE	Union of Jews for Resistance and Mutual Aid (Union des juifs pour la résistance et l'entraide)
UNRRA	United Nations Relief and Rehabilitation Administration
UPA	United Palestine Appeal
USNA	United Service for New Americans
Vaad	Vaad Hatzala
WJC	World Jewish Congress
YMCA	Young Men's Christian Association

A "JEWISH MARSHALL PLAN"

INTRODUCTION

"Whoever says he wasn't afraid during the Occupation, it isn't true, because even the most courageous were afraid. We knew that at any minute you could be . . . we never considered that by the evening, we would still not be arrested. It was everyday, everyday, everyday. It was something we really lived. And the feeling when America stepped foot here, now we could talk about tomorrow, and not only 'at four o'clock, what is going to happen?' It is something that one cannot transmit, it's something that one cannot transmit. One can't, it's like if you wanted to describe [*raconter*] your blood and your bones—there are no words."[1]

ALMOST SIXTY YEARS AFTER THE liberation of France, former Jewish resistance member Gaby Wolff Cohen recalled the Occupation and the significance of the arrival of "America." Wolff was seventeen years old when she and her family were evacuated from their native Alsace. She finished high school in Limoges and then enrolled at the university to study medicine. By then, however, Vichy's antisemitic legislation had established a *numerus clausus*, limiting the number of Jewish students in higher education. Wolff's dream of becoming a doctor would be deferred, indefinitely. In the meantime, she decided to follow in the footsteps of other young women she knew from the Jewish Scouts of France, who were assisting foreign Jews. She trained to become a kindergarten teacher and began working in the children's homes of the Jewish public health organization Children's Relief Agency (Oeuvre de secours aux enfants, OSE). When Nazi-Vichy deportation measures made the homes too dangerous, Wolff and her colleagues sought out hiding places for the children in non-Jewish settings, coached them on their new identities, and led them to safety. Wolff acted out of solidarity with foreign Jews, realizing only later that she was also a target. Almost eighty thousand Jews were deported from France to Nazi death camps or executed on French soil during World War II.[2] The liberation ended four years of persecution, fear, and death. But for Gaby Wolff Cohen and other French Jews, there was much more to the "America that stepped foot" in France than one might expect.

American participation in France's liberation represents an important part of the postwar story. What is less known is that American Jewish individuals and organizations also mobilized in the name of reconstructing European Jewish life after the Holocaust. For Wolff and other Jews, the American Jewish presence in France, especially the main American Jewish philanthropic organization, the American Jewish Joint Distribution Committee (JDC, Joint), shaped postwar lives. Wolff explained: "[American Jews] were protective papas and mamas. With them here, we were safe. [. . .] In this period that was really quite agitated, it gave you meaning, a solid basis somewhere. Nothing could happen now. . . . As people said, 'Where is the Joint?' Whenever there was the slightest problem, they said 'Where is the Joint?' So, even as a joke, to get a laugh, when something terrible happened 'Oh, he spilled all the jam!' we used to say 'Where is the Joint?' by which we meant it could repair anything."[3]

Orchestrating a philanthropic endeavor of unprecedented magnitude, Jewish Americans sent over $194 million to Europe from 1945 to 1948.[4] France, for distinct reasons, took on a privileged place in their aid efforts. When compared to Belgium or the Netherlands, France had a considerably higher survival rate, making it the largest Jewish population in Western Continental Europe with roughly between one hundred eighty and two hundred thousand individuals.[5] France's ports provided access to the Americas and Palestine, turning the country into an important crossroads for postwar Jewish migrations. As a result of such migrations, France was one of the few places in Europe to recover its prewar Jewish demographics, albeit with an entirely different population.[6] Finally, while liberation marked the beginning of a painful period in which Jews emerged from hiding and waited, often in vain, for the return of loved ones, most did not suffer in isolation. A diverse network of Jewish welfare organizations survived the war, helping individuals recover their lives and communities. These organizations provided an infrastructure into which American Jewish aid could be infused. While observers of Jewish life initially focused on the "surviving remnant" in Displaced Persons camps, over time, as a result of these demographic and structural factors, American Jews came to see France as one of the only hopes for reviving European Jewish life. Paris therefore became a hub for American Jewish reconstruction work.[7]

In the decade following World War II, American Jewish organizations gave over $27 million to French Jews.[8] This little-known Franco-American encounter, retroactively labeled a "Jewish Marshall Plan," sheds new light on the American presence in postwar France. While there are certainly parallels between American Jewish initiatives and US foreign policy, American Jewish programs actually predated the Economic Cooperation Act of 1948 by four years. Likewise, there was only a tangential link between the United States' Marshall Plan and private American Jewish aid.[9] I am thus using the term "Jewish Marshall Plan" here as an analogy to describe the extensive aid program established by American Jews to assist their European brethren in the aftermath of the Holocaust. While solidary indisputably grounded the "Jewish Marshall Plan," it also incited—like the larger Marshall Plan—a lively debate in France, especially when American Jewish organizations sought to reform French Jewish life according to an American model. To my knowledge, the term was not used by individuals during the period, with one exception: in 1949, French Jewish leaders suggested to an American Jewish organization, not without some chutzpah, that they needed a "Jewish Marshall Plan!"[10] Many years later, in the late 1990s, JDC leader Ralph Goldman used the analogy to describe the American Jewish initiative to reconstruct European Jewish life after the Holocaust.[11]

Opening a debate on the influence of American Jews on contemporary French Jewish life, I argue that the reconstruction of French Jewish life can only be fully understood in a transnational perspective. Not only did American Jewish organizations bring needed funds but they imported structures and methods from the United States that have left a lasting mark. The reconstruction of French Jewish life engaged French and American Jews in interactions that were as complex as they were intense. Far from passive aid recipients, French Jews fought to reconstruct after the Holocaust according to their own vision(s), often resisting, but sometimes embracing, American models. By examining the actions of American Jewish members of the US Armed Forces and American Jewish organizations abroad, including the JDC, the American Jewish Committee, and the National Council of Jewish Women, among others, this book explores how these American Jews adapted their philanthropy to the concrete challenges of post-Holocaust Europe, the Cold War, and the establishment of the State of Israel.

The "Jewish Marshall Plan" was very much a product of postwar American Jewish life. As American Jews moved in great numbers from cities to suburbs, they faced a moment of uncertainty. Fears of domestic antisemitism, the challenge of integrating mixed suburban neighborhoods, and new access to elite institutions fueled anxiety and debate on the Jewish future.[12] In this moment of transition, American Jews also had to come to terms with genocide, a concept that emerged during this period to describe the Nazi attempt to exterminate the Jews.[13] Many of the organizations in this book had been active in the fight against Nazism since 1933, yet few were prepared for the magnitude of destruction they witnessed on the ground or in reports. While American Jews had played an increasing role in the Jewish diaspora since World War I, the Holocaust shifted the center of the Jewish world from Europe to the United States.[14] As they adjusted to this new leadership position, American Jewish individuals and organizations seized the opportunity to help European Jews. Coming to France not only allowed them to respond to the Holocaust but also provided them an opportunity to hone their institutional identities and assert their place in both the American Jewish community and the postwar world.

AMERICAN JEWISH PHILANTHROPY IN POSTWAR FRANCE: LINKING TWO POLES OF THE DIASPORA

Historian Nancy Green has pointed out that philanthropy creates "intersection points," placing the giver and the receiver in a "symbiotic relationship."[15] Philanthropy represents a collective activity that links individuals (both the needy and the philanthropists) to the group. These observations are particularly appropriate for Jewish philanthropy in both the United States and Europe, which has had to respond to internally and externally imposed requirements on Jews to care for their own—even after Jewish political emancipation.[16] Responding collectively to this requirement, and more importantly, deciding as a group who should be helped and how, has served as a natural forum for larger discussions on group solidarity, identity, and survival. The collective nature of philanthropic action proves as interesting as the actual assistance provided.

The case of the American Jewish presence in postwar France serves as a particularly poignant example of how philanthropy bridges populations by creating a symbiotic relationship that benefits beneficiary and benefactor alike. Helping the surviving Jews of Europe was a means for American Jews, the majority of whom of Eastern and Central European descent, of expressing their solidarity, anxiety, and guilt over the fate of their families in Europe after the Holocaust. Participating in philanthropic activities also helped them affirm their own Jewish identities in this moment of transition, engaging in what one scholar called the "civil religion of American Jews."[17] The relationship binding American Jews to those in France was at times purely symbolic; most American Jews never actually met the Jews they assisted. They gave funds to the United Jewish Appeal, their central fundraising organization, to support *European* Jewish reconstruction, not French Jewish life. During the period under study, however, the relationship between the givers and receivers became less symbolic and more tangible. American Jewish chaplains and GIs in the US Armed Forces sought out Jewish survivors as they liberated France, becoming in many cases deeply involved in the communities they helped rebuild. Others, especially American Jewish women, organized clothing and food drives, sent packages, and corresponded with Jewish children.[18] Some philanthropists even traveled to France to better understand the needs of those they were helping.[19] These grassroots efforts remain difficult to quantify yet coexisted with a larger organizational response. While this book seeks to explore the actions of Jewish individuals and organizations, my primary focus is on the work of the latter. As such, my observations on American and French Jews, based on the records of Jewish organizations, as well as oral histories I conducted with the former employees of the latter, represent only a partial view. As more than one scholar has pointed out, one should not assume that Jewish organizations were the mirror of the populations they claimed to represent.[20]

The philanthropic relationship linking French and American Jews may have been symbiotic, but it was not equal. The "Jewish Marshall Plan" took place during a period of intense American expansionism. Like other Americans who sought to influence French society and foreign policy through the Marshall Plan,[21] American Jews used their philanthropy as an incentive for change. Under American Jewish auspices, philanthropy and social work became conduits for the diffusion of American savoir faire and practices that at times created tensions with the French. However, unlike the larger Marshall Plan, which was a response to the Cold War, the American Jewish initiative emerged in the aftermath of the Holocaust, a crisis unprecedented in the modern Jewish experience. The "Jewish Marshall Plan" was thus in large part improvised on the ground. Multifaceted, it reflected the diversity of American Jewish life.

A DIVERSE MOBILIZATION

With its focus on Jewish welfare, this book proposes a bottom-up understanding of Americanization in postwar Europe, highlighting an area of activity that has received little scholarly attention: the social sector.[22] American Jewish organizations, the JDC in particular, served as "vectors" in this process, importing welfare structures and practices from the United States.

Established in the United States at the outbreak of World War I to aid Jews in Eastern Europe and the Middle East, the Joint Distribution Committee quickly became the official overseas representative of American Jews.[23] In the interwar period, the JDC was especially active in the Soviet Union and Poland and only played a minor role in France until 1933. After this date, the JDC moved its European headquarters from Berlin to Paris, where it helped French Jews confront the Central European refugee crisis. When Nazi Germany invaded France in May 1940, the JDC moved its offices from Paris to the Unoccupied Zone, where it helped coordinate aid in the French internment camps. After Vichy and the United States broke off their diplomatic ties in November 1942, two French citizens represented the JDC. With the help of individuals in Switzerland, they smuggled JDC funds into France, allowing the organization to finance an estimated 60 percent of the French Jewish resistance.[24]

Paris was liberated in late August 1944. By December, American JDC representatives had returned to Paris and had begun responding to the needs of Jewish children and refugees by funding a network of Jewish welfare organizations of diverse ideological affiliations, including those of Jewish Communists. The JDC did not simply write a check to the organizations it assisted. Influenced by American principles of philanthropy and self-help, the JDC aid philosophy stressed the importance of building autonomous, self-sufficient Jewish communities.[25] In order to achieve this goal, it played a hands-on role in the French Jewish organizations it subsidized. For the JDC, training local Jews was as important as assisting them financially.

After the war, the JDC reestablished offices throughout Europe. It transferred its European headquarters from Lisbon to Paris. This indirectly magnified France in the JDC program, providing French Jewish leaders with greater access to JDC officials at its European headquarters. In 1945 alone, the JDC estimated it aided fifty thousand individuals in France, which represented between 25 and 28 percent of the Jewish population at the time.[26] According to its own estimates, the JDC supported 72 percent of the expenses of French Jewish welfare organizations in 1946, 54.5 percent of these costs in 1949, and still 40 percent in 1952.[27] One can therefore comprehend the importance of this organization among French Jews and its central place in this study.

However, the JDC was not the only American Jewish organization to establish a program in postwar France. The Hebrew Sheltering and Immigrant Aid Society (HIAS) was also active in France in the interwar and war years under the name HICEM. This organization helped Jews emigrate from Europe. In the postwar period, HIAS reestablished offices throughout France but a lack of resources and immigration possibilities limited its efforts. The American Jewish Committee, founded to protect Jews' civil rights, established a Paris office in 1947, where it sought to develop a French counterpart to monitor antisemitism.

It actively tried (and failed) to convince French Jews of the dangers of communism. In the same period, the National Council of Jewish Women established a home for "unattached" Jewish women in Paris and organized a scholarship program for European Jewish women to study welfare-related subjects in American universities. Other American Jewish organizations, such as the Jewish Labor Committee and the orthodox Vaad Hatzala, worked closely through their ideological partners in France, directing aid to the members of their respective groups. Still other organizations, such as the World Jewish Congress, were not technically American, yet they are considered here because the majority of their funds, as well as the drive behind their French programs, came from the United States.[28]

This book seeks to understand the activities of these American Jewish organizations in their larger political and social contexts. At times, they found themselves in conflict in France. Their goals and missions overlapped and resources were limited. Tensions existed, mirroring divisions within American Jewish life. Helping the Jews of France was a means for these American Jewish organizations to secure their place within what political scientist Daniel Elazar has called "the organizational dynamics of American Jewry."[29]

RECEIVING AMERICAN JEWISH AID: FRENCH JEWISH EXPECTATIONS

The philanthropic endeavor that brought the American Jewish presence to France was not a one-sided affair. I argue in this book that the scope and nature of the American aid was determined in large part by its French reception. French Jews were more than aware of the fact that the reconstruction of French Jewish life was largely being financed by American Jews. On one hand, they expected, and even demanded, this aid, as seen in a November 1944 article from the Jewish Communist newspaper *La presse nouvelle* entitled "A Message to Our Brothers from the United States," which clearly stated: "The Jews of France, the first large liberated community of Europe, expect efficient aid from their brothers from the United States that will allow them to rise up from their ruins."[30] Yet on the other hand, French Jews grappled with how to position themselves with regard to this assistance. Some French Jews considered American aid as an exchange from which both parties benefited. Reflecting upon American Jewish assistance in this manner helped those who were diminished by the war regain a sense of dignity.

Yet in general, American Jewish organizations and individuals were less concerned about restoring French Jews' sense of dignity than they were about efficiently meeting their welfare needs. American Jewish organizations, especially the JDC, expected teamwork and compliance from French Jews. As solidarity flowed from the United States, French Jews struggled with a conflicting sense of gratitude and resentment as they met the obligations their benefactors imposed on them.

Gaby Wolff Cohen's postwar path provides a singular example of how the "Jewish Marshall Plan" shaped French Jewish lives. After risking her life to save others during the Occupation, Wolff continued to care for Jewish children living in OSE homes subsidized by the JDC after World War II. In 1947, she received a scholarship from the National Council of Jewish Women to study child development at the University of California, Berkeley. After her return to France in 1949, she worked for the JDC, supervising French Jewish childcare organizations. Several years later, she transferred to the United Jewish Social Fund (Fonds social juif unifié, FSJU), a newly created French Jewish fundraising apparatus modeled directly from the United Jewish Appeal in the United States. American Jewish organizations influenced each step of Wolff Cohen's postwar career. As seen from her example, the American Jewish presence also helped feminize French Jewish welfare by allowing women new leadership roles in communal organizations.

If most French Jews did not benefit from Wolff Cohen's level of contact with American Jewish organizations and individuals, a considerable number received American Jewish aid indirectly, either by seeking help from a subsidized Jewish welfare organization or by benefitting from one of the American-funded, interest-free loans that helped some 23,500 Jewish individuals rebuild their lives.[31] American Jewish members of the US military played an even larger role than American Jewish organizations in certain areas of France. In Reims, for example, a sustained military presence helped spark the renewal of the small Jewish community and bring Jews from all walks of life to the synagogue—and American Jewish soldiers into French Jewish homes.

THE HISTORIOGRAPHY OF THE AMERICAN JEWISH PRESENCE IN POSTWAR FRANCE

This book represents a fully revised and expanded edition of its French version, first published in 2013.[32] Until its publication, American Jews and their organizations had gone unnoticed in studies on the American presence in France.[33] Furthermore, the case of France was neglected for many years in historical studies of European Jews after the Holocaust, which understandably focused on the "surviving remnant" in Displaced Persons camps in Germany, Austria, and Italy. More recent contributions to the historiography have sought to correct this by focusing on the reintegration of European Jews into their countries of origin.[34]

The period immediately following the Holocaust remained in the shadows of the historiography of Jews in France for many years due to the fact historians understandably engaged in the study of the Jewish population under Nazi occupation and the massive arrival of North African Jews as the French colonial empire was dismantled, which brought an estimated two hundred and twenty thousand Jews to France.[35] The magnitude of the North African Jewish migration caused historians, in the words of Maud Mandel, to "oversimplify the picture,"[36] creating the perception that it was the North African immigration that rekindled the rebirth of French Jewish life after the Holocaust. This book contributes to a growing body of literature showing the reconstruction process was well underway, even "completed" by the early 1960s.

Because the Holocaust and decolonization have marked French Jewish life so profoundly, historical analysis of the immediate postwar period emerged only in the 1990s.[37] In 1996, Bernard Wasserstein published *Vanishing Diaspora, The Jews in Europe since 1945*, in which he contended that Jewish life in Europe was disappearing as a result of the Holocaust, emigration, disaffiliation, and weak demographic growth.[38] Wasserstein opened a debate on the nature of postwar European Jewish societies that fueled new scholarship on France.[39] The growing historiography on the postwar period, most notably Maud Mandel's *In the Aftermath of Genocide: Armenians and Jews in Twentieth Century France* (2003), has analyzed the complex relationship between Jews and the French state. Other important contributions have explored Jewish children, gender, Holocaust memory, and postwar communal institutions.[40] Katy Hazan's, and more recently Daniella Doron's, work on children demonstrates the symbolic function they played in the reconstruction process.[41] A new generation of French scholarship on the postwar period, which I have incorporated in this edition, furthers the understanding of how Jews in France rebuilt their lives and communities.[42] This burgeoning historiography demonstrates the depth of French losses during the Holocaust yet also the vitality of French Jewish life in the years following the war.

Nonetheless, the historiography has painted a false impression that reconstruction was a strictly French affair, involving French Jews, their communal institutions, and the Republic. This book represents the first full-length study on the role of American Jews in the reconstruction of French Jewish life after the Holocaust.[43] It explores how American and French Jews worked together. What were their sources of conflict? What role(s) did national and Jewish identity play for the individuals who sought to rebuild French Jewish life? By studying the actions of the US military and American Jewish organizations in their political and social contexts, I hope to break with the institutional history approach that has characterized part of the historiography. As a social history of French Jewish welfare, a field that expanded and took on new meaning in the aftermath of the Holocaust, this book also explores a significant shift in French Jewish identity.[44]

Scholars have contemplated the extent to which the Holocaust caused French Jews to rethink their identities. In the interwar period, France boasted vibrant and diverse Jewish communities, in which Jews of French and foreign descent debated multiple and divergent definitions of Jewishness in religious, cultural, political, and social contexts. As scholars have pointed out, interwar French Jewish life resisted most attempts at coordination, even if some collective efforts to assist refugees were successful after 1938.[45] While there was never only one way of conceiving of Jewish identity in France, the native French Jewish establishment officially endorsed a religious definition of Jewishness during the nineteenth century and the decades leading up to the war. Furthermore, since Jews in France disagreed on most issues, Jewish organizations coexisted without necessarily attempting to unite in common structures. The Occupation provoked a major upheaval and uprooted individual Jews from their homes, subjecting them to internment, arrest, and deportation. In its drastic reconfiguration of French Jewish life, the Holocaust led to new forms of organizing—both involuntary and voluntary—that fostered a link between the diverse Jewish groups. In November 1941, Nazis, with significant help from Vichy authorities, compelled French Jews to establish the General Union of Israelites in France (Union générale des israélites de France, UGIF). As a *Judenrat*, it placed almost all cultural and social Jewish organizations under a common umbrella, forcing them to participate in the persecution process.[46] Later in the war, in the winter of 1943 and early 1944, Jews clandestinely established an organization to represent them politically, assembling the divergent elements of French Jewish life (religious, cultural, and political groups led by French and foreign Jews) that had previously refused to associate. As scholars have pointed out, the Representative Council of Israelites in France (Conseil représentatif des israélites de France, CRIF) represented a significant break with the strictly religious definition of Jewishness that had dominated before the war.[47]

In this book I often refer to "French Jews" in opposition to "American Jews" for reasons of linguistic simplicity while recognizing that it would be more accurate to discuss "Jews in France," a term that acknowledges the strong presence of foreign Jews.[48] Nonetheless, this book demonstrates the continuing geographic, political, and ideological diversity within French Jewish life in the postwar period yet also shows that the trend of working together continued after the Holocaust, deepening the communal bond that linked Jews and their organizations. Even during a period rife with conflict, Jews in France proved more willing to endorse a capacious definition of Jewishness that included religious and nonreligious forms of identification and continued to invest in structures designed to centralize and unify French Jewish life. As I will show in these pages, American Jewish organizations, especially the JDC, proved determinant to these shifts.

RECONSTRUCTING THE AMERICAN JEWISH PRESENCE

This book's transnational approach deepens current understandings of French and American Jewish life in the postwar period. Scholars concur that there was indeed a "transnational turn" beginning in the early 1990s in the social sciences but not all agree about its relevance to the field of Jewish history.[49] One could argue that the concept of transnationalism had been there all along. Isn't the field of Jewish studies, the study of an "extraterritorial group," in essence, transnational? Others have distinctly shown how transnational approaches can renew a body of scholarship that has been heavily invested in integrating Jews into their respective national histories.[50] Here a transnational approach helps contribute to debates on the "myth of silence"[51] of American Jews regarding the Holocaust by documenting their concrete response to the catastrophe. Extending the gaze across borders also allows new perspectives on the place of Jews in the French republic. French Jews' reintegration into the nation-state after the Holocaust was facilitated and, one could posit, even mediated by American Jewish organizations. Somewhat paradoxically, however, this moment of expansion of the French welfare state saw a concomitant explosion of the private Jewish welfare sector. The specific Jewish experience during the Occupation—often overlooked by the French state in the postwar period—created a pressing need for American aid and an equally strong desire among Jews to care for their own, leading to a parallel welfare system.

As transnational as this moment may have been, national contexts remain relevant. The American Jewish presence in France after World War II also tells the story of two branches of the Jewish diaspora, each imbedded in its distinct national history. If a comparative approach to American and French Jewish life undergirds this analysis, my primary goal is to understand what happened when American Jews and French Jews encountered each other in France. The *histoire croisée* method, theorized by Michael Werner and Bénédicte Zimmermann, provides a particularly useful approach due to its emphasis on the dynamic nature of encounters between groups and an awareness of the unequal power relations that can characterize interactions.[52] American Jews brought a distinct vision and savoir-faire to France that was specific to their experience as Jews, Americans, and welfare professionals. Their sense of identity was perhaps sharpened when they encountered France and its Jews. French Jews received, rejected, and/or adapted what their American helpers sought to teach them according to their own experiences as Jews, members of French society, victims of the Holocaust, and/or members of the resistance. With time, and as a result of contact with the other, all of the actors changed, yet French Jews were arguably more affected by the encounter than American Jews.

The sources I have used to reconstruct the American Jewish presence in France reflect the *histoire croisée* approach. I have studied the archives of both American and French organizations, not only for their descriptions of postwar France but to identify French perceptions of the American presence. This approach seeks to deconstruct the JDC archives, which until now have served as an important source for historians working on postwar France. Here, the source becomes an object of study in itself, revealing the American vision of French Jewish life, which has been used by historians to write the narrative of French Jewish renewal. Furthermore, I conducted over fifty oral history interviews with French and American individuals who worked in or with American Jewish organizations.[53] These sources each help untangle the American Jewish presence in its complexity through a variety of perspectives.

Finally a note on periodization: While the liberation of France provided a natural starting point, deciding on an endpoint proved more difficult. I have chosen to end this study in 1954 for several reasons. Exploring the first decade after the war allowed me to closely follow the contours of reconstruction, as emergency aid in the immediate postwar period gave way to long-term planning. This decade also included the establishment of Israel. By studying the years before and after this event, it was possible to discern the shifts that occurred in American and French Jewish life as Jews made the transition from a "stateless Diaspora" to a "state-based Diaspora."[54] Likewise, this period marked the beginning of the Cold War, which forced American and French Jewish organizations to reaffirm their ideological positions. Another important reason for ending this study in 1954 is linked to the increasing migrations of North African Jews to France as a result of the decolonization of the French Empire. These migrations drastically transformed French Jewish communal dynamics and opened a new chapter in French Jewish life that deserves its own place in the historiography. Finally, the exclusive relationship that bound American and French Jews in the aftermath of the Holocaust technically ended in 1954. This was the year that French Jews began receiving settlement funds from the Federal Republic of Germany as part of the Conference on Jewish Material Claims against Germany.[55] Claims Conference funding began a new chapter in postwar reconstruction and changed the dynamic between American and French Jewish organizations. While American Jewish organizations continued to support French Jewish life after this date and the JDC exercised a large influence over how Claims Conference funds were distributed in France, American Jews were no longer the primary benefactors of French Jewish welfare.[56] Furthermore, as the administrator of part of the Claims Conference funds, the JDC was accountable to the Claims Conference board, which included four French representatives.[57] Thus the 1944–1954 period was one in which American Jews shared a privileged relationship with French Jews.

The "Jewish Marshall Plan" is a Jewish story in the context of a global one about the rise of American interventionism, both humanitarian and otherwise. It occurred in a moment of intense American Empire building, a period characterized by a new American hegemony in the circulation of knowledge and cultural transfers. Building on experiences abroad during the First and Second World Wars (chap. 1), American Jews, like other Americans who sought to influence French society and foreign policy, used philanthropy as a means of inciting reform. American Jewish members of the military, eager to assist Jewish survivors, asserted their own conceptualizations of Jewish life and shaped the contours of French Jewish reconstruction in the immediate aftermath of the Holocaust (chap. 2). American Jewish organizations soon replaced these individual efforts. American JDC representatives returned to France to rebuild European Jewish life by distributing JDC aid widely. Not all American Jews felt the JDC would represent their voices, a fact that prompted a diverse mobilization (chap. 3). Under American Jewish auspices, philanthropy and social work became vectors disseminating American know-how and practices (chaps. 4 and 6). Yet unlike a great deal of the historiography on Americanization, this book does not only address American Jewish aid in France but is equally interested in French responses. The structure of French Jewish life still bears the mark of this encounter (chaps. 4 and 6). If American policies led to lasting change, it was the result of long-term, complex negotiations between the representatives of American Jewish organizations and French Jewish leadership. Such negotiations were by nature political and influenced by the communal dynamics in the United States and also the larger Cold War period (chap. 5).

The study of the "Jewish Marshall Plan" in France thus helps better comprehend the shifts that occurred within the Jewish world in the aftermath of the Holocaust—and also more generally as the United States moved into a position of global dominance—contributing not only to our knowledge of French and American Jewish life but also to the field of transnational history.

ONE

BEFORE THE "JEWISH MARSHALL PLAN"

Considering the Diaspora

IN NOVEMBER 1944, SHORTLY AFTER the liberation of Paris, a group of delegates from the newly formed Representative Council of Israelites in France (Conseil représentatif des israélites de France, CRIF) traveled to New York to meet with American Jewish leaders. Over several meetings with the Joint Distribution Committee (JDC), the main overseas American Jewish philanthropic organization, the French leaders discussed what had happened during Nazi occupation and how to begin the task of reconstructing French Jewish life. Rabbi Jacob Kaplan, one of the French delegates, proved surprisingly optimistic. Instead of emphasizing their hardships, Kaplan insisted that French Jews had been "self-supporting before the war and proud to respond to all appeals that were addressed to [them]. The funds that JDC sent to France before the war were used for the refugees from Germany." Perhaps in an attempt to reassure the JDC, he stated, "The French Jews will do their best to pay their debts to JDC either directly or by sending aid to the needy of other countries."[1]

Kaplan's statement shows that at the war's end, some French Jews still presented themselves as philanthropists. The disconnect between this image and the reality of French Jewish life after the Holocaust, which forced French leaders to continually ask for funding from American Jews, is a fitting place to begin exploring the encounter between American and French Jews after the Second World War. Why would French Jews, diminished in number and weakened by over four years of Vichy and Nazi persecution, present themselves as capable of self-sufficiency or sending funds to other Jewish communities in need? Why were they even having this conversation with American Jewish leaders? After all, French Jews could have stayed home in Paris, turning to the newly re-established republican government to meet their needs. Likewise, American Jews could have focused exclusively on their domestic situation during this time of uncertainty.

The "Jewish Marshall Plan" was an encounter between French and American Jews and their organizations in the aftermath of World War II, shaped by longstanding philanthropic traditions. Indeed, French and American Jews were not meeting for the first time in 1944. Their first real encounter actually occurred in the interwar period as a result of the Central European Jewish refugee crisis. If French Jews could boast of a centuries-long tradition of Jewish philanthropy that had served as a model for American Jews, the refugee crisis, followed by the outbreak of World War II, forced French Jews into a new position of dependence. With the goal of analyzing the shared experiences that undergirded their postwar encounter, this chapter will argue that in spite of French Jews' overwhelming dependence on American Jewish aid, they never fully relinquished their self-image as equal partners to American Jews. Considering Jewish philanthropy in France and the United States in historical and comparative perspective provides important clues to understanding how each group perceived its position within the Jewish diaspora in the aftermath of the Holocaust. Wartime experiences also informed the postwar encounter between American and French Jews and prove essential to understanding their complex relationship as they faced reconstruction.

Before focusing on the intersections and connections of these two groups, it is important to define my usage of the term *diaspora*. Scholars have criticized the notion as all-encompassing and vague,[2] yet precisely for these reasons, actors in my study mobilized the term to refer to Jews living in other countries—and after 1948, outside the State of Israel—and as an abstract concept to speak of Jews collectively. The notion of the diaspora as both a physical space, divided into branches, and as an abstract concept to describe the Jewish world is useful here, especially since it took on real and tangible manifestations for those in this study.

FRENCH AND AMERICAN JEWS: PARTNERS IN THE DIASPORA?

On a certain level, the French and American branches of the Jewish diaspora share important commonalities. From 1654, the date of the first Jewish settlement in the North American colonies, and 1791, the date of French Jews' emancipation, Jews in the United States and France have benefited from the promise of full civil rights—albeit compromised during certain periods—which led to citizenship in the modern nation-state. Like all postemancipatory Jewish societies, Jews in these countries continually sought to prove allegiance to the state while remaining Jewish, with varying outcomes. Furthermore, both groups lived in countries that conceived of themselves as civic, as opposed to ethnic, nations. Beyond these fundamental similarities, both France and the United States have acted as traditional reception countries for multiple waves of immigrants. Their Jewish populations have been renewed through immigration from Central and Eastern Europe, the Middle East, and in the case of France, North Africa throughout the nineteenth and twentieth centuries. Immigration not only increased the number of Jews in France and the United States but also led to confrontations between established Jewish leadership and newcomers, provoking a continual redefinition of communities and institutions.[3] Finally, as two subsets of the Jewish diaspora that obtained civil rights at home, Jews in France and the United States grew concerned with the fate of Jews living in other nations. Both groups designed a philanthropic infrastructure to address the needs of less privileged Jews and saw themselves, with some variation, as benefactors.

Though the Jewish populations of France and the United States considered themselves privileged members of the Jewish diaspora, looking closer reveals some important differences. As more than one scholar has observed, American Jews hold the unique status of the only Jewish community born into emancipation.[4] In other words, they were not burdened by the legacy of a separate regime for Jews that conditioned Jewish life in pre-emancipatory Europe. American Jews have hence operated with a symbolic clean slate; the baggage of long-term discrimination was perhaps imported to this country by its Jewish immigrants but could not be wholly attributed to the American experience. This contrasts deeply with the extensive debates, discussions, and legislation that resulted in the emancipation of the Jews of France and, more importantly, with the preceding centuries of discrimination during which the Jewish condition was dependent on the whims of local power. Pre-emancipatory discrimination—or lack thereof—conditioned the relationship of this minority group to the state and influenced public discussions and private interpretations of the status of Jews in modern society.

The structure of religious life also reflects important differences: the centralization of religious authority in France contrasts with its absence in the United States. In France, for example, the Central Consistory was established in 1808 to act as liaison between the state and French Jews in order to "regenerate" and centralize French Jewish life. This central structure and local Consistories ceased to exist as official public institutions after 1905, but they continued as voluntary associations, and maintained their role, at least symbolically, as representatives of French Jews. In contrast, no such organizations were established in the United States. As such, decisions associated with Jewish life were made at the local level, and regional differences became the norm.[5]

Immigration also created several key demographic differences in French and American Jewish societies. If both countries served as poles of reception, the United States was certainly considered the *goldene medine* (the golden country) by the masses of Eastern European Jews that fled political instability and antisemitic violence from 1881 through 1924.[6] France remained more of a selective choice until the American immigration restrictions of 1921 and 1924, as demonstrated by the occupational statistics of Jewish immigrants.[7] Immigration from Eastern Europe transformed Jewish demography in both places. However, while the United States received almost two million Jewish immigrants from 1881 to 1914, only an estimated thirty-five to forty thousand arrived in France during this period.[8] France, which counted more Jews than the United States until the mid-nineteenth century, lost a considerable part of its Jewish population as a result of the German annexation of Alsace-Lorraine in 1871. The return of these territories to France in the aftermath of World War I, coupled with interwar migrations primarily from Eastern Europe and the Central European refugee crisis, caused the Jewish population of France to grow to an estimated three hundred thirty thousand individuals. Deportations and flight during World War II tragically reduced the Jewish population of France to between one hundred eighty and two hundred thousand Jewish individuals, whereas in 1945, the United States' population included 4.8 million Jews.[9]

After the Holocaust, as members of the world's largest Jewish community, American Jews considered themselves leaders of the Jewish diaspora and therefore responsible for reconstructing European Jewish life. Their post-Holocaust philanthropy originated, however, with World War I. Following the example set by French Jews in the nineteenth century, it was at this time that American Jews developed an infrastructure to help Jews abroad.

AMERICAN JEWS AND THE FIRST WORLD WAR: TURNING OUTWARD

The outbreak of World War I marked a new era in American Jewish communal life as the focus shifted from meeting the domestic welfare needs of Eastern European immigrants to addressing the international crises brought about by the war. Until this period, American Jews saw themselves and were seen as the younger sibling of European Jewish communities. French Jews had been setting an example of international philanthropy since 1860 with the creation of the Alliance israélite universelle (Universal Israelite Alliance, AIU, Alliance). Founded in the aftermath of the 1858 Mortara Affair, the Catholic baptism and removal of a young Jewish boy from his family,[10] the Alliance conceptualized its work in political, as opposed to philanthropic, terms.[11] Its leadership sought to construct political influence through the creation of an international network of schools that fostered an identification with France through its language and culture.[12] An enthusiastic response from Jews outside of France quickly surpassed French participation levels, yet the leadership and the direction of the organization remained firmly seated in the French civilizing mission. The AIU emphasized emancipation through regeneration, a concept influenced by the Haskalah movement and enlightenment thinking that sought to educate Jews and further their integration into their surrounding societies. In order to regenerate nonemancipated Jews, the Alliance developed a network of schools throughout the Ottoman Empire and North Africa. By the outbreak of the First World War, it was running 183 schools attended by 43,700 students.[13]

Unlike French Jews, American Jews did not initially take on a leadership role when they mobilized on behalf of Jews outside of the United States. As it had in the Jewish communities of Western Europe, the 1840 Damascus Affair solicited a dramatic response among American Jews, who petitioned the US government to aid the accused. Likewise, the 1858 Mortara Affair led to public protests that numbered two thousand individuals in New York City alone, requesting that President Buchanan intervene on the family's behalf. In 1878, American Jews requested US government help for the Jews of Romania, and just two years later, they began to draw attention to the mistreatment of Jews in the Russian empire. The Dreyfus Affair also solicited an important mobilization among American Jews and non-Jews alike, as did the Kishinev pogrom of 1903. The concern of American Jews for the fate of Jews in Eastern Europe continued over the next decade. However, at the outbreak of World War I, there existed no permanent organization for American Jewish overseas relief.[14]

World War I challenged this situation and sparked a massive mobilization among different factions of the American Jewish community. American Jews of Zionist orientation concerned with the worsening conditions of Jews in the Ottoman Empire organized the first war relief organization on August 30, 1914, which they called the Provisional Executive Committee for General Zionist Affairs. The American Jewish Committee (AJC), led by the "uptown" Jews of German descent, who were primarily anti- or non-Zionist, concurrently responded to a request by US Ambassador to the Ottoman Empire Henry

Morgenthau Sr. by pledging $50,000 to Jews in the Ottoman Empire. In October 1914, the AJC established what it hoped would become a representative committee for the relief of Jewish war victims: the American Jewish Relief Committee (AJRC). Like its parent body, the AJRC represented the wealthiest Reform Jews yet also received support from diverse factions of American Jewry, including some socialist and orthodox groups.[15] Several weeks before the AJRC was established, an even larger faction of Orthodox Jews had chosen to establish the Central Committee for the Relief of Jews Suffering through the War (CCR).[16] On November 27, 1914, the AJRC convinced the CCR to coordinate their efforts while maintaining independence. This established the Joint Distribution Committee of the American Funds for Jewish War Sufferers (JDC), which would distribute funds raised by these organizations and operate a relief program in war-torn areas. In August 1915, working-class Jews affiliated with the labor and socialist movements established the People's Relief Committee. This group joined the JDC on November 29, 1915.

The JDC, or "the Joint," which would become the predominate American Jewish overseas relief agency, was therefore created from a tenuous collaboration of three opposing factions of American Jewish life, divided by social class and political and religious ideology. Ironically, the success of this partnership stemmed from the divided nature of the endeavor that, in theory, allowed each group to raise funds without stepping on the others' toes. The AJRC was able to target donors of the affluent classes, usually affiliated with the Reform movement, while the Orthodox CCR addressed synagogue-attending, middle-class Jews and the PRC solicited funds from secular, working-class Jews. Together these organizations contributed to a common pool of resources that was then distributed by the JDC.[17] The war relief efforts represented an unprecedented fundraising success. By the end of 1915, the JDC had collected $1.5 million and by the end of 1918, $16.5 million.[18] In addition to this organized relief, individuals sent cash remittances to their relatives on the front via organizations such as the JDC and the Hebrew Sheltering and Immigrant Aid Society.[19] Significantly, for the first time, American Jews also solicited non-Jews for help.[20]

The success of the Joint during World War I demonstrated that American Jews of all classes and ideologies showed concern over the fate of overseas Jews. This sense of shared responsibility was facilitated by the significant growth of the Jewish population between 1881–1914 as a result of Eastern European immigration, which deepened American ties to the areas affected by the war. Furthermore, the democratization of philanthropy throughout the United States during the First World War validated the idea that all social classes could become philanthropists. This enabled American Jews to expand their

Federation movement, which centralized fundraising for Jewish organizations on a citywide level and eventually established a nationwide philanthropic infrastructure that allowed for an unprecedented division of labor and coordination.[21] These developments made the American Jewish mobilization during World War I different from previous periods and marked this moment as the formal entry of American Jews onto the world stage.

Ten million of the world's fifteen million Jews lived in areas affected by World War I.[22] The JDC distributed its aid primarily in the territories that would soon become Poland, the Soviet Union, and Palestine. According to one JDC report from March 1919, from the outbreak of hostilities until 1919, the organization had spent $14 million of its $16 million budget in Eastern Europe and Palestine.[23] After the conflict, the JDC joined forces with the American Relief Administration (ARA), the official American postwar aid body established under Herbert Hoover. In exchange for a contribution of $3.3 million, the JDC was able to send their officials to Europe as ARA workers.[24]

THE INTERWAR YEARS AND THE STRUGGLE FOR UNITY

During the interwar years, American Jewish life had grown progressively more divided. The Zionist movement had gained new support among the increasingly middle-class and acculturated Eastern European immigrants and their descendants, as well as among some prominent American-born communal leaders. This created new tensions regarding the distribution of resources, especially those directed for overseas aid.

Two conflicting visions essentially split American Jewish leadership: one that supported Jewish life in the diaspora and a second that endeavored to create a Jewish state in Palestine. Tensions surged when the JDC—technically apolitical but controlled by largely anti- or non-Zionist donors—began an ambitious plan to promote Jewish agricultural resettlement in the Soviet Union. In a period of four years, from 1924 to 1928, the JDC resettled fifty-six hundred Jewish families in Ukraine and Crimea.[25] The decision of the JDC to direct its funding to the Soviet Union enraged American Zionists, who responded by establishing a separate fundraising campaign in 1925, the United Palestine Appeal (UPA). The Jewish Agency, enlarged in 1929 to mediate relations between the Jewish settlement in Palestine (*Yishuv*) and the diaspora, distributed the funds collected in the United States.

Torn by these ideological differences, American Jews attempted to unite for overseas Jews only when international crises appeared insurmountable. In 1929, after anti-Jewish riots in Palestine, an attempt was made to unite the fundraising campaigns for the JDC and the UPA. A second attempt occurred in 1934 in response to Hitler's 1933 rise to power. The November 9–10, 1938, pogrom finally brought unity to American Jewish fundraising for Jews overseas. This somber event prompted the JDC, the UPA, and a new organization for refugee aid, the National Coordinating Committee Fund, to form the United Jewish Appeal for Refugee and Overseas Needs (UJA) in January 1939. By uniting the fundraising campaigns of these three organizations, the UJA raised over $15 million, marking a huge increase over the total of $7 million collected previously in separate campaigns.[26] This money was then distributed to the three agencies according to predetermined percentages. In general, the JDC obtained slightly more than 50 percent of these funds. Significantly, the UJA used the national infrastructure of the Council of Jewish Federations and Welfare Funds, established in 1932, to coordinate the Federation's local campaigns. The domestic and international branches of American Jewish philanthropy thus began working together in new ways.

While communal unity was still a distant ideal during this period, American Jewish philanthropy and the welfare activities it supported had developed into a more centralized, efficient machine by linking organizations within communities and cities within regions through the Federation movement. This strong domestic network enabled American Jews, who had previously followed the lead of older and larger Jewish communities in Europe, to mobilize with unprecedented vigor on behalf of Jewish war victims. The establishment of the JDC in 1914 and the UPA in 1925—two institutions designed to channel local support for Jews overseas—marked the official turn outward. The establishment of the UJA in 1939, which united and streamlined the overseas fundraising campaigns by linking them to the domestic philanthropic infrastructure, amplified American Jewish overseas aid.

WAR, RECONSTRUCTION, AND REFUGEES: THE AMERICAN JEWISH JOINT DISTRIBUTION COMMITTEE IN FRANCE (1914–1939)

Concern over the fate of Jews during WWI and its aftermath brought American Jewish organizations and their representatives to Eastern Europe. France was not central to their aid programs, and the thriving nature of French Jewish life in the 1920s certainly did not reflect a portrait of need.[27] The afterglow of French Jewish participation in World War I, which furthered the integration of Jews into French society, set an optimistic tone for Jewish life in the following decade. Perhaps the greatest challenge French Jews faced during this period was heightened immigration from Eastern Europe, which had increased after the American immigration restrictions of the 1920s. Interwar immigration to France challenged the power dynamics within French Jewish life, as new immigrant institutions emerged.[28] One of the most important organizations to develop during this period was the Federation of Jewish Societies of France (Fédération des sociétés juives de France [FSJF]), which pursued the efforts to unite the immigrant landsmanshaftn and helped boost the representation of immigrants in communal politics.[29] New leadership from immigrant circles questioned the ways of the established native Jews, who conceived of their Jewishness in more restrictive and private terms, as a religious—as opposed to an ethnic—identity. Nevertheless, native Jews did assume public roles representing Jewish institutions and dominated the leadership of the Central Consistory and the Alliance. Even as they struggled with their increasing diversity, French Jews saw themselves as privileged members of the diaspora and equal partners of American Jews when occasions to collaborate arose.

Reconstruction efforts after World War I provided such opportunities. The JDC set up an institutional presence in Paris in 1919, although it moved its Paris office to Vienna in 1921. It possibly reopened in Paris in 1922.[30] The Alliance archives reveal a tone of respectful collaboration with the JDC centered on the exchange of information and mutual aid. For example, when JDC employee Miss H. Goldman was sent to Greece under the auspices of the Red Cross to investigate the situation of its Jewish population in 1918, the JDC provided her a letter of introduction to the Alliance in Paris. The latter had been informed directly by the JDC of her arrival with a request to aid her if necessary.[31] More importantly, the two organizations had clearly established—and respected one another's—spheres of influence. When a school in Baghdad, presumably operated by the Alliance, was unable to receive funding from British sources, the JDC contributed to it on at least one occasion.[32] Likewise, the JDC's philanthropic infrastructure in the Soviet Union allowed the Alliance to send F100,000 to be distributed there by the JDC in 1923.[33] The upheavals of the next decade would challenge this relationship, making the American Jewish community more influential than ever.

THE CENTRAL EUROPEAN REFUGEE CRISIS: A NEW ERA

Hitler's ascent to power in Germany in January 1933 forced the JDC to shift its attention from Eastern to Western Europe. By April 1, 1933, Dr. Bernard Kahn, the European director of the JDC, had decided to move the European headquarters of the organization to Paris.[34] Between thirty-seven and forty-five thousand Jews left Germany in 1933, over half of whom migrated to France.[35] The arrival of these refugees corresponded with the reinforced presence of the JDC on French soil and marked a new era of collaboration between American and French Jews. The responses of the organized community to the arrival of Central European Jewish refugees from 1933 to 1939 are important because they show the increasing interactions between the JDC and French Jewish organizations.[36] While Vicki Caron and others have focused their analyses on French governmental policy, public opinion, and the responses of French Jewish leadership to the refugee crisis, the goal here is to read these events in relation to the shifting power dynamics in the Jewish diaspora. As the refugee crisis gave way to World War II, the JDC took on an increasingly influential role in French Jewish welfare by assuming an important financial role and challenging the French Jewish leadership to embrace a more welcoming stance on refugees.

French Jews initially greeted newly arriving German Jews with warmth and encouragement. Organizations affiliated with the Jewish immigrant community were the first to protest the Nazi antisemitism and provide aid for refugees.[37] The native Jewish establishment, represented by the Alliance and the Central Consistory, also set up a series of committees, establishing first the Comité d'accueil et d'aide aux victims de l'antisémitisme en Allemagne, which then merged into the Comité National français de secours aux réfugiés allemands victimes de l'antisémitisme (National Committee).[38] While members of the Central Consistory, including Robert de Rothschild and Jacques Helbronner, led this second committee, it was endorsed by several non-Jewish politicians and presented itself as a nonsectarian body.[39] From 1933 until its dissolution in 1935, the National Committee was the principal aid provider for Jewish refugees and recognized by the French government as such. The international Jewish organizations ORT and Union OSE also played an important role in the direct care and vocational training of Jewish refugees.[40] By spring 1933, there were fifteen refugee aid committees in Paris alone.[41]

In spite of this initial response, enthusiasm was already beginning to wane by the end of 1933. The conservative members of the National Committee (labeled by Caron as "hardliners") actively sought to disprove accusations of a double allegiance that would place Jewish solidarity over national interests. They refused to consider France as anything more than a stopover for the refugees and endorsed the emigration and repatriation of German Jews, instead of their resettlement and vocational training in France.[42]

European JDC director Dr. Bernard Kahn did not see things in the same light. He sought to shape pro-refugee policy and used JDC funding to do so. Upon his arrival in France in 1933, he convened a conference with partner

Table 1.1. JDC Aid to France, 1933–1939 (in US dollars of the 1930s)

Year	France (in US Dollars) (a)	Total Global JDC Expenditures (in US Dollars) (b)	Percentage of Global JDC Expenditures Spent in France
1933	95,657	665,754	14%
1934	285,070	1,382,326	21%
1935	70,106	983,343	7%
1936	115,910	1,904,923	6%
1937	147,629	2,883,759	5%
1938	112,486	3,799,878	3%
1939	698,761	8,490,516	8%
Total	1,525,619	20,110,499	8%

Sources: (a) American Jewish Joint Distribution, *Catalogue*, n.d., France 1939–1944; (b) Bauer, *My Brother's Keeper*, 140 and 306. There are some discrepancies in the sources for 1933, 1938, and 1939. Bauer estimates the JDC spent $125,000 in France in 1933; $130,884 in 1938, and $589,000 in 1939.

organizations and raised F3 million from the participants ($160,000 at the time).[43] In 1933 alone, the budget of the National Committee reached $477,000, of which more than 20 percent stemmed from the JDC, while one third was provided by Robert de Rothschild.[44] Over the next three years, from 1933 to 1936, French Jews raised almost F15 million (roughly $800,000).[45] During the same period, the JDC contributed approximately $567,000 to French Jewish welfare.[46] (See table 1.1.) In this short period, the JDC had become a major benefactor of French Jewish welfare.

Extensive JDC funding led to unprecedented interaction with French Jewish leadership and institutions. Even if the JDC claimed an official policy of political neutrality, including in local Jewish politics, its activities in France during this period show that the organization actively sought to make French Jewish policies toward Central European Jewish refugees more accommodating. When the National Committee renewed its request for JDC support at the end of 1933, the JDC imposed a condition on both the French government and the National Committee: the JDC would continue its support but only if France's borders were kept open and refugees were granted work permits.[47] As seen by the severe anti-immigration measures taken by the French government in 1934 and 1935 and the National Committee's own embrace of repatriation policies, these conditions were not respected. In 1934, Kahn protested to his superiors in New York that French Jewish leaders "disapprove [of] every attempt to help the refugees constructively, no matter what the project may be."[48] In 1935, the National Committee closed its doors. The refugees, and Kahn himself, greeted this event with anger and desperation. In June 1936, Kahn's sense of exasperation seems to have peaked, leading him to exclaim that, apart from the JDC, "nobody cares about the German Jewish refugees in France, neither ICA [Jewish Colonization Association], the Jewish community, the British [Jews], nor any other organization."[49]

The rise of Léon Blum's Popular Front government in May 1936 nonetheless helped Kahn take advantage of the more favorable political situation in order to renew French Jewish aid efforts.[50] Kahn approached French Jewish leaders to establish a new refugee committee. At first he obtained negative results. He then resorted to more direct techniques, threatening to cut all JDC funding to France. Simultaneously, however, he promised that if French Jews complied with his plan to form a new committee, the JDC would provide 50 percent of the new committee's funding. Finally, Kahn imposed a set of conditions that would guide the work of the new committee, including vocational training and, more importantly, new leadership. Kahn took pains to block the most conservative leaders of the National Committee, such as Jacques Helbronner, who as a member of the Conseil d'État (Council of State) and France's representative on the High Commission for Refugees from Germany had systematically sabotaged pro-refugee initiatives. Raymond-Raoul Lambert was the only National Committee member to serve on the new Committee, and the addition of a representative from an immigrant organization, the Zionist Israël Jefroykin, then president of the Federation of Jewish Societies, and a woman—*chose rare* in French Jewish leadership—the feminist journalist Louise Weiss, reinforced his liberal stance on the refugee problem.[51] These JDC-imposed conditions led to the establishment of the Comité d'assistance aux réfugiés (CAR) in July 1936, which functioned as an important fixture in French Jewish welfare throughout World War II. Once established, the CAR coordinated material aid to Jewish refugees and dealt with the twists and turns of French refugee policy, maintaining a moderately pro-refugee stance. The JDC's critical attitude toward the French Jewish leadership seems to have been replaced with one of satisfactory support.[52] This is not surprising, since Kahn had handpicked the CAR's board, indirectly giving more power to those outside the establishment—including an immigrant and a woman—all of whom reflected Kahn's own reading of the refugee crisis.

The demise of the Popular Front gave way to a more restrictive period in April 1938. The new Daladier government issued a series of anti-immigrant decree laws in May, June, and November 1938, limiting the right of foreigners to engage in commerce and preventing further entry of new refugees while expelling others. The most shocking of the laws legalized the internment of illegal refugees who could not be expulsed. The annexation of Austria in March 1938, followed by the Munich Agreement in September, led to Nazi Germany's expansion into Austrian territories and the Czechoslovakian Sudetenland. These events, followed by the November pogrom and the enactment of racial laws against Jews in Italy, forced even greater numbers of Jews to seek refuge in France. By the end of 1938, an estimated sixty thousand Jewish refugees of Central and Eastern European origin were in France.[53] Faced with these new challenges, French Jews took a further step toward unity. After the November pogrom, two new committees were established to orchestrate relief and fundraising.[54] According to Vicki Caron, the diverse factions of French Jewish life moved toward consensus in 1939 when they fought the decree laws, albeit with limited success.[55] The outbreak of World War II ultimately crushed any hope of improving the situation for Central European refugees in France.

THE *ST. LOUIS* TRAGEDY: THE JDC AS INTERNATIONAL COORDINATOR

A highly symbolic event occurred in spring 1939, which provides one final example of the JDC intervention in French Jewish life on the eve of the Second World War. On May 13, 1939, 907 Jewish refugees fleeing Nazi Germany boarded the SS *St. Louis* for Havana, Cuba, hoping to ultimately find refuge in the United States. All passengers had Cuban entry visas in hand, and 743 held affidavits or immigration papers for the United States. Yet these refugees were denied the right to disembark in Cuba because their Cuban entry visas had been issued illegally by a corrupt immigration official in Havana. The ensuing monthlong drama has come to symbolize what one historian has called an "impossible exile."[56]

With the hope of finding refuge for his passengers in the United States, the captain of the *St. Louis* slowly guided the ship along the Florida coast. This sparked media coverage and an outpouring of concern among Americans, who solicited their government to allow the refugees to disembark without success. Among American Jewish organizations, the JDC played the most active role in advocating on behalf of the refugees. It intervened with the Cuban and American governments and offered the former over half a million dollars to accept the refugees.[57] In spite of these efforts, both Cuba and the United States denied entry to the refugees, and the *St. Louis* was forced to make its way back to Europe.

Determined to prevent these refugees from returning to Nazi Germany, the newly installed European director of the JDC, Morris Troper, Bernard Kahn's successor, centralized negotiations from his Paris headquarters.[58] Troper worked closely with Louise Weiss, a prominent French journalist. As seen above, she had been working with the JDC since 1936 as a CAR board member. Weiss's own distinct background enabled her to bridge vastly different groups. She openly discussed her Jewish and Protestant family in her 1937 memoirs, allowing both religious groups to claim her as their own. However, what seems to have mattered most to Weiss herself was her ability to make her own decisions.[59] According to Weiss's biographer, she had romantic relationships with several politicians, including Foreign Affairs Minister Georges Bonnet.[60] This helps explain how Weiss could have, according to her own account, "forced" Bonnet to establish the pro-refugee Central Committee for Refugees (Comité central des réfugiés) in December 1938. Her strategic position in French political life and fluency in English—she had studied at Oxford—made Weiss a valuable asset to the JDC.[61] The male-dominated JDC leadership overlooked Weiss's gender, making her one of the rare women in its orbit, which was possibly due to sheer necessity.

Troper's and Weiss's advocacy on behalf of the SS *St. Louis* refugees led to a breakthrough on June 10, when Belgium agreed to accept 200 of the refugees, provided they had possibilities for emigration. Holland seconded this response by promising to accept 194 refugees. England followed and accepted 250. France, perhaps emboldened by these commitments, announced it would accept the remaining refugees and that it would have, in fact, accepted all of the passengers had these other countries not stepped forward.[62] The JDC was thus able to announce a temporary reprieve for the *St. Louis* refugees.[63] The incident made the JDC's ability to negotiate across local, national, and international boundaries evident to all. While not entirely bypassed, French Jewish organizations were somewhat eclipsed by the JDC, which had taken over negotiations with the French government. Still, the Europe of 1939 was quickly becoming a trap, and in light of the oncoming crisis, the JDC's presence most likely lent a sense of protection to French Jewish leaders.

With the continued rise of antisemitism and the spread of authoritarian and fascist regimes throughout Europe, Jewish refugees fled their home countries for France, looking for safety. By the end of 1940, France counted an estimated three hundred and thirty thousand Jews, including one hundred and ninety to two hundred thousand French nationals and one hundred and thirty to one hundred and forty thousand foreigners, most of whom came from Eastern and Central Europe.[64] The overwhelming task of caring for the growing number of refugees was further complicated by a new government measure after France's entry into World War II on September 3, 1939, which led to the internment of eighteen thousand male "enemy aliens" aged seventeen to sixty-five.[65] In May 1940, this extended to women as well. As the political and living conditions of Jewish refugees in France grew more somber, American Jewish aid increased to compensate the budgetary insufficiencies of French Jewish aid organizations. By 1939, the JDC was supporting 90 percent of the CAR budget.[66] Over the course of a decade, American Jewish aid had become a crucial fixture in French Jewish life: the well-being of many individuals now depended on it.

"GUIDE AND MOTIVATOR" OR "CENTRAL TREASURY?"[67] THE ROLE OF THE JDC IN FRANCE DURING THE SECOND WORLD WAR

The JDC became an indispensable actor in French Jewish welfare during the interwar period, yet the Second World War complicated its role in France. Mounting numbers of refugees and forced internment increased the need for Jewish welfare organizations exponentially, yet these challenges proved minor compared to the antisemitic legislation put in place by Nazi and Vichy authorities that would further marginalize Jews in France and eventually lead to the deportation of seventy-six thousand individuals, in addition to the death of another four thousand who were executed on French soil or perished in French internment camps.[68]

The outbreak of World War II forced the JDC into a delicate situation: How could it negotiate its place as both a Jewish and American organization in France while maintaining a semblance of political neutrality? The predicament of neutrality became even more acute with the increasing tensions between Washington and Vichy after the entry of the United States into World War II in December 1941. Nevertheless, the United States maintained a diplomatic presence in France until the Allied invasion of North Africa, which led to the rupture of diplomatic ties in November 1942.[69] This imposed new limitations on the JDC's actions because it triggered the application of the American "Trading with the Enemy Act," which drastically reduced the funds the JDC could send to France. How could the JDC negotiate the dilemma of saving lives while following American laws and regulations? To what extent did the JDC resist—in this case, its own institutional policy of neutrality and American regulations—in order to save lives? The answers to these questions are important here as they determined how French Jews would view the American organization in the aftermath of the war. The fact the JDC managed to send funds, even during the heightened 1942–1944 period, positioned the American organization as a faithful partner in the eyes of French Jews. However, the chaotic distribution of JDC aid during the Occupation, and the fact it was French Jews who took charge after 1942, caused the line between American and French Jewish aid to blur.

THE JDC IN WARTIME FRANCE, 1939–1942: ASSISTANCE IN CONTINUITY

After the outbreak of the war, JDC representatives began to prepare for their possible departure from Europe. Morris Troper and his deputy, Dr. Joseph Schwartz, quickly toured Europe in May 1940, meeting with Jewish leaders in several countries. They appointed Saly Mayer, head of the Federation of Jewish communities of Switzerland, to act as a JDC representative should it be forced to withdraw from Europe.[70] The JDC also established an office in Lisbon to serve as its European headquarters. The Nazi invasion of France in May 1940 forced the JDC to close its Paris office. After retreating to Angers and then Bordeaux, the JDC, like other American organizations, reestablished itself in the Unoccupied Zone, in Marseilles. During the first half of the war, American JDC worker Herbert Katzki led operations for France, assisted by Jules (Dika) Jefroykin, the son of immigrant leader Israël Jefroykin, who was hired by Dr. Schwartz in December 1940.[71] The JDC thus strategically braced itself for war, maximizing its chances to continue functioning if American organizations were forced to flee. Yet in 1939 and 1940, few individuals could have predicted—let alone prepared for—the catastrophe that would occur in Nazi-occupied Europe.

In France, Nazi occupation and Vichy rule radically reconfigured individual lives and Jewish communal institutions.[72] Jewish welfare has not entirely escaped historical analysis, yet it remains enmeshed in the highly polemic debates on the Nazi-Vichy imposed Jewish Council, the General Union of Israelites in France (Union générale des Israélites de France, UGIF), established in November 1941 to oversee French Jewish communal life.[73] Yet long before this, as a result of invasion, French Jews faced an overwhelming welfare crisis: in addition to the Jews who had abandoned their homes to flee the hostilities, French Jewish leaders had to deal with the Nazi expulsion of three thousand Jews from Alsace-Lorraine in July 1940.[74] The demographic upheaval caused by the Nazi occupation forced Jewish organizations to shift their mission to aiding all Jews, not just foreigners.[75]

From 1940 until 1942, French Jewish welfare focused on sending relief to those interned in camps and the larger, displaced Jewish population, and providing emigration aid. JDC aid during the first part of the war followed this pattern, although its efforts have largely escaped attention.[76] Importantly, as the status of Jewish organizations became more precarious, the JDC began to reinforce its relationship with other American organizations, such as the Young Men's Christian Association (YMCA) and the American Friends Service Committee (the Quakers), which were active in France.[77] By building horizontal collaborations, the JDC repositioned itself as an American voluntary organization working in France during this period. This did not fool Vichy or Nazi authorities, who continued to see the JDC as an international Jewish organization, but it did facilitate relief work on the ground.

The increasing number of foreign Jews in French internment camps as a result of the October 4, 1940, Vichy law allowing for the internment of "foreigners of the Jewish race," regardless of age, especially concerned the JDC. In the same month, the Nazis expulsed sixty-five hundred Jews from the Baden and Palatinate regions of Germany to internment camps in the Southern Zone of France. As a result, whereas Jewish internees in the Southern internment camps numbered five thousand of the eight thousand total internees in spring 1940, they represented twenty-eight thousand of the forty thousand at the end of 1940. By February 1941, the number of Jews had reached forty thousand out of a total internee population of forty-seven thousand.[78] In response, the JDC funded French Jewish welfare committees to provide food and medical care for internees.[79] Finally, in November 1940, on Donald Lowrie of the YMCA's initiative, the JDC united with twenty-four other organizations (French, American, Swiss, and various religious affiliations) to establish a nonsectarian structure to coordinate welfare in the camps.[80] Known as the Nîmes Committee, its leaders included Donald Lowrie of the YMCA and Herbert Katzki of the JDC, among others. The committee encouraged specialization to minimize the duplication of services: the Unitarian Service Committee worked with the OSE to provide medical services, HICEM worked on emigration, and so on. The ecumenical aspect of the committee served as an advantage since its work depended on access to the camps and the authorization of Vichy authorities, which, according to JDC representative Herbert Katzki, was more readily provided to Christian organizations. In addition to its participation in the Nîmes Committee, the JDC maintained its support of French Jewish welfare, which it funded primarily through the CAR and Federation of Jewish Societies. During the first half of the war, the JDC estimated that it indirectly assisted thirty thousand Jews in internment camps and forced residence, provided cash allowances to thirty-five thousand individuals in forty-one cities, and helped sixty-five hundred children daily.[81]

Increasing pressure from Vichy and Nazi authorities to establish a Jewish Council placed relief work at risk. As discussed above, the UGIF was established on November 29, 1941. While this structure differed in significant ways from the Judenräte in Eastern Europe, the creation of the UGIF ended the era of independent French Jewish welfare. Now under law, all Jewish philanthropic and welfare organizations became subordinate to Vichy's General Commissariat for Jewish Affairs and all Jews in France were forced to pay dues to the UGIF. Furthermore, profits resulting from sales of confiscated Jewish property funded the UGIF. As a foreign organization, the JDC escaped membership; however, as it did with similar structures in other occupied countries, the JDC chose to fund the UGIF in order to continue providing aid while continuing to fund Jewish organizations outside of this structure.[82]

While the JDC maintained an official relief-based program from 1939 to 1942, its policies had, in fact, begun to change during the summer of 1942. The massive Vélodrome d'Hiver round up in Paris on July 16 and 17, 1942, during which 12,884 Jewish men, women, and children were arrested, shifted perceptions. While the first deportations to Nazi concentration and death camps began in France in March, their intensity increased in July 1942. Dr. Joseph Schwartz, who had become the chief of JDC overseas operations in February 1942, came to France to intervene. Breaking with the JDC's neutrality, Schwartz met with American officials to prevent future deportations and French Jewish leaders to emphasize the need for Jewish unification and a limited role for the UGIF, directing relief programs outside of official channels.[83] Schwartz's actions during this trip indicated a willingness to depart from the fully legal stance the JDC had followed until this point.

THE JDC UNDER FRENCH LEADERSHIP: RESISTANCE AND RESCUE (1942–1944)

The Allied invasion of North Africa in November 1942 led to the Nazi occupation of the Southern Zone of France and the rupture of diplomatic ties between Washington and Vichy. The American employees of the JDC were forced to leave France; the JDC office in Marseille was closed, and subsequently stormed by the Nazis.[84] Jules (Dika) Jefroykin, who became the JDC representative for France in spring 1942 and his assistant, Maurice Brener, found themselves the sole representatives of the JDC in France, with limited possibilities for communication with Dr. Schwartz.[85] The "Trading with the Enemy Act," the American law dictating interactions with enemy nations, was now in effect, limiting the amount of funds the JDC could legally send to France.[86]

The role played by the JDC in France from 1942 to 1944 demonstrates the tensions related to the shifting notions of legality as the conditions of the war changed. These notions shifted depending on the period in the war, the place of the act, and the nationality of the actors. Americans and American organizations—even outside the United States—were bound to the evolving regulations determined by their government. Therefore, a Swiss national transferring money into Nazi-occupied territories could acting legally, yet it would still be illegal for an American. These shifting notions of legality led to a general lack of clarity that acted as both a hindrance and a help to rescue and resistance—a hindrance because conservative leaders of the JDC preferred to "draw a fence" around American laws to demonstrate their strict adherence to them. For example, in 1939, James Rosenberg, the vice chairman of the JDC, wrote, "Our rule must be, when in doubt, ask the State Department."[87]

Yet shifting notions of legality were also helpful because those who preferred to challenge these laws were able to use the ambiguities and gray areas to their advantage, all while claiming the JDC had acted according to the law. For example, Dr. Schwartz, director of JDC European operations, explained in an oral history interview the strategic decision to rely on a Swiss citizen to represent the JDC during the hostilities: "Saly Mayer, because he was Swiss, was able to do a lot of things that we couldn't do and we were always able to say look, we can't control the Swiss. After all, we try as much as we can, but communications are bad, and so on and so forth. An awful lot of things were done."[88]

One could also interpret Schwartz's decision to name Jules (Dika) Jefroykin as the JDC's French representative as a gesture in support of resistance. Jefroykin's distinct profile strongly suggests he was not arbitrarily selected. Close to the leadership of the Federation of Jewish Societies of France and after its creation in May 1942, president of the Zionist Youth Movement, Jefroykin represented the more radical, Zionist, immigrant faction of French Jewish life. As seen above, his father, Israël Jefroykin, had also worked closely with the JDC as a leader of the CAR. By 1941, while working for the JDC, Jules (Dika) Jefroykin had become a leader in the Jewish Army (Armée juive), the Jewish resistance organization.[89] It is difficult to assess to what extent Dr. Schwartz was aware of Jefroykin's political activities or even if Jefroykin was the JDC's first choice as a director. Strangely, Raymond-Raoul Lambert, former leader of the CAR and head of the UGIF in the Southern Zone, noted in his diary that he was asked to represent the JDC in France at the end of November 1942.[90] Even if he were pro-refugee, Lambert represented native Jewish circles and, as seen from his tragic involvement in the UGIF, was more obedient to Vichy and Nazi regulations. In the end Jefroykin directed the JDC in the absence of its

American representatives, suggesting that Schwartz distinctly chose to support the more radical immigrant faction of French Jewish life that was organizing resistance against Vichy and the Nazi occupation.

On a trip to Lisbon in June 1942, Jefroykin was given carte blanche to borrow funds in the name of the JDC, which would be reimbursed after the war. On this occasion, the JDC told Jefroykin that it would not fund armed resistance.[91] Yet the JDC, under Jefroykin, did fund armed resistance, rescue, and relief. Indeed, Jefroykin fled to Nice and met with the heads of the major Jewish organizations to determine how JDC funding should spent. He recalled in 1963 in an oral history interview:

> I was cut off [sic] the direction of the Joint and I didn't want to take on, I didn't think I could take on all the responsibility. So I asked a certain number of leaders of the Jewish community to help me by giving me their advice and experience, I was still pretty young still [sic] at the time, and I took the initiative to constitute a sort of advisory board of the Joint [...]. I wasn't prepared to allocate all of the budget to official organizations and I asked for their moral approval so that a part of the budget on which I would decide would thereafter be allocated not only to underground activities but also to armed struggle. [...] It was after this meeting in Nice that all of the reorganization of the JDC work I directed was modified. This is when I started being able to give money to the Zionist Youth Movement network [...] and that we could allocate a large part of the budget to underground activities.[92]

In spring 1943, a JDC council was formed to distribute JDC funds, comprised of Jefroykin, representatives from the Central Consistory, Union OSE, the Federation of Jewish Societies, the CAR, and the Zionist Youth Movement and other Zionist Organizations.[93] According to Jefroykin, the JDC was not aware of his decision to divert funding for clandestine purposes and armed resistance, although he eventually cleared this unofficial activity with Dr. Schwartz.[94] But how did he obtain this funding if American regulations strictly limited the transfer of dollars into Nazi-occupied territory?

RESOURCES FOR RESCUE

Through its French representation, the JDC was able to fund relief, rescue, and resistance through various sources. The first and most important was by reestablishing what the JDC called a "loan après" system, which the organization had used during World War I. Under this system individuals who wanted

Figure 1.1. Nina and Jules (Dika) Jefroykin in Spain in 1944 after having crossed the Pyrenees. Mémorial de la Shoah, Collection ARJF.

Figure 1.2. Maurice Brener, Mémorial de la Shoah.

to loan out their money would lend it to the JDC in exchange for repayment after the war.[95] A second means of JDC funding became operational for France in summer 1943 via Switzerland. In light of American restrictions, Swiss JDC representative Saly Mayer suggested in February 1942 that the JDC double its subsidy for Switzerland, which would allow Swiss Jews to transfer their resources into Nazi-occupied territories. This plan received authorization from the US Treasury Department in March 1942.[96] Mayer was only in contact with the French Jewish leadership, however, after the arrival of Zionist Marc Jarblum in March 1943 and Dr. Joseph Weill of OSE in May 1943.[97] Jarblum, the second president of the Federation of Jewish Societies and the French representative for the World Jewish Congress (WJC), had been "nominated" for membership in the UGIF. He fought this appointment and joined the Jewish Army in 1943.[98] A well-connected socialist and seasoned negotiator, Jarblum began a vigorous letter-writing campaign from Switzerland to raise funds for clandestine activities in France, especially those of the Federation and the Jewish Army.[99] While Mayer viewed Jarblum with suspicion and showed a preference for Dr. Weill's work with the OSE, he supplied funds to both men. Weill was able to smuggle the funds across the border to JDC representative Maurice Brener with the help of a resistance group led by a pro-Gaullist pharmacist from Geneva and a priest, who, thanks to creative use of his wooden leg, was able to perform this task with efficiency. Jarblum used the services of a professional cyclist and a mechanic, who received a commission on the funds they delivered. Jarblum's funding, procured from the JDC, the Vaad Hatzalah of the Jewish Agency for Palestine, and the World Jewish Congress, went directly to the Jewish Army and was deposited at a newsstand operated by this organization in Lyon, which sold collaborationist newspapers while doubling as an arsenal and meeting point.[100]

The JDC also channeled some funding through other international organizations for specific activities. For example, the Quakers received $100,000 from the JDC to "help children out of France to Spain and possibly Switzerland,"[101] which the Quakers provided to the Jewish Army for this purpose. Finally, it appears that the JDC was able to send some funds directly to France during the 1942–1944 period. According to Schwartz, the transfer was quietly facilitated by the US Treasury Department.[102] American restrictions eased after the establishment of the War Refugee Board in January 1944 by the Roosevelt administration, a government body that was largely subsidized by the JDC.[103]

The JDC allocations in France appear exceptionally high when compared to those of other occupied countries and can be explained by the complex geographic, political, and social conditions that made rescue, relief, and resistance possible in France.[104] According to one estimate, the JDC provided 60 percent

Table 1.2. JDC Funding for France (1941–1944) by Source and Year (in US Dollars of the 1940s)

Year	Official JDC Allocation for France (in US Dollars)	JDC Allocation from Switzerland to France (in US Dollars)	Total Global JDC Expenditure (in US Dollars)	France Allocations as Percentages of Total Global JDC Budget
1941	793,384	—	5,716,908	13.8%
1942	872,682	—	6,318,206	14%
1943	1,748,500	149,935	8,470,538	31.7%
1944	1,657,223	1,056,930	15,216,643	10.9%
TOTAL	5,071,789	1,206,865	35,722,295	14.2% to 19.8%

Source: Bauer, *American Jewry*, 244.

Note: Bauer's table unfortunately lacks clarity and contains an error: for the year 1943, he reaches the figure 31.7% by adding the official $1,748,500 with an exceptional and unofficial $789,599 with the figures from Switzerland ($149,935). Yet for 1944, he does not add these figures but considers the money from Switzerland as included in the official figure for France ($1,657,223). It is therefore not possible to know if the money from Switzerland was in addition to or included in the official allocations. In 1943 there was an additional unofficial allocation for Jefroykin's loans: $789,599. It is unclear if Bauer included this figure to arrive at the official $1,748,500 or if this is in addition to this sum. I established a range to account for the ambiguity in Bauer's original table.

of the funds of the Jewish resistance in France.[105] As seen above, other international Jewish organizations contributed to France as well, such as the World Jewish Congress and the Vaad Hatzalah of the Jewish Agency for Palestine; however historians have been unable to determine the extent of their aid.[106] One internal memo noted the WJC provided a total of $90,000 for rescue in France.[107] The history of how these funds were used—from border crossings to armed resistance—has been explored in numerous works on Jewish resistance in France.

CONCLUSION

Aware of their privileged position in the Jewish diaspora, French and American Jews mobilized internationally to help Jews outside of their borders over the course of the nineteenth and twentieth centuries. During their encounter in France in the interwar period, these groups considered themselves equal partners—members of an exclusive club—even if the resources of American

Jews soon surpassed those of the French. When Rabbi Kaplan presented French Jews as capable philanthropists in New York in November 1944, he was alluding to the sophisticated philanthropic infrastructure French Jews had developed long before the Americans, asserting the dignity of French Jews. But the postwar reality proved more complex.

Increasing dependence on American Jewish resources shaped French Jewish welfare in the interwar period. The JDC strongly influenced the French Jewish response to the Central European refugee crisis by imposing conditions on its funding and through daily involvement in communal politics. The JDC cultivated a new generation of leadership within the French Jewish population, leading the Zionist immigrant faction to a new prominence in Jewish life. One could argue the JDC also helped make room for female leadership. Key moments in this transition include the appointment of Israël Jefroykin and Louise Weiss to the CAR followed by the selection of Jules Dika Jefroykin as JDC representative for France in 1942. As seen in the *St. Louis* Affair, the JDC's strength came not only from its close work with French Jewish refugee committees but from its international presence and capacity—thanks to Louise Weiss's help—to negotiate across borders and governmental hierarchies. The outbreak of World War II, followed by the Occupation in June 1940 and the rupture in diplomatic ties between Vichy and the United States in November 1942, complicated the JDC's capacity to operate in France. Yet despite American regulations and its own policy of political neutrality, the JDC remained active. The 1942–1944 period is key for understanding how the JDC's American representatives managed to return to France and speak with credibility.

Several observations on French and American Jews and their organizations are necessary to contextualize their postwar encounter, which was not a first meeting but a reunion of seasoned partners. In the aftermath of the Holocaust, French Jews came to the table with the pain and trauma of the preceding years and deep gratitude for the support of the JDC. Yet no matter how thankful French Jews were for the continued support of their American brethren, the Americans had not been present in France during the most intense period of the persecutions. The Americans had not risked their lives in the Jewish resistance nor, for the most part, had they lost their loved ones. JDC aid was distributed under French auspices, and French Jewish leaders naturally emerged from the Occupation with a sense of ownership regarding their actions in the name of the JDC. For these French Jewish leaders, the line between American and French Jewish aid had blurred. The American JDC representatives, however, did not share these experiences or perceptions. For them, JDC aid represented an American Jewish response to the Holocaust. These differing perceptions shaped the postwar encounter between American and French Jews, taking both by surprise when the Americans returned to France with energy and zeal, ready to reconstruct French Jewish life.

American JDC representatives would have to wait, however, until the Allied Forces granted them access to liberation France. In the meantime, American Jewish chaplains and GIs would take the lead, ensuring the continuity of American Jewish aid to France.

TWO

JEWISH ENCOUNTERS IN LIBERATION FRANCE

Chaplains, Soldiers, Survivors

IN FALL 1944, AMERICAN JEWISH chaplain Isaac Klein, recently arrived in France, sat in the center square of Chartres, opened his Yiddish newspaper, and began to wait. Having been told that all of the local Jewish families had been deported, Klein had no hope of finding survivors. Only after he was asked to translate for a man, trying first in French, then German, and finally Yiddish, Klein learned that twelve Jewish families were in fact hidden in the town, unaware of each other's existence. Klein therefore decided to have his helmet painted with his chaplain's insignia—the tablets of the ten commandments with a star of David—"with colors that looked like neon lights."[1] He then went to the center of town and opened one of the Yiddish newspapers from the United States. When Klein greeted the families who cautiously emerged out of hiding and approached him in the center square of Chartres, he was initiating both a real and symbolic connection between American Jews and the survivors of the Holocaust.

American Jewish chaplains and GIs were among the first on the scene to witness the destruction of European Jewish life. As they liberated Europe with the US Armed Forces, they reached out to surviving Jews and provided precious assistance before the reestablishment of aid programs run by American Jewish organizations. While it is difficult to quantify the aid provided by American Jewish chaplains and GIs, French and American accounts suggest a form of help whose significance derived from its highly personalized nature. Unlike the efforts of American Jewish organizations, which indirectly assisted French Jews by offering funds to French Jewish organizations during and after the Occupation, American Jewish chaplains and GIs entered into close contact with surviving Jews. In the chaos of liberation, American Jewish chaplains and

GIs, as members of the US Armed Forces, had considerable power to assert their visions of both Jewish reconstruction and postwar justice.

By focusing on chaplains, soldiers, and French Jews in Reims, where the US military had a sustained presence, this chapter will argue that the close encounters between American and French Jews in liberation France represent an expression of diaspora solidarity that was driven by American Jews' intense desire to respond to the Holocaust. American Jews often liberally reinterpreted their military responsibilities in order to reach out to Jews in France. Offering food and blankets, assistance in retrieving stolen property, and religious leadership, chaplains and GIs shaped the earliest moments of Jewish reconstruction, in some cases becoming part of the communities they sought to rebuild. Although I am not the first to consider the interaction between Jewish members of the American military and Jewish survivors that took place after the Holocaust,[2] I seek here to draw out the French responses to American Jewish aid through a case study of Reims. This approach allows me to make an equally important argument on French Jews: no matter how desperate they were for help, they were never passive aid recipients. This chapter will show how French Jews carefully selected which American GIs would be allowed into their homes, keeping a watchful eye over their daughters.

Researchers working on Jewish survivors' experiences in the aftermath of the Holocaust have been understandably drawn to Displaced Persons camps in Germany and Austria.[3] In comparison, Jewish survivors in liberation France have received less scholarly attention. The historical literature on the interaction among American Jewish military personnel and European Jewish civilians in the aftermath of the Holocaust stresses the positive and productive relationships that developed between these two Jewish groups. Such historical studies present a striking contrast from the historiography on the broader US military presence in Europe after World War II. Studies of liberation France have highlighted the primarily negative perception of the US military among the French civilian population, which was characterized by many as the "American Occupation."[4] As one scholar recently put it: "In garrison towns and large cities, American GIs made life miserable for French civilians by drinking too much, acting as a magnet for prostitutes and visiting upon the innocent a violence they had learned in war."[5] According to this historiography, a significant number of American GIs transposed the violence of the battlefield into civilian interactions as they liberated Europe.

The case of Jewish survivors in postwar France provides the opportunity to reconsider these two distinct historiographies by interrelating them. Members of the American military first encountered considerable numbers of Jews among the civilian population in France, where American Jewish soldiers were allowed to mingle freely with Jewish survivors.[6] Broader Franco-American military-civilian relations provide a backdrop for understanding the first postwar encounters between American and French Jews. American Jewish soldiers and chaplains offered surviving Jews material aid and recognition of their suffering during the difficult transition from war to peace. American Jews may have been members of the American military, but their actions hardly reflected a formal American military policy. These were much smaller scale, at times individual, responses to the suffering encountered.[7] Their assistance laid the groundwork for later Franco-American Jewish reconstruction efforts by establishing a physical connection between the givers and receivers and fostering the expectation among French Jews that help was on the way. The larger mobilization of American Jewish organizations in France put in place after liberation, beginning in early 1945, can only be understood in the context of this initial response by Jewish servicemen; they ensured the continuity of American Jewish aid to France by bridging the gap between the JDC's aid during the Occupation and the postwar mobilization of organizations.

Documenting this initial postwar encounter is possible thanks to a variety of sources. Oral history interviews conducted with twelve of the thirty-six American Jewish chaplains who served in France in the US Armed Forces during the immediate postwar period, conducted by historians in the 1960s and 1970s, and the first-person accounts written by chaplains who served in France proved to be of great significance.[8] These accounts provide rich details on the immediate postwar reconstruction of French Jewish life and demonstrate the important contribution of American Jews to this process. However, as oral and written first-person accounts, such sources raise a certain number of methodological problems. In many cases, these interviews were conducted with chaplains at least twenty-five years after their military service in France. Furthermore, as subjective accounts, they demonstrate the interplay of memory and the presentation of self—one observes a tendency to present collective efforts in individual terms. Finally, like the American historiography on the liberation of France, the historical literature on Jewish military-civilian interaction has been largely based on American sources, which cast members of the US military in a positive light, or at least, the center of the action.[9]

While recognizing such limitations, these sources provide precious clues and can be juxtaposed with other narratives.[10] A case study of the city of Reims shifts the perspective from those who provided aid (Americans) to those who received it (French). Oral history interviews conducted with French Jewish families reveal the microlevel interactions that help ground the chaplain's first-person accounts to local realities.[11] The aim is to understand the narratives French and American Jews wove as they began reconstructing French Jewish life.

REENTRY INTO THE NATION:
FRENCH JEWRY AT LIBERATION

The transition from war to peace and the immediate postwar period is crucial for understanding the larger themes that influenced postwar Jewish reconstruction.[12] The slow liberation of France began with the Allied landing in North Africa in November 1942, intensified with the arrival of Allied troops in Normandy in June 1944, and concluded in the most eastern regions of France in February 1945. While the world would have to wait another year for the end of the war, Paris and the majority of French cities were at last free by fall 1944. The autumn and winter months of 1944 and 1945 announced a period of extremes that would characterize the immediate postwar period. The jubilation of liberation, the transition to democratic order, and the reunions of loved ones could only be contrasted with the severe material and psychological tolls of the Occupation that continued to weigh on people, and the long wait for those who would never return. The support for the resistance grew among the general population after 1943, followed by calls for national unity at liberation, and coexisted with deep-seated and opposing political views that had divided the country into *la France collaborationniste* and *la France résistante* (and within the resistance, into Gaullist and Communist factions).[13]

These political divisions exacerbated the human losses and material shortages the nation faced at liberation. The population of France, which totaled 41,600,000 in 1936, had declined by 1,500,000 during the war due to departures and deaths related to armed struggle, deportations, and bombings.[14] In 1944, 35,317 civilians were killed in bombings.[15] In addition, after the war, 2,150,000 French citizens, including prisoners of war, forced laborers, and deportees needed to be repatriated from Germany.[16] Food was scarce, especially in cities. One out of three children in large cities demonstrated growth-related difficulties and the adolescents of 1945 were seven to eleven centimeters shorter and seven to nine kilograms lighter than their 1935 counterparts. Housing had become a major crisis: 25 percent of real estate capital in France had been destroyed during the war, leaving one million families homeless. Those who still had homes lacked heat because coal production had decreased considerably during the war and its importation remained difficult. Finally, just going home was a luxury because the entire French transportation system had been severely damaged.[17] As 1944 came to a close and more than four years of Nazi occupation ended, the French were cold and hungry, often far from home or even homeless. As they emerged from hiding, Jews attempted to reenter a society of need, not bounty.

Liberation ended four years of humiliation and hardship for the majority of the French population, yet the immediate postwar era did not promise a rapid improvement of living conditions. To move beyond the losses of war, the leadership of the French provisional government set forth a conciliatory tone that recognized the collective suffering of the nation while stifling attempts to address injustices that had been committed against specific groups. For General de Gaulle, the ultimate goal of national cohesion required that French society see itself as a collective victim of the Occupation. Once reincorporated into the republican legal framework, individual groups and the suffering they had incurred went unrecognized, as this challenged the founding myth of postwar French society. For Jews, this created a strong argument for silencing the recent past, even if, as scholars have begun to reveal, they did assert Jewish difference and voice their singular wartime experiences in the immediate postwar period.[18] Significantly, the discriminatory racial categories used by Nazi Germany and Vichy France had been annulled by an ordinance on August 9, 1944, suppressing a legal category that had enabled antisemitic policies and the deportation of Jews to Nazi death camps.[19] Nonetheless, while the 1944 legislation technically provided the legal grounds for Jews to recover their full rights, it also served to erase a category whose effects were still quite real in the aftermath of the war.[20] Furthermore, the August 1944 ordinance did not allow Jews to reclaim their stolen property. As Shannon Fogg has recently noted, "The French government elaborated a restitution process in 1944 and 1945," yet its "early laws and ordinances did not provide any monetary compensation for the losses."[21]

On the surface, the conditions of the Jews emerging from hiding resembled those of the majority of the French population. As Jewish artist Henri Schinzer wrote to his "maître" from Paris in November of 1944, the inability to find a room and the lack of money, food, and clothing represented primary concerns, prompting him to ask, like his compatriots, "How can I live? How can I live? Personally, my situation resembles the Jewish proverb that, translated literally, signifies 'feeling along the wall.' I'd like to paint and I don't have a place to live, I'd like to rent a room and I don't have any money, and one has to eat, and the torturous problem of clothing!"[22]

And yet, the content and urgent tone of Schinzer's letter evokes a suffering that goes beyond the material and touches on the specific experience of Jews during the Second World War. Liberation represented the first of many postwar challenges for the Jews of France, who, in the words of Schinzer, were unable to share in the collective joy:

> Our condition is, for the most of us Jews, that of people who have lost everything in a monstrous fire, who have been thrown into the streets without resources. [...] Now, because of the damned Krauts, I no longer have parents, I no longer have friends, I no longer have money? I must say, that here, in France, until now very little has been done to help Jews in distress, only personal initiatives. The poor Jew shares his poverty with his brothers, even more dispossessed than him. A great Jewish solidarity was born out of these mortal years. Everyone in his own unhappiness consoles his neighbor, we have to hold on, hold on tight, to avoid falling into an abyss, I assure you.
>
> And yet we are free. Those of us, who for four years of cruelties and darkness dreamed of this day, no longer hoping that it would come, are not able to taste the happiness, too much death, too much blood, too much suffering haunt our souls.[23]

For Henri Schinzer and other Jews, survivors of genocide, the most important thing was "to hold on tight to avoid falling into an abyss."[24]

The execution of the Nazi Final Solution in France profoundly altered the demographics of its Jewish population. By 1940, the Jewish population of France numbered roughly 330,000 individuals, comprising 190,000 to 200,000 French nationals and 130,000 to 140,000 foreigners. During the war, 75,721 Jews were deported to Nazi death camps from France, of whom 56,500 were foreigners. Only 5 percent, or 3,943 individuals, deported from France survived.[25] In addition to those who had been deported, 10,000 to 15,000 Jewish prisoners of war were being held in German POW camps. Before and during the war, approximately 30,000 Jews had found refuge in Switzerland, while others had departed to London and Algiers, New York and elsewhere. Annette Wieviorka and others estimate the Jewish population of France in 1944 at just under 200,000.[26] The geography of the Jewish population had also changed as a result of the war. Whereas Paris had been home to the majority of the Jewish population since the end of the nineteenth century, only 20,000 registered Jews (excluding those in hiding) still lived there in August 1944.[27] During the war, Jews had migrated to cities in the provinces, especially in the Southern Zone. As a result, after the war, cities that had not had a Jewish population for centuries now had a Jewish presence, whereas other cities had lost their Jewish population entirely. Parisian Jews slowly returned home once hostilities ended, yet the geographic dispersion left its mark.

Not only were they scattered and diminished in number, Jews in France were survivors of genocide and as such faced losses whose consequences cannot be easily summarized or measured. Entire families were separated and destroyed, leaving children orphaned and individuals without friends or family and devoid of a support network. In 1944, an estimated five thousand to fifteen thousand Jewish orphans needed care.[28] Family members searched for loved ones and waited for others to return; others were unable to care for their children due to physical or mental illness. Material problems resulting from the legacy of Vichy's antisemitic legislation compounded these human losses. Businesses and belongings had been confiscated and "Aryanized," leaving those who were able to work without workshops or tools. Vichy legislation had also targeted those in civil service, the media, and liberal professions, depriving an estimated 50 percent of the Jewish population of a means of employment by the summer of 1941.[29] Apartments and homes that had belonged to Jews before the war were often occupied and difficult to reclaim at liberation, in spite of legislation passed in November 1944 to facilitate the restitution of Jewish property.[30] In Paris alone an estimated sixty-five thousand Jews had their homes ransacked or sold.[31]

Religious and organizational life had also undergone tremendous changes during the course of the war. Twenty synagogues had been destroyed, ten had been vandalized and looted, and many others damaged.[32] Twenty-three of the sixty rabbis who had been members of the Central Consistory in 1939 were killed in deportation and two others had been shot.[33] Jewish welfare organizations fared slightly better. Forced to join the Nazi-imposed UGIF, many developed clandestine branches that received funding from the JDC and other organizations. In both the Northern and Southern Zones, the line between Jewish welfare and resistance had blurred as the common goal of Jewish survival required illegal activities; welfare organizations mobilized for resistance work and resistance groups, at times, distributed money for welfare. In the Southern Zone, Jewish welfare organizations and resistance networks of Bundist, Zionist, and Communist orientation merged into the Comité général de défense des juifs (CGD) in July 1943. Following the lead of those in the south, welfare and resistance groups in the Northern Zone unified as the Comité d'union et de défense des juifs (CUDJ) in January 1944. Together, the Central Consistory and the CGD established the Conseil représentatif des israélites de France (CRIF) in the winter of 1943 and 1944.[34] The CRIF represented a radically new way of thinking about French Jewish life. Until its creation, only the Consistory had claimed to represent the Jews of France. In reality, however, the Consistory had traditionally represented native Jews and their interests, often disregarding the considerations of immigrant Jews. In contrast, the CRIF was designed to represent and defend the political interests of both immigrant and native Jews of all ideologies. As historian Annette Wieviorka has pointed out, this was not the first time immigrant and native Jews worked in a collective structure—the UGIF also forced immigrant and native Jews together—yet this was the beginning of their voluntary collaboration. Born out of the war years, this new yet fragile collective marked a turning point for Jews in France, showing their desire to overcome their internal differences in order to be recognized as a group.

With the dissolution of the UGIF in August 1944, the leaders of the surviving Jewish organizations attempted to provide for the remaining Jews of the Paris region. In September 1944, French JDC representative Maurice Brener, who had recently arrived in Paris, wrote to Dr. Joseph Schwartz, the general director for overseas operations of the JDC. His letter sheds light on how the needs of the remaining Jews were perceived. Brener estimated that one hundred thousand Jews had been deported "towards an unknown destination that for many would mean death; those who stayed here were constantly hunted, persecuted, drained [minés]."[35] Cut off from the rest of France, Brener described the situation of Jews in Paris, whose numbers he estimated at forty thousand. Of these surviving Jews, Brener estimated that ten thousand were in need of material goods and money. He therefore requested aid for the Jewish welfare agencies in Paris, including the Federation of Jewish Societies, which was providing meals and financial aid to five thousand individuals, the OSE and the Jewish Scouts of France, which were caring for eight hundred and two hundred children, respectively, and Madame Juliette Stern, former UGIF member, who was overseeing the care of nine hundred children.[36]

One scholar estimates that 9,630 individuals were being assisted by Jewish organizations in Paris immediately before the liberation, yet by September 1944, this number had increased to 29,786.[37] Brener had thus severely underestimated the population in need of help, showing how difficult it was to prepare for the large-scale needs of the Jewish population after the war.

Victor Bienstock, an American war correspondent, reported on the conditions of Jews in the south of France, where he traveled in September 1944. In urgent tones, he wrote to the JDC about the seven thousand remaining Jews in Marseille and the six to eight thousand in Nice, many of whom did not hold French citizenship. While initially concerned that, as both Jews and foreigners, these populations would have difficulty accessing government aid, he was reassured by US Armed Forces Civil Affairs staff that these Jews were receiving aid without discrimination. Yet in Bienstock's eyes, this aid was horribly insufficient and could not address the magnitude of need he encountered among Jewish survivors. "They are in terrible shape, for the most part, and need all kinds of help—moral, financial, etc. You can imagine the situation when I tell you that a group of Jews was found in an internment center who, though free to leave, were afraid because they had no clothes, no money, and didn't know where to go or what to do."[38]

As these accounts indicate, the war years represented for the surviving Jews of France a psychological, geographical, and economic rupture. Parents, children, friends, and family could not be replaced. Trust in the nation and, on the local level, in one's neighbors, was shattered for many. The dismal economic conditions that plagued the entire country at liberation, coupled with the legacy of the antisemitic legislation, made the challenge of reconstructing individual lives even greater. In addition to difficulties in accessing government aid, surviving Jews suffered from the French provisional government's embrace of the notion of collective suffering, which deprived them of the cathartic recognition of their specific experience as victims of genocide. As Jews embarked on the journey back to their prewar homes and lives, they looked to other Jews for help.

AMERICAN JEWISH MEMBERS OF THE US MILITARY AND JEWISH SURVIVORS IN FRANCE

Isaac Klein, the chaplain discussed above serving in Chartres, was a Hungarian-born American rabbi trained in the Conservative movement.[39] He volunteered to provide religious counsel to the roughly five hundred and fifty thousand Jewish American men and women who had enlisted in the US Armed Forces.[40] At the outbreak of World War II, only twenty-nine rabbis were serving in the Reserve forces of the American military. This number increased dramatically during the war: 311 Jewish chaplains were mobilized, representing all three major branches of American Judaism (of the 311 Jewish chaplains, 147 were Reform, 96 were Conservative, and 86 were Orthodox). Over two-thirds of qualified and able American rabbis were involved in the war efforts.[41] The extremely high participation rate of American rabbis magnified and personalized the war experience for American Jews, who were eager for news from their relatives in the "old country" and their sons and daughters in the Armed Forces.

While American Jewish military personnel in general showed a particular interest in the situation of European Jews, those in the chaplaincy had greater freedom and were particularly able to help those in need. Active throughout Europe, chaplains accompanied Jews in France as they began the delicate process of reintegrating into French society. Through letters, reports, and press conferences, they organized an informal public information campaign on the needs of Jewish survivors and encouraged their troops and congregants at home to contribute to their efforts. Beyond the concrete aid chaplains provided, they sought to improve the morale of survivors and strengthen the bonds between the Jews of America and Europe through friendship, and even marriage. As representatives of American Jewish life, they hand delivered the humanitarian response to the Holocaust that American Jews had been attempting to provide, with only frustratingly limited success, during the war years.[42] The mission infused this solidarity with emotional intensity that moved both giver and receiver as chaplains' and GIs' efforts to provide material aid to surviving Jews will demonstrate.

MATERIAL AID TO SURVIVORS

As they set out to help surviving Jews, American Jewish chaplains and GIs shaped the early reconstruction of French Jewish life from the inside through close relationships with local Jewish leaders. Helping survivors was an overwhelming task, and chaplains and their Jewish troops faced a difficult balancing act. Chaplains were accountable to both the US military and the National Jewish Welfare Board, a private American Jewish communal organization that granted ecclesiastical endorsement to American rabbis for the chaplaincy through its Commission on Jewish Chaplaincy, which later became the Committee on Army-Navy Religious Activities (CANRA). Chaplains stationed in Europe were coordinated through the US Armed Force's Office of the Theatre Chaplain in Paris, where Rabbi Judah Nadich, a thirty-two-year-old Conservative rabbi who later became Eisenhower's advisor on Jewish affairs, was serving as senior Jewish chaplain.[43] Nadich's actions show to what extent chaplains became entangled in local Jewish affairs and influenced the earliest moments of reconstruction.

Nadich arrived in Paris ten days after its liberation on September 5, 1944. By evening the next day, he had been to the former JDC offices and had met with representatives of the Federation of Jewish Societies and Rabbi Julien Weill. Among other activities in his first week, he received Maurice Brener and members of the CUDJ, attended the liberation service at the rue de la Victoire synagogue, and requisitioned France's only Reform synagogue on the rue Copernic for the use of American troops. He also held several press conferences on the conditions of Parisian Jews, addressed the Zionist Youth Movement in Hebrew and Yiddish, and visited Parisian Jews in the canteens on the rue de Rosiers.[44] Throughout his stay in Paris, Nadich maintained an open-door policy for local Jews, whom he received daily in his quarters. He thus set an example that chaplains and soldiers could emulate and demonstrated that direct aid to Jews in France would not be punished by the military, or at least, that it was possible to render it under certain circumstances.

Like Nadich, Captain Edward Warburg, who was responsible for setting up refugee centers in France, benefitted from a prestigious position both in the military and in American Jewish life. Warburg had a longstanding relationship with the JDC through his family. His father, Felix Warburg, was one of the JDC's founders and had served as its honorary chairman until his death in 1937. Edward Warburg followed in his father's footsteps and served as JDC chairman from 1938 until his mobilization in the US Armed Forces. Warburg, in the days after the liberation of Paris, naturally went to the former JDC offices on the rue de Téhéran. There, he authorized French JDC representative Maurice Brener to borrow more funds in the American committee's name. In order to find food for the JDC to distribute, Warburg later recalled taking Brener to a military supply officer to whom he explained, "Here you have the whole Jewish population neatly organized. If you give them the amount of food they need, they can get the soup kitchens in the streets tonight [. . .]."[45] According to Warburg's account, the supply officer saw the logic in Warburg's suggestion and began providing food for the Jewish canteens in Paris.

Individual chaplains' and soldiers' acts to help survivors in France appear modest when compared with the feats of Nadich and Warburg, yet for many, the opportunity to respond to the Holocaust formed their prime motivation for enlisting. The American public had learned of the Nazi plan to annihilate the Jews in Europe in late 1942 and was well aware of the magnitude of Jewish suffering there before this time.[46] This knowledge incited American Jews to join the war effort. Chaplain's Assistant Israel Joel Philips, who was initially stationed in Normandy, explained, "I had volunteered to go to Europe eventhough [sic] I was pretty sure I could stay out of going. I felt that I wanted to be a soldier rather than a boyscout. I knew that Jews were in Europe, I myself was born there. I wanted to get there."[47] Deborah Dash Moore has shown how young American Jewish men struggled to overcome internal barriers, such as family responsibilities, and external ones, such as antisemitic stereotypes that cast doubt on the ability of Jews to fight, in order to enlist.[48] The strong participation rates of American Jews show to what extent World War II was a personal matter for them and can help explain their desire to help the surviving Jews of Europe.[49] Many American Jewish soldiers realized that the Jews they would encounter in Europe were victims of persecution and the remnants of European Jewry.[50] This emboldened Jewish GIs to operate as literal foot soldiers for chaplains. Chaplain Meyer Miller, a Reform rabbi from Connecticut who arrived in France in July 1944, explains, "Jewish GIs went out of their way to seek Jewish survivors, and did everything possible to help them. Not only did they give me their parcels, not only did they get clothing and blankets and other material for them, but they gave them [*sic*] themselves. They went out of their way to search out—and very often I remember soldiers coming to me and telling me that they had found Jewish survivors and families in various homes, and then I was able to call on them, visit them."[51]

Chaplain's Assistant Israel Joel Philips's quest to find survivors took him to a farm between Sainte-Mère-Eglise and Saint-Laurent-sur-Mer, where he had learned of a camp survivor who had been hiding as a French farmer. After an initial visit, Philips quickly returned to bring this person new boots.[52] To thank Philips, this individual taught him a prayer that had been sung in the camps, *Ani Maamim*, and offered him the yellow star he had been forced to wear by the Nazis. Chaplain Meyer Miller found a Jewish family of three hidden in Bayeux to whom he brought food, blankets, and clothes. He then helped a woman in Caen, who was also assisted by a group of American Jewish GIs. When passing through Paris, he sought out artists and important religious and communal figures. He provided food to the Lubavitcher rabbi, rabbis Jacob Kaplan and Julien Weill, and the sculptor Chana Orloff and Jewish literature and periodicals to other communal leaders. Miller met with local Jews in a restaurant in the *Pletzl*, the Jewish immigrant neighborhood in Marais, who provided Miller the addresses of their relatives in the United States. Miller wrote to their families to send news. In Fontainebleau, where Miller was stationed next and where the local synagogue had been destroyed, Miller helped four Jewish families resettle and included them in military celebrations of Jewish holidays. He also located fifteen Jewish children in hiding and arranged for their transfer into a Jewish children's home. Finally, Miller, who took over the chaplaincy of several units from Judah Nadich, arranged to donate several thousand francs that had been raised by American Jewish troops to a Jewish school near Paris.[53] Miller's aid distribution did not follow a given strategy; he simply helped those who crossed his path. Other chaplains, such as the Russian-born Reform rabbi Isadore Breslau, grew overwhelmed with individual requests and decided that the most efficient way to aid Jews in France was to help those already organized in groups.[54]

Modest initial efforts of many chaplains and soldiers soon gave way to more organized attempts to aid greater numbers of Jews. In addition to asking for contributions of food and money from their GIs, chaplains turned to congregants, family, and friends in the United States with lists of needed supplies. Because the civilian postal service was not yet operational, American Jews sent packages to individual chaplains. Chaplains, such as Chaplain Eli Bohnen, encouraged this practice by writing thank-you notes to the senders: "This is to acknowledge the receipt of your package which will be used for the relief of the Jewish survivors of Nazism. On behalf of all these Jews I extend my heartfelt thanks. May I express the hope that you will continue to send similar packages to me. The need here can never be adequately filled. Your help will go a long way toward helping the unfortunate Jews who look to you for aid in their moment of need."[55]

Packages addressed to American Jewish chaplains drew negative attention from both the military and the Jewish Welfare Board as army regulations prohibited the use of the army postal system for civilians. Furthermore, the direct solicitation of American Jews by chaplains caused tensions at the Jewish Welfare Board because it violated the centralized fundraising policy of the American Jewish community.[56] Chaplains often chose discretion as a means of getting things done. A double-wrapped package scheme was devised in which packages were addressed to individual soldiers and then distributed to the individuals whose address appeared on the second layer of wrapping.[57] Chaplain Abraham Haselkorn, who was particularly active in aiding Jewish children and those en route to Palestine, received a negative response when he wrote to the Jewish Welfare Board in New York, requesting clothing for the Jews he encountered.[58] He took matters into his own hands by asking Nadich to send him to London, where he organized a clothing drive and brought back a "planeload of clothes." Later, through his wife, he appealed to the women's Zionist organization, Hadassah, for food for Jews awaiting immigration to Palestine in *hachsharot*, kibbutz-like settlements in France designed to train future immigrants for life in Palestine. The president of this organization refused to get involved but referred Haselkorn to a woman who subsequently organized a shipment of seventy boxes of "religious supplies" containing the needed food.[59] Others, who were in close proximity to army warehouses, were able to access supplies without the hassle of shipping. Ralph Goldman, member of the 66th Infantry Division and who later would become known as "Mr. Joint" due to his role as executive vice president of the JDC, explained how he and other GIs were able to access army surplus to distribute to survivors:

> They would get a truck in the afternoon for the Chaplain, go to various government storehouses, and just take what we wanted. [...] And so, we would order sheets, blankets, [...] they would give it to us. In one particular instance I got, I don't know, 44,000 boxes of Milky Ways [the chocolate bar]. The manufacturer of Milky Ways in the United States put one wrapper around it instead of two. American soldiers could not eat any candy that did not have two wrappers, and therefore it was "*pas sûr*" [not safe]. And consequently, I picked up all those candies for the DPs.[60]

While it may have been relatively easy to channel damaged goods to survivors, others learned how to make precious commodities available from Catholic chaplains, who seem to have established a precedent.[61] Like Ralph Goldman, Chaplain Isadore Breslau, who was stationed in Marseille, managed to go to Nice regularly in spring 1945, where an estimated five thousand camp survivors had arrived. Thanks to a Catholic chaplain, Breslau had learned that simply kicking a box of supplies would damage it, which made it available to civilians. In this manner, he distributed powdered milk, oil, and coffee to Jews he met in Nice, who would then trade them on the black market for the supplies they needed. Breslau's Catholic colleague also showed him how to flash (but not give) his authorization pass to the soldiers guarding the supplies warehouse, therefore keeping it for future use.[62]

As these examples show, the US military maintained a tolerant policy toward Jewish aid efforts in France, as long as discretion was applied and non-official routes were used. Yet chaplains, like soldiers, ran the risk of being court-martialed, and this threat remained real for the duration of their service.[63] Political and religious ideology appear to have played a role in determining the extent of risk-taking, as did place and circumstance.

If solidarity fueled the distribution of American Jewish aid, it goes without saying that American Jewish chaplains and GIs were part of the larger "American Occupation" and represented, like all uniformed members of the US Armed Forces, the new face of power. American Jewish chaplains and GIs actively sought out newly liberated Jews; the latter, lacking basic resources and moral support, looked to these soldiers with hope, eager to enter into relationships. However, such relationships were not devoid of the moral ambiguities of the period, as seen in the case of the Lichtman family. As recent Polish immigrants, working in the garment industry from their apartment, the Lichtmans were especially vulnerable at the outbreak of World War II. Like many foreign Jews, Jacob Lichtman volunteered for the French Foreign Legion. He was killed in combat in June 1940 near Soissons. The newly widowed Hélène (Hana) Lichtman spoke Yiddish and only a little French. Dependent upon her neighbors, she spent the war years hiding in a maid's room in the third arrondissement of Paris. The family placed their only son, René, born in 1937, in hiding with a Catholic family in a northern suburb of Paris, Le Vert Galant. René was almost seven years old when he was reunited with his mother. As seen in their photograph, his mother and one of her girlfriends, also a Polish Jewish immigrant, found camaraderie in a group of American Jewish GIs. The group communicated in Yiddish, and clearly, as seen in the photos they took at the Place de la République and in a professional studio, they found their friendships meaningful enough to record. Young René, whom I interviewed in his late seventies, recalled that all of the American soldiers were married. Some of the women were as well, I later discovered.[64] With their wives at home in the

United States, helping out a group of Jewish women, one widowed with a young child and a second awaiting the return of her POW husband, the US soldiers in René Lichtman's photo album demonstrate the morally ambiguous nature of this aid: To what extent could surviving Jews say no to this needed help? What was demanded in exchange? How did gender influence how and when aid was provided? The photos point to an obvious, yet easily overlooked, fact: the individuals capable of providing aid were men. Those in need represented a more diverse bunch: women, men, young and old, of various linguistic and national backgrounds, as well as political and religious ideologies. The ability of the latter to obtain help was largely dependent on fitting into the larger goals and ideology of the aid provider. Nothing shows this more than aid to children.

AID TO CHILDREN

The chaos of liberation coupled with local Jews' acute needs provided chaplains with the power to shape reconstruction according to their own political and religious ideologies. This becomes clearer when examining the aid provided to Jewish children, which stands out as somewhat different from the other forms of aid provided by American Jewish chaplains and GIs. As seen above, aid from American Jewish members of the military was channeled to Jewish survivors in France through informal networks, chance meetings, and more organized structures, such as *hachsharot* and synagogues. Yet the military was on the move; its members rarely stayed in the same place for long periods of time. This made it difficult to provide consistent aid to those most in need or collaborate with French Jewish organizations. However, aid to Jewish children provides an example in which help came continuously, with responsibilities passed on from chaplain to chaplain. American-born chaplain Abraham Haselkorn, a Reform rabbi and staunch Zionist from New York, proved especially active on the behalf of children.

Late in August 1944, Haselkorn arrived in Le Mans, where the difficulties of his job soon became clear to him. He wrote to Philip Bernstein of the Jewish Welfare Board in New York that he "[could] be busy 48 hours a day taking care of the administrative job which I have, plus trying to serve the Jewish men in this area." But it was the Jewish refugee problem that "takes up much of my time and is growing to such proportions that it will be impossible for me to do justice to it, much as I should like."[65] Especially disturbed by the situation of Jewish children, Haselkorn took up the care of a group that had been hidden in the area surrounding Le Mans, a responsibility he inherited from Chaplain S. Appelbaum, who had taken over after the departure of Chaplain David Max Eichhorn.[66] Thanks to a former member of the Jewish resistance

Figure 2.1. A group of friends, American Jewish GIs and Polish Jewish Women, Place de la République, Paris, circa 1945. The group of friends spoke Yiddish together. The child, René Lichtman (*first row*), was recently reunited with his mother, both had survived the war in hiding. Private collection of René Lichtman.

Figure 2.2. The same group of friends posing together in a private studio, circa 1945. Private collection of René Lichtman.

named Trachtenberg, Haselkorn located additional Jewish children who had been hidden in local farms during the Occupation. Many of these children had been placed by Père Devaux of the Notre Dame de Sion order while the Jewish childcare organization OSE, in turn, had paid a monthly pension to the farmers who had hidden them.[67] Reflecting both Zionist and more widespread Jewish views, Haselkorn grew increasingly determined to reclaim the hidden children in the name of the Jewish people. Along with his assistant and Trachtenberg, Haselkorn searched the countryside and found over thirty-six children. In encounters with farmers, Trachtenberg posed as an unofficial US Army representative. If farmers resisted, Haselkorn and his team did not hesitate to threaten them—Haselkorn's American military uniform added weight to his words. When necessary, Haselkorn paid the farmers with his own funds in order to get the children back. In spite of these efforts, some farmers understandably refused to release the children without permission. After all, who were these soldiers and why should they be trusted? Having protected the children during the Occupation, some famers quite legitimately questioned Haselkorn's intentions. He did not find this acceptable.

Père Devaux, the priest in charge of Notre Dame de Sion also proved determined to keep the children under the auspices of his order. In late September 1944, Père Devaux met with Chaplain Judah Nadich to ask him to intervene against Haselkorn's efforts, arguing the children needed to remain with their host families until their parents returned from deportation.[68] Nadich, also a Zionist, suspected Père Devaux of wanting to convert the children to Christianity and sided with his chaplain. Haselkorn arranged a meeting with Père Devaux in Paris in November 1944 with the help of the American Jewish writer and war correspondent Meyer Levin, who later described this encounter in his autobiography:

> I was present in Paris a few days later when the rabbi confronted the priest, demanding, in the name of the Jewish community, the full list of the rescued Jewish children. It was a humiliating scene for both, and for humanity. For these men of God were at first polite with each other, the rabbi thanking the priest for his great humanitarian work in rescuing the children, and the priest insisting that he had done it all as part of his normal moral duty, without ulterior thought.
>
> But as the rabbi became insistent in his demand for the entire list, the priest began to hedge, saying he would first have to get in touch with any survivors in the childrens' [sic] families, to secure their consent. Soon their colloquy became a professional struggle over the souls of the surviving children; and beneath the surface of their words, it seemed to me that there was a primitive

hatred streaming from the most remote sources, going all the way back to all the legends of Christ-killing, and all the tales of Jew-burning.

[...] It was, to me, an ugly commerce. And this too would be leaving its scar on every soul, squabbled over for one god or another.[69]

Levin's portrayal of this interaction placed the rabbi and the priest on the same level, pointing out that their respective ideologies motivated both. Instead of the children's needs, these men were interested in their souls, representing an "ugly commerce" indeed. Still, Zionists like Haselkorn were not alone in their ardent belief that Jewish children should be returned to and cared for under Jewish auspices. Most Jews in postwar France held this conviction, leading to organized search committees and even legal battles.[70] One researcher has recently concluded that Devaux turned over most of the four hundred children saved under his auspices but did indeed refuse to return those who had been converted or who were in the process of conversion at the end of hostilities.[71]

Persisting in their quest, Haselkorn and Trachtenberg decided to open a home for the children they had found. The mayor of Le Mans offered to rent the local Château Mehancourt on the condition that Haselkorn would cover the $500 a month operating expenses for a period of at least three months.[72] Haselkorn agreed to these terms and began collecting funds. In September, he organized High Holiday services for American troops at the Le Mans Opera, which fourteen hundred soldiers attended. There he asked soldiers to contribute francs (as asking for dollar contributions was against army regulations) and collected the equivalent of about $5,000. In November 1944, the chaplain continued his fundraising by hosting a cocktail party (*vin d'honneur*) at the château. The Army post exchange (PX) provided Haselkorn with butter, chocolate, and cigarettes that could then be traded on the black market.[73] GIs regularly visited the children in the château and enlisted their own families in the United States to help provide needed supplies. Haselkorn's assistant, a cantor named Morton Shanok, gave lessons on Yiddish, Hebrew, and Judaism. Fifty to sixty children, ages three to sixteen, lived in the château and benefited from this American Jewish aid.

Haselkorn reflected widespread American Jewish concerns when he tried to reinstill the children with a sense of Jewish identity. As a Zionist, he also hoped to send them to Palestine. He imposed these views on the children, describing the "wailing and the howling" that took place when they decided to "strip" the children of their Christian medallions, especially among the youngest children, who felt the medallions would protect them from harm.[74] Haselkorn's draconian methods stood in stark contrast with the work of other

French Jewish childcare organizations during and after the Occupation as they purposefully sought to avoid sudden ruptures in identity.[75] Local French Jews and the children themselves may have been against Haselkorn's methods but were not in a position to complain.

The demands of Haselkorn's military service, however, restrained his zeal. He received transfer orders in December 1944 and attempted to contact French Zionist Marc Jarblum with the hope of sending the children to Palestine. When this fell through, Haselkorn contacted the Jewish childcare organization OSE, which then took over the home.[76] The efforts of Chaplain Haselkorn and his network of GIs led to a long-term solution for Jewish children that was integrated into the French Jewish social service network. Their actions represent a display of American Jewish power in liberation France but also the emotional nature of their solidarity.

AIDING THE ZIONIST CAUSE

Both French and American Jews in general agreed upon the need to return Jewish youth to the communal fold, while a more controversial agenda motivated other American Jewish chaplains in France. They assisted the Mossad le'Aliyah Bet, the prestate immigration organization of the Haganah, the Jewish Brigade of Palestine, and others in efforts to smuggle Jews and arms to Palestine. In the postwar period, France, due to its ports, became a crossroads for such activities.[77] The Jewish Agency, the de facto government of the Jewish settlement in Palestine, reestablished an office in Paris as early as October 1944; it was operated by Marc Jarblum, David Shaltiel, and Ruth Klüger (Aliav).[78] In his diary, Chaplain Judah Nadich reported regular meetings with these individuals, especially after March 1945. Nadich also met often with Sylvia Neulander, an American Jewish Zionist who had been recruited by Ruth Klüger to pose as a soldier's club organizer on behalf of the Red Cross in Pilsen, Czechoslovakia. There, with the help of Chaplain Eugene Lipman, she directed Jewish DPs toward camps in the American Zone.[79] From Paris, and later Germany, Nadich helped organize the convoys of DPs, provided them with supplies, and facilitated their entries into France, where they could then await passage to Palestine. Nadich's distinct Zionist outlook also shaped American policy on Jewish survivors. In June 1945, for example, Anna M. Rosenberg, a manpower and industrial relations consultant, came to Paris on behalf of the Truman administration to inquire about surviving French Jews. Nadich met with her at the Hôtel Ritz, where they decided Rosenberg would take back a memorandum to President Truman. Nadich turned to Klüger, Shaltiel, and Jarblum to prepare this document, demonstrating his role as conduit for postwar Zionist networks.[80]

Next to Nadich, Chaplain Abraham Haselkorn, seen above in Le Mans, was perhaps one of the most active of the American Jewish chaplains in France. Stationed in Marseille in July 1945, the Mossad approached Haselkorn to aid them in their efforts, which he did until his departure in early 1946. Among other tasks, he helped establish four *hachsharot* in the south of France and provided them with food and supplies. He used American military channels to obtain equipment for a clandestine radio station in Toulon so that members of the Mossad could communicate with Tel Aviv, passing on messages from his own office to the Jewish Agency in Paris by telephone. Finally, Haselkorn helped collect one to two hundred guns and, on one occasion, helped the Jewish Brigade smuggle arms they had purchased from Communists to a safe house inside a *hachshara*.[81] Chaplain's Assistant Robert Handwerger also reports collecting arms with Chaplain Hersh Livazer, a Polish-born Orthodox rabbi from New York. According to Handwerger, soldiers returning to the United States had the right to take home only one "souvenir" (weapon) and were supposed to return all others to the adjutant general's office. Instead, soldiers "returned" their guns via Livazer and Handwerger, who would smuggle them out of their living quarters at the Hôtel Majestic in Paris in boxes of clothes and candies.[82]

It has been argued that the US military encouraged chaplains to seek out a "nation building" role in the postwar period.[83] Surely, however, it did not intend them to take this role literally by smuggling arms to Palestine. As the chaplains sidestepped military guidelines, they became actors in the larger postwar geopolitical situation. It was more common, however, for chaplains to embrace the job for which the US Army and their rabbinical training had prepared them: organizing religious life.

RELIGIOUS RENEWAL: STRENGTHENING THE BONDS OF DIASPORA

American Jewish chaplains had not been emotionally prepared for the acute needs of the Jewish populations they encountered in Europe and often reported feeling inadequate and overwhelmed. As seen above, they improvised solutions to help survivors by turning themselves into one-man aid committees, foster parents, and arms smugglers. If there was one domain in which the chaplains were truly prepared, however, it was in the religious realm. Indeed, as rabbis, chaplains used synagogues to their fullest potential, capitalizing on Jewish holidays to foster a sense of community and solidarity between two branches of the Jewish diaspora. In the name of providing religious services to their troops, American Jewish chaplains sought to salvage what remained of French Jewish life, raised funds to rebuild synagogues, reinstated (and at times created) religious instruction for children, and called on their soldiers to bolster synagogue attendance. Of course, religious activities cannot be easily separated from politics. A strong belief in the Jewish people, which revealed an ethnic conception of the group and at times tinged with Zionism, shaped the help the chaplains provided.

In France, the official practice of Judaism, while never completely extinguished during the war, had existed in a moribund state for over four years.[84] The literature on postwar Jewish religious life in France has emphasized this period's continuity with the war years, underscoring the decline of the Consistory and heightened disaffiliation with Judaism.[85] Although useful in their general analyses, these studies have not taken into account the atmosphere of religious renewal that reigned immediately after the war, in large part due to the presence of American Jewish chaplains and soldiers. From famine to feast, in less than a month after the liberation of Paris, Jewish life in France underwent a total transformation. Synagogues that had been desecrated, bombed, or burned during the Occupation bustled with new life and energy as they resumed their intended function. An anecdote from a chaplain stationed in Marseille evokes an image closer to that of a Baptist church in the Southern United States than of a stark, declining Jewish community in France:

> The people in Marseilles... the Jewish community in Marseilles were so grateful to us—we took over their synagogue. [...] And we used to sing at that time *Adon Olam* [a traditional Jewish hymn] in this new jazzy music where there is response and re-response. And the boys on the right hand—well, I used to get about six or seven hundred boys on a Friday night in Marseilles. We were a staging area. There were a lot of boys. And they would shout *Adon Olam* and the people on the left would answer. One day, one of the little women, a little old woman from the civilian group were [sic] sitting in front of me ran up on the pulpit and put her arms around me and said, "*Vive le juiv* [sic]*! Vie* [sic] *le american, Vive le* ..." Everything. It was so exciting.[86]

The Jewish high holidays of 1944 fell in late September. According to Chaplain Judah Nadich, over three hundred individuals had attended the liberation service held at the rue de la Victoire synagogue in Paris earlier that month. But some three thousand, including a thousand members of the US military, came to this synagogue less than two weeks later to celebrate Rosh Hashanah, the Jewish New Year. Nadich, as the official representative of the American Jewish chaplains, spoke at the rue de la Victoire synagogue, and then continued on to the Sephardic synagogue on rue St. Lazare, where a thousand individuals, including two hundred GIs, had come to pray. The next day Nadich attended services at the rue Montevideo synagogue and concluded the holiday at the synagogue on rue Notre Dame de Nazareth.[87]

The strong mobilization of American Jewish soldiers was not out of sheer piety: Paris had been off limits to most of the American military since its liberation. Jewish soldiers, who were granted a three-day leave from the chaplain's headquarters in order to attend Rosh Hashanah, were thus given the opportunity to visit the City of Light. As Deborah Dash Moore notes: "As they piled into their 6-by-6 trucks, their thoughts focused less on Judaism than on 'clean sheets and hot showers.' After three months of living in tents and foxholes, a chance to enjoy civilization exerted more appeal than an occasion to pray."[88] Mary Louise Roberts also suggests that such enthusiasm was not exactly religious: "Most GIs did not give a damn about the *Mona Lisa*. They came to Paris for one reason and one reason only: sex."[89] In a recent interview, 101-year-old Hyman Fox, a former Jewish GI who was stationed in Nancy with the Army Signal Corp, recalled his excitement at being allowed to go to Paris. It was the Place de l'Etoile and its traffic that impressed this young Detroiter.[90] Regardless of what drew Jewish GIs to Paris, many found the time to contribute to revivifying French Jewish life with their presence and new melodies. Even more numerous at Yom Kippur services—twelve hundred GIs attended the rue de la Victoire synagogue on the eve of the holiday for the *Kol Nidre* service, according to Nadich—American Jewish military personnel also distributed prayer books in French from the Jewish Welfare Board and gave two large packages of mezuzot (encased scrolls, typically placed on the doorposts of Jewish homes) to local Jews, which could be used in the traditional fashion or worn as necklaces.[91] Such public displays of belonging suggest that the encounters between French and American Jews held a symbolic meaning, serving as proof of the vitality and resilience of Jewish life in the aftermath of the Holocaust.

Outside of the capital, other chaplains worked to reconstruct religious life in diverse ways. The US military, which saw religious practice as a means of maintaining order and unity, encouraged the celebration of Jewish holidays.[92] Chaplains organized the celebration of Jewish holidays in cities throughout France, including Rouen, Le Mans, Chartres, Valenciennes, St. Quentin, and Reims, among others. Cities were selected according to their proximity to troops, not the needs of local Jewish communities. Soldiers and officers leapt at the chance to take advantage of furloughs and created an impressive showing. Previously mentioned Hyman Fox, the Army Signal Corps wire chief from

Detroit, was one of six or seven GIs who regularly attended Shabbat services in Nancy during his nine-month mission in town. American GIs outnumbered the local community at the 1945 Passover seder, providing an altogether different image of the American Jewish presence.

Preparing for the holidays, finding a venue that could hold several thousand individuals, and in the case of Passover, preparing the seder fell on the shoulders of chaplains, who turned to local Jews for help. Chaplain Klein sought to obtain kosher meat for between one and three thousand people for the Passover seder of 1945 in St. Quentin, and when this proved too difficult, his "boys" told him a meal of borsht and gefilte fish would suffice. After considerable footwork, Klein found a locale large enough to host the event. Klein's account of his exchange with the owner of the restaurant demonstrates the complicated yet comical problems of reproducing American Jewish culinary culture in postwar France. When asked by the owner why he wanted to bring his own personnel to prepare the food, Klein responded:

"I want to cook Jewish food."

He [the owner] said, "There is nothing that a French chef can't cook."

I said, "Do you know how to make gefilte fish? [...] Gefilte fish is the way Jews make fish."

[the owner]: *Mais oui! Fish à la Yid.*

So I said, "You tell me what's *fish à la yid*." I found out that *fish à la yid* was what we call breaded fish. I said, *Monsieur, fish à la Yid ce n'est pas gefilte fish and gefilte fish ce n'est pas fish à la yid.* [Sir, *fish à la Yid* is not gefilte fish and gefilte fish is not *fish à la yid*]

Alas, Klein concluded, "You better let me bring my own cooks." With a thousand kilos of fish and two local Jewish women to prepare the food, Klein and his troops were able to "make the Seder, in style."[93]

Restoring religious life plunged French and American Jews into a close collaboration, rendering the bonds of diaspora more tangible. In 1945, Chaplain Isaiah Rackovsky, an Orthodox rabbi in his late thirties, was sent to Biarritz, where the US Army operated a university for three thousand students until March 1946. There, he raised money among the American Jewish students to help rebuild the local synagogue and then officiated at Yom Kippur services for the local Jews, which they permitted on the condition that he learn their traditional melodies for *Ne'ilah*, the closing service. He also made great efforts to organize a circumcision for a child who had been born during the war, again

Figure 2.3. Army Signal Corps wire chief Hyman Fox, circa 1945. Private collection of Hyman Fox.

Figure 2.4. Passover in 1945 in Nancy drew American troops from throughout the region and was held in the local synagogue. Private collection of Hyman Fox.

with the financial help of his soldier-students.[94] In the same period, Chaplain Carl Miller, a Reform rabbi from Ohio, was stationed in Nice, where he spoke at the consistorial synagogue about Jewish life in the United States. Miller also received special permission and an army bus to take a group of Jewish children for an afternoon of play in Monaco.[95]

Contact between local Jewish youth and American Jewish GIs appears to have been cultivated by both the French and Americans with the hope of creating more lasting ties. In Paris, Chaplain Judah Nadich organized a Chanukah service and dance in December 1944 that was attended by six hundred people, including one hundred and twenty-five young French Jewish women. In Nadich's words, this was "a very successful function with the Jewish soldiers and officers meeting the French, [sic] Jewish girls."[96] One year later, in December 1945, Chaplain Carl Miller held a Chanukah party at Poznanski's kosher restaurant in Nice for a hundred and fifty GIs, officers, and young civilians. Miller wrote to his family that the party had a menu of fish, salami, potato pancakes, and Coca-Cola with singing and dancing until midnight. This chaplain, who appears to have placed great value on linking communities within the diaspora, replaced Chaplain Rackovsky at the Army University in Biarritz in January 1946. There, Miller organized a group of nineteen American soldier-students to meet with the Jewish Student's Association of Bordeaux, with whom they toured the city and held a dance. The American Jews were hosted by French Jewish families, who served them sumptuous meals, some of which included shellfish (doubly forbidden, one might add, because in addition to being unkosher, it came from the black market).[97]

The systematic study of ketubot (marriage contracts) of the Paris Consistory for this period reveals that such events led to lasting connections between American and French Jews. Jewish members of the American military breached military policies that discouraged marriage and tied the knot in consistorial synagogues.[98] The Paris Consistory allowed American chaplains, such as Irwin Hyman and Harry Essrig, to perform marriages in its synagogues on several occasions. At least ten marriages involving at least one American spouse took place in 1945 in Parisian consistorial temples, representing at least 5 percent of the total marriages performed that year in these institutions.[99]

American Jewish chaplains emphasize their ability to help French Jews, a situation facilitated by the chaos of liberation, the lax attitudes of the military, and the acute needs of surviving Jews. Their accounts downplay the agency of local Jews, presenting them as grateful, yet passive, aid recipients. Paying attention to French voices offers a more complex view of early reconstruction efforts.

AMERICAN AND FRENCH JEWS IN REIMS: "CROSSING" THE NARRATIVES

The small Jewish community of Reims, 140 kilometers east of Paris, provides an opportunity to explore Franco-American Jewish interaction from a French point of view in order to question how the extended presence of the American military affected the local Jewish populations. This city maintained an important American presence because it served as a hub for the US Armed Forces and for a period housed the Supreme Headquarters Allied Expeditionary Force (SHAEF). In mid-May 1945, 24,500 military personnel were stationed in Reims alone, consisting primarily of American forces but also Allied forces and prisoners of war liberated by the Allies as they advanced into German territory.[100] The American and British military employed almost nine thousand French workers, leading to even greater contact between the civilian population and the military.[101] Contrary to the rest of France, which saw a decrease in the American military presence after VE Day, Reims remained an important military hub, serving as a stopover for troops en route to Asia. These conditions placed the Reims Jewish community in contact with American Jewish military for a two-year period.[102] The small size of the Jewish community in Reims led to the development of strong social networks; these were attested to in the oral history interviews I conducted with multiple generations of individuals.[103] Without claiming to be representative, these local accounts, in addition to those of the American Jewish chaplains who served in Reims, generate a rare body of sources that help shift the gaze from American narratives to those of the French. By looking at Jewish survivors in Reims, French Jewish perceptions of the American presence come to the fore and shed light on the actions of local Jews in the early reconstruction process.

At liberation, Madame Berthe Harrari, a young widow in her early thirties, was living in Reims with her elderly parents and young son. Before the war Harrari trained as a nurse by the French Red Cross. These credentials and her fluent knowledge of German helped to protect her and her small family during the war. During part of the Occupation, she worked in a German-run hospital in Reims, where she hid her Jewish identity at considerable risk.[104] At liberation, her small family reclaimed its home, which had been emptied of most of its contents, and made do with ration tickets and limited furniture. While the family was not particularly religious, Berthe Harrari's father, Paul Grass, was elected president of Reims' Jewish community after the war. Describing herself as "not too synagogue," Harrari nonetheless attended the local synagogue in the months following the liberation.[105] There, she encountered other local Jews, such as the Marx family, who had survived the war in hiding near the Spanish border and returned to Reims in 1944. Like the Grass family, the Marx family was originally from Alsace-Lorraine and had moved westward to remain French after 1871. A proud French citizen, Georges Marx had fought in World War I, an experience which earned him not only a sense of patriotic fulfillment but lasting ties to non-Jews. In exchange for their valuables, Marx's former lieutenant hid the family during the Occupation.

At liberation, when the family returned to its empty home in Reims, the daughters, Denyse and Nicole, were thirteen and seventeen years old, respectively.[106] Only slightly older than the Marx girls were Hélène Lerner and Solomon (Serge) Ejnès. Unlike the Grass and the Marx families, the Ejnès and Lerner families had recently immigrated to France from Poland and spoke Yiddish at home. The Ejnès family arrived in France in 1933 when their son, Solomon, was eight. The family stood out in the small Jewish community as one of the only ones who maintained an Orthodox approach to Judaism and kept kosher. As naturalized French citizens who spoke French with difficulty, this family was considered foreign, both within and outside of the Jewish community. During the war, the family dealt with this increased vulnerability by sending their three children to the Southern Zone separately. Thanks to a Protestant friend's papers, Solomon changed his name to Serge and managed to avoid forced labor in Germany by finding employment in a factory. In the meantime, Hélène Lerner, a young woman of eighteen at liberation and the first of her family to be born in France, was near Lyon. There, she assisted in the resistance work organized by the French Jewish scouting movement. In April 1944, Lerner's brother, Louis, was arrested and deported to Buchenwald. These individuals, each with their unique trajectory and war experience, returned to Reims after the war, where one hundred Jewish families had been members of the Consistory in 1939 and where only forty-eight Jewish families were living in 1945.[107] Almost two-hundred Jews were deported from the city, and only seven returned.[108] Hélène Lerner's brother, weighing barely thirty-five kilograms, was one of the lucky few.

The Centrality of the Synagogue

As different as they may have been, these Jews were all drawn to the local synagogue in the months following Reim's liberation. The synagogue, which had been pillaged in March 1942 and used as storage—for airplane engines or possibly explosives—was restored to its original function by the Jewish inhabitants of Reims and Jewish members of the American military.[109] Chaplain Isaac Klein, who had enthusiastically greeted the Jewish survivors of Chartres, was

Figure 2.5. Chaplain Isaac Klein (*left*) and his assistant (*right*) with the members of the Reims Religious School, December 1945. Private collection of Denyse Marx.

transferred to Reims after the Jewish High Holidays in September 1944. As he roamed around the synagogue and contemplated the destruction of the Jewish community, he felt as if he were "in a museum rather than in a living institution."[110] Klein reported in letters, his memoirs, and an oral history interview how he proceeded to infuse his energy into reestablishing the communal life of the synagogue.[111] With the help of his soldiers and his congregation in Springfield, Massachusetts, funds were raised to establish a free-loan association to help the returning families. Communal leaders organized a formal board and committee to evaluate the loan applications. When the board asked Klein to become the community's official rabbi, at first he declined, turning to the Central Consistory to find a French rabbi. When the Consistory proved unable to do so, he "assured them that Uncle Sam would be very glad unofficially to allow me to give them all the assistance in my power and to serve their religious needs."[112] Klein reinstated Friday-night services, which drew French civilians and American military personnel together, filling the synagogue with three to four hundred individuals weekly. A curiosity about Americans and a longing for community drew new faces to the synagogue, including many who had not attended regularly before the war. When Klein gently reprimanded those talking during the services, one local woman, Madame Mosel, told him (according Klein's account), "*Monsieur le Chaplain*, in America, when you conduct the services and you speak to your congregation, they understand what you are saying and listen to you. Here we sit bored because we do not understand a word of what you are saying."[113] Indeed, until that point, Klein had conducted services as he had in the United States—in English and Hebrew. After consulting his troops, he decided to speak in slow, "unamericanized" Yiddish every other week. He remarked with some mischievousness that this forced the French Jews to ask the foreign Jews to translate, thus inverting the hierarchy between French and foreign Jews that had carried over from the interwar period. Several months after his arrival, Orthodox rabbi Hersh Livazer, the Zionist arms smuggler, joined Klein. Thereafter, the chaplains took turns officiating Friday-night services and shared the role of planning Jewish holidays. Chanukah 1944, followed by Purim, Passover, Rosh Hashanah, and Yom Kippur of 1945, were celebrated under American auspices, with Livazer taking over after Klein's departure in spring 1945.

Opening Jewish Homes?

The synagogue created a space where local Jews of diverse political and ideological stances could interact with American Jews. Such encounters were not, however, limited to the synagogue. When young Berthe Harrari opened the door of the Grass family home to a group of American soldiers she had seen at the shul (synagogue), she was embarrassed to tell them that she had nothing to offer them to eat. They attempted to put her at ease, explaining they would be happy with just a cup of tea. Yet Berthe Harrari did not even have tea. This provided the soldiers with a good excuse to return, this time, with the packages sent from home—fittingly, each with a box of tea.[114] Regularly thereafter, the Grass family received twelve to fifteen American Jewish soldiers in their home each evening. Most of the family's furniture had been stolen, but the GIs piled their coats and weapons on the floor and gathered around the remaining piano, exchanging songs, stories, and pictures of family. American Jewish soldiers were welcome not only in the Grass home but also at the Marx's, where fifteen to twenty soldiers were received each evening in the garden under the watchful eye of Monsieur and Madame Marx, who did not feel that an American soldier would make a suitable match for their seventeen-year-old daughter. The Ejnès home also became a meeting place for the most Orthodox of the American GIs.

Chaplain Livazer spent a great deal of time there, helping the family secure kosher food and enjoying the fruits of his labor.[115]

The accounts of these French Jews focus on the friendships they developed with the Americans in Reims after the war. Unlike the accounts of the American chaplains, these emphasize exchanges that occurred in homes rather than synagogues. They use words such as *trust*, *comfort*, and *family* to characterize these relationships. Berthe Harrari recalls that the soldiers would drink their tea and then go into the kitchen to do their own dishes.

The vast material inequality that separated American Jews and French Jews encouraged sharing. In the words of Berthe Harrari, "They brought us ice cream, they brought us oranges, they brought us everything they had because they had everything in abundance and we still had nothing at that moment. We still had ration tickets."[116] Yet those interviewed refused to describe their relationships with Americans in solely materialistic terms and, without being prompted, violently criticized those who took advantage of this solidarity by reselling food on the black market. "We didn't take advantage,"[117] repeated Denyse Marx over ten times in the course of our interview.

In their accounts, the Jews of Reims recognized the material aid they received from American Jewish soldiers yet refuted the idea that aid was unilateral. Instead, French Jews described these encounters as an exchange in which both parties had something to offer. Most importantly, French Jews offered their hospitality to Americans, which, as intangible as it may have been, served to balance out the inequalities that divided them. Berthe Harrari explained, "One day, one [an American] came over and brought a friend from shul. [...] We were all at the table with this young man, [who said] 'I am really proud, it's an honor to be here.' And so his friend [...] told him 'You know, the first time is not an honor. The second time is an honor. Many have come a first time, but if you are invited again, if they say to come back, then that is an honor.' That really flattered me. I was happy."[118]

French Jewish families provided hospitality on their own terms, attentive to respectful behavior and shared affinities. A general suspicion pervaded these interactions, especially those involving young women, coherent with the larger atmosphere of sexual violence experienced in French cities with a US military presence during the postwar period.[119] Denyse Marx, while only an adolescent at the time, recalls that those deemed to have acted inappropriately with her older sister were not invited back. Lillian Schoem, the wife of one of the American Jewish soldiers received in the Marx home, spoke of her husband's pride at finally receiving permission to take the Marx girls for ice cream.[120] In addition to their hospitality, French Jews offered solace to

Figure 2.6. Young Denyse Marx and soldiers Harry Stein and David Schoem, Reims, January 13, 1946. The inscription reads, "As a souvenir of our friendship, [hoping] to see you again soon." Private collection of Denyse Marx.

American soldiers, who were battle weary and far from home. Both Marx and Harrari remembered soldiers weeping in their homes and proudly reported having created a sense of family for them.

Establishing a New Order?

Beyond the direct benefits of the food and solidarity, accounts of the American Jewish presence in Reims suggest this presence offered a sense of protection and freedom to the Jewish community. This helped French Jewish teens reclaim the joie de vivre associated with a normal coming of age, which they were deprived of during the Occupation. Still, accounts show young women and men did not experience the newfound freedom in the same manner, signaling the gendered nature of aid from American Jewish GIs and chaplains. Interestingly, in spite of their wary parents, women of three different generations shared anecdotes involving jeeps, a symbol of both America and freedom. Adolescent Denyse Marx chose the name Jeep for her beloved dog. Berthe Harrari proudly spoke of her special authorization to ride in American military jeeps in order to translate for soldiers. Hélène Lerner, who was taking the baccalaureate examination on

June 6, 1944, in Lyon and threw her exam in the air when she learned of the Allied invasion, had to repeat her final year of high school in Reims. American Jewish soldiers helped her prepare for the philosophy and English sections of the baccalaureate. On the day of the exam, they accompanied her to school in their jeep. This prompted the disapproval of her teacher, who told her she was "going down the wrong track."[121] Riding in American jeeps provided freedom of movement, sent a visual example of protection to former collaborators, and for women, offered the additional thrill of challenging gender conventions.

Still, Jewish girls and young women were under surveillance by their parents, teachers, and at times, even the chaplains. In one case, a chaplain broke up a relationship between a local Jewish girl and a Jewish GI by telling the girl's parents the soldier in question wasn't good enough for her; in another anecdote involving a chaplain and a local woman, the parents intervened, preferring their daughter not marry a rabbi.[122] Not all parents prevented their daughters from getting involved with American Jewish GIs. In the nearby town of Nancy, Hyman Fox was invited to meet the parents of Simone, a local Jewish woman with whom he spent his free time. This time it was the soldier and not the parents who grew wary. After meeting her parents, Hyman lied and told Simone he had a fiancée back in Detroit. She wrote to him a few months after his departure, her almost flawless English revealing a hint of bitterness:

> I'm sure you're living your new life again, and I guess that all the nice hours you spent over here would'nt [sic] tempt you anymore.
> Perhaps my new address will surprise you. Well, I'm back home. I had found through the medium [sic] of friends of mine a very nice job as librarian in a camp around Reims with people who were very pleasant to work with. I did'nt [sic] enjoy it for a long time for I got an "ultimatum" from my parents and I had to come home "tout de suite" [...]. I'm no more talking English and I do regret it as much as I do regret the delightful hours I spent in Nancy and Reims. I'm living in this town you have seen, where entertainments are just a "souvenir."[123]

It was one thing for Simone's parents to allow her to date a prospective marriage partner in Nancy; it was another to let her extend this experience by working in what was most likely a military camp outside of Reims. Indeed, the accounts of the general population of Reims focus on the water and electricity shortages, drunken soldiers, violence against local women, and the requisitioning of private and public buildings, leading locals to speak of the "American Occupation."[124] Jews were also aware of the potential dangers of the American presence. Denise (Caraco) Siekierski, who worked in a Jewish aid committee in Marseille after the war wrote about what she also labeled the "American occupation": "We were helped a little by the Jewish chaplains of the American Army, which was practically occupying Marseille. But the American Occupation wasn't too fun [drôle]! I was twenty-years-old, and for a woman of my age, walking around alone at night in the streets of Marseille was at least as dangerous as it was during the German Occupation. The Americans drank too much ... an extremely unpleasant atmosphere dominated the city."[125]

Franco-American Jewish solidarity coexisted with and was informed by this larger context. Still, without excluding the idea American Jewish military personnel may also have carried out acts of violence against French civilians, the more prevalent image that emerges from Jewish sources is one of a dual protection: Jewish GIs and chaplains helped Jewish survivors recover from Nazi Occupation, just as they helped protect them from the excesses of the "American Occupation." In both of these roles, Jewish GIs and chaplains, as well as survivors, were aware of the power of the uniform.

In Reims, in the period before formal court proceedings for the return of Jewish property, Chaplain Klein reported helping several individual Jews reclaim their homes and businesses, adding military authority to their moral pleas.[126] Furthermore, local Jews relied on the presence of American Jewish military in their homes to act as a buffer from the bothersome and potentially violent American soldiers who provoked local disapproval. American GI David Schoem, who served in the Oise Intermediate Command and was stationed in Reims in 1945, remembered breaking the fast after Yom Kippur in the Lerner's home when a group of drunken soldiers tried to come in, thinking it was the entrance to a bar. "Everyone was frightened," Schoem wrote, "but I went to the door and convinced them that they were making a mistake, and they left without making any trouble."[127]

Beyond these concrete examples reported by Americans, in which American Jewish troops took the defense of local Jews, their presence also symbolized a new postwar era in which the Jews, and not the Nazis, wore the uniform. The symbolic benefits of the American Jewish presence are seen clearly in accounts of Passover 1945, when Chaplain Livazer organized a seder for several thousand individuals in the social hall on rue Gambetta of Reims. The chaplain's written account focuses on the difficulty of planning this event, especially because of the rumors that it would be attended by General Eisenhower. Livazer proudly detailed the help provided by his military colleagues in obtaining the necessary materials for the seder and his ingenious use of army bedsheets, which created lovely white tablecloths, and the glass encasements from German mines, which made perfect soup bowls.[128] The accounts of local Jews also highlight the atmosphere of collaboration and the work required for such an event. The food was stored at the Grasses' home, and Berthe Harrari and Hélène Lerner, along with six other local women, helped prepare the meal. Yet what stands out most in these accounts were the German prisoners of war who had been assigned by the American military to help in the preparations, both to pluck the poultry and peel the horseradish for the seder plate. This strong herb, which is eaten during the seder to evoke the bitterness of enslavement in Egypt and provokes tears while grated, made the German prisoners of war cry. The unexpected German tears brought the Jewish community to the site, where they took turns watching the Germans cry.[129] This example of the new postwar order, situated during the holiday in which the Jews of Reims celebrated the escape from Egypt and the transition from slavery to freedom, took on a particularly symbolic meaning for French and American Jews alike.

CONCLUSION

Oral history accounts of the encounter between American and French Jews in liberation France demonstrate the close interactions that shaped mutual perceptions. While the examples presented here represent only a small sample, they suggest that in Reims and elsewhere, American Jewish chaplains contributed to reconstructing French Jewish life by providing concrete aid, especially to children and the Zionist cause, and rekindling Jewish religious life. Unlike the aid efforts of American Jewish organizations, which would begin in early 1945 and were centralized in Paris, aid from Jewish members of the American military reached Jews in remote areas of France. As seen in the case of Reims, a new postwar order was felt intensely when the small Jewish community became host to a large number of American Jewish troops. For Jews in France, these efforts created the expectation that American Jews would send more help.

For American Jews, especially those who chose to enlist to fight the Nazis, the liberation of France provided them with the long-awaited chance to *do something*, even if the Holocaust had already transpired. Chaplains served as ambassadors for American Jews. They mobilized a large stateside audience. In reports, press conferences, letters, and sermons, they convincingly argued that an organized approach to aiding European Jews was needed and that France, as home to the largest survivor population in Western Europe, deserved this aid.

However welcome it may have been, the actual aid from the American Jewish military personnel remains difficult to quantify. Anecdotes gleaned from oral histories suggest that the distribution of this aid, while at times abundant, was piecemeal and arbitrary: some were able to benefit immensely, while others remained in need. Jewish artist Alfred Aberdam thus wrote from Paris in

November 1944, "They talk to us about America. In the meantime, all that we see from America is a few soldiers, that's all. We aren't sure to benefit [from this assistance], in spite of the fact that we have so deeply suffered."[130] It should also be noted that the GIs and chaplains providing aid were all men, whereas the recipients were not. Gender dynamics surely exacerbated the unequal power relations inherent in philanthropic aid.

Nonetheless, it would be anachronistic to minimize the importance of such aid because it was not distributed systematically, especially in light of its important significance in the eyes of both giver and receiver. American aid allowed for the establishment of individual and, at times, intimate relationships between two groups who had experienced the war under extremely different circumstances. In the case of Reims, these bonds remained intact long after the demobilization of the American troops. American Jewish soldier Harry Stein sent his daughter to learn French at the Marxes' home in the late 1960s. In 1974, Denyse Marx traveled with her family to visit the Stein family in Stratford, Connecticut, before going to Washington, DC, to see David Schoem and his family.[131] The Schoem family attended the marriages of the Marxes' children. Berthe Harrari Créange also maintained correspondence and sent her children to visit the families of former soldiers in the United States. The commemorative efforts led by Serge Ejnès, Françoise Nochimowski, and Jacqueline Husson to publish a memorial book for the Jewish community of Reims mobilized Jews on both sides of the Atlantic, who contributed letters, photos, and anecdotes.[132] This continued contact, long after the immediate postwar period, dedicated to remembering shared events provided both French and American Jews multiple occasions to forge narratives of the postwar period that emphasized primarily positive memories and feelings of belonging to a larger group. As seen in a telling account, chaplains Klein and Livazer sought to cultivate a sense of Jewish peoplehood in their interactions with local Jews. Indeed, on VE Day the Jewish youth decided, against the wishes of their parents, to march in the liberation parade as Jews, under a blue-and-white flag. Local youth Serge Ejnès later recalled that "as soon as our flag and banner appeared to the first people packed at the corner of the Boulevard [...] we heard 'Oh, the Jews...', and then a silence, and then 'long live the Jews,' once, twice, ten times, a hundred times and the clapping touched us to the heart. That was unbelievable but true. That very day, at that very time, we were no longer outcasts. For that crowd, we were the most tangible symbol of the regained freedom, and that crowd was for us the embodiment of the re-born human brotherhood."[133]

If, for Ejnès, marching as a Jew led to a cathartic reentry into the French nation, Chaplain Isaac Klein, who had left Reims several months before and had heard about the parade, interpreted it differently. For him, this event showed that his teachings had indeed been integrated: "These were the youngsters that I had influenced, and a sense of pride welled up in me when I heard the story."[134]

These findings add nuance to the historical narrative on civilian-military interaction in postwar France, which casts American GIs in an exclusively negative light, just as the historiography on Jewish civilian-military interaction is rendered more complex when we address how local Jews perceived those who assisted them in the aftermath of liberation. American GIs were not just liberators nor were they only vectors of violence and misbehavior. Some, motivated by solidarity, interacted closely with Jewish civilians in order to provide material aid. Distinct circumstances in liberation France provided American Jewish military personnel with a great deal of power to help local Jews. However, the ideology of the provider clearly influenced the aid, and there were certainly abuses of power. Helping civilians was not an exclusively Jewish experience, although further studies are needed to document how Protestant and Catholic chaplains approached their work in postwar France. In the case of Jews in Reims, American aid responded to deeply felt material and psychological needs at a moment when larger French society downplayed Jewish suffering. Yet Jews remained wary of American GIs, even if they shared a Jewish bond, and carefully selected those whom they permitted to enter their homes. Still, in many cases, American Jewish members of the military offered a sense of protection during this chaotic transition.

The history and memory of the first postwar contact between American and French Jews suggests that for the American and French Jews who were active in their respective military and civilian Jewish communities, expressing solidarity across national lines was a way of affirming a sense of belonging to the Jewish people and a means of responding to the Holocaust. In spite of their strikingly different wartime experiences and material situations, these individuals made the first steps in reconstructing French Jewish life. While awaiting a more organized solution, Jewish members of the American military eased the burden of individual Jews in France in important ways, which led to a primarily positive perception of American Jews. The institutionalization of American Jewish aid would add a new element of complexity to Franco-American Jewish relations, since American Jewish organizations had to develop partnerships with French organizations in order to distribute their aid. The days of simply sharing a box of tea were over.

THREE

EMERGING FROM CATASTROPHE

American and French Jewish Welfare in the Immediate Postwar Period

A YOUNG WOMAN OF SIXTEEN when Hitler came to power, Lolita Eschborn and her family left Germany to seek refuge in Portugal in 1933. In 1940, she was tutoring students in English, French, and German when the head of the Portuguese Jewish community suggested she contact the newly opened offices of the American Joint Distribution Committee (JDC). During her interview with Dr. Joseph Schwartz, soon to be head of JDC's European operations, she admitted she didn't know why she had come and claimed she didn't really have any skills. Annoyed, Schwartz asked her current profession and began to smile when he realized her fluency in the languages the JDC needed in order to conduct business (German, French, Spanish, Portuguese, and English). Schwartz offered Eschborn a significant increase in salary, and Eschborn—as secretary, interpreter, and jack-of-all trades—became the first local employee of the JDC in Lisbon. Her 1941 marriage to an American JDC employee, Melvin Goldstein, who later became the assistant secretary of the JDC's European executive council, linked Lolita Goldstein to the JDC long after she resigned from her position. Indeed, in light of her husband's increasing importance in the organization, and indicative of the traditional gender dynamics there, both Lolita Goldstein and her husband felt it was preferable for her to resign from her position in 1946.[1] But in summer 1945, Lolita Goldstein was still a JDC employee, making her way from Lisbon to Paris. Her baggage included the files of the JDC European headquarters.

With the war officially over in Europe, the JDC decided to move its European headquarters back to Paris. This choice would lead to the Goldsteins' relocation, followed by that of other Americans, such as Herman and Charmion Stein and Blanche Bernstein, reestablishing an American environment in the

Figure 3.1. The employees of the JDC in Lisbon celebrating the end of the war, May 8, 1945. Lolita Goldstein is holding the flag of her new country. Private collection of Lolita Goldstein.

Parisian JDC offices. Dr. Schwartz and his American staff lived in requisitioned hotels, obtained their food in Army post exchanges (PXs), and dined regularly in Parisian restaurants. They held evening meetings, over whiskey, in Dr. Schwartz's hotel room, where the day's work was reviewed and important decisions on European reconstruction were made.[2]

Sandwiched between World War II and the Cold War, historians have only recently begun exploring the role of humanitarian organizations during this transitional period.[3] Building on previous scholarship on the JDC in France,[4] this chapter marks the first analysis of the postwar transition from French to American leadership, which is key to understanding the larger themes in the reconstruction of French Jewish life. The JDC embraced a different mission than the other nongovernmental organizations, such as the United Nations Relief and Rehabilitation Administration (UNRRA), which sought to rebuild nation-states and promote internationalism in the aftermath of war.[5] In France, the JDC sought to reanchor Jews in the nation-state as a means of ensuring European Jewish survival after the Holocaust. Its main concern was salvaging

European Jewish life, but its solutions, at least in France, took the form of reintegrating local Jews into the nation by providing economic aid and insisting, without much success, that the French provisional government share responsibility for the welfare of this population. This can be contrasted with JDC policy in Germany and Austria, where it provided assistance to German and Austrian Jews willing to stay, but especially facilitated Jewish emigration.[6]

Analyzing who was providing aid to Jews points to larger issues of Jewish belonging in postwar France. Though historians have developed increasingly complex approaches to the French state during the Nazi Occupation, they have only recently begun to deconstruct the attitudes of the postwar French provisional government on Jews.[7] The growing body of research suggests that Jews remained a distinct group in this period, both in the eyes of the agents of the Republic and the Jews themselves.[8] Indeed, as observers have pointed out, Vichy's discriminatory categories may have been annulled in August 1944 but their effects remained quite real. Trapped in a "strange silence,"[9] an expression coined in September 1945 to describe the absence of Jews from French public discourse, Jews struggled to address their specific legal and welfare needs against the dominant discourse of universal French suffering. Understanding the JDC's relationship with the French provisional government sheds light on how Jews and the Republic faced the paradox of Jewish belonging in the aftermath of the Holocaust.

Questioning the transition from French to American leadership at the JDC, and the relationship the organization cultivated with Jews in France, also provides the opportunity to explore postwar Americanization from the bottom up. While the JDC remained active in France throughout the war years, its French representatives were more or less cut off from its American direction after 1942. What shape had French Jewish welfare efforts taken in the absence of American JDC leadership? At the end of hostilities, the French Jewish leaders who had been involved with JDC operations during the war were confronted with a series of challenges. First and foremost, they were helping needy populations and managing what they considered an unprecedented humanitarian crisis. At the same time, the management of the JDC in New York wanted to know what had happened during the war, both to the Jews of France and in the name of the JDC. The important question of finances—assessing how much money had been spent, how many loans had been contracted in the name of the JDC, and how they would be repaid—was of major importance. Finally, the question of the return of American personnel was being negotiated with American and French government authorities. While battle-weary Jewish leaders eagerly awaited the return of American leadership, this would also relieve French Jews of the important place they had occupied in this powerful organization. After risking their lives in the name of French Jewry, would French Jewish leaders simply be dismissed by those who had not lived through the Occupation? Would these newcomers now tell them how to run their community?

Such questions did not initially concern the French individuals who had led the JDC during the war. Nonetheless, this chapter will show that the bond of solidarity that had linked American and French Jews throughout the war proved within a short time to be more fraught than all parties had imagined. In contrast to the highly personalized help offered by American Jewish members of the US military, the efforts of the JDC to set up its wide-scale humanitarian program in France required engaging with organizations and administrations, both private and governmental, of multiple ideologies. Indeed, even though French Jews had created a centralized, representative body, the CRIF, the need for welfare services largely surpassed its political mission. In order to reach those in need, the JDC thus bypassed the CRIF and distributed its funding directly to a myriad of local Jewish organizations. This had the effect of exponentially increasing the welfare offer since organizations competed with one another for the seemingly limitless JDC funding, inevitably leading to an exacerbation of tensions among French Jews. It also pushed the American Jewish organization into a central role in postwar French Jewish life.

At the same time, the JDC was asserting itself as the primary conduit for American Jewish aid to Europe. Indeed, the centralization of American Jewish welfare made the JDC one of the main beneficiaries of the American Jews' main fundraising body, the United Jewish Appeal. Yet not all Jews in the United States agreed that the JDC represented their views. As seen by the presence of the Orthodox committee Vaad Hatzala, the Jewish Labor Committee, and the Hebrew Sheltering and Immigrant Aid Society (HIAS), the JDC soon had competition in Paris from initiatives stemming from the immigrant faction of American Jewish life. I argue here that internal contradictions in the JDC's early postwar program led to a paradoxical situation: the organization sought to distribute its aid as broadly as possible, yet at the same time, its funding led to an explosion of Jewish welfare initiatives and provided an excuse for states and international organizations to renege on their responsibilities toward Jews. JDC management, aware of the problems created by its own funding, spent considerable energy trying to fix them: on the one hand, by centralizing local welfare initiatives, on the other, by negotiating with states. While doing so, it struggled to maintain its position as the sole American Jewish aid provider in France.

THE FINAL HOURS OF THE JDC UNDER FRENCH LEADERSHIP

The Parisian JDC offices on rue de Téhéran, occupied by the UGIF during the Occupation, reopened in September 1944. There, as seen in chapter 2, French JDC representative Maurice Brener immediately began assessing the needs of the surviving Jewish population in Paris.[10] During this period the JDC primarily funded the the Comité d'assitance aux réfugiés (CAR) and the General Defense Committee (CGD), which distributed general aid to the Jewish population. An estimated thirty-five thousand individuals received regular monthly assistance from one or both of these organizations in the last quarter of 1944.[11] Of the organizations concerned with providing aid to the approximately eleven thousand Jewish children in need of assistance, the OSE received the majority of JDC funding.[12]

Brener's efforts on behalf of the JDC coincided with those of the French Jewish leaders who had grown increasingly depressed and overwhelmed. When Marc Jarblum, president of the Federation of Jewish Societies of France (FSJF) and French representative of the World Jewish Congress (WJC), returned to France from Switzerland in fall 1944, he immediately began working to alleviate the conditions of French Jews. Discouraged, he wrote to his friend and WJC founder, Nahum Goldmann, in November 1944, assessing the daunting challenges ahead:

> Things here are in a complete mess, in incomprehensible disorder. Organizations and agencies are growing like mushrooms. This competition creates a duplication of services, and the results are pretty meager.
>
> The situation for Jews is far from good. Vichy law has been abolished, but from a material point of view, the return of Jews to their belongings and to their homes will not happen quickly. Everything is slow and while we wait, thousands of Jews remain in the same situation as before. They have, of course, recovered their liberty and safety. But this is not enough. Those who occupy the places left by Jews who were pushed out and hunted are not in a hurry to give them back. While we wait for governmental decisions, we need to do something about this ourselves.
>
> All of this is quite sad. I don't know how to get out of this situation.[13]

French Jewish Welfare in the Aftermath of War

Jews in France needed food, housing, medical care, and clothing, in addition to loans to reestablish a livelihood or aid for professional reinsertion. Often, legal advice was necessary when attempting to reclaim housing and former businesses. Jews of foreign descent who had their nationality revoked during the Vichy regime or who had never obtained French citizenship were in a particularly dire situation after the war.[14]

Children shared many of these needs yet also required stable care, affection, and guidance their parents would have provided. Many children had been hidden with non-Jewish families or in Christian institutions under false identities, under both the auspices of Jewish and non-Jewish organizations. At liberation, the children's homes that had been used to shelter refugee children in the interwar period were reopened, along with new homes. French Jews established search committees to locate the Jewish children who were living in Christian families and institutions. The end of the war meant that these children would have to change their surroundings yet again and come to terms with their former (and perhaps forgotten) identities. Reunification with surviving parents or family members also proved painful for many children.[15] Beyond these specific needs that made children an urgent priority, youth represented the hope of continuity for the future. As Daniella Doron has shown, their Jewish identity and education understandably became a central issue in postwar reconstruction.[16] Respecting the memory of missing parents gave Jewish aid committees a strong justification for their work. In the name of providing the education their wards would have received at home, more recent organizations of Bundist, Zionist, and Communist leanings gained new legitimacy. Newly created children's programs thus coexisted with more established Jewish institutions that had worked with youth in the interwar period, such as the OSE and the Jewish scouts of France. This also justified the political indoctrination of children, prompting one JDC leader to suggest that "agencies [were] interested in taking the children for their political machines."[17]

While children were a priority for all organizations, with several important exceptions, Jewish aid organizations—especially those created in immigrant circles—sought to provide an all-encompassing array of services. The FSJF exemplifies this cradle-to-grave approach. This organization unified the landsmanshaftn of the Jewish immigrant populations in the interwar period and provided extensive assistance to its members during the war. At the end of 1945, it counted eleven cultural associations, forty-eight aid societies in Paris, and thirty-five aid societies outside of the capital among its affiliates. The FSJF and its affiliated aid societies offered a network of care that included general relief, temporary housing, canteens, clothing banks, and medical and legal aid, in addition to an extensive program for children run primarily by the Program for the Protection of Jewish Children (OPEJ). The FSJF also ran a service for returning deportees, providing family relocation services, administrative assistance, and professional placement. The total cost of these services in 1945 amounted to almost $2 million, made possible by an impressive list of international benefactors.[18] In addition to its monthly newspaper, *Quand même!*, board members and close affiliates of the FSJF ran two important postwar publications, the Yiddish daily *Unzer wort* (Our Word) and *La terre retrouvée*, both of Zionist slant. This vast social service network therefore connected to a clearly articulated political ideology.[19]

Fiercely opposed to the socialist FSJF was the more recent Union of Jews for Resistance and Mutual Aid (UJRE), which had emerged out of the Jewish Communist resistance. The UJRE developed a network of services, including medical dispensaries and legal assistance for recovering stolen property. Its Central Commission for Children operated six children's homes in 1945.[20] It also published a daily newspaper in Yiddish, the *Naye presse*. Smaller in number and wholly opposed to the Communists, Bundists (the General Jewish Workers Union of Lithuania, Poland, and Russia), Jewish socialists with a distinct concern for Jewish peoplehood and the preservation of Yiddish, also maintained a network of children's homes run by their mutual aid society, Workmen's Circle (Arbeter Ring/Cercle Amical), and a newspaper, *Unzer stimme* (Our Voice).[21]

As this overview suggests, in the immediate postwar period, instead of reinforcing the communal bond that began to develop during the Occupation, Jewish welfare was developing along ideological lines and in continuity with the interwar period during which each faction of French Jewish life maintained its own welfare network and fundraising campaigns.[22] Parallel Jewish self-help networks both reflected and enflamed internal divisions, even if the CRIF, created at the end of the war, symbolized a new way of thinking about Jewish life. By placing diverse ideologies together in a representative committee, the CRIF suggested that the Jews of France were willing to publicly present themselves as a unified group. While this may seem obvious to some, a collective Jewish group identity was in fact a large departure from the terms of Jewish political emancipation—upheld in public by native French Jewish organizations—which framed Judaism as a religion and Jews as individual French citizens. In reality, however, Jews in France had variegated approaches to Jewish identity and belonging, embracing a group or individual conception, or at times both, depending on the context.[23] Older political divisions that threatened to destabilize the very leadership of the CRIF, whose leaders each held important positions in their own ideological camps thus crippled the postwar road to unity and this new more collective way of thinking about Jewish identity. Nonetheless, as the only organization that could claim to represent the Jews of France, the CRIF slowly gained legitimacy, in part through its first official visit to the United States.

Paris–New York: The CRIF Delegation in the United States

As the first liberated country with a considerable Jewish population, France captivated American Jews. Learning what had happened to Jews in France provided those in America with direct information on Nazi persecutions. The JDC understood the importance of this direct encounter in a more practical light. The visit of French Jewish leaders would allow the JDC's New York management the opportunity to understand what exactly had occurred during the war in its name and, more specifically, with its money. Loans would have to be repaid—but to whom and how much? How would reconstruction be financed?

As important as the JDC may have been to French Jewish welfare, the idea of bringing the group of French delegates to the United States was actually conceived of by Marc Jarblum, the French WJC representative. He suggested the CRIF send a delegation to attend the WJC's War Emergency conference held in Atlantic City in late November 1944.[24] Jarblum advanced the costs for the trip and with the help of André Blumel, a former member of Léon Blum's cabinet, managed to obtain visas for Léon Meiss, Guy de Rothschild, Rabbi Jacob Kaplan, and Joseph Fisher.[25] With travel orders authorized by General Eisenhower, the delegation left for the United States in late November 1944.[26]

At least two meetings between the French delegation and the JDC's New York management took place during this trip. Here, Joseph Fisher, the French representative of the Jewish National Fund (KKL) proudly informed the JDC of its role in financing legal and illegal resistance activities during the 1942–1944 period.[27] In describing the JDC's wartime activities in France, Fisher spoke without hesitation on behalf of the JDC: "We [the JDC] did not go out of existence," he declared. "We, just like other Jewish organizations, continued to work illegally."[28]

Though the JDC's response to Fisher's speech remains unknown, its concern over the financial aspects of reconstruction appears in notes from an internal discussion that took place the following day. The JDC considered the French individuals who had been wealthy enough to loan them money during the war as a possible solution to the massive reconstruction costs. While the JDC planned on reimbursing these loans, American JDC leaders hoped these same individuals could be persuaded to provide the money that was currently needed for reconstruction and, in turn, pressure their own government to guarantee its participation.[29]

At a second meeting with the CRIF delegation, JDC officials announced they had approved a monthly budget of $250,000 for operations in France, in addition to a F10,000,000 loan fund, known as a loan *kassa*, to help individuals reestablish themselves. Furthermore, the JDC had purchased thirty thousand pairs of shoes.[30] With funding attributed to cover welfare needs, Central Consistory president Léon Meiss and Rabbi Jacob Kaplan turned to the financial plight of their institution. "It looks as if French Judaism will be the only one to survive in Western Europe," stated Léon Meiss, "and we want it to accomplish its religious mission."[31] Yet to do so, they needed funds. JDC officials refused to commit to funding on the spot and while promising to look into it suggested that French Jews participate financially in the reconstruction of their institutions.[32] They cited the example of the Jewish community of Rome, which had raised funds locally which were then matched by the JDC. French Jewish leaders proved skeptical, noting that the wealthy members of their community had not yet returned to France, and besides, the Central Consistory needed to raise money for small communities, not the larger, wealthier Parisian one. Over the short period during which the CRIF delegation was in the United States, the "we" that had been used by Joseph Fisher to describe the JDC's rescue efforts during the war had evaporated. French Jewish leaders, who had for the past two years had a say in how the JDC funding was spent, now found themselves on the other side of the fence.

RETURNING TO FRANCE: THE JDC UNDER AMERICAN LEADERSHIP

As the French delegation became acquainted with different aspects of American Jewish life, the upper levels of JDC management became familiar with the various governmental and intergovernmental bodies that would dictate their return to France. Even before the liberation of France, in late February 1944, JDC representative Noel Aronovici began to outline the arguments of why such a return would be necessary. He wrote from New York that

> after the liberation of Europe, the task which will confront us will be of such magnitude that no one government will be able to cope with it. Only the united efforts of all free nations may be able to meet the needs of the millions of destitute, starving people in occupied Europe. We feel that in addition to the activities of the UNRRA [United Nations Relief and Rescue Administration] and other governmental bodies, there will exist a need for specific forms of aid which can be rendered only by private agencies with

experience in the field of relief and rehabilitation. As the major American Jewish agency for relief and rehabilitation with almost thirty years of uninterrupted activity behind it, the JDC is prepared to continue its work after this war in France as well as in other European countries to the utmost extent of its financial capacity.[33]

Aronovici and others expected that the UNRRA, the forty-four member intergovernmental organization created in November 1943 to address the postwar needs of displaced persons of Allied nations, would function in France and feed, clothe, and shelter the uprooted populations. Nonetheless, Aronovici argued that "special assistance will be needed by the Jewish populations to solve their special problems such as care of orphans and other detached children who are hiding from the Gestapo. According to information from occupied Europe, many thousands of children have been left because their parents were deported to unknown destinations. Another difficult problem will be presented by the situation of Jews who have been deprived of their citizenship and are now stateless."[34]

In late August 1944, Aronovici met the representative of the French provisional government in the United States in charge of relief and welfare, Madame R. Pleven, at a meeting of the Council of American Voluntary Organizations. Aronovici invited Pleven to the JDC offices in New York in early September to discuss the plans of the French authorities.[35] His efforts to convince Pleven of the JDC's utility to the French provisional government were successful; Madame Pleven later cabled the Public Health Ministry in Paris to request help in obtaining authorization for the entry of JDC's director of overseas operations, Dr. Joseph Schwartz, and newly appointed country director, Arthur Greenleigh. "The support of the Joint Distribution Committee," she wrote, "is in my opinion one of the most important to obtain for reconstruction."[36]

As the JDC solicited the help of the French authorities in the United States, its representatives in Europe began seeking authorization from the US Armed Forces to enter what was still considered a military zone. Former JDC chairman Edward Warburg, now a captain in the US Armed Forces in charge of displaced persons, advocated for the reentry of the JDC to the US military as well as to the leadership of the Intergovernmental Committee on Refugees (IGCR) and UNRRA.[37] Warburg reported to JDC chairman Paul Baerwald that these organizations were eagerly awaiting the arrival of Dr. Schwartz and that in his opinion, the American military would not be concerned with the presence of JDC personnel as long as proper authorization had been obtained from the US government. In fact, Warburg's letter warned the JDC of a new problem: by gaining access to Europe, the JDC would essentially relieve other organizations of their responsibilities. He explained:

> What I have heard and seen makes me feel that great care must be exercised by JDC to make it's [sic] grants conditional upon the participation of the quasi-governmental and inter-governmental agencies and that the community organize itself properly so that such funds meet all needs and do not build up one group to the exclusion of some others. [...] You will be deluged from all sides for grants as all other funds are dependent upon the slow wheels of one or more governments turning and turning favorably. While the funds are desperately needed and cannot be withheld, it is of the utmost importance that all agencies who can be used for meeting these problems clearly define their fields of action so that there is the minimum of overlapping and our funds be conserved for the big picture and no unfortunate precedents be set. I get the impression that everyone is talking big but in the end we will have to foot the bill.[38]

Aronovici's belief in the capacity of the JDC to address the specific needs of Jewish survivors, such as caring for orphans and the stateless, while UNRRA took care of basic necessities, such as food and clothing, was not shared by Warburg, whose observations soon proved to be correct. UNRRA, which established camps in France to recruit personnel to send to German DP camps in summer 1944, was eventually not allowed to provide direct aid in France, even if its employees were assigned to work in French organizations.[39] The SHAEF was therefore primarily responsible, at least for the first months following liberation, for providing for the displaced persons in the country.[40] According to an October 1944 *New York Times* article, the SHAEF turned this responsibility over to the French provisional government, whose "nonrecognition has made it sensitive to accepting outside help."[41] Furthermore, according to this source, five hundred thousand individuals without French nationality were homeless in France and waiting for help, yet the French provisional government appeared more concerned with repatriating its own nationals than helping foreigners. David H. Sulzberger, a member of the SHAEF's civilian affairs division, confirmed this impression in a letter to the JDC, stating that the French government showed no interest in helping foreigners and that while it was not discriminating against Jews, it made no distinction between "those who had lost everything and have no resources and those who haven't and have some."[42] In this context, the JDC's attempt to reenter France was seen as a solution to a potentially explosive DP problem. The IGCR and UNRRA, established to assist refugees yet limited by their mandates, echoed this attitude, as seen in their message to the JDC, sent via the War Refugee Board in November 1944:

1. We deem it necessary that the JDC should renew monthly remittances to the office in Paris as soon as possible; the minimum requirements at the present time are ten million French francs and this will probably prove to be insufficient.
2. We deem it to be most desirable that [JDC employee] Greenleigh should take over in Paris at as early a date possible; we understand that difficulties in the way of his coming are being removed.
3. We deem it to be very advisable that [head of JDC European operations] Schwartz should visit Paris at as early a date as is practicable in order to survey the entire position and make arrangements accordingly.[43]

In addition to these intergovernmental organizations, Jewish individuals, including members of the US Armed Forces but also survivors in camps and concerned Europeans living in the United States, pressured the JDC to send American personnel to France. In April 1945, a group of 115 Jewish survivors interned in the Natzweiler-Vaihigen/Enz concentration camp wrote to the French Army, demanding to be put in contact with the JDC in Paris.[44] In what may have been sheer pragmatism, or maybe an attempt to settle a personal score, Isaac Naiditch, a French Jewish exile in New York and member of the French committee of the WJC, wrote to Dr. Schwartz of his disappointment in hearing that Jefroykin and Brener had been appointed JDC representatives in France and argued that only an American male would have the necessary influence with American, British, and French authorities: "In these extraordinary times for the french jewry [sic], it will be of the greatest moral and practical support for the remaining jews [sic] in France, that the JDC has an authoritative american [sic] representative in Paris, particularly in the first most confused months after the liberation."[45] Once "the right man for the job" was found, Naiditch advised, the JDC should "send this gentleman to Paris immediately."[46] To Naiditch and many others, it was not yet conceivable that a woman could be this person, a fact that would eventually change.

Multiple forces—from camp survivors to the members of the highest echelons of intergovernmental organizations—encouraged the JDC to establish a large-scale program under American direction in France. In November 1944, two Americans were granted permission to enter France: Dr. Joseph Schwartz, who arrived at the end of the month, and Arthur Greenleigh, who arrived in late December. This marked a new chapter in the history of the postwar JDC program.[47]

The JDC Program under American Auspices: Dealing with the Emergency

As Europe was being liberated, Dr. Joseph Schwartz continued to use the JDC European headquarters in Lisbon as his base as he traveled throughout the formerly occupied countries to meet with surviving communal leaders. He assigned the responsibility of launching the postwar reconstruction program in France to an American social worker in his forties, Arthur Greenleigh. In 1944, Greenleigh had worked with the JDC in Italy organizing aid for Jewish displaced persons, and previous to this, in the United States he was the assistant executive director of the National Refugee Service and Roosevelt's War Manpower Division.[48] Two UNRRA employees lent to the JDC for a period of several months, Cecilia Razovsky Davidson and George Rooby, also played an important role. UNRRA hired Razovsky in September 1944 as a displaced-persons specialist for the European mission and arrived in February 1945.[49] Razovsky was not new to humanitarian crises. One of the only women to break the glass ceiling in American Jewish welfare, she rose to a position of authority in the 1930s due to her four decades of experience working with Jewish immigrants in the United States and Latin America, including an important role counseling the passengers of the *SS St. Louis* when Cuba refused permission to disembark in 1939.[50] Along with a handful of French employees, Greenleigh, Razovsky, and Rooby set out to reestablish JDC operations in France under American auspices.

Greenleigh and Razovsky, who surely knew each other from the National Refugee Service, where they both had worked in the early 1940s, shared a rationalized approach to the Jewish welfare crisis in France. The JDC offices had been ransacked. Their first challenge was to gather materials and needed personnel. In early 1945, the JDC had to compete with the black market for employees. Razovsky reported having offered F5000 a month for a secretary, to which one "girl" responded: "Why should I? See this bag on my arm? If I sell six bags, I make 500 francs, and I sell 6 bags easily. So why should I work in an office all day long?"[51] By April 1945, the difficulty of finding local employees seems to have diminished, yet Greenleigh insisted to the JDC in New York that more Americans were needed:

> I know from past experience that with just a few Americans here, we can provide a far better service for many more disadvantaged people and at the same time can save the JDC millions of francs and can provide some training for local staff. We have many French persons available, but none have the professional training nor experience necessary to do the big job that faces us now. And one of the very serious difficulties with most of those that we

have is that they are so politically minded that they cannot be objective in situations in which objectivity is imperative. It is a handicap which is becoming increasingly evident and acute.[52]

Greenleigh's request for more American staff shows his initial prejudice against the French, whom he considered too political and insufficiently professional to become good employees. His assessment suggests an ignorance of the continuity between wartime resistance and postwar welfare work, which were, by nature, political endeavors. Greenleigh's worldview instead reflected American social work norms of the 1940s, which valued a neutral and rational approach to aid.

This contrasted with the realities of postwar France. Indeed, beyond the primary difficulty of finding "qualified" employees, American JDC staff soon encountered another problem: the lack of efficiency of their new recruits. Often, letters that had been dictated in the morning had not been typed by the end of the day. The reason for this, however, was soon discovered, revealing the Americans' unawareness of the conditions under which French Jews had been living under the Occupation: "When we pressed them to work hard and fast we found them fainting on our hands and then we learned that they did not ever get enough to eat. [...] The relief expert was sitting in a staff meeting one day and fainted away. He was in the hospital unconscious for two days and we found it was all due to malnutrition. He had lived on potatoes for eleven months; no butter, no milk, no bread."[53]

Problems of this nature prompted Greenleigh to set up a canteen, supplied with food from the black market, for the JDC staff. This way, they were able to "get results, a half-day's work a day, anyhow."[54]

Local Jews, in contrast, viewed their own alleged inefficiency with distance and at times even humor, as seen in a comic sketch written for Razovsky on the occasion of her departure from France. The sketch, entitled "Scherzo Capriccioso in AJDC Major," mocks the functioning of the JDC office in Paris. Its director, Arthur Greenleigh, is portrayed as a time-obsessed taskmaster. In one instance, he yells, "Damn! These people here do nothing but lose their time and not only their time. When he arrives, get him in my room, immediately. I'll raise hell. What kind of organization is this?" To which Liselotte, a French secretary and most likely the author of the sketch, responds, "You don't expect an answer, Sir?"[55]

Such examples, even when comical, suggest that French and American Jews approached the problem of reconstruction from different perspectives. American JDC staff arrived with the standards of efficiency and professionalism that had governed their working lives in the United States. No matter how sensitive these individuals may have been to what Jews in France underwent during the war years, their lives and careers had not been interrupted by the Occupation, allowing them the detachment to treat postwar reconstruction as a rational problem to which time-tested social work methods could be applied. Americans saw the perceived inefficiency, lack of objectivity, and training of French hires as barriers to reconstruction that had to be overcome immediately, not symptoms of the deeper wounds of the Holocaust, which would take time to heal. More generally, these observations could be the product of broader Franco-American cultural differences regarding work.[56]

Many Jews in France were still awaiting news from family members and getting by without proper food, housing, or resources. For some of those involved with the JDC, reconstruction work was a peacetime carryover of resistance work. Others simply needed a job. Little is known about how the French representatives of the JDC, Maurice Brener and Jules (Dika) Jefroykin, perceived the arrival of Greenleigh and his American staff. Did Greenleigh respect their intimate knowledge of French Jewish welfare? Neither the archives nor oral histories allow for answers to these questions, although it is clear that both Jefroykin and Brener remained in close contact with the JDC in the following years. The silence of the sources seems to confirm that a new era had indeed begun with Greenleigh's arrival.

Greenleigh's preoccupations were not about establishing a smooth transition from French to American management, nor from occupation to peace, but in reestablishing JDC programs in France and throughout formerly occupied Europe. While Dr. Schwartz traveled throughout Europe to achieve this goal, Greenleigh, from the strategic location of Paris, was assigned the task of facilitating JDC efforts and bringing aid to survivors of Nazi concentration and death camps, who were now in Displaced Persons camps in Germany and Austria, in addition to organizing an efficient welfare program in France.[57] Greenleigh dealt with these tasks concurrently.

The JDC's objectives in postwar France were somewhat paradoxical. On one hand, it endeavored to aid all needy Jews; on the other, it fought to stimulate government aid for this population. Likewise, while it initially sought to distribute its aid as widely as possible by funding a large number of Jewish aid organizations, it soon began centralizing Jewish welfare when its own funding led to overlapping services.

Organizing French Jewish Welfare

For the JDC, the conditions of France's Jewish population did not inspire the same urgency as those who had experienced the horrors of the Nazi death camps and were now interned in DP camps. Whereas French Jews understandably had a more acute perception of their wartime experiences and postwar needs, the JDC saw their situation in the larger European context, casting France in a more hopeful light. As home to the largest surviving Jewish population in continental Western Europe, France came to represent the future of European Judaism and a priority for the JDC. As seen above, three-quarters of the Jewish population had survived the Holocaust in France, compared to roughly one quarter of the prewar Jewish population of Holland.[58] A vast network of Jewish aid organizations had survived the Occupation. After the liberation, others had sprung up, in the words of Marc Jarblum, "like mushrooms,"[59] as each ideological faction of French Jewish life sought a response to the problems of its members.

In the immediate postwar period, most French Jewish aid organizations showed expansionist tendencies, even those specializing in a certain domain or population, such as vocational training or children. The OSE, the largest Jewish children's organization in France, ran seventeen children's homes in March 1945 and had over three thousand children under its care.[60] By January 1946, this organization had twenty-four children's homes and offices all over France, where it provided medical care, professional orientation services, and recreational activities.[61] The French Jewish scouting movement had developed an extensive resistance network during the war known as "la Sixième." In March 1945, this organization still had five hundred children in its care. After the war, this organization also opened a social service for unattached adolescents and young adults, the Social Service for Youth (Service social des jeunes, SSJ) and created the Ecole Gilbert Bloch in 1946, a school to train future Jewish communal workers, all while expanding its scouting programs in France and North Africa.[62]

From the American perspective, the ever-increasing number of Jewish welfare agencies of such different political ideologies appeared both baffling and counterproductive. Greenleigh thus set out to bring order to the organizations that, in his opinion, willingly accepted JDC funding but remained reticent on the details of their work. Echoing Jarblum's observations, Greenleigh wrote about the French Jewish welfare organizations in his correspondence with the JDC in New York: "The one characteristic almost all have in common is the tendency to 'empire building' as we used to say in public administration. Each agency is continually reaching out for new fields of activity even though there may be three or four already in that field and no need existing for any additional agencies. There has been in many cases a political motive, either communist [sic] or Zionist or bundist [sic], etc. And we are expected to foot the bill."[63]

The burgeoning network of French Jewish welfare agencies defied the social work principle that had governed American Jewish welfare since the interwar period: the centralization of services. Furthermore, it was considered inefficient and expensive. In their letters to New York, both Greenleigh and Warburg spoke of the JDC having "to foot the bill" for French Jewish welfare, hinting at a resentment that the JDC was expected to pay for reconstruction. Because the JDC was "footing the bill," it did not hesitate to control how its money would be spent. The JDC thus began its efforts to streamline French Jewish welfare by encouraging organizations to specialize and centralize and slowly began to establish common standards and reimbursement rates for all agencies. Accountability, through regular audits of financial records, also became a major priority for the JDC.

The Centralization of General Relief: COJASOR

In an attempt to centralize services, Dr. Schwartz met with leaders of the three major aid committees, the CAR, the CGD, and the FSJF, in January 1945. With Greenleigh's mediation, these agencies at first resistant finally accepted a merger, establishing the Jewish Committee for Social Action and Reconstruction (COJASOR), which was functioning by March 1945 under the direction of Maurice Brener. COJASOR opened twelve offices throughout France and by the end of June had a national caseload of 24,287 individuals, of whom 35 percent were French, 27 percent were Polish, and 9 percent were formerly German. In its first months, COJASOR provided financial and material aid and ran four reception centers for returning deportees, two convalescent homes, and an old-age home, in addition to operating sixteen canteens in Paris. The organization also provided legal aid to Jews seeking help in matters of restitution.[64] COJASOR's existence eliminated some of the overlap of services, yet the FSJF and OSE continued to provide financial assistance to special categories of individuals, such as intellectuals, students, and physicians. Likewise, the FSJF maintained its own network of convalescence, old-age, and children's homes, reception centers, and canteens throughout France.[65] By 1946, COJASOR had expanded its programs, running a total of 49 regional offices and in Paris alone employed 174 individuals.[66] As a recipient of IGCR funding, COJASOR became the organization of reference for the increasing number of Jewish refugees and stateless persons arriving en masse from Poland and DP camps.[67] In April 1946, COJASOR established a special service, the Special Service for Immigrants (SSI), to help these populations.

Extensive financial and administrative support from the JDC, which covered 84 percent of its budget for the period between 1945 and 1948, gave

COJASOR importance.[68] The JDC did not hesitate to transfer the few direct services it operated to COJASOR, and if COJASOR performed poorly, the JDC intervened and managed those services in its place.[69] According to one source, COJASOR obtained the lion's share of JDC funding in 1945 (39.5%).[70] Through these agencies and others, the JDC reported its assistance of an estimated fifty thousand Jews in France in 1945 (one out of four of the estimated population of two hundred thousand), of whom nineteen thousand were under the age of eighteen.[71]

Former JDC representative Maurice Brenner became the director general of COJASOR. However, he resigned in July 1945, suggesting that the efforts of the JDC to increase the efficiency of French Jewish welfare came at a price. Centralization meant that resources were redirected away from smaller aid committees, furthering divisions among French Jews. Maurice Brenner did not portray the JDC and its policies positively in his resignation:

> After several months of experience at Cosjasor, I have come to the conclusion that because of a deplorable spirit of competition among the different Jewish organizations in charge of social questions, and because of what I consider a lack of understanding on the part of the Joint about the different problems of French welfare, and also due to the lack of solidarity of almost all of French Jewry [*judaïsme*] towards our needy fellow Jews and its lack of comprehension of the depth of problems that we must affront, and finally, due to the lack of technical personnel truly qualified for this job, it is basically impossible [*exclu*], under the current conditions, to perform concrete social work, the only kind that interests me.[72]

While the circumstances leading to Brener's departure from COJASOR remain mysterious, they suggest that the JDC's methods, while well-intentioned, added pressure to an already conflict-ridden environment, ending Brener's extensive collaboration with the JDC.[73]

AND THE STATE? THE JDC, THE FRENCH, AND THE AMERICANS

As Arthur Greenleigh attempted to decode the communal dynamics of French Jewish life, a larger problem resulting from the very presence of the JDC in France confronted him. On one hand, the JDC had sought actively to reintegrate Jews into the nation, advocating for their right to public social services and indemnities; on the other, the JDC's very recognition of specific Jewish needs, and its programs to address them, reinforced the separate treatment of Jews, which some government-mandated agencies then took as permission to abandon their responsibilities. With several exceptions, the JDC refrained from funding organizations not run by Jews.[74] Postwar JDC funding allowed for an unprecedented expansion of Jewish welfare organizations in France, but this created a new problem for the JDC: Greenleigh now had to shield attempts of French governmental agencies to send all Jews, regardless of their right to public assistance, to the JDC or its subsidized agencies for help.[75]

This is seen clearly in the relationship of the JDC to the Social Aid Committee for Resistance Organizations (Comité des oeuvres sociales de la résistance, COSOR). COSOR grouped together the aid committees established under the Occupation to care for resistance members and their families. In the postwar period, the French Ministry of Prisoners of War, Deportees and Refugees mandated COSOR to provide for the families of individuals who had been deported from France, regardless of nationality. In practice, however, COSOR discriminated against foreigners, many of whom were Jews. For example, when funds were low, COSOR decided to cut its aid to non-French individuals.[76] To advise COSOR on matters concerning Jews, the CRIF established a liaison committee.[77] This did not keep COSOR from turning to the JDC for help. In March 1945, Greenleigh received two COSOR board members, accompanied by the welfare chief of UNRRA for France. They explained that their organizations had not received the necessary government funding and as a result were requesting that the JDC assume responsibility for all Jewish families. Greenleigh responded negatively to this request explaining that it violated JDC policy and furthermore would not be in "the best interests of the nation for the Jewish persons in a certain category to be given different treatment and from a separate agency than is the case for those not Jewish in the same general category."[78] These officials temporarily accepted Greenleigh's argument. However, at a later meeting, members of COSOR stated that they would have to discontinue aid to non-French families, despite their mandate. Greenleigh saw this as an attempt to send more individuals to the JDC for help: "It was evident in the discussions that unless we were adamant we would be forced to take on a load distinctly that of the government. In order to bring the issue to a head, I announced that because of our financial stringency, we would have to stop giving assistance to any families of deportees after the end of May. I find that I have to play a bit of poker with these agencies, or we shall never get out from under a load that should never be ours."[79]

Like COSOR, the French Ministry of Prisoners of War, Deportees and Refugees (MPDR) seems to have been overwhelmed by its mission, which led to an ambiguous policy on Jews. Historian Annette Wieviorka notes the low percentage of Jews among the returning victims of deportation: "About forty thousand for resisters and political prisoners... a little more than two thousand for Jewish survivors. One French person out of one thousand experienced Nazi concentration camps, one Jew out of one-hundred living in France in 1945 was a survivor of a death camp [centres de mises à mort]."[80] Historians have since revised the number of Jewish camp survivors to roughly four-thousand, yet the fact remains that next to the other categories of deportees, Jews represented a small minority.[81] Correspondence showing the ministry's slow response to a British organization seeking to provide aid to Jews in France can be interpreted as a sign of inefficiency.[82] However, the ministry's September 1944 decision to centralize care to all "Jewish deportees" at the same address, even though this legal category did not technically exist, shows that Vichy's discriminatory categories died a slow death.[83] A recent study of French policies for returning camp survivors suggests an ambivalent attitude that defies easy generalizations; the MPDR did indeed establish a section dedicated to generating statistics on Jewish deportees. While severely understaffed, it was intent on elucidating what had transpired.[84]

In the eyes of the JDC staff, however, the MPDR's attitude was less than cooperative. A central location index, containing information on individuals who had been deported from France, was one of the key tools needed to reunite families in the immediate postwar period. American organizations and Jewish individuals sent their inquiries through the JDC, which received the addresses of survivors in DP camps from members of the US military who were passing through Paris.[85] The MPDR kept an alphabetical index but listed Jews separately, according to their date of deportation, camp, and convoy, making them extremely difficult to locate on the list. While the JDC offered to pay for labor costs to integrate the Jews into the alphabetical index on the condition of receiving a copy of the list, the MPDR never responded to its offer. As a result, Razovsky worked with local staff to establish a search index for the JDC's own use.[86] This had the indirect result of bringing the JDC directly in contact with the most diminished Jews in France. These individuals came to the JDC offices in search of lost family members, turning the JDC into a hectic crossroads of the diaspora.[87] One former American employee recalled that on her first day at the JDC offices, a camp survivor showed her his tattooed arm. Startled, the young woman did not notice she was dangerously close to the stove, which burned a hole through her skirt.[88]

The study of the JDC's relationship with the French government and its mandated care organization, COSOR, underscores what historian Karen Adler has pointed out regarding the ambivalence toward Jews and the continuities of Vichy rhetoric during the "long liberation" of France. If the postwar universalist discourse sought to stifle differences, government actions maintained Jewish distinctiveness by asserting that Jews' care should remain under Jewish auspices. At the same time, as Daniella Doron's findings on custody battles over Jewish children show, French Jews also fought ardently to care for fellow Jews.[89] This situation speaks to the multifaceted and complex nature of Jewish belonging in postwar France. Paradoxically, private Jewish welfare helped Jews meet their specific needs and regain a sense of hope for the future but was also used to justify cost cutting on the part of the government.

Even though the JDC was officially registered in France as an association, it escaped the notice of the Paris police when, in December 1947, the latter was asked by the Minister of the Interior to report on foreign populations living in Paris.[90] In a forty-two page report on the "American colony" in Paris, the author described the some twenty-nine hundred American citizens in Paris who "belong almost exclusively to the upper class [and] hold, for the most part, official functions or important positions in industrial companies, banks, insurance companies, films, newspapers, etc."[91] While the report described many American organizations, ranging from the American Club of Paris to the Rockefeller Foundation, the JDC was not mentioned. The French government obviously knew about the JDC, and yet the Paris police did not consider it an American organization. This suggests, yet again, a certain Jewish distinctiveness in the postwar period.

The JDC: An American Organization?

Even if it didn't make it into the Paris police's report, the JDC was indeed one of many American voluntary organizations that came to help reconstruct France after World War II.[92] The ambiguous relationship between the JDC and the French state raises the question of the JDC's place in the larger constellation of American voluntary organizations that had come to reconstruct France. These organizations faced similar challenges in France and made both formal and informal efforts to coordinate their work. To what extent did the JDC develop horizontal alliances with fellow American organizations to further its work on behalf of Jews?

As seen above, even before France was liberated, the JDC sent a representative to a meeting of the France committee of the Council of American Voluntary Organizations. Once in France, Arthur Greenleigh maintained the JDC's presence in American relief circles. In February 1945, for example, Greenleigh attended a meeting of the Cooperative Committee of Foreign Voluntary

Societies in Paris. There, he renewed contact with many of the organizations the JDC had worked with on the Nîmes committee, which had coordinated relief work in the French internment camps during World War II.[93] At the meeting, representatives from American organizations shared their problems. All had difficulties bringing their personnel to France and many voiced their concerns over the inadequacy of French public aid. The group decided that Greenleigh would gather information on this problem and the Cooperative Committee would organize a meeting with SHAEF representatives and French officials.[94] The JDC remained active in the Cooperative Committee during the immediate postwar period and was described, along with twenty-two other member organizations, in the committee's 1949 report.[95] The JDC was thus wholly integrated in the American aid networks that were creating the foundation on which the Marshall Plan would build.

Indeed, the Marshall Plan represented a real opportunity for American organizations, including the JDC, since the European Recovery Program provided them with reimbursement for expenses related to their relief activities in France. American voluntary organizations therefore decided to work together to learn how to qualify for the provisions offered by the 1948 Economic Cooperation Act. In April 1948, the American Council of Voluntary Agencies created a special committee on the Marshall Plan. This US-based, five-person committee was chaired by an employee of the JDC and had a second JDC employee as a member.[96] In Paris, a group of American voluntary organizations met regularly with Irving Fasteau, the Special Welfare officer at the American Embassy. Again, a committee was established to help plan and implement the Economic Cooperation Act, and again, the JDC was one of the seven represented organizations.[97] These efforts paid off—the JDC was able to benefit from reduced fees for the shipping and storage of food and materials under the Marshall Plan, saving considerable amounts of money.[98]

The JDC clearly did not hesitate to play an active role among the American voluntary organizations in France, reflecting its longstanding reputation in welfare circles and, more generally, the legitimacy that Jews were rapidly gaining in postwar American society. Yet the JDC was not the only American Jewish organization active in postwar France. The presence of smaller American Jewish initiatives suggests a more complex picture: communal divisions across the Atlantic were fueling competition for the JDC and thus influencing the dynamics of French Jewish welfare. Like the Jews of France, communal divisions prevented American Jews from speaking in one voice; the "neutral" JDC was not legitimate in the eyes of all. France thus became a space where American Jewish organizations could assert their distinct visions of Jewish life.

COMPETING WITH THE JDC? AMERICAN JEWISH WELFARE INITIATIVES IN EARLY POSTWAR FRANCE

Analyzing Jewish welfare in postwar France requires paying attention to the shifting dynamics in postwar American Jewish life. Historians have generally agreed that at the end of World War II, American Jews "crossed a threshold,"[99] leading to an unprecedented level of integration into American society. Nonetheless, the same historians disagree about the persistence of communal divisions among American Jews, notably the divide between the so-called German elite and those who arrived after 1881 from the Russian Empire.[100] By 1945, most of the 4.8 million American Jews were the descendants of Eastern European immigrants,[101] yet the German elite continued to exert power, especially in the field of philanthropy. One's geographic origins, while far from determinant on the individual level, did have some sociological implications. Broadly speaking, in the 1940s American Jews of Central European origin tended to eschew Zionism, belong to the middle or upper classes, and affiliate with the Reform movement. Eastern European Jews and their descendants were a religiously and politically diverse group more likely to embrace Zionism, or be violently opposed to it. Fiercely secular identities coexisted with multiple (and opposing) strands of orthodoxy, even if the descendants of religious Jews were slowly joining the Conservative movement.[102] This upwardly mobile group was becoming middle class, yet in the immediate postwar period, there were still Jewish workers, even though the Jewish labor movement was rapidly declining.[103] The diverse American Jewish population naturally produced more than one solution to help surviving Jews in Europe.

As seen in chapter 2, some American Jews responded to the Holocaust by joining the US Armed Forces; others stayed home but shipped food and clothing or corresponded with Jewish orphans.[104] The perceived urgency of the postwar period led to unprecedented donations to the centralized fundraising organization, the United Jewish Appeal (UJA). This organization had been unable to raise $20 million in 1939, yet it collected over $100 million in 1946.[105] These funds were then distributed to three competing arenas: overseas aid (which included Europe), the *Yishuv* in Palestine, and domestic welfare. The JDC was the UJA's sole mandated recipient for overseas aid to Europe, enabling the former to distribute over $194 million between 1945 and 1948.[106] As seen above, JDC funding infused Jewish organizations in France with needed cash to face the postwar emergency, helping to compensate for weak public assistance. Yet in spite of the centralization of overseas welfare, the JDC was not the only American Jewish organization that came to France.

American Jewish organizations transposed both the diversity and ideological divisions of American Jewish life to French soil. For example, the Reform movement's World Union for Progressive Judaism and the Synagogue Council of America initiated their own programs for renewing religious life in France.[107] The World Jewish Congress and the American Jewish Committee launched French programs in 1945 and 1947, respectively, each with ambitious political objectives (see chap. 5). Likewise, the National Council of Jewish Women set up initiatives in Paris offering services and training to young women (see chap. 6). The presence of these organizations multiplied the forms of aid available to French Jews.

Three additional organizations, the Orthodox Vaad Hatzala (Vaad), the Jewish Labor Committee (JLC), and the Hebrew Sheltering and Immigrant Aid Society (HIAS), challenged the JDC's status as the sole overseas representative of American Jews. Each of these groups merit, yet have not all received, ample scholarly attention.[108] While their leaders would most likely not appreciate being placed at the same table, three shared characteristics justify their analysis here. First, each had a history of aiding Jews in Europe that predated the postwar period. HIAS had the longest standing European presence. This organization, established by Russian immigrants in New York in 1882,[109] adapted to the American immigration restrictions of the 1920s by establishing a collaboration with the Jewish Colonization Organization (ICA) and Emigdirect, a Berlin-based emigration organization, under the name of HICEM. In 1927, HICEM set up offices throughout Europe to assist Jews in their migrations.[110] The JLC was created in 1934 by leaders of the Jewish Labor Movement as a response to Nazism and was active in Europe during WWII, especially in France, where it facilitated the flight of labor leaders.[111] The Vaad Hatzala, established by the Union of Orthodox Rabbis (Agudat Harabanim) in November 1939, also worked actively to evacuate yeshiva students and rabbis from Eastern Europe during World War II.

Second, all three of these organizations, run by American Jews of Eastern European descent, mobilized a self-help discourse in order to defend a distinct way of providing aid. Each organization therefore ran independent fundraising campaigns, generally outside of the United Jewish Appeal.[112] Even HIAS, which assisted all Jews with their migration needs, was funded through donations from those it had helped. Continually struggling for funds, HIAS's underdog status seemed to reflect older animosities between the German elite and the Eastern European immigrants.[113]

Finally, what unites the organizations here is their refusal to accept the JDC's legitimacy as the sole provider of American Jewish aid in Europe. If the JDC was perceived, inaccurately, as a bastion of the German elite,[114] Jews of Eastern European origin in the United States pushed back, not explicitly as Eastern Europeans but as Orthodox Jews, Bundists, or in the case of the HIAS, simply as outsiders. In doing so, they changed the shape of French Jewish welfare.

The Vaad Hatazla: Defending Orthodoxy

There has been little written about the Orthodox element in French Jewish life, which developed outside of the consistorial system over the course of the nineteenth and twentieth centuries. Alex Grobman, on whom I rely to discuss the Vaad Hatzala's efforts to aid Orthodox Jews in postwar France, estimates that 25 percent of the Jews in postwar France were Orthodox.[115] This figure is difficult to substantiate, and perhaps even more difficult to define. *Orthodox* could mean the traditional Jews associated with the Consistory, or rather those who embraced Haredi forms of Orthodoxy and as such took issue with the compromises the consistorial synagogues made to accommodate modernity.[116] Franco-Judaism shocked the traditional Jews arriving at the end century from the Russian Empire. These individuals, along with a few others from Alsace and Lorraine, set out to defend their own approaches to orthodoxy by establishing oratories and synagogues outside of the consistorial system.[117] This faction of Jewish life was significant enough in the postwar period to establish, in 1952, a structure to federate thirty-six different organizations, the Representative Council of Traditional Judaism of France (Conseil représentatif du judaïsme traditionaliste de France, CRJTF).[118]

Of equal importance to the French context was the larger European situation: Paris was quickly becoming the center of postwar Jewish migrations, especially after the 1946 Kielce pogrom. Jewish individuals were crossing France's borders daily from Poland and the DP camps, bringing new forms of religious diversity to French Jewish life. The Vaad Hatzala had representatives traveling throughout Europe within the transnational networks maintained by Haredi Jews. The Vaad's work in France must be understood in the larger postwar European context that was turning Paris into a new hub for Jewish migrations.

The Vaad Hatzala sent its first representative, Dr. Samuel Schmidt, to Paris in 1945. While born in Kovno, Schmidt immigrated to the United States as a child and held degrees in public health and biology from MIT. He participated in the JDC's mission in Poland after WWI, which helps explain why the Vaad would send this "non-observant"[119] Jew to Europe to help evacuate yeshiva students and rabbis in 1940. Schmidt apparently underwent a religious transformation during his wartime travels and became more religious.[120] In the postwar period, he stayed in Paris for several months in 1945 and then returned again in October 1946 to stay for eight months. While Schmidt was in Paris, a second Vaad emissary, Stephen Klein, the Austrian refugee who founded Barton's Candies, embarked on a self-financed tour of Europe, where he stayed from October 1946 to February 1947. Under Klein the Vaad offices were housed at the Hôtel Moderne and had a staff of five.[121] These observations on the Vaad Hatzala in Paris suggest the organization ran a small program on a shoestring budget.[122]

The goals of the Vaad Hatzala in France were threefold: First, it fought for visas for Orthodox Jews, both to enter France and the United States;[123] second, it supplemented the material assistance provided by COJASOR and the JDC for Orthodox Jewish refugees in France;[124] and third, it helped Jewish children through a subsidiary organization it established in June 1946, Rescue Children, Inc. This seemingly independent structure shared leadership with the Vaad and sought to transmit "Torah-true-Judaism" in its multiple homes throughout Europe.[125] In France, Rescue Children, Inc. ran between five to nine structures, including children's homes and yeshivot.[126] Curiously, two of its homes in the Paris region were actually run in collaboration with the non-Jewish resistance organization COSOR, which, as seen above, annoyed the JDC with its continual requests for funds.[127] The unlikely collaboration between the French resistance group and the Orthodox Vaad needs to be further explored.[128] It is possible COSOR was a silent partner: multiple organizations typically funded Jewish children's homes, which allowed each to claim the home as its own. To finance its structures, Rescue Children, Inc. set up an extensive child-sponsoring program, matching the children in its homes with families in the United States, thus personalizing the connection between French and American Jews.[129]

The JDC did not appreciate the Vaad's incursions onto what it considered its own territory. Not only did the Vaad threaten the JDC's singular role in French Jewish welfare, but the JDC felt the Vaad was undermining the United Jewish Appeal by conducting an independent fundraising campaign. When the JDC accused the Vaad of duplicating its services, a representative of the latter observed, "It is not we who are duplicating, but it is Joint who is trying to imitate and duplicate us."[130] Such tensions led the JDC in New York to set up the Central Orthodox Committee in July 1947 to advise the JDC on its allocations concerning Orthodox Jews.[131] While this only seemed to exacerbate tensions, the JDC and the Vaad signed an agreement in early 1948 stipulating that the Orthodox group would entrust the management of its children's division,

Rescue Children, Inc., to the JDC. This agreement ceased the independent fundraising on behalf of children that the Vaad had conducted outside the auspices of the UJA. Never passive, the Vaad accused the JDC throughout 1948 of sending the children to non-Orthodox Jewish organizations or returning them to their parents, where they would not keep kosher. In 1949, Rescue Children, Inc. provided a donation of F200,000 to COSOR.[132] A possible sign of the end of the Vaad's work in France.

The Jewish Labor Committee: Supporting Yiddish Voices

Just as the Vaad Hatzala sought to bolster the Orthodox faction in French Jewish life, the Jewish Labor Committee returned to France to lend support to those with whom it shared a common ideology. Historians Catherine Collomp and Constance Pâris de Bollardière, on whose work I primarily draw upon here, have shown the strong influence of the Bund on JLC leadership. Founders David Dubinsky, president of the International Ladies' Garment Workers' Union, and Baruch Charney Vladeck, city councilman and general manager of the Yiddish daily *Forverts* (The Forward), were both affiliated with the Bund in the Russian Empire before immigrating to the United States in 1911 and 1908, respectively. The two men traveled extensively throughout Europe during the 1930s and alerted the larger American labor movement about the rise of Nazism. The JLC managed to enlist the American Federation of Labor in its fight to save European labor leaders, allowing it to obtain emergency visitors' visas to the United States for European labor leaders. As a result, the JLC helped more than fifteen hundred individuals immigrate to the United States during World War II.[133]

France, where many of the hunted political activists had sought refuge, thus came to occupy an important arena of activity for the JLC during World War II. The committee returned in the postwar period and once again found France a ripe terrain for its activism, even if its actual presence was limited to the visits of its representatives.[134] Instead of setting up an office, the JLC relied primarily on the French Jewish Bundist mutual aid society, Workmen's Circle (*Cercle amical or Arbeter-ring*). In 1945, JLC representative Nahum Chanin appointed Workmen's Circle leader Fajwel Schrager to serve as the committee's representative in France.[135] Schrager was assisted by Bertha Mering, with whom he had worked in the Jewish resistance.[136]

Like the Vaad Hatzala program, the JLC program was small and its aid almost exclusively directed at the Yiddish-speaking community in postwar France. The JLC's ties to the French Bund were obvious as both organizations embraced a diaspora-nationalist perspective that was grounded in socialism, secular Yiddish culture, and anticommunism. Zionism, however, was a more contentious issue; in 1943, the JLC withdrew from the American Jewish Conference after its vote in favor of a Jewish commonwealth in Palestine.[137] Nonetheless, some individuals in the JLC network were affiliated with Left Poale Zion, the Zionist movement that, depending on the place and time, embraced communism. Thus, all while remaining staunchly anti-Communist, the JLC supported Bundist and some Zionist initiatives in France.[138] For example, in 1949, the JLC was partially or fully funding sixteen organizations, including a small monthly grant to support the Bundist Medem Library in Paris. It also helped meet basic needs by sending packages distributed by the Workmen's Circle and Left Poale Zion.[139] Yet the heart of its program focused on helping children.[140]

The JLC supported multiple children's institutions in France, including three children's homes run by the Workmen's Circle that were also funded by the OSE and JDC.[141] One of the homes, acquired in May 1945 and used initially as a summer camp, was a sanatorium in Brunoy named after JLC founder and former president, Baruch Charney Vladeck. In May 1945, another home was opened in Le Mans, which was moved to the Paris region in 1948, where the JLC opened a third home.[142] In 1952, these three homes alone cared for a total of 220 children and received $71,000 from the JLC.[143] The JLC also regularly supported children's homes run by the School Colony (*La colonie scolaire*) and the Left Poale Zion's Jewish Workers' Home (*Arbeter heim, foyer ouvrier juif*) and provided a one-time grant to the OSE. The JLC's support of these institutions shows the complexity of postwar organization dynamics, in which multiple organizations were involved in—and claimed credit for—the same projects. As seen above, both COSOR and the Vaad Hatzala could claim ownership of their children's homes. Likewise, the Jewish Workers' children's home, named after the sculptor Naoum Aronson, in Les Andelys (Normandy), was also part of the Youth Aliyah network, an organization that emerged to evacuate children from Nazi Germany to Palestine in 1933. In the postwar period, Youth Aliyah continued sending Jewish children to Palestine and ran a network of homes in France, where they could await their departure.[144] The JLC, however, claimed the Aronson home as its own because it provided a significant part of its funds, while the FSJF counted it as part of its children's program because the Jewish Workers' Home was an affiliated society.[145] To further complicate matters, the JDC was also funding these organizations for their aid on behalf of children. Recent work by Constance Pâris de Bollardière shows the intricate balancing act required to maintain such arrangements.[146]

Like the Vaad Hatzala, the JLC expanded its work in France and other European countries to include a child "adoption" program in 1947, which involved sponsorships, not actual adoptions.[147] American workers, and at times entire unions, sponsored European Jewish orphans, collectively raising the $300 per year fee to feed, clothe, and school "their" child. This JLC program helped twenty-five hundred children in France, Belgium, Italy, Israel, and Poland in its first ten years.[148] In 1951 alone, 556 children were sponsored in Europe, 322 of them were in France.[149] The program also included non-Jewish orphans, providing the JLC an occasion to bolster intraethnic solidarity within the traditionally Jewish unions where Jews had become a minority.[150]

The JLC program in France coexisted, at times uneasily, with the larger JDC program.[151] With its small infrastructure and even smaller budget, the JLC did not seek to compete with the JDC; it sought to defend its own. As seen above, the JDC worked actively to streamline French Jewish welfare and pressured "competing" organizations, such as the Vaad Hatzala, to withdraw from child welfare work. The JLC, however, was curiously allowed to maintain its program in France. Several reasons can explain this, one of which being the proximity between the JLC leadership and the principal Yiddish newspaper of the United States, *Forverts*.[152] Out of both pride and pragmatism, the JDC was extremely sensitive to criticism in the American Jewish press. As I explore in chapter 5, the JLC's importance to the JDC increased in proportion to Cold War tensions.

In France, the Bundist Workmen's Circle, which benefitted from both the JDC and JLC's funding, quickly understood it could use the JLC's leverage to its advantage, and, at times, even snubbed the JDC.[153] For example, after unsuccessful attempts to increase funding from the JDC, the Workmen's Circle continued to refuse to show the JDC its financial records.[154] The JDC eventually discovered that the Bundist homes were receiving JLC funding, and though annoyed, it did not terminate its support for the organization. Finally, in summer 1947, the Bundist newspaper *Unzer stimme* published two defamatory articles on the JDC's financial support of Jewish Communist organizations. In spite of such "behind the back tactics" that did "a lot of damage in the United States,"[155] the JDC maintained its funding to the Workmen's Circle. The JLC program in France thus succeeded in creating a counterbalance to the JDC that French Jewish Bundists used to their advantage. As a minority voice in French Jewish politics, Bundists found needed support from the JLC. With the JLC as an ally, French Bundists defended their right to "reconstruct according to their own values and cultural references,"[156] transmitting Yiddish and Bundist heritage to the children it assisted, until its children's homes were closed in the early 1960s.[157]

The specific nature of the Vaad Hatzala's and JLC's aid programs provided both organizations with a raison d'être. The HIAS, however, while established by Russian Jews in the United States for those fleeing the Russian Empire, expanded its assistance in the interwar period to include Jews fleeing Nazism. Nonetheless, just as the Vaad and JLC had, the HIAS could also claim to fill a niche in Jewish welfare through its specialization in migration matters. Would this be enough to guarantee its coexistence with the JDC program in postwar France?

The Hebrew Sheltering and Immigrant Aid Society in France: Rival or Partner?

As seen above, HIAS had operated in France since the 1920s as a partner in HICEM, whose headquarters were in Paris.[158] At the outbreak of World War II, HICEM's Paris office was being run by Wladimir Schah, a Russian-born French citizen.[159] After the fall of France, HICEM reestablished its operations in Marseille and employed a staff of seventy-seven individuals. Between July 1940 and December 1941, HICEM helped 9,922 people emigrate from Europe, of which 3,482 emigrated from France.[160] Like the JDC, HICEM also opened an office in Lisbon in June 1940, where Dr. James Bernstein and Ilja Dijour oversaw the organization's European operations. It remained active in France throughout the war and unlike the JDC was forced to join the Vichy-Nazi UGIF. The HICEM office in Marseilles was eventually transferred to the UGIF office in Brives (Corrèze). HICEM staff, comprised primarily of foreign Jews, some of whom active in the resistance, were targeted for deportation during this period.[161] HICEM's wartime experiences were strikingly different than the JDC's; the organization was perceived as European and not American, which had tragic consequences.

On September 10, 1944, Wladimir Schah wrote to his colleagues in New York from Meyssac, a small village in Corrèze:

The time has come to resume our work. The task ahead is immense.
[...] Whatever the new laws may be that will settle the fate of the Jews, tens or hundreds of thousands of them will not want to remain in Europe. Too many griefs, too many awful memories will hang like a nightmare for a long time to come [...]. Too great a distrust will survive in their hearts for them to work in peace for the reconstruction of their desecrated, burned, annihilated homes. [...]
We who have remained here are awaiting your information on this subject. We suppose that you have posed this old problem, now more tragic than in the Middle-Ages, to the governments, and that you have obtained results. We are therefore expecting your information and instructions because we shall

soon be submerged by the mass of requests of these unfortunate people. We fear their questions: "What have our representatives done, what have they obtained to alleviate our sufferings?" What must we answer them?[162]

According to Schah, European Jews had suffered too intensely to stay in Europe, leaving emigration, and thus the revival of HICEM, as the only solution. Efforts to reinstate the French committee of HICEM had actually begun in North Africa in July 1944, where a provisional board had been established.[163] This body was overseeing HICEM's activities in North Africa and sought to facilitate its reinstatement in metropolitan France. By April 1945, HICEM had reestablished headquarters in Paris, set up regional offices in Lyon, Marseilles, and Nice, and had seventeen correspondents in order to assist Jews in France with their migration.[164] Additional regional offices were later opened in Montauban, Montpellier, Toulouse, Limoges, and Bordeaux.[165] In November 1945, HIAS and the ICA dissolved their collaboration, terminating the existence of HICEM and leaving HIAS solely responsible for European operations. From its Paris headquarters, HIAS director Dr. James Bernstein and sixty-five-year-old Wladimir Schah negotiated with consular authorities to obtain visas for HIAS's "protégés."[166] HIAS also worked closely with local Jewish child welfare organizations to coordinate the immigration of children.[167] In addition to these immigration-related matters, HIAS continued to serve as an intermediary between American Jews and their European relatives by delivering packages and cash remittances.[168] Soon, HIAS-France employed a staff of over one-hundred individuals.[169] With the exception of correspondence between the executive director and the local director, HIAS business was conducted in French. In continuity with the war period, HIAS seems to have been embedded in French Jewish life, a fact that set it apart from other American Jewish aid committees.[170]

As much as the postwar situation confirmed its need, structural problems limited HIAS's ability to fulfill its mission of moving Jews out of Europe. France, due to its ports and liberal immigration policies, became the central destination for Eastern European Jews, DPs, and other refugees. Many crossed French borders hoping to go elsewhere or finding family. For example, COJASOR assisted approximately seventy-five thousand "transients" and "infiltrees" from 1945 to 1955.[171] An estimated thirty-five thousand Jews settled in France in the 1944–1949 period.[172] This figure can be explained in part by the limited immigration possibilities of the immediate postwar period. As one historian has pointed out, HIAS was only as strong as existing immigration legislation.[173] After the war, immigration to the United States remained difficult in spite of the 1945 Truman Directive and the DP Act of 1948.[174] The latter, while representing a major evolution in US immigration law in its attention to migrants' political status, nonetheless discriminated against Jewish DPs. Only 68,700 of the 339,000 DPs resettled in the United States under this act were Jewish.[175] HIAS's postwar record reflects these structural constraints: of the 20,000 individuals assisted by the organization in 1949, 2,559 individuals were of French nationality or permanent residents of France.[176] It moved a total of 447 people from France to Palestine in the "postwar era."[177] In 1951, according to historian Mark Wischnitzer, there were still over 50,000 Jewish individuals in France awaiting emigration, many of whom ultimately settled there.[178] This figure shows the limits of the HIAS immigration program in France.

Such limitations created frustrations among HIAS officials in France, who looked upon the extensive JDC program with envy. The tensions between these organizations can be explained by the overlapping scope of their work yet also speaks to older animosities and, of course, funding disparities.[179] In the United States, HIAS "retained its image as an arm of the East European immigrant community"[180] and received the majority of its funding in the form of donations from this faction of the American Jewish population. However, more established American Jews of German origin ran the JDC, and it received most of its funding from the United Jewish Appeal. HIAS's request to participate in the UJA was rejected in 1940.[181] For the year 1945, HIAS's annual *global* budget was roughly $1.5 million (less than the JDC allocation for France alone for the same year).[182] During periods of crisis, HICEM received JDC funds, making HIAS somewhat indebted to the JDC.[183] Furthermore, by 1945 the JDC had obtained the status of agent of the IGCR, along with five other American voluntary organizations. This meant that the JDC was eligible for IGCR funding for its work on behalf of stateless individuals. HICEM was excluded from this agreement and "felt slighted," according to one official.[184] As seen above, the Truman Directive of December 1945 created new immigration possibilities for individuals in DP camps in Austria, Germany, and Italy, yet it furthered the conflict between the JDC and HIAS, which both sought to provide emigration services.

While the leadership of these organizations sought to resolve the conflict through official talks throughout 1946, their representatives in the field were left to negotiate on their own terms. On the ground, the JDC always seemed to fare better. In France, where the JDC initially benefited from an agreement with UNRRA to obtain more personnel, HIAS had to resort to recruiting individuals who it hoped would obtain favors from the American authorities, such as Mrs. Jones, a physicist who was married to the American Consul of Berlin and hired by HIAS in Marseille because of her "intimate relations with all of the American personalities from the Army, War shipping and the Consulate."[185]

In France, the small world of Jewish welfare created multiple occasions for employees from HIAS to bump into those from the JDC. The departure of 815 people for Palestine in July 1945 brought representatives from the Jewish Agency, FSJF, OSE, and JDC to Marseille. Joseph Dubrowitch, the HICEM representative, improvised a reception attended by forty individuals. His justification of its cost to his superiors is revealing:

> First of all, the OSE and the Federation had already organized receptions and plus I wanted to show to the other organizations (the Palestinian Office, the JDC, Jewish Agency) that we have all the help necessary here to take care of relations with the Americans and that it wasn't necessary to spend a crazy amount of money for eighteen people to travel from Paris and elsewhere to Marseille.
>
> It was also absolutely necessary to show to the press the role that the HICEM played in this departure, as it had been poorly informed by the other organizations [...]. Finally, reconciling and calming the mood [*les esprits*] also was important.[186]

This example shows that American Jewish aid organizations were as concerned with turf as the French. Conflict surged when the JDC opened an office in Bordeaux in summer 1946—the city where HIAS processed most of its immigration cases for the United States. HIAS officials therefore thought Bordeaux should be off-limits to the JDC. Adding insult to injury, the JDC set up its office in the same building as HIAS, which also housed the offices of COJASOR and OPEJ. Concerned with maintaining good relations with the American Consul, who warned HIAS that he did not want to see rivalries among emigration organizations, the HIAS representative in Bordeaux wrote to his superiors in Paris for clarification on how to deal with cases that concerned both organizations.[187] This prompted the director of HIAS-France to forward this letter to his superiors in New York to show them the "effect made by [the] appearance of another 'competing' organization." He continued,

> You certainly will be aware of the shade of contempt in the words of the Bordeaux Consul when saying "that they don't want, under any pretext, 'rivalry' between different organizations in order to get a success more or less important [*sic*]."
>
> I understand indeed that in order to make peace you need at least two parties, but to make war, the wish of a single one is quite enough, I dare say that peace does not depend only on you. I believe useful to show in

discussions that there was no sense in creating a new organization in Bordeaux: As said before hand, the total amount of emigration cases in the Bordeaux district has been centralized by our office and the lack of complaints and, on the contrary, lots of compliments we get, show that our Office works at [sic] everybody's satisfaction.[188]

This incident illustrates the gap between the JDC's discourse and its actions. By opening an emigration office in Bordeaux, it was engaging in the same practice it had criticized among French organizations: the duplication of services. Such conflicts persuaded HIAS to better publicize its work by employing the same tactics as the JDC, which had a public relations department in Paris. Lewis Neikrug, executive director of HIAS's European operations sought to hire "two competent young Americans, a sort of combination handymen and 'trouble shooters'" in the field of public relations. "With a pair of youngsters like that around I think I could start things humming in the Central office. [. . .] I feel it is incumbent that I keep probing into situations and keep developing and capitalizing every opportunity for good HIAS publicity."[189]

The "war" between HIAS and the JDC continued throughout Europe until the passage of the DP Act of 1948. Now faced with what they thought was a real possibility to evacuate the DP camps, the JDC and HIAS finally joined forces and established a shared office in Frankfurt in July 1949.[190] Outside of the "DP countries," these organizations continued to operate independently. In the United States, HIAS had worked outside of the established circuits to help settle their "protégés," while the National Refugee Service and the Service to the Foreign Born of the National Council of Jewish Women worked through more recognized channels to accomplish the same task. In 1946, these latter two organizations merged to create the United Service for New Americans (USNA). USNA began to work with HIAS in December 1953, merging to create the United HIAS service. The terms of the merger allowed HIAS to continue its independent fundraising yet also receive funding from the UJA. Perhaps the ultimate victory is that the merger forced the JDC to relinquish its migration work. After years of feeling like the stepchild of American Jewish welfare, HIAS was finally able to enter "mainstream" American Jewish communal work, all while continuing its mission overseas.[191]

This study of HIAS in France, when analyzed along with the Vaad Hatzala and the Jewish Labor Committee, shows that tensions between the German elite (embodied by the JDC) and Eastern European Jews were not completely extinguished in the immediate postwar period in the United States. As Jews moved progressively into the American mainstream, one can see that Eastern

European Jewish visions of the Jewish future were not suppressed but incorporated into the fold. France thus played an important role for American Jewish organizations, serving as a site where each actor could stake out a territory and defend its particular vision. While this led to new compromises in the United States, it also influenced the shape of French Jewish welfare, lending weight to minority voices during the crucial emergency period following the Holocaust.

CONCLUSION

The JDC, which had remained active in France during World War II, underwent major changes in the postwar period. French Jewish leaders who had run the JDC during the war continued its work in its aftermath, allotting funds to feed, clothe, and shelter surviving Jews. The return of American personnel to France marked a new era in this Franco-American Jewish collaboration. Different wartime experiences and perceptions of postwar needs transformed the collective "we" (the Jews) into "we" (the French), as opposed to "you" (the Americans). Suddenly, French Jews were being asked to return to a normal existence after years of persecution in order to conform to American social work principles, which valued efficiency, centralization, and accountability.

Arthur Greenleigh, who directed the French JDC program from December 1944 to May 1946, began the importation of these concepts. Greenleigh established several policies to coordinate French Jewish welfare and integrate Jews into the larger French public aid system. He also sought to increase the accountability of the French Jewish agencies that received JDC funding by requesting they recognize it on their letterhead. From January 1946 onward, funded agencies were required to submit monthly and annual reports. Finally, under Greenleigh, the JDC established the Social Service Exchange, a centralized index system that registered those seeking aid in a common file. Jewish welfare agencies had to consult this file before providing services to an individual, reducing the fraudulent use of the French Jewish social service network. The JDC made its funding contingent on adopting these practices. As a result, French Jewish leaders maintained a complex relationship with the JDC, in which feelings of gratitude often coexisted with resentment. This period stood in stark contrast to the informal aid offered by American Jewish GIs and chaplains, characterized by the simplicity of exchanges among individuals.

The JDC may have inspired ambivalent feelings among French Jews, but one cannot deny its importance in postwar French Jewish life, especially in light of the French provisional government's largely unsatisfactory response to Jewish welfare needs. The return to republican order and annulment of Vichy's discriminatory policies, even if imperfect, created a paradoxical situation in which the specific needs of Jews either went unaddressed or were handled in an extremely discreet manner by the provisional government.[192] Furthermore, even the purest intentions could not make up for France's dismal financial situation. Strapped for resources, government-mandated agencies such as COSOR saw the JDC as the solution for helping Jews, even if this encouraged excluding eligible Jews from their programs. Finally, it should also be noted that in the aftermath of genocide, Jews were also wary of the state and clearly did not want to leave the responsibility of raising the next generation in its hands.[193]

During this complex time, the JDC responded to multiple needs by fueling Jewish self-help and philanthropy. It distributed almost $2 million in 1945 and $2.8 million in 1946 to approximately thirty-six Jewish welfare organizations, which in turn provided services to the Jews of France through their aid networks.[194] In May 1946, the JDC was indirectly assisting 40,500 individuals in France, including more than 12,000 children.[195] By far, the JDC was the primary benefactor of Jewish welfare. In 1945, the JDC estimated it had subsidized 73 percent of total costs.[196] While problematic, JDC data on 1946 reveal the organization's continued importance, whose contribution to French Jewish welfare had decreased only slightly—to 72 percent. As seen in figure 3.2, meager contributions from the French government (5%), the IGCR (10%), and private contributions (13%), left the primary responsibility for aid on the JDC's shoulders.[197]

These JDC statistics reflect only its own funding. As the study of the Vaad Hatzala, the Jewish Labor Committee, and the HIAS shows, other American Jewish organizations were also providing aid to French Jews. French Jews had an interest in omitting other sources of funding when they opened their books to the JDC.

The JDC was indisputably a central player in Jewish and American welfare circles in postwar France, yet it was not working in a vacuum. Its actions in France were observed closely, influenced by the dynamics in American Jewish life. The HIAS, for example, perceived the omnipresence of the JDC in the field of emigration as an affront yet was unable to change the situation until New York leadership ironed out a compromise. The JDC's important role among other American voluntary organizations to obtain Economic Cooperation Act funding shows that the Jewish organization was fully integrated into larger American circles. This echoes the dynamics of postwar American society, in which Jews increasingly entered the mainstream.

Arthur Greenleigh left France in May 1946. After almost one and a half years in France, he was able to conclude, "The situation has passed from an emergency basis to a more stable one and permanent long time plans can now be made with the objective of assumption by the local Jewish community of the

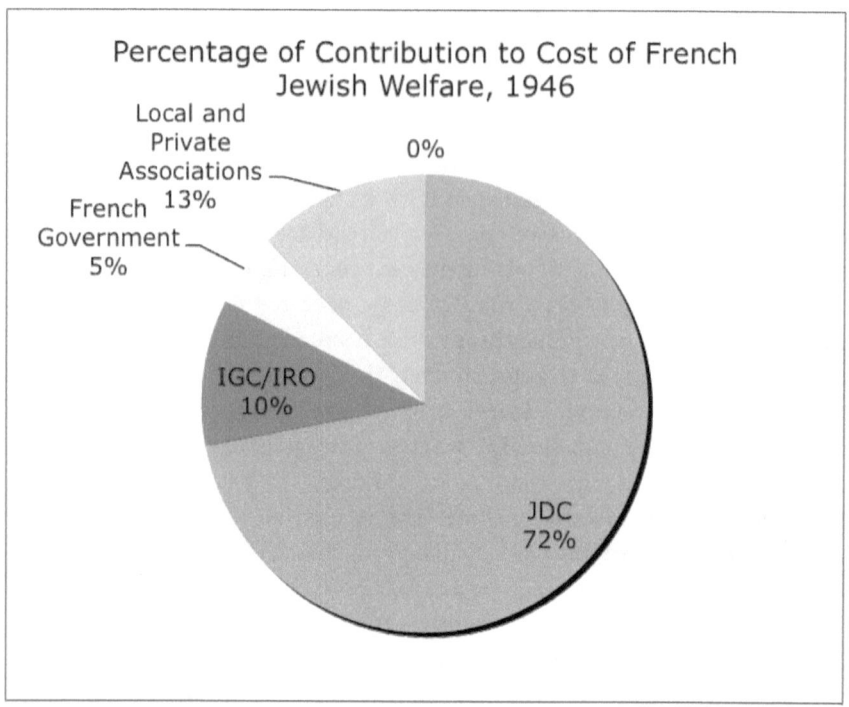

Figure 3.2. Contribution to French Jewish welfare by organization, 1946. JDC-I, Laura Margolis Jarblum Archives, uncatalogued, Statistical Report, France, Country Directors Conference, October 1952.

major responsibility for direction, supervision, and finance."[198] An increasing distance began to develop between French Jewish leaders and the top American leadership of the JDC in Europe, even though certain French leaders bypassed bureaucratic channels and solicited Dr. Schwartz directly, drawing his attention to their needs. Claude Kelman, a leader of the FSJF, recalled, "We would often enter his [Dr. Schwartz's] famous angle office on the rue de Téhéran, overwhelmed and discouraged by the weight of the misfortune and its aftermath, but we always left these walls, where so many cries of distress had echoed, so many nightmarish accounts, reassured, comforted, encouraged."[199] French Jewish leaders may have been welcomed by Schwartz, but their direct solicitations influenced the JDC decision to physically separate its European headquarters from its "Office for France" in April 1946.[200] The arrival of Laura Margolis, who directed the JDC Office for France from 1946 until 1953, announced a new era that would favor long-term reconstruction with the goal of rendering French Jews self-sufficient.

FOUR

LONG-TERM RECONSTRUCTION

The End of French Dependence?

"I AM IN THE MIDST of my second day in Paris and I feel as though I have been working here for a year. I arrived at 9 o'clock Wednesday night and 9 o'clock Thursday morning I was behind a desk. [...] I will continue to give you impressions which is all I am able to do at this time; as Laura [Margolis] says, 'the important job now for me is just to understand the confusion that exists;' I am devoting myself to this objective for the present,"[1] wrote Harry Rosen to his JDC colleague in New York in May 1948. An American Jewish fundraising expert and specialist in what American social workers called "community organizing," Rosen had come to France to help the local Jewish population establish their own centralized fundraising organization based on the American model of the United Jewish Appeal. The new organization would serve to coordinate the multiple French Jewish welfare and cultural organizations.[2]

Harry Rosen was one of several experts hired to implement JDC policies as they shifted from providing emergency relief to the long-term reconstruction of French Jewish life. As discussed in chapter 3, the urgent welfare needs of French Jews inspired a chaotic mobilization among French Jewish welfare organizations, leading to the "confusion" Rosen had observed. Beyond the practical problems, the question of who would reconstruct Jewish life—and how—was ever present. The strikingly different visions of what the future should look like also complicated matters. The creation of the CRIF, which placed French native and immigrant Jews of multiple and divergent political and religious ideologies together, provided hope that the Jews of France would rise above their divisions. While the war years led Jews to reconsider tensions related to national origin, the growing possibility of a Jewish state in Palestine and the Cold War enflamed political divisions.[3] Contrasting notions of Jewish identity influenced Jews on the individual and collective levels. Some Jews, especially immigrants, conceived of their identities in ethnic terms, whereas others considered themselves French citizens of the Jewish faith. After the Holocaust, a fractured sense of trust in the state forced Jews to reevaluate their national and Jewish identities and ask whether it was possible to remain in France. While some decided to start anew elsewhere, the majority chose to remain, even after the creation of Israel in 1948.[4] Though most Jews in France chose to reinvest their hope in their nation, this was not the case for Jewish survivors in Central and Eastern Europe, who fled postwar, anti-Jewish violence and the closing of the Iron Curtain. By late summer of 1946, France had become one of the primary destinations for about one hundred thousand Polish Jews who had fled their country. While many of these individuals came to France before moving on to other destinations, approximately thirty-two thousand Eastern European Jews settled in France, bringing their specific wartime experiences, conceptions of Jewish life, and politics to an already diverse population.[5]

On the collective level, ideological diversity manifested itself in a rich network of Jewish aid organizations. The difficult coexistence of these organizations and their new importance to the Jews of France challenged the very definition of the term *community* as it had been previously applied to French Jewish life. Before the war, the term referred to members of synagogues, keeping with the notion that Judaism was a religion, not a people. Furthermore, the "French of Jewish faith" may have expressed their Jewishness at home and the synagogue, but elsewhere, they were French.[6] As a result, France had many Jewish communities.[7] The notion of a singular Jewish community encompassing a larger scope of activities and ideologies, including secular Jews, implied that a bond existed between these individuals because they belonged to a common people, not faith. While this way of conceptualizing Jewish life was common in the United States and Eastern Europe before World War II, it represented a new understanding of Jewish identity in France. Indeed, as seen above, the seeds of a "communal bond" had been planted during the war, when Jews from divergent ideological factions, after having been forced to establish the UGIF, actually *chose* to establish the CRIF. After the war, surviving Jews sought to honor the memory of missing parents by providing orphaned children with the education they would have received had the war not taken place. This sacred duty created a strong argument for pluralism, supporting the claim that even the smallest voices had the right to exist alongside more established Jewish institutions. Yet in the immediate postwar period, it was unclear whether such diversity would lead to the reestablishment of Jewish communities or a unified one.

Even though American Jews were struggling with similar divisions in the early postwar period, the JDC perceived the absence of a unified Jewish community in France as a barrier to self-sufficiency. If the JDC withdrew from France, who would coordinate the welfare organizations, distribute funds, and plan for the future? In 1947, Laura Margolis, the newly arrived director of the JDC's Office for France, felt the time had come to address this question. The answer, she believed, was to import social welfare structures and practices from the United States. Though Margolis was a newcomer to France, having arrived in 1946, she and other JDC officials knew that their ideas would have a better chance of being accepted by French Jewish leaders if they were perceived as originating from local sources. They therefore worked indirectly to educate French Jews on what kind of "Jewish community" they should reconstruct.

The JDC's "importation" of a unified fundraising and distribution agency based on the United Jewish Appeal, which in France took on the name of the Unified Jewish Social Fund (Fonds social juif unifié, FSJU), provides a rich example of the JDC's efforts to influence local Jewish life. This was not the JDC's only "importation" project. In May 1947, the JDC established an "American" nursing school in the Rothschild Hospital in Paris for foreign Jewish women.[8] In October 1949, the JDC opened the Paul Baerwald School of Social Work in Versailles to train Jewish social workers in American methods, which I will explore in chapter 6. While these schools influenced French Jewish life by providing American training to individuals who worked in local institutions, the FSJU arguably left the greatest mark because it changed the actual structure of French Jewish welfare.[9]

Labeled retroactively by one American Jewish communal leader as a "Jewish Marshall Plan,"[10] the JDC program in France is an example of American philanthropy in Europe. There is little debate among historians on the emergence of a hegemonic American presence in Europe following World War II. A growing body of literature has documented the role of philanthropy in Americanization.[11] Historian Maud Mandel has questioned the place of American hegemony in Jewish philanthropy in her analysis of the influence of the JDC on French Jewish life after World War II. Noting the JDC's success in importing American structures and methods to France, she argues that the JDC functioned "like many American philanthropic organizations of the twentieth century, spreading its own cultural agenda through its activities abroad."[12] Focusing on the outcome of the JDC's importation efforts, Mandel's research suggests that JDC aid, though well intended, was a form of cultural imperialism.

This chapter, which will focus exclusively on the JDC, will argue that shifting the emphasis from the outcome to the *process* of Americanization tells a more complex story, one in which French Jews have a lead role. This approach requires paying greater attention to how the receiving society perceived and reacted to American aid.[13] Instead of thinking of cultural transfers in binary or hegemonic terms, the purpose here is to see how JDC policies were implemented from the perspective of the French and Americans. To do so, it is first necessary to analyze the shifts in the JDC program under Laura Margolis. Her efforts to reform Jewish aid organizations created new conflicts, and it is only by understanding these tensions that one can grasp why local Jews would agree to establish an American structure to organize French Jewish welfare. French Jews did indeed Americanize but did not passively submit to the whims of their American benefactors. Instead, they played a central role in the establishment of the FSJU.

THE JDC OFFICE FOR FRANCE UNDER THE DIRECTION OF LAURA MARGOLIS: A NEW ORDER?

As director of the JDC Office for France from 1946 to 1953, Laura Margolis can be considered the architect of the JDC's long-term reconstruction efforts. She was also one of the first women to penetrate the masculine worlds of the JDC and French Jewish welfare. Her unique personal and professional background provided her with the tools for this task. Born in Constantinople in 1903 to Russian Jewish parents, Margolis arrived in the United States at the age of five, "speaking all the languages of the Middle East but not a word of English."[14] She grew up in Ohio, earned a degree in social work from Western Reserve University, and began her professional career in the Jewish communities of Cleveland and Buffalo before being hired by the National Refugee Service to help Jewish refugees in Cuba in 1938. In January 1939 Margolis sailed for Havana, where she organized welfare services for the growing number of refugees and managed a staff of over one hundred. The 1939 *SS St. Louis* tragedy proved a trying beginning to her career as an overseas social worker.[15]

In April of 1941, the JDC contacted Margolis requesting her presence in Shanghai, where over twenty-thousand Central European refugees had fled. Interestingly, it was the US State Department that had noticed Margolis in Havana and suggested she be sent to Shanghai. Margolis benefited from good relations with US consular officials once in China, with whom she was supposed to negotiate immigration matters. Once in contact with the refugees, Margolis reoriented her assignment to organize a welfare program with them.

As the Japanese invasion of the Shanghai International Settlement grew imminent, the JDC did with Margolis in China what it had done with Jefroykin in France—it authorized her, in case of war, to borrow funds in the name of the JDC that would be reimbursed afterward. Following the Japanese invasion of the Shanghai International Settlement in December 1941, she worked closely with the refugees to set up their welfare program. In January 1943, Margolis and her American JDC colleague were interned as enemy nationals. Margolis was sent to camp outside of Shanghai, where she worked in the kitchen and surrounding fields. While treated fairly, after half a year, Margolis found a way to be transferred to a hospital where, with the compliance of her doctor, she recuperated from camp life and received visits from the representatives of the refugee aid committees. In December 1943, Margolis was traded as a prisoner of war and repatriated to the United States. She smuggled out crucial information on her work in Shanghai on a piece of toilet paper that she had rolled up and placed in the elastic band of her underwear.

Reunited with the JDC staff in New York, Margolis learned for the first time of the mass murder of European Jews. While en route to Washington, DC, to be interviewed by the Department of the Treasury and UNRRA on her activities in China, she made the JDC agree to send her to Europe, which Joseph Schwartz arranged in March 1944. Margolis's first assignment was to operate a children's home in Barcelona that had been opened by the JDC to receive children who had crossed into Spain from France.[16] Margolis was later sent to Sweden, where she organized a parcel program for the Jews interned in Bergen-Belsen and Theresienstadt. In March 1945, Margolis was assigned to the postwar JDC program in Belgium, where she worked until she suffered a breakdown.

After a week in an army hospital and a return visit to the United States, Margolis was sent to France in June 1946. After Cuba, China, Sweden, Spain, and Belgium, she immediately recognized the potential of France. She recalled in a 1976 oral history interview:

> JDC was spending ten million dollars [sic] in France, and I could see the possibility of creating something permanent. Before the war I'd been working in an emergency situation and during the height of the war there was no possibility of thinking in terms of rebuilding the community. You met problems and emergencies as they arose, you were glad to save people's lives. But now the war was over and I began to think in terms of reconstructing a community, as well as preparations for Aliyah. [...] But it was obvious that there were people who were going to stay in France, a part that belonged to France.[17]

Indeed, while a committed Zionist who later immigrated to Israel, Margolis set out to organize and rebuild a community for that "part that belonged to France."

"The JDC Is Not Santa Claus"[18]

Laura Margolis's wartime experiences shaped her perception of France. Her battle record—especially her experiences in Shanghai—followed her to her new assignment, and perhaps helped communal leaders overlook her gender.[19] Her tough reputation, strong sense of diplomacy, and very importantly, her mastery of French gave her the credibility her position required. Upon arrival, she criticized the current JDC program in France by saying, "The policy of 'laissez-faire,' practiced for almost two years vis-à-vis the French subventioned [sic] agencies, has resulted in huge cumbersome and badly administered structures from which structures it is difficult to extract the simplest financial or statistical facts so necessary to us in our planning of the social service program as well as budgetary needs."[20]

Referring to the 1944–1946 period as "the Halcyon days" for French Jewish agencies,[21] she assigned a JDC staff member as a liaison to each of the local welfare agencies. Still critical in early 1947, Margolis assessed the JDC program in France, echoing her predecessor Arthur Greenleigh's 1945 observations:

> I think that the program in France is a little chaotic. It was not until June of last year that France had a staff and a structure that was completely separate. By that time, however, the agencies in France had gotten into the habit of not having too many questions asked. So that we now have 34 or 35 separate organization [sic], each are doing everything. Our job has been to get basic statistics and basic facts of what the agencies are doing with our money. [...] I look at it from a long range point of view, to what we will leave behind in a country as we pull out. You have terrific conflicts in this country between political parties. We spend 90% of our effort and our time in trying to understand the politics rather than the social work program. [...] I think the time has come in France where, if we can crystallize our policies and define our program, the time has come when that kind of crystallization of policy is the only answer to really establish a program in France of which the JDC can say after a couple of years that we have created something. Up until this time we have done a job in terms of life saving, feeding, housing, taking care of emergencies. I think that period has ended.[22]

Margolis was seeking support from JDC leadership to establish a long-term program for France. She had three major goals that she progressively set into action. The first was to continue streamlining French Jewish welfare; the second was to increase cooperation among aid organizations; and the third was

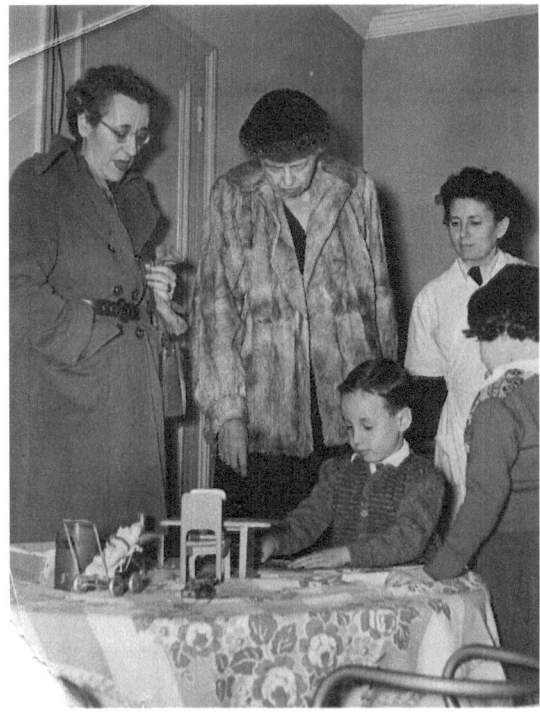

Figure 4.1. Laura Margolis (*left*) with Eleanor Roosevelt visiting an OSE children's home (most likely after 1946). OSE collection of the Mémorial de la Shoah.

to encourage French Jews to assume greater responsibility for their welfare programs, which were, in her opinion, too dependent upon American funds.

The JDC and the Jews of France: "'Shocking' our agencies into facing reality."[23]

Even though the JDC valued centralization and self-sufficiency, its program in France grew steadily from 1944 to 1947. Record donations from American Jews to the United Jewish Appeal (UJA) made this possible. As seen in table 4.1, UJA donations jumped from $33 million in 1945 to $103 million in 1946, of which the JDC received 57 percent.[24] The unprecedented success of the 1946 UJA campaign can be seen in France, with a record JDC grant of $5.9 million in 1947.[25] However, predictions of a recession and a slow going UJA campaign in the United States, coupled with an increase in the cost of living in France, forced the JDC to start radically cutting back its programs in 1947.

Table 4.1. JDC Program in France Compared with Global JDC Expenditures and United Jewish Appeal Results (1944–1948)

Year	Total United Jewish Appeal Campaign Results (in US Dollars) (a)	JDC Global Expenditures (in US Dollars) (b)	JDC Contribution to France (in US Dollars) (c)	Evolution between years of JDC contribution to France as Percentages
1944	27,000,000	15,210,000	1,657,223	—
1945	33,000,000	28,300,000	1,998,000	20.6%
1946	103,000,000	54,100,000	2,831,000	41.7%
1947	125,000,000	75,700,000	5,906,000	108.6%
1948	150,000,000	70,600,000	3,583,000	−39.3%

Sources: (a) For 1944–1945, Karp, *To Give Life*, 77–85; for 1946–1964, Raphaël, *A History of the United Jewish Appeal, 1939–1982*, 136–141; (b) Bauer, *Out of the Ashes*, xvii–xviii; and (c) for 1944, Bauer, *American Jewry and the Holocaust*, 244; for 1945–1948, Bauer, *Out of the Ashes*, xviii.

While a financial necessity, JDC budget cuts were also a means of provoking a response from the agencies it funded, as seen in one JDC childcare specialist's assessment of its progress in limiting the duplication of services:

> In retrospect, we can safely say that we have made progress in developing this principle [limiting the duplication of services] in our continued relationships with our agencies during the past two years. This progress we feel did not come only from teaching through a consciously planned educational approach. The pressures, complexities and size of our program was such that we had neither time, money, nor sufficient personnel to rely on the educational process only. Where persuasion and interpretation brought only halfhearted acceptance of our ideas, the thing which actually made our agencies face reality, was budget cuts. Although these budget cuts were frequently essential, based on budgetary limitations which headquarters imposed on the Office for France, we must admit that in some situations, we cut budgets with a conscious purpose of "shocking" our agencies into facing reality. Thus, we used the subvention [*sic*] as a tool in treating an agency in much the same way as relief has been used as a tool in treating the individual client.[26]

Margolis's new policies brought her closer to her goals. For example, COJASOR shrunk from 49 local agencies with 363 employees in 1947 to 5 local agencies with 187 employees in 1949.[27] During the same period, the ties linking the various aid organizations increased. The employees of French Jewish agencies established a professional association for Jewish social workers in 1947 whose membership grew from 260 in that year to 600 in 1949.[28] The JDC's Social Service Exchange, the collective file designed to curtail the "wandering beggar," grew to include 87,000 entries by 1949.[29] Most importantly, French Jewish aid organizations began to consider themselves as part of a larger entity. When faced with the enormous challenge of Jewish immigration from Poland, which escalated in summer 1946, Jewish organizations in France first mobilized individually and then, at the request of the JDC and the French government, created the Interagency Council to Aid Jewish Migrants and Transients (Conseil interoeuvres d'aide aux immigrants et transitaires juifs). The council was wrought with infighting and accusations of corruption and did not prove efficient—the first convoy of Polish Jews sponsored by the council arrived eight months after its creation.[30] Nonetheless, this body grouped together seventeen Jewish organizations and represented a new way of working together that, even while unsuccessful, slowly established the norm of acting collectively.

French and American Jews may have been partners in the reconstruction of French Jewish life, but by cutting budgets, the JDC flexed its financial muscle, reminding French Jews of the differences that separated them. While French Jewish leaders graciously accepted JDC aid, and growing obligations to obtain its funding, by 1947 signs of unrest were growing obvious in France and elsewhere.[31] Having worked collectively to help Polish Jews, French Jewish leaders were beginning to understand that unification was the only way to create a counterweight to the JDC behemoth. As early as December 1946, Léon Meiss, president of the CRIF and the Central Consistory, expressed his concerns about the JDC's work in France. Meiss proposed the CRIF establish a JDC Committee (Comité auprès du joint). The latter then formed a three-person committee.[32] In February 1947, he spoke out again: "The JDC, while providing a considerable amount of aid for France, does so in 'splendid isolation' and is accomplishing its mission without consulting French Jewry [*judaïsme de France*]. Yet the moral responsibility of the Jews of France is still being engaged, and not just their moral responsibility: the current JDC budget for France is 50 million [francs], yet it cannot carry out this effort in the long run. French Jews will have to be the ones to shoulder this responsibility."[33]

Evoking the dysfunctional nature of French Jewish welfare and the injustices in the JDC's distribution of funding, Meiss suggested in February 1947 the CRIF should enlarge its three-person committee into an advisory committee on the JDC, comprised of representatives from the major French Jewish welfare organizations.[34] While Meiss's suggestion provoked some debate among the

CRIF board members, the latter voted to establish the JDC Advisory Committee in September 1947.[35] Importantly, it was then suggested the committee should have a fundraising role and even, in the words of Léon Meiss, "an analogous action to the United Jewish Appeal."[36]

During the same period, individual organizations began responding to the JDC's budget cuts. Protests came from unlikely corners of French Jewish life. The OSE, a long-term partner of the JDC, showed its resentment after a meeting with them in April 1947, at which OSE leaders learned that the JDC would curtail its funding of certain activities. Furthermore, the JDC had determined the monthly cost of caring for a child. The OSE, whose costs amounted to F6,900 a month per child, was more expensive than other agencies, which managed to deliver their services for F4,500 a month per child. The OSE would therefore only receive F5,500 a month per child.[37] One month later, the OSE received confirmation of its funding from the JDC. Instead of the anticipated cut, it had been granted more funding than expected. Nonetheless, the unilateral manner in which the JDC had decided on the OSE budget had shocked OSE leaders. In addition, the JDC fixed the total OSE budget, allowing it to reduce its contribution if the OSE obtained funding from external sources.[38] Soon thereafter, one OSE official noted that the JDC was attempting to "transform the OSE into its own agency" and declared that "the moment had arrived to strongly oppose this tendency."[39] This context of communal turmoil allowed for the creation of the Unified Jewish Social Fund (Fonds social juif unifié, FSJU).

THE CREATION OF THE UNIFIED JEWISH SOCIAL FUND (FSJU)

The sense of urgency that had characterized the immediate postwar period was starting to subside by early 1947.[40] The evolution of JDC funding for France reflects this shift. In 1948, for the first time since liberation, the JDC decreased its budget—a trend that continued over the following 1949–1953 period. JDC budget cuts incited French Jews to voice their criticisms. As seen above, from December 1946 through September 1947, the CRIF's leadership engaged in debate on how to influence JDC policy.[41] A shared frustration about the JDC's meddling provided a centralizing force for French Jewish leaders, who realized that by unifying they could establish a formidable counterweight to the JDC. Instead of each aid organization negotiating individually, they felt collective bargaining through one representative body would yield better results.

While French Jewish leaders debated this issue, JDC director for France Laura Margolis spent the summer months of July and August 1947 in the south of France, coordinating aid for the forty-five hundred passengers who had boarded the *Exodus 1947* and were taken to Hamburg in British prison vessels. Upon her return to Paris in fall 1947, Margolis felt the moment had come to start discussing the long-term reconstruction of French Jewish life by establishing a central fundraising, distribution, and social-planning structure based on the UJA. In the postwar period, even though Jews represented only 3 percent of the American population, the UJA had become the most successful American philanthropic organization.[42] In 1939, the UJA campaign raised $16 million. In 1948, it raised more than $200 million.[43] Arguably, the postwar success of the UJA led American Jewish social workers to see this model as the solution to the disorganization and divisions of French Jewish welfare.

French Jewish leaders had been familiar with the UJA long before JDC employees attempted to import it to France. Indeed, UJA fundraising campaigns in the United States used eyewitness accounts by European Jewish survivors to spark the generosity of American Jews.[44] France, with its strong record of Jewish resistance and burgeoning postwar Jewish life, provided American Jewish donors with a particularly optimistic vision of the future. Two young French Jewish women, Franceline Bloch and Gaby Wolff Cohen, obtained scholarships from the National Council of Jewish Women (a beneficiary of the UJA) to study in the United States. During their stays, they were often called upon to speak on their experiences in the French Jewish resistance. Likewise, Robert Gamzon, founder of the Jewish Scouts of France (EIF), traveled to the United States to help raise funds for the general 1946 UJA campaign. From there, in a UJA-sponsored article, Gamzon asked American Jews, "Don't you want to be the American uncle of a Jewish child [in Europe]?"[45] Gamzon (and consequently, the UJA) did not hesitate to evoke feelings of guilt to raise funds:

> You Jews of America owe it to the Jews of the world to care for them, to be the rich uncle who supports his nieces and nephews throughout the world. You have to earn the right to your happiness. You cannot know what it means to live in constant fear, under a false name, to be afraid to turn around in the street lest you should be followed, arrested and tortured, or to come home to an empty house and find your whole family deported. No, you cannot know what it means to die of cold and hunger or to come home from Hell finally and not to find anybody or anything and to feel, as one of the returning deportees put it, as naked as a newborn baby. You can thank God you have a home and a free life and a free country. I speak, not for those who gave their money, but their lives, when I say that life has meaning only if it serves a definite purpose. Let us give a value to our lives and let us show the world that Jewish fraternity is not a word but a fact and by so doing show Israel's contribution to mankind.[46]

To help raise funds for the UJA, the French Jewish Scouts produced a film, with the JDC's support, on its wartime activities entitled *Hazak* ("strong," in Hebrew). Destined for American audiences, the film underscored the image of French Jews as resistance fighters, and even though it arrived too late for the 1946 UJA campaign, the film produced "good results"[47] when it was finally shown in the United States. Supporting the UJA was clearly in the best interest of French Jews; they pleased their American benefactors by helping them raise money to finance French Jewish welfare and, at the same time, made valuable contacts for their organizations in the United States. For Gamzon, the fruit of these efforts was an exchange program organized in collaboration with the Jewish Education Committee in New York City, which recruited American Jewish youth to serve as "educators" in the children's homes run by the French Jewish Scouts, the OSE, and other children's organizations.[48] Eventually, however, French Jews began to study and emulate instead of assisting the UJA's fundraising efforts.

In November 1946, four months after Laura Margolis's arrival at the JDC Office for France, Jacques Pulver, the producer of the Jewish Scout's film *Hazak*, submitted a report to the JDC on his recent trip to the United States. In it he wrote, "The main purpose of my trip to the United States was to study American fundraising methods in order to adapt those methods to France in the organization of a central Jewish fund raising body as quickly as possible."[49] After two weeks spent learning about American fundraising in JDC and UJA offices in New York, Pulver traveled across the United States to see how the theory applied in the field. Intrigued yet unconvinced that American methods could be applied in France, Pulver explained the major barrier to establishing a centralized fundraising organization in France to his American benefactors: "I am ashamed to admit that some of our French agencies might reason as follows: 'What is the use of raising money if it is only to have the Americans, who can afford it, give less.'"[50] In spite of his doubts, Pulver laid out a detailed plan on how he would lead French Jews toward an American fundraising model, estimating that the first united campaign would take place six months later, in May 1947. Pulver did not achieve his goal.

At almost the same time, the CRIF was establishing its JDC advisory committee. Margolis took advantage of this development to reiterate her wish to see a UJA-like structure in France. When she approached Dr. Schwartz, head of JDC operations in Europe, with her idea, he reportedly responded, "Laura, are you going to try to make good Americans out of the French?"[51] Margolis recalled her response: "My answer to him was that I never expected them to take over the American total pattern. But I was convinced I could sell them the idea of building something more permanent. They would be the heirs of the

JDC."⁵² Margolis's reflections suggest she genuinely felt a centralized structure would help the French.

Margolis and Schwartz were clearly aware of the perils of transferring an American model to France. Without pronouncing the term "American imperialism," Schwartz and Margolis seemed to have sensed that this accusation would sabotage their efforts. Margolis proceeded slowly. After private talks with leaders, such as Baron Guy de Rothschild,⁵³ Margolis convened a meeting attended by the leadership of the primary Jewish institutions of France: the CRIF, the Central Consistory, the FSJF, the recently formed Zionist Federation of France, and possibly the Communist Jewish UJRE.⁵⁴ An ad hoc committee led by Léon Meiss was established, and in March 1948, it decided to name the structure it was creating the Unified Jewish Social Fund (Fonds social juif unifié, FSJU).⁵⁵ Laura Margolis had capitalized on French Jewish leaders' desire to influence JDC's policy: the CRIF's advisory committee on the JDC—designed to curtail its influence—essentially became the ad hoc committee of the FSJU, a project envisioned by the JDC.

In May 1948, at Margolis's request, American social worker Harry Rosen arrived from New York to take the lead in creating the FSJU. In a letter informing Léon Meiss of Rosen's arrival, one can infer that Meiss had not been consulted about the JDC's plan to bring Rosen to France. Even though Margolis informed Meiss of her decision instead of asking for his opinion, the respectful tone, choice of language (French), and content of her letter provide an example of her diplomatic attempt to avoid the charge of American imperialism.⁵⁶ Clearly, her goal was to make the French feel as if they were in charge. Quite possibly, as one of the JDC's only female experts, Margolis had learned to walk softly, honing her ability to negotiate with powerful men.

Importing American Expertise: Harry Rosen and the FSJU

"I would like to draw your attention to the fact that French Jewry has its own traditions and methods of work, which even if there are some exterior similarities with what we know in the States, are profoundly their own,"⁵⁷ wrote one seasoned JDC employee to Harry Rosen in the days before his departure for France in May 1948, where he would take over the JDC's work with the budding FSJU. This warning, accompanied by a detailed analysis of the different ideological factions present in French Jewish life, did not prevent Rosen from discovering Franco-American Jewish differences on his own. An expert in community organizing, a method embraced by American social work in the interwar period, Rosen was trained to cultivate consensus out of conflict.⁵⁸

Nonetheless, with its ideological diversity and staunch resistance to coordination, French Jewish life represented a challenge to even the most experienced community organizer. After a month, Rosen reported having spoken with two-hundred individuals and presented his program on the FSJU to a thousand people![59] He kept his superiors and colleagues in Paris and New York abreast of his progress. His success was of course dependent on convincing French Jews of the necessity of the FSJU. Therefore French Jewish leadership failing to meet his expectations frustrated him: "I think I am making headway. But, God bless these French Jewish leaders, one can never be sure! They are-shall we say- fickle, unstable?"[60] Rosen went on to complain to his New York colleague about

> the blessed French temperament which our French Jews have absorbed. It isn't exactly a *"mañana"* attitude. It isn't even one of not being concerned. I can't pin it down. Suffice it to say that the situation needs constant supervision and follow-up. What makes this doubly difficult is the fact that I have to conduct myself as a *"grand technicien"* a consultant who is available for advice and giving *"daihes,"* [opinions] but who is not trying to tell these folks what to do.
>
> [...] My conclusion in the face of these difficulties is that the job of organizing French Jewry upon a truly community basis must be done—and that it can be done. [...]
>
> They have learned from Joint, learned the hard way, but learned, certain disciplines and controls. I can say it can be done because I am convinced that there are enough men of good will in the French Jewish community who want the job done.[61]

With his sharp judgment of French Jewish "temperament" and his direct attitude, Rosen fit the stereotypical American trope prevalent in postwar France. In fact, his arrival corresponded with the early stages of the Marshall Plan, a policy that incited a great deal of debate and media coverage throughout the country. One year after its ratification, only one-third of non-Communist French supported it.[62] The rest of the nation perceived the Marshall Plan as a veiled attempt of the United States to dominate the French economy.[63] French Jews were certainly not indifferent to these larger political tensions. Furthermore, while a politically diverse group, a vocal segment of the Jewish population did affiliate with the French Communist Party, which was engaging in an active campaign against the Marshall Plan. Of the three postwar Yiddish dailies, the Communist-Jewish *Naye presse* boasted the highest circulation figures.[64] Many French Jewish leaders were therefore sensitive to the deeper implications of American aid and drew a parallel between the Jewish

American aid on which they depended and the larger American program.⁶⁵ A newcomer like Rosen may not have been aware of these dynamics. In a letter to his superior, Dr. Schwartz, Rosen used a teacher-student metaphor to describe the cultural transfer that he felt was occurring between the JDC and French Jews: "The subventioned [sic] agencies have learned a few things from their association with Joint. I have had an opportunity to observe at firsthand the 'teaching' process. The 'pupils' were not always good students and they had strong motivations against 'learning.' Nevertheless, the agency leadership has developed some concepts of standards and selective intake. They have acquired some measure of understanding of and respect for the budgeting process. Some of them even express a yearning for 'American' administrative techniques."⁶⁶

While it is unclear if Rosen shared his "teacher-student" analogy in his talks with French Jewish leaders, it does seem he was aware of everything in French Jewish life except the effect of his words on the French. Margolis and Schwartz, as seasoned overseas staff who showed sensitivity to the complexities of French Jewish life,⁶⁷ may have hoped that Rosen's first impressions of France would fade into a more nuanced portrait. In the meantime, they clearly approved of his methods. Two months after Rosen's arrival, Schwartz cabled New York requesting Rosen's stay be extended to a minimum of twelve months.⁶⁸ By late September 1948, Rosen seems to have been humbled into a little self-criticism: "There are times that I wonder at my *chutzpedig* [nervy] optimism in thinking that a campaign could be set up and run here in France within a matter of months after undertaking such a program."⁶⁹

Harry Rosen worked closely with the FSJU ad hoc committee, training them in American Jewish fundraising techniques. He taught them to divide the Jewish population of each city into small professional and cultural subgroups (for example, garment workers, furriers, women, Sephardic Jews). Volunteer leaders were appointed within each group. This system was designed to maximize peer pressure in order to establish new philanthropic norms.⁷⁰ The manner in which the JDC would support the FSJU was also clarified: the JDC would advance the operating costs of French Jewish welfare agencies until the FSJU had successfully completed its campaign. In addition, the JDC would underwrite the first two years of the FSJU's administrative costs and provide a location for its offices at their 19 rue de Téhéran address.⁷¹

Léon Meiss: Adapting the American Model

As president of the ad hoc committee of the FSJU—as well as the CRIF, the Central Consistory, and multiple other Jewish organizations—Léon Meiss worked closely with the JDC and was clearly the key French Jewish mediator in the its importation of American welfare practices. It should be recalled that Meiss was not an unequivocal supporter of American Jewish organizations in France. Meiss led the CRIF's efforts to organize the advisory committee on the JDC. In early February 1947, it was Meiss who declared to his fellow CRIF members that the JDC was working in "'splendid isolation' and [wa]s accomplishing its mission without consulting French Jewry."[72] Meiss also confronted the American Jewish Committee regarding its diplomacy on behalf of North African Jews, considered by many as the domain of the CRIF or the Alliance.[73]

And yet Meiss became one of the major proponents of importing the American UJA to France. According to Gaby Wolff Cohen, who worked for the JDC and the FSJU after her return from the United States, Meiss was one of the few individuals who understood the JDC's message and vision.[74] His refusal to blindly accept the actions of American Jewish organizations perhaps gave him the credibility to judge certain of their ideas appropriate. In an attempt to build consensus among the Jews in France (not just their organizations) on the need for the FSJU, a series of interviews with FSJU leaders were published in the Jewish press. In a 1949 interview, Meiss showed his willingness to serve as a spokesman for a new vision for French Jewish life. He described the FSJU as a means "to make French Jewry conscious of its responsibilities in regard to Jewish misery [*misères juives*],"[75] clearly restating the JDC leitmotif of self-sufficiency. Yet more significantly, Meiss spoke of the FSJU goal of "preparing and ensuring the future of our community."[76] This is the first time in my postwar sources that a French Jewish leader used the term *community* in the American sense, that is, to describe the loose body of organizations and individuals that made up French Jewish life. As mentioned earlier, in the period leading up to World War II, French Jews referred to synagogues and their members as "communities." A unified concept of community thus represents a turning point in French Jewish history. One should question who actually wrote this interview; it may have been Harry Rosen. However, Meiss, in signing it, obviously approved of its content. His usage (or approval) of the term *community* demonstrates that French Jews were beginning to adopt American Jewish vocabulary (and, in fact, a certain vision of Jewish life) to discuss their own institutions.

On October 22 and 23, 1949, after almost two years of planning, the FSJU held its national constitutive assembly in the presence of leaders from 250 Jewish organizations.[77] Meiss's role as mediator in the Franco-American Jewish cultural transfer can be seen in his opening address. Recognizing the FSJU's origins in the JDC, Meiss asked the Jews of France for their support in adopting a new model of fundraising:

We do not hide the fact that this project, of extreme importance, is somewhat revolutionary, since it is so new for our French Jews. We do not hide the fact that it means making acceptable to [French] Jewish society a system, which even though it has proven itself in other countries, may disturb our habits, especially our habit of doing what comes easiest [*habitudes de facilité*]. An individual is encouraged, according to his temper and his sympathies, to take interest in specific agencies and sometimes individual miseries. Today we come to ask him to ignore this fully respectable sentiment, to a certain extent, and to place himself above these particular contingencies in order for him to see before him one goal only: to help all in need [*tous les malheureux*], relieve all misfortunes, support every cultural endeavor.[78]

Meiss's remarks suggest that French Jews had moved toward consensus on the American methods, yet the notion of a unified community did not quell their political divisions. Even though Jewish Communists had participated in the FSJU from its beginnings, they withdrew their support at the constitutive assembly. Nevertheless, the FSJU charter was ratified on October 23, 1949, and on February 15, 1950, the organization was officially registered.[79] As promised, Meiss saw the FSJU through its initial phases. He then turned over its leadership, and the presidency of the Central Consistory, to Baron Guy de Rothschild, who was elected president of the FSJU on January 18, 1950.[80] Rothschild, who had spent the war years in the United States and whose own parents had volunteered for the UJA during that period, spoke English perfectly and was highly familiar with American culture. This background, coupled with his family's historical role in French Jewish life, made him a natural successor to Meiss and a key collaborator of the JDC.[81] Julien Samuel, an Alsatian Jew from an Orthodox background, was recruited to be the FSJU's director. Before the outbreak of World War II, Samuel had worked in the insurance industry. During the war, he began working with the OSE, playing an important role in the organization's clandestine work. At liberation, Samuel remained active in Jewish communal work and became the director of the OSE's sociomedical department. Samuel's business experience combined with his intimate knowledge of Jewish welfare provided him with the credibility needed for the FSJU directorship.[82] With its ratified charter and new leadership, the FSJU slowly took shape. However, the FSJU was not a guaranteed solution to the problems affecting the "French Jewish community." For this, the organization would have to prove capable of raising funds and maintaining unity. As seen in Jewish Communists' decision to withdraw from the FSJU at its constitutive assembly, ideological divisions remained. The young state of Israel also threatened its fragile equilibrium.

ISRAEL VERSUS THE DIASPORA?
INSTITUTIONALIZING THE FSJU

In May 1948, several days after Israel declared its independence, thirty thousand Jews gathered in the Vélodrome d'hiver to celebrate.[83] Perhaps even more significantly was *where* this event took place. The Vélodrome d'hiver was where the Jews who had been arrested in the massive roundups in Paris in July 1942 were held before being sent to Drancy or internment camps in the Loiret and subsequently to deported Auschwitz. The creation of the new Jewish state, in the words of Guy de Rothschild, "decolonized not only the Palestinian Jews, but also, emotionally and psychologically, millions of Jews of the Diaspora."[84] Breaking with his family's prewar position on Zionism, Rothschild celebrated this moment by marching on the Champs-Elysées with his wife, Alix de Rothschild, and Madame Mendès-France, most likely the wife of future prime minister Pierre Mendès-France.[85] Such a public embrace of Zionism by a representative of the traditionally anti-Zionist French Jewish nobility helped quell a conflict that had divided French Jews for over five decades. In June 1948, Léon Meiss invited Israeli president Chaim Weizmann to the Consistory's rue de la Victoire synagogue, where a special service was conducted in Weizmann's honor, against the wishes of the traditionally anti-Zionist Consistory. "The organ played and to the delight of many and probably the consternation of the Consistoire the theme of Hatikvah [the Israeli national anthem] was woven into the music that the organ played," observed one employee of the American Jewish Committee, who added that "all rules of decorum were broken at the end of the service when Weizmann left the auditorium of the synagogue to the accompaniment of shouts of affection by the gathering and the spontaneous singing by some of Hatikvah."[86] Received with joy, the news of the young state nonetheless raised the question of the viability of Jewish life in France: Would the existence of Israel destabilize the fragile reconstruction process or would it generate new energy for renewing Jewish life, even in the diaspora? The institutionalization process of the FSJU provides a concrete means of exploring this question since its objective was to centralize fundraising for the both the young state and French Jewish welfare. How would FSJU leadership negotiate the tensions surrounding these two very different missions?

The FSJU emerged at the same time as the Jewish state; the FSJU's ad hoc committee was established in the months following the 1947 Exodus Affair. Harry Rosen arrived in Paris in May 1948, within days of Israel's Declaration of Independence. The national constitutive assembly of the FSJU occurred only months after the Israeli War of Independence had reached its conclusion.

While the timing of these events was coincidental, those involved in the FSJU's creation followed the development of the new state closely. Furthermore, while many objective criteria had led Laura Margolis to advocate for the importation of a UJA-inspired structure to France, Margolis was a self-proclaimed "starry-eyed Zionist."[87] Margolis's own father had emigrated from Russia to Palestine in 1892 before going to Constantinople to establish *hachsharot* (training camps) to prepare future immigrants for life in Palestine. Margolis's family then immigrated to the United States, having decided not to return to Palestine as long as it remained under Ottoman rule.[88] In the summer of 1947, Margolis found herself at the heart of the Exodus Affair and soon after vacationed in Palestine.[89] With the Jewish state on the horizon, Margolis had undoubtedly strong personal reasons for encouraging the autonomy of French Jews. Once the latter were capable of standing on their own feet, she would feel free to leave for Israel. As she wrote in a 1981 essay on the founding of the FSJU, she saw the French structure as the framework into which the JDC program could be slowly transferred, granting both independence to the French and allowing her to fulfill her family's dream of returning to Israel.[90]

For Harry Rosen, French enthusiasm over Israel was a sign that the FSJU would work. He wrote to his superior, Dr. Schwartz, that "the birth of *Medinat Israel* [the state of Israel] has captured the imagination and fired the hearts of the vast majority of Jews in France" and represented "the strongest single cohesive force in French Jewish life."[91] Rosen added that in multiple fundraising campaigns for Israel the Jews of France had raised F200 million in 1948, a sign that raising large sums of money was indeed possible in France.[92] These examples suggest that instead of threatening the diaspora, Israel had inspired a new sense of unity and pride. The low number of French emigrants to Israel— only 3,050 from 1948 through 1951—supports the notion that Israel did not harm the reconstruction of French Jewish life.[93] The FSJU, which provided a framework for collective action for this ideologically divided population, certainly benefitted from the newfound energy.

Nonetheless, French Jews' strong support for the new state now had to be translated into concrete fundraising agreements that would dictate how resources were allocated. Two decisions had to be made: the first regarding whether campaigns for local needs and Israel should be united or held separately and the second regarding the ratio for distributing the funding between local and Israeli needs if the campaigns were held jointly. At the creation of the FSJU, these questions had still not been resolved. To further complicate matters, the leadership of the FSJU included the top Zionist leadership of France: Marc Jarblum, Jules (Dika) Jefroykin, and Claude Kelman, who were also the leaders of the Federation of Jewish Societies of France, which was also a local welfare provider.[94] Unwilling to wait for the official launch of the FSJU, Zionists had begun raising money in France in the spring of 1948 for a fund called "Help for Israel," which had been set up by the Jewish Agency. As a result, the JDC's Dr. Schwartz felt that the FSJU should conduct its first campaign for local welfare only.[95] Furthermore, the Jewish Agency refused to consider a joint campaign. It was therefore assumed that there would be two separate campaigns. Negotiations began to determine at what point in the year each group would launch its campaign. The Jewish Agency sent a representative to France and insisted on its right to conduct its campaign throughout the year, leaving only the summer months for the FSJU, which the latter would not accept. In an attempt to avoid a "war" between Israeli and local needs, the FSJU renewed its offer to conduct a joint campaign yet did so by imposing an ultimatum on the Jewish Agency: if the latter did not agree to participate in the FSJU campaign, the FSJU would still include the needs of Israel in its campaign. Fearing it would not receive French funding, the Jewish Agency conceded to a joint campaign for 1950.

However, the thorny and symbolic issue of how the funds would be distributed remained. Unable to resolve this issue, the FSJU launched its first campaign on February 15, 1950. According to Laura Margolis, the distribution was eventually decided at sixty/forty in favor of Israel for the first F500 million and evenly split on the next F100 million; everything over that amount would go to Israel.[96] The agreement favored Israel and reflected the UJA's distribution ratio in the United States, which had shifted in favor of Israel after the creation of the new state.[97] This ratio also corresponds to the FSJU's initial offer, showing its determination to impose its vision on the Jewish Agency while defending the diaspora.

1950 and 1951: The First Campaigns

In the United States, the launch of the FSJU was covered by the American Jewish press with pride, as seen in the Jewish Telegraphic Agency's article, "French Jews Emulate United Jewish Appeal, Launch Their First United Fundraising Drive."[98] Harry Rosen predicted the first FSJU campaign would gross between F500 and 800 million, so the campaign goal was set at F500 million.[99] Laura Margolis also showed optimism when she wrote to "My Dear Mr. Rothschild," announcing that the JDC planned on transferring files on all past and current JDC-funded agencies to the FSJU.[100] Both the JDC and the FSJU faced an unpleasant surprise as the first campaign drew to a close: 4,214 individuals out of an estimated Jewish population of 250,000 had donated to the campaign, which grossed only F109 million.[101] After distributing the Jewish Agency its part and reimbursing expenses, the FSJU was only able to contribute between F27 and 38 million to local welfare.[102]

The extent of the failure of the first FSJU campaign can be fully understood when one considers its result in relation to the total costs of French Jewish welfare. For 1950, the Jews of France contributed 7.5 percent of the total costs. This can be compared with their 1949 contribution, which amounted to 21.5 percent.[103] Ironically, the FSJU, which was designed to increase the financial participation of French Jews in their local welfare needs, had the opposite effect. This particularly frustrated the American JDC employees, who had closely followed French Jews' economic reconstruction and judged them capable of financing their own welfare programs. JDC statistics supported its employees' assessments: whereas in the last months of 1944, thirty-five thousand individuals sought some form of assistance from the two major welfare organizations subsidized by the JDC, by 1951 only fifteen thousand individuals were receiving assistance from JDC-funded agencies.[104] The reduced number of needy Jews was in part a result of the JDC's support of two loan funds, which helped individuals reestablish themselves. From 1945 through 1950, these two funds loaned out F470 million to Jews in France, benefitting 23,500 individuals, including the families of the borrowers.[105] To the JDC, these statistics indicated that French Jews, while not fully recovered from the war, were certainly headed in the right direction. Furthermore, according to Laura Margolis, French Jews "[could] practically count millionaire for millionaire with the Americans."[106] While it is not possible to know exactly why the first FSJU campaign failed without access to its archives, it is possible to speculate that Jews in France maintained deeply entrenched loyalties to specific welfare organizations and, in spite of the JDC's assessments, did not feel economically secure. Even though the FSJU unified almost all of the welfare campaigns (Communist Jews remained apart), it is unclear to what extent Jews in France understood the new system. Donating to the FSJU may have felt like betraying the very organizations that had stood by them in their most dire hour.

Though the first campaign of the FSJU was considered a failure, it inspired a subtle shift in French Jewish life. Funds from the JDC were no longer considered grants but loans that would have to be repaid after the campaign. When this proved impossible, French leaders requested that the JDC transform their loan into a gift. While the end result remained the same, a shift in mentality had occurred. Instead of it being considered normal that the JDC fund French Jewish welfare, outright grants from the JDC were starting to be seen as exceptional.[107]

Laura Margolis supported local leaders in their attempts to cover the costs of the struggling welfare agencies during the campaign and advocated on their behalf to her superiors.[108] In doing so, she seems to have earned the trust of the FSJU leadership. However, this could not be said for all JDC employees. At one point in 1950, Guy de Rothschild sent a delegation to Margolis to announce the refusal of the FSJU to work with "the person" Margolis had brought from New York. While Margolis did not name the individual in her account of these events, Harry Rosen is the only person who fits this description. According to Margolis, the delegation provided her with an ultimatum: "Either you get him out or we break up; we're not going to work with this man."[109] Guy de Rothschild reportedly told Margolis, "We're going to have our own man. You can teach him, you can work with him. We'll work with you and we'll work with him, but we don't want another American here."[110] Rosen had clearly failed to win over local support. Margolis, of course, was an American and a woman, and the fact this had momentarily escaped Rothschild's notice testifies to her acceptance by the FSJU leadership. Gender quite possibly played a role here. As a woman, Margolis did not fit the French stereotype of the domineering American man but the "can-do" American woman.[111] Plus, she spoke the French Jewish leaders' language (French) and was, as one of the only female directors in a male-dominated organization, skilled at negotiating with powerful men. Margolis accepted the FSJU's refusal to work with Rosen, who was eventually sent back to the United States—a fact that seems to have improved the JDC-FSJU working relationship.[112] After Rosen's departure, Margolis took responsibility for teaching the new organization the "ins and outs" of raising and distributing funds and worked closely with Julien Samuel and the FSJU board.[113]

In a meeting between Schwartz, Margolis, Rothschild, and the FSJU board in June 1950, it was decided that the two organizations would follow a common policy in France and consult each other on important decisions. The FSJU leaders publicly reported having received "full and total comprehension" from the leaders of "the great American organization."[114] The close working relationship between the JDC and the FSJU was maintained through the hire of a liaison, Tito Cohen, in April 1950.[115] Cohen was a Greek Jew who had been raised in Vienna. Trained in law, Cohen survived the war in France under a false identity and in its aftermath expressed his solidarity with fellow Jews by working for the Program for the Protection of Jewish Children (OPEJ) and the Federation of Jewish Societies of France.[116] In addition to being one of the rare Sephardic Jews who understood Yiddish, Cohen also had fluent command of English. His legal training, language skills, and experience in Jewish welfare brought him to the attention of the FSJU board and the JDC.

For the 1951 campaign, all parties agreed that two separate campaigns, one for Israel and one for local welfare, would prove more effective. An estimated F338 million were needed to support local welfare in 1951. The JDC agreed to contribute F200 million with the understanding that the FSJU would cover the remaining F138 million.[117] In an attempt to raise this amount, the goal of F150 million was set for local needs, considerably more realistic than the previous goal of F500 million total in 1950. In the end, F88 million were raised from 3,671 donors for local welfare.[118] Even though the FSJU did not meet its goal, the 1951 campaign showed a net improvement over 1950, increasing the local contribution of French Jews to their welfare network to 25.5 percent.[119]

"An Entirely New Chapter"[120] in French Jewish History?

With the goal of providing increased motivation to the FSJU leaders and French Jewish donors, the JDC mobilized the American fundraising technique of matching funds, offering to provide four francs for every franc raised above 120 million in the 1952 campaign. According to Margolis, this "gave the FSJU the challenge it required."[121] Indeed, the FSJU ran its first successful campaign in 1952, exceeding its goal of F150 million by raising F176 million.[122] This increased the participation of the Jews of France to 39 percent of the total welfare costs.[123] The JDC rejoiced in these results and the blossoming FSJU. In the words of one JDC official, "My own view of the situation in the FSJU is that this community has begun an entirely new chapter in its history. It is still using JDC money but is also making its own contribution and is certainly facing up to its responsibilities itself. [...] I believe we can still help them with some guidance but I no longer feel that the complete burden is that of JDC."[124]

While the JDC remained enmeshed in French Jewish life, the American organization could begin transferring its various departments to the FSJU, advancing its goal of permanently withdrawing from France. In April 1953, the JDC transferred the Social Service Exchange and its Personal Service Department (its family location service) to the FSJU.[125] By July 1953, the JDC reported the transfer of more departments, observing that "the direct responsibility for communal planning and the distribution of funds collected locally and contributed by JDC has been placed in the hands of the community."[126] French JDC employees were transferred to the FSJU, including two National Council of Jewish Women scholarship recipients who had been working for the JDC since their return from the United States. Gaby Wolff, who later married JDC-FSJU liaison Tito Cohen, and Edith Odenwald Kremsdorf thereafter codirected the FSJU's social service department, where they worked until their respective retirements. The JDC reduced its Office for France considerably, from a total of seventy-two employees (fifteen foreign and fifty-seven local) in 1949 to twenty-six employees (four foreign and twenty-two local) in 1952.[127]

With its success, the FSJU began to take on a new independence. It affirmed its institutional identity with a bimonthly publication, *la Revue du FSJU*, published from 1953 through 1956, and thereafter, its monthly periodical, *l'Arche*. The evolution of the FSJU can be traced through the increasingly diverse themes explored in each issue of the *Revue*.[128] Its first issue was dedicated to social services for children, and following issues remained closely tied to the theme of welfare. Yet from mid-1955 on, corresponding to a new institutional policy on cultural programs, topics completely unrelated to welfare were explored, which broadened the scope of the publication.[129] In this manner, the FSJU allowed for what Maud Mandel has observed and what this research independently confirms: a legitimization of sociocultural expressions of Jewish identity, breaking with the strictly religious definition of Jewish identity encouraged by the Consistory.[130]

A successful and strong FSJU meant that Laura Margolis would be free of her self-imposed obligation to construct a lasting program in France and could leave for Israel. She did not, however, do so alone. In the course of her work with French Jewish welfare organizations, Margolis, who hadn't married, developed a relationship with Zionist leader Marc Jarblum, a widower. The announcement of their marriage in 1950 shook up quite a few Jewish leaders for several reasons. First of all, the marriage, which took place in a civil ceremony—not in a synagogue—was announced after the fact, breaking with French protocol. More striking was the fact union called into question the JDC's political neutrality since the JDC's Office for France was now, at least unofficially, "in bed" with the FSJF, the French Zionist Federation, the Jewish Agency, *Unzer wort*, and the other endeavors in which Jarblum was involved. Finally, as a woman over forty, Margolis clearly refused the tacit agreement that allowed a woman to have a career as long as she forfeited a family life. Margolis clearly refused the fate of the old maid. *Stupéfaction* was the response of most communal leaders, according to Tito Cohen. Guy de Rothschild, hurt that Margolis had not informed him of her plans, continued to call her "Mademoiselle." Another more mischievous person, who knew that Jarblum had been a frequent visitor at Margolis's home before their marriage, sent Margolis a telegram, quoting from the Passover seder *Ma nishtana ha-lilah ha-zeh*? (Why is this night different from all other nights?).[131] Amid the commotion, Margolis graciously accepted the mazel tovs of her colleagues at the JDC and wrote to them from her honeymoon in the French Alps, signing her letter, "Laura Margolis-Jarblum."[132]

Over the next three years, French Jewish leaders had time to get used to Madame Margolis-Jarblum, and when she announced her departure for Israel at the end of 1953, they honored her as both a friend and a professional in a ceremony held at the FSJU. Guy de Rothschild praised Margolis-Jarblum's achievements and dedication, and then addressed her directly:

> You have managed not only to establish your leadership [*vous imposer*], but to calm conflicts that would have been unresolvable without you. In a community such as ours, you have successfully provided a model, admired by all, that we commonly refer to as the social worker: a civil servant devoted to the public Jewish cause, a form of service that did not exist here before the war that you managed to legitimate in the eyes of all [*gagner la consideration générale*]. Your sense of responsibility and your personal devotion will remain an example for all of our social workers who consider you with great gratitude. We will continue to honor you for a very long time to come with our grateful memory.[133]

They presented Margolis with a gift inscribed, "On behalf of the Jews of France, June 1946–December 1953."[134] Her departure symbolized the end of an era. Joseph Schwartz had left his position at the JDC in 1951 to return to the United States to lead the UJA. French Jews thereafter became acquainted with Moses Beckelman, who replaced Schwartz in the European headquarters. Auren Kahn, an American social worker, replaced Margolis as director of the Office for France. Beckelman and Kahn, while certainly competent, had not shared in the ups and downs of French Jewish life like Schwartz and Margolis had. A less intimate, more professional relationship would come into being between the JDC and its new partner, the FSJU.

CONCLUSION

The creation of the FSJU in France is an example of the JDC's importation program in action. Maud Mandel suggests that the JDC used its financial weight to influence the structure of French Jewish life.[135] I have also underscored the ways in which the JDC used its funding as a carrot to encourage compliance with its policies. From this point of view, the evolution of the FSJU, from its embryonic stages to its first successful campaign, can be understood as yet another example of the JDC flexing its financial muscle.

Nonetheless, focusing on the importation process gives nuance to this hegemonic vision of the JDC by demonstrating the central role French Jews played in the creation of the FSJU. Once the emergency of the immediate postwar period abated, both French Jews and the JDC looked to unification as the solution to their problems but did so for different reasons. For the JDC, strongly influenced by American welfare practices, unifying French welfare under one umbrella was the only means of ensuring long-term reconstruction of French Jewish life. For French Jews, unifying welfare organizations, first within the CRIF and then within the FSJU, was a means of counterbalancing the JDC's power. Some grew convinced unification also represented a more efficient means of funding welfare. French Jews' decision to create the FSJU should thus be understood as a result of a complex negotiation process and not just a result of the JDC's financial power. French Jews were recipients of American aid, but they were not victims.

This detailed look at the JDC's importation effort has also shown the central role of individual interactions in this Franco-American project. Laura Margolis and Joseph Schwartz showed a real awareness to the critique of cultural imperialism. While this quality could not correct the power imbalance between American and French Jews, it did guide the process of creating the FSJU through its most delicate stages. Léon Meiss, Guy de Rothschild, Julien Samuel, and Tito Cohen were well aware of the dominance of the JDC yet still chose to work with it in order to gain access to both the funding and new tools that would help their community. Cultural imperialism may explain why the JDC sought to import an American structure to France, yet it cannot explain how the structure was implemented and why French Jews adopted it. More subtle (and subjective) questions of individual background and personality appear to have helped both the American and French overcome the power imbalance that separated them. Beyond these factors, the paradoxical role of gender played a part in this process. As one of two women on the overseas staff of the JDC in 1945, Laura Margolis provides a key example of the emergence of women into positions of responsibility in the JDC after World War II.[136] The powerful role of Laura Margolis in the creation of the FSJU (and at the JDC in general) can be juxtaposed with the reactions to her marriage with Jarblum, suggesting that her gender played a significant role in how her ideas were received by French Jewish leaders. Indeed, the French stereotypes associated with Americans were gendered. While American men were framed as agents of empire, American women benefitted from a positive image based on their work reconstructing France in the aftermath of World War I. Léon Meiss spoke of Margolis's "finesse" and "comprehension" when discussing her with fellow CRIF members, which suggests she knew how to impress important men.[137]

The success of the JDC in imposing its model in France, when seen in a comparative perspective, is even more noteworthy. The policies that guided the JDC in France also dictated its work in other European countries. In both Holland and Belgium, the JDC attempted to establish a similar, UJA-inspired model to coordinate Jewish welfare. While efforts were successful in Holland, leading to the creation of the Joodse coördinatie commisssie, the JDC never managed to establish a similar structure in Belgium.[138] Indeed, Veerle Vanden Daelen has shown that the JDC attempted to centralize Jewish welfare in Brussels, home to the country's largest Jewish population, and failed. What the JDC neglected to take into consideration was the smaller, more religious Jewish population of Antwerp, which had its own welfare tradition predating the war. Fighting among Jewish aid committees in Brussels and Antwerp finally forced the JDC to open an office in Antwerp. Once in contact with Antwerp's Jews, however, the JDC realized that local welfare efforts were already highly efficient. Concluding that what was lacking in Antwerp was funding, not advice, the JDC quickly closed its Antwerp office and permanently abandoned the idea of establishing a UJA-style structure in Belgium, although it maintained its funding.[139]

The Belgian example shows that financial dependence on the JDC did not automatically subject European Jews to the JDC's agenda. Indeed, the case of Belgium points to the importance of structural factors (in this case, geographic, religious, and economic) that tempered the JDC's ability to impose centralized welfare. In Belgium, the Jewish population was not concentrated in one city. Furthermore, distinctly different levels of religiosity divided the Jews of Brussels and Antwerp. Finally, the diamond trade in Antwerp and this economic sector's strong connections to New York allowed Antwerp's Jews to exert pressure on the JDC through their American-based colleagues. The JDC's desire for centralized welfare simply could not compete with these structural factors.

If one applies these findings to France, one sees structural factors that support a centralized welfare system. Since the end of the nineteenth century, French Jewish life had been fairly centralized in Paris. Even though the Nazi Occupation of France uprooted Jews and modified the geography of its Jewish population, at the end of the 1940s (and before the massive immigration of North African Jews in the early 1960s), Paris was again home to the majority of French Jews.[140] While a vibrant Jewish life with its own distinct culture and structure had reemerged in Alsace-Lorraine after the war, the Paris-centric bias, present in French society in general, may have helped both the JDC and Parisian Jews forget their brethren in the East. While Strasbourg could have been France's Antwerp, this clearly did not occur, although future research should explore why. Finally, Jews in postwar France, while a politically and nationally diverse group, did prove more homogeneous from a religious point of view. Though pockets of orthodoxy existed, the postwar period saw a reduction in affiliation with the Consistory and, more generally, a decrease in religiosity.[141] These structural factors help explain why the JDC and French Jewish leaders were able to find support for the FSJU.

The history of the FSJU shows that the creation of Israel did not threaten life in the diaspora as many had feared and, on the contrary, may have encouraged a new investment in European Jewish life. The new state served as a cohesive force in French Jewish society that helped Jewish welfare agencies work together in unprecedented ways. The fact Jews could now stay in France or emigrate to Israel turned living in the diaspora into a conscious choice. Ironically, American Zionist Laura Margolis masterminded the structure that was designed to ensure the future of French Jewish life.

Once successfully institutionalized, what did the FSJU mean for the Jews of France? Historian Colette Zytnicki, and later Maud Mandel, have observed how this new organization influenced French Jewish identity. Zytnicki notes that "with the creation of the CRIF in 1944 and the FSJU in 1950 [sic], new institutions appeared that largely exceeded the religious framework inherited by the Napoleonic structures, which sought to provide a more extensive meaning to the notion of community, understood not only as a grouping of individuals of a same religion, with the synagogue as center, but as the expression of a Judaism recognized as protean, by both the diversity of its origins and of each person's commitments: religious, secular, Zionist."[142]

If the FSJU helped broaden the contours of Jewish identity, it also furthered the integration of Eastern European Jews into French Jewish life. The FSJU's creation also marked a subtle yet significant shift in language. After World War II, American Jews used the expression "the French Jewish Community" to describe Jewish life in France, whereas French Jewish leaders spoke of the "Jews of France," which emphasized the inclusion of the French *and* foreigners, "French Jewish life," and "community" in the plural form to speak of synagogues and their members. In the process of establishing the FSJU, however, French Jewish leaders finally adopted the American vocabulary. "The French Jewish Community" was officially born with this organization and with it a more inclusive vision of Jewish life that grouped together native and immigrant Jews of diverse ideologies in an ethnic bond.

A new reality accompanied this linguistic shift: individual Jews were able to express their belonging to the "French Jewish Community" by simply writing a check.¹⁴³ In 1951, 3,761 individuals supported the FSJU, and by 1955, 6,255 were doing so.¹⁴⁴ In 1963, after the mass arrival of Algerian Jews, 15,000 individuals donated to the FSJU.¹⁴⁵ More than ever, French Jewish welfare was a collective enterprise. Nevertheless, working together in new ways did not suppress the strong political divisions continuing to divide Jews in the aftermath of the Holocaust, both in France and the United States.

FIVE

AMERICAN JEWISH ORGANIZATIONS AND THE POSTWAR WORLD

A Political Presence

"JUDAISM IN FRANCE IS IN a condition of crisis for the overcoming of which there does not seem to be any immediate plan in view," wrote a representative of the American Jewish Committee (AJC) in Paris in 1949. In a memorandum to his colleagues, he explained:

> They [The Jews of France] have to be given hope and a program. If no existing body is capable or willing to do it, then despite the abundance of organizations, a new one must be formed. [...]
> Such a new group, if properly selected, could fill the present gap as the representative spokesman for French Jewry. It could serve as a bridge between certain divergent Jewish elements which today have no real organizational meeting-ground. It must, by example as well as by precept, clarify for the Jew his position and relationships within the body politic and culture of the country. This must also be explained to the non-Jew, perhaps by a regular publication available to the public, and also by special documentary efforts. When more people will be exposed to explanations and information about Judaism, perhaps the swing to the extreme left politically, or towards the doctrine of Catholicism, will be arrested. [...]
> Unless a complete all-out attempt along these lines is initiated, it is difficult to envisage a future here for the Jewish way of life [...] If the same enthusiasm spent on the Israeli effort could be focused on it, there is every reason to hope for the possibility of establishing a solid Jewish community.[1]

These observations illustrate the fact American Jewish organizations in France were not just interested in welfare matters. In the aftermath of the war and the liberation of the camps, American Jews faced a newfound responsibility to lead the diaspora.[2] Several organizations, such as the American Jewish Committee, took this challenge seriously and sought to shape French Jews' politics in order to establish a "solid Jewish community." The definition of this concept, of course, differed according to the speaker's political outlook.

As the very concept of genocide began to emerge, American and French Jews struggled to reconcile the magnitude of this event with their prewar ideologies. A quest for continuity and survival may have inspired new forms of unity among Jews, yet political divisions remained salient. In the period between 1945 and 1948, the idea of a Jewish commonwealth in Palestine started to garner support from formerly anti-Zionist or non-Zionist circles, yet the issue remained contentious.[3] While "the Jewish street"[4] had largely accepted Zionism, what did that mean for the future of Jewish life in the diaspora? Diaspora nationalism, the notion that Jews should develop an autonomous political voice in their countries of origin, emerged at the turn of the twentieth century in Eastern Europe, a place that no longer held the promise of a vibrant Jewish future.[5] Nonetheless, the postwar period did not extinguish the diaspora nationalist fight for Jewish political autonomy. This can be seen in the struggle for the survival of the Yiddish language and also in the political representation of Jews as Jews in negotiations with states and international bodies. The diaspora nationalist worldview shared a notion of Jewish peoplehood yet coexisted, at times uneasily, with Zionist perspectives that, for the most part, saw the Jewish future exclusively in a Jewish state. Those who considered Jewishness a religion and not a form of peoplehood competed with these divisive ideologies. For the latter, discriminatory barriers preventing Jews from thriving in their respective nation-states needed to be removed so they could again embrace their national identities. These divisions, internal to the Jewish world, coexisted with larger national and international political movements. As Cold War tensions grew, so did animosities between Socialists and Communists in France, adding a new layer of infighting to French Jewish life. The situation was quite different for American Jews, who had supported the Democratic Party since the 1930s. The latter faced the Cold War by distancing themselves further from the extreme left and embracing the postwar liberal consensus.[6] Such conflicting political visions turned reconstruction after the Holocaust into a battleground and caused reconstruction efforts to take on a missionary status—coming to France provided American and international Jewish organizations with an opportunity to assert their respective worldviews and shape the Jewish future. French Jews, embroiled in the same political conflicts, seized this occasion to further their own agendas.

Though all aid—no matter how modest—is inherently political in that it is designed to influence the receiver's present and future, the political stakes of this period were particularly high. While assistance is designed to help individuals, the manner in which it is provided always advances the belief system of the provider. Furthermore, the act of providing aid is a de facto response to the contentious question of who should be responsible for caring for the needy.[7] As seen in chapter 3, by the late 1940s, the JDC had become the main provider of American Jewish aid to Europe. Still, smaller American Jewish organizations also established programs in France, transposing both the diversity and ideological divisions of American Jewish life to French soil. Assistance from the Jewish Labor Committee (JLC) and the Vaad Hatzala advanced the different agendas of these organizations by supporting, respectively, the survival of Bundist and Orthodox voices in the postwar Jewish world. Even the HIAS, by providing migration services to all Jews, influenced the European Jewish future by enabling those who wanted to leave Europe for greener pastures. JDC aid especially, while claiming to be apolitical, had considerable power to sculpt Jewish reconstruction and unwittingly gave the French state an excuse to shift public responsibilities onto private shoulders. Nonetheless, while inherently political, these organizations, perhaps with one exception, considered themselves as aid providers, not political organizations.[8] This separates JDC work from two other organizations that came to Paris in the aftermath of the Holocaust, each with a clearly articulated political agenda for French Jewish life: the World Jewish Congress and the American Jewish Committee.

Both of these organizations can, to a certain extent, trace their origins to the United States. Established to advocate Jewish civil rights in a period of increasing tension over immigration, the American Jewish Committee (AJC) thrived as one of the most powerful Jewish organizations in the United States since its origins in 1906. Scholars have noted its distinct social and political characteristics, linking it to upper-class (non- or anti-Zionist) American Jewish men of German descent, who generally affiliated themselves with the Reform movement. The AJC fought for the right for Jews to live as full citizens in the United States and saw Judaism as a religion, not an ethnicity. For the AJC, Jews were an integral part of their respective nation-states, not a nation apart.[9]

The World Jewish Congress, established in Geneva in 1936 to "unify Jews and strengthen Jewish political influence in order to assure the survival of the Jewish people,"[10] was an international organization, as its name suggests. In its attempt to become a representative body for all Jews, the WJC hoped to recreate the Committee of Jewish Delegations, which had attempted to unify Jewish organizations during the 1919 Paris Peace Conference. Though some of its leaders hailed from Europe, the WJC can be considered an emanation of the American Jewish Congress, the organization established in 1918 to represent American Jews during the Paris Peace talks and reestablished in 1922 under the leadership of Rabbi Stephen Wise.

In the interwar period and throughout World War II, the AJC and the American Jewish Congress came to embody two fundamentally different conceptions of Jewish life.[11] Under Wise, the American Jewish Congress mobilized primarily Eastern European Jewish immigrants and their offspring through its vocal, ethnic definition of Jewishness that embraced a vision of Jewish peoplehood that included both diaspora nationalists and Zionists. If the American Jewish Congress represented the downtown masses, the American Jewish Committee continued to be associated with the uptown elite, even after its 1944 decision to break with its committee format and establish local chapters throughout the country.[12] During World War II, the two organizations disagreed on most issues, from the call to boycott German goods to the tactics that should be used to raise public awareness on Nazi persecutions of Jews. The American Jewish Committee preferred discreet, "behind the scenes" diplomacy, whereas the American Jewish Congress preferred more direct appeals, designed to incite public outrage. American Jewish leaders tried to set aside their differences on multiple occasions in order to establish a common agenda. Their final attempt, the American Jewish Conference, convened in late August 1943. While the organizers agreed to avoid the divisive Jewish commonwealth resolution, Zionists forced a vote on this very issue. The American Jewish Committee withdrew from the conference after the resolution was endorsed, ending the possibility of unity.[13]

Unable to find common ground during the war, how would these organizations approach the postwar world? Who would lead the diaspora and according to what political vision? How did the vastly changing geopolitical situation trickle down and shape the organizational dynamics on the Paris street? By exploring the attempts of the World Jewish Congress and the American Jewish Committee to influence French Jewish life according to their respective worldview, this chapter argues that France served as an arena where they could confront their visions of the Jewish future. French Jews, far from passive bystanders, played an important role in this battle for dominance. They served as crucial allies to the outsider organizations, all while using these same organizations to settle their scores and advance their own political goals.

In its consideration of politics, this chapter also revisits the JDC program in France in light of the Cold War. As seen above, while the JDC was clearly embedded in the organizational dynamics of American and French Jewish life, it avoided taking a stance on political matters in the countries where it operated, considering itself an apolitical welfare organization.[14] The JDC-led "Jewish Marshall Plan" had only a tenuous link to the American government's Marshall Plan, viewed by many in France as a Cold War political maneuver.[15] While the JDC didn't consciously push the American way of life, it did have to reckon with Cold War tensions. As the latter increased in the early 1950s, and eventually seeped into the French general press, local Jewish organizations forced the JDC to recognize the inherently political nature of its work.

THE WORLD JEWISH CONGRESS: THE QUEST TO REPRESENT

Based in Paris at its establishment in 1936, the World Jewish Congress was never an American organization but an international one. As seen above, the WJC's goal to represent Jews as Jews reflects a sense of Jewish peoplehood that appealed especially to Zionists and diaspora nationalists. According to Zohar Segev, the WJC leadership "wished to shape the structure of the Jewish people according to the model of Diaspora nationalism, in parallel to the Jewish state rather than in its place. [They] actively engaged in integrating Jews within their countries of residence while underscoring their cultural characteristics and need for an organizational structure that would ensure the rights of Jews in particular and of all minorities."[16] While Americans held two of the top three positions in the WJC—Judge Julian Mack and Rabbi Stephen Wise—Jews from France, in particular the Zionist immigrant leadership of the Federation of Jewish Societies of France (FSJF), played an important role in the WJC.[17] One estimate shows that French support for the WJC on the eve of the Second World War had grown to include affiliations with eighty Jewish organizations and five thousand individuals.[18] In 1941 the war forced the WJC to move its executive offices from Paris to New York, where the pro-Zionist American Jewish Congress provided the lion's share of its funding. The WJC remained active in Europe during the Holocaust from Switzerland, channeling funds to France through its French representative, the Zionist leader Marc Jarblum. While historians have refrained from quantifying the amount of WJC aid to European Jews, one internal document from 1945 estimates that it spent $90,000 for rescue in France during the war.[19] As the conflict ended, the WJC faced a choice: Should it return to France, and if so, how should it reinsert itself into French Jewish life?

An equally important concern was how French Jews would perceive the WJC's return. Would its presence destabilize the CRIF, the recently formed body for the political representation of French Jews? As seen in previous chapters, this organization was established during the war and represented a break from the past for two reasons. First, it established a representative body that institutionalized the collaboration between immigrant and native Jewish leaders. Second, and most significantly, the CRIF broke with previous conceptions of Jewish identity that framed Jewishness in strictly religious terms and eschewed all ethnic definitions of Jewish peoplehood. The fact native Jewish leaders, including members of the anti-Zionist Central Consistory, had accepted that Jews needed political representation as Jews shows to what extent the Holocaust caused Jews to reconfigure their prewar ideologies.[20] Nonetheless, the extreme conditions that had created the CRIF's unity had ended with liberation. The WJC's return sparked intense negotiations, revealing an internally divided Jewish world.

The WJC's War Emergency Conference in Atlantic City in November 1944 provided an opportunity to discuss the future and start raising funds for reconstruction.[21] As seen in chapter 3, Marc Jarblum, upon his return from Switzerland, took up the cause of the WJC in France by sponsoring a French delegation to attend the conference. With the exception of Joseph Fisher, the delegation did not draw from the immigrant Jewish leadership that had supported the WJC in the interwar period but instead included the CRIF's and Consistory's native French leadership, including Léon Meiss, Guy de Rothschild, and Rabbi Jacob Kaplan.[22] In the United States, the delegation met with JDC and WJC leadership. Contrary to the talks with the JDC that discussed the actions of French Jews during the war, those with the WJC focused on the future. As a body claiming to represent world Jewry, the WJC was naturally intrigued by the newly formed CRIF.[23] Would the CRIF interfere with the mission of the WJC by claiming to represent the Jews of France instead? Would the CRIF affiliate with the WJC and allow it to represent the CRIF on the international level? Or would the CRIF try to limit the WJC's presence in France? Interestingly, and unlike any of the other organizations in this study, before reestablishing itself in France, the WJC asked and tried to resolve these questions. Marc Jarblum facilitated this through his overlapping roles: He was simultaneously the WJC representative for France, president of the FSJF, editor of the Yiddish daily *Unzer wort*, and a key intermediary between the French government and the Jewish Agency with regard to emigration to Palestine. Jarblum's importance to French Jewish life had resulted in an invitation to become the vice president of the CRIF. Yet before committing himself, and indirectly the WJC, Jarblum preferred to wait until negotiations between the two bodies had reached a conclusion.[24]

Upon his return to France from the War Emergency Conference, Léon Meiss, president of the CRIF and the Central Consistory, wrote to Rabbi Stephen S. Wise, chairman of the executive committee of the WJC: "With the prestige attached to your position, with your charming personality, and with the powerful authority emanating from the uncontested head of American Judaism, you have succeeded in making our relationship one of mutual trust and confidence, and in binding more closely together our two communities."[25] Yet Meiss's warm note could not mask the dissent within the CRIF on its potential affiliation with the WJC. In March 1945, Jarblum wrote to WJC leader Nahum Goldmann to update him on the progress of his negotiations with the CRIF. Meiss, according to Jarblum, was impressed with the work of the WJC, its political networks, and the intelligence of its leaders. "But... and here begins a long but," Jarblum wrote, explaining Meiss's reserves, "1. The WJC doesn't represent all American Jews [...] 2. The Congress has very few non-Zionists and is almost a Zionist organization. 3. Very few countries belong to the Congress."[26] Internally divided over Zionism in spite of its endorsement of the movement in its charter, the CRIF proposed that the WJC modify its structure to include a larger representation of non-Zionist organizations.[27] In return, the CRIF would join the WJC and request other nonaffiliated organizations to do the same. Jarblum expressed his skepticism of this proposal and also questioned the veracity of an agreement that Meiss had reportedly made with the WJC while in New York, whereby the WJC would refrain from reestablishing a physical presence in France and instead nominate a French delegation that would consult with the WJC's New York executive committee.

Jarblum's skepticism was justified. At the same time, the CRIF was trying to persuade the Alliance israélite universelle, which continued to balk at ethnic conceptions of Jewishness, to join its ranks. In an attempt to win over the Alliance, Meiss reassured the its leadership that the CRIF would not "create a ghetto" and that it was important that "French *israélites* be the ones to interpret French Judaism to public officials and shape opinion, not the foreign *israélites*."[28] Meiss may not have personally believed this discourse; he was open-minded enough to use the polite yet soon to be outdated term *israélite* for both native and foreign Jews, instead of reserving this term for French Jews only.[29] As a member of French native circles, he knew the kind of argument that would bring the Alliance to the table. The Alliance's decision to join the CRIF in July 1945 shows that Meiss had correctly assessed the situation.

With the Alliance as a new partner, the CRIF's affiliation with the WJC was even more contentious. Internal conflict was rife since Communist and Zionist leaders encouraged the CRIF to join the WJC, whereas the native leadership sought to collaborate, not affiliate.³⁰ As a result, the WJC broke the agreement made with the CRIF in New York and set up a French office in Paris. "The majority of these organizations represented in the CRIF are in favor of the Congress," Nahum Goldmann wrote to Léon Meiss in September 1945, notifying him of the WJC's decision. "If the CRIF can maintain its unity only by letting itself be ruled by the negative attitude of this community, this is its business and its right, but it would really mean a dictatorship by a minority."³¹ In this manner, the WJC justified its return to Paris at 83 avenue de la Grande-Armée, where it shared an office with the Jewish Agency, *Unzer wort*, and several other Zionist organizations.³² The WJC appointed Dr. Sylvain Cahn-Debré, a French citizen, to direct its local section.

The reestablishment of the WJC in France in September 1945 introduced a new source of conflict among CRIF members, some of whom continued to fight for the supremacy of the WJC. Why would French Jewish leaders undermine the CRIF, their "own" organization? Jarblum, pragmatic, was concerned that the Consistory did not fully appreciate the importance of the CRIF and that its indifference would limit the CRIF's capacity to fulfill its crucial mission of representing the Jews of France.³³ The coexistence of the WJC and the CRIF also seems to have sparked old animosities between immigrant and native Jews, the former tending to support the WJC, the latter still uncomfortable with ethnic conceptions of Jewishness and Zionism. Pragmatic support of the WJC soon gave way to partisan attitudes, as seen in one of the FSJF leader's explanations for the lack of progress in building support for the WJC among the Jews of France. Writing to a member of the WJC executive committee several months after the establishment of its French office, he explained:

> Our lack of success was also due to the fact that, at the time of our attempt, the CRIF had not yet sufficiently discredited itself (but it has since made progress in this direction).
>
> To advance in our direction, it was at the same time necessary to give the CRIF time to demonstrate its inertia (disappointment and disaffection would follow naturally) and meanwhile to act through the medium of the Federation of Jewish Societies of France. Steady and skillful propaganda tending [sic] to identify the Federation with the Congress. This is obscure labor, long and exacting, but sure to bear fruit.³⁴

The organizations representing the immigrant faction of French Jewish life had independently joined the WJC³⁵ and, as Kelman's letter shows, defended it over the CRIF. Nonetheless, in January 1946, Cahn-Debré organized the WJC's French delegation, an act that generated negative publicity for the WJC. The

FSJF was strongly represented in the delegation in order to keep the influence of the CRIF to a minimum.[36] However, the manner in which the WJC delegation was selected (and not elected) angered its Communist members, who had previously supported the WJC. They denounced the WJC's undemocratic methods in an article that appeared in the Communist Jewish press in Yiddish and French.[37] In response, Nahum Goldmann of the WJC decided to limit the powers of the French delegation to a consultative role, which in turn sparked criticism from both Jarblum and Cahn-Debré, who felt the body should have a decision-making capacity.[38] French immigrant support of the WJC was therefore not unconditional.

Both the WJC and the CRIF clearly wanted to avoid conflict by working out an agreement to better define each organization's scope. Meiss and Cahn-Debré met in April 1946 to negotiate. As described by the latter in a letter to his superiors, which may have minimized any compromises the WJC had made, Cahn-Debré reported the outcome: the CRIF would limit its scope to France alone and not interfere in any government matters that could compromise French diplomacy. The WJC, reported Cahn-Debré, would not limit its activities, since its very nature was international.[39] Such an ambiguous agreement was naturally difficult to uphold. Furthermore, the CRIF had reached a similar agreement with the Alliance, granting the latter jurisdiction over all matters concerning Jews outside of France's borders.[40] In exchange for dominance on the national level, the CRIF claimed it would let others take the lead internationally. In practice, however, the CRIF, AIU, and WJC continued to step on each other's toes on international matters. Each participated in the Jewish delegation during the 1946 Paris Peace conference, which, as I will explore below, convened to establish peace treaties with Germany's former allies.[41]

Defending its place in the international arena, the WJC lobbied for the restitution and protection of Jewish civil rights in the newly created United Nations and for the reconstruction of religious and educational dimensions of Jewish life to be considered as part of the UNESCO mission. In March 1947, the WJC obtained consultative status with the Economic and Social Council of the United Nations, legitimizing its voice on matters concerning Jewish life in the diaspora and the creation of a Jewish state in Palestine.[42] Perhaps most significantly, through the leadership of Nahum Goldmann, the WJC played a primary role in negotiations with the German Federal Republic in obtaining reparations for the victims of Nazi persecution; this resulted in the Conference on Jewish Material Claims against Germany (or Claims Conference). Funding from the Claims Conference, which was made available to European Jewish organizations primarily from 1954 through 1964, transformed French Jewish life. France was the greatest beneficiary of this funding, receiving $22 million of the $65 million distributed to the diaspora during the ten-year period.[43]

The World Jewish Congress Program in France

While the WJC's primary focus was political, in the years following the war it also contributed to the general relief of French Jews and endeavored to promote Jewish culture and education.[44] The WJC kept scrupulous records on the food and clothing it sent to France, showing to what extent it sought to document its relief work.[45] It remains unclear how this aid was distributed, but it quite possibly moved through the children's homes the WJC supported.

As with most Jewish organizations, children occupied a large place in the WJC's reconstruction work. Mrs. Louise Waterman Wise, the wife of Rabbi Stephen Wise, mobilized the Women's Division of the American Jewish Congress, creating the American Committee for the Rehabilitation of European Jewish Children. The goal of this committee, funded by the Women's Division, was to establish or fund children's homes and, when possible, encourage the reunification of children with their surviving relatives. This committee used the European infrastructure of the WJC, and through it opened eleven homes in four countries.[46] In France, the WJC worked in collaboration with Zionist and Communist organizations to run six children's homes.[47] In addition to the 255 children being cared for in these institutions in the spring of 1947, the WJC was supporting 410 children with foster families.[48] In an effort to personalize the connection among Jews in the diaspora, the WJC encouraged American Jews to sponsor and correspond with Jewish children in Europe. By May 1948, a total of 10,880 American children and adults were writing to Jewish children in eleven countries. In France, between September 1945 and April 1948, a total of 1,168 children corresponded with American Jews under the auspices of the WJC.[49]

The WJC's welfare work annoyed the JDC, which considered itself the direct (and the only legitimate) emanation of American Jewish aid to European Jews. These two organizations had fought bitterly over who would assist the children who had escaped from France to Spain during World War II.[50] In early 1945, the WJC actually approached the JDC to suggest they create a multiorganizational advisory committee for the "rescue and rehabilitation" of Jewish life in Europe. The JDC rejected this offer, stating, "Our consistent policy has been not to associate the JDC formally with any organization or committee with a political character or having political objectives."[51] In the postwar years, the leaders of the two organizations appeared more willing to work together. In 1946, Nahum Goldmann wrote to a colleague that he was working with the JDC's Joseph

Schwartz to establish "good neighbor relations and friendship."[52] In 1947, these efforts led to an agreement by which the American Jewish Congress, the primary supporter the WJC, agreed to cease its independent fundraising in the United States and join the United Jewish Appeal. In exchange, the JDC would finance the homes previously funded by the WJC and the American Jewish Congress while allowing these organizations to continue managing them.[53] As seen in chapter 3, the JDC orchestrated a similar agreement with the Orthodox Vaad Hatzala in the same period, thus affirming its place in European Jewish welfare while reinforcing the United Jewish Appeal in the United States. Such actions indicate a new consensus within American Jewish life that progressively incorporated outliers into the philanthropic fold.[54]

Between its political work and relief efforts, the French section of the WJC worked to infuse the Jews of France with its pro-Zionist, diaspora-nationalist outlook, supporting both the State of Israel and Jewish ethnic solidarity within the diaspora. It highlighted the conditions of Jews in France and throughout the world in its publication, *La vie juive*, published from 1946 through 1964. In 1957, the WJC began organizing an annual conference for French-speaking Jewish intellectuals.[55] By 1962, the French section of the WJC had, according to one estimate, eleven affiliated organizations and approximately forty local chapters throughout France.[56] In the words of one commentator writing in the early 1960s, "The WJC doesn't represent the entire community at all, but it aspires to do so."[57]

The WJC was not the only organization actively defending Jews in the legislative and political spheres. The American Jewish Committee (AJC) worked in the United States and on the international level on the same problems. However, though the missions of the two organizations were similar, their working methods and ideologies were diametrically opposed. The AJC's presence in France was motivated by solidarity with French Jews but also by the fear they might be influenced by the wrong camp.

THE AMERICAN JEWISH COMMITTEE: EXERTING AN INFLUENCE?

In the United States, no organization was as politically opposed to the WJC as the American Jewish Committee, not to be confused with the American Jewish Congress. The American Jewish Committee (AJC) thrived as one of the most powerful Jewish organizations in the United States, having grown by 1949 to include thirty-eight local chapters with eighteen thousand members. In spite of this growth, the AJC's postwar organizational style and membership profile, which was described as "moderate, judicious, deliberate, with a preference for anonymity and an aversion for the dramatic,"[58] remained similar to the interwar period.

The AJC participated in the 1919 Paris Peace Conference but did not operate in Europe during World War II, unlike the JDC and WJC. Instead, the AJC worked from the United States to help facilitate the entry of Jewish refugees and reduce domestic antisemitism. It also began planning for the postwar period. In 1940, the AJC recruited Dr. Max Gottschalk, a Belgian Jew who had served on the central committee of the Alliance, to direct its Research Institute on Peace and Post-war Problems.[59] Gottschalk's affiliation with the Alliance was not a coincidence—the AJC was modeled after the French organization. The two organizations maintained a working relationship, united in their belief that Jews deserved full civil rights in their respective nations.[60] Both the Alliance and the AJC defended Jews against the accusation of dual loyalties by stressing a strictly religious definition of Jewish identity and ties to their respective nations. After the Holocaust, the AJC and the Alliance remained diametrically opposed to the brand of Jewish peoplehood endorsed by the WJC.

In the immediate postwar period, the AJC was initially content to follow French Jewish affairs from afar. In November 1945, it hired former head of the Southern Zone's UGIF, Raymond Geissman, as its Paris correspondent. The fact the AJC picked Geissman at a moment when French Jews were conducting honor courts to determine the role of UGIF leaders during the Occupation suggests the AJC was somewhat ignorant of French Jewish affairs.[61] The AJC seems to have broken off its relationship with Geissman in November 1946 but for a different reason: he was not opening the AJC mail.[62] Furthermore, France was proving to be too important a place in postwar European Jewish life to ignore.

Indeed, the Paris Peace Conference, held during the summer of 1946, was one of several postwar conferences that allowed the participation of nongovernmental organizations. The advisory conference was designed to determine the peace treaties with Germany's former allies, including Italy, Romania, Hungary, Bulgaria, and Finland. While the stakes were notably lower than the 1919 Paris Peace Conference, American and International Jewish organizations flocked to Paris, eager to shape the postwar world.[63] The AJC delegation, led by its president, Jacob Blaustein, eventually united with ten other Jewish organizations to propose amendments to the treaties that would better protect minorities from discrimination and establish legislation for the restitution of stolen property.[64] While at the conference, the AJC reconnected with the Alliance and grew acquainted with the CRIF, which also participated in spite of its promise, as seen above, to stay out of international affairs. The AJC also temporarily buried animosities with the WJC. Still, one can imagine the surprise of the AJC's leaders when they realized the WJC had a strong presence in France, its Paris office having been reestablished almost one year before.

Eight months after the Paris Peace Conference, in April 1947, the AJC opened its Paris office on 30 rue la Boëtie, under the supervision of its European Director of Foreign Affairs Joel Wolfsohn. Zachariah Shuster, a Polish-born writer, publicist, and former AJC delegate at the Paris Peace Conference, came to France to direct the new office. It is possible that Shuster's language skills helped him earn this appointment since he "spoke everything," including Russian, German, and French.[65] In 1951, Abraham Karlikow, a young American journalist who had been working for the JDC's public relations department in Paris, began working for the AJC.[66] He eventually became the director of the office, which at its peak never employed more than a dozen individuals. Under the direction of Shuster and then Karlikow, the Paris office of the AJC served as a base from which it could closely observe the political situation of Jews behind the Iron Curtain and in North Africa. The situation in metropolitan France, while less urgent, quickly became a more central preoccupation.

Upon his arrival, Shuster immediately set out to fulfill his organization's mission: "Prevent the violation of Jewish civil and religious rights, provide Jews assistance and undertake useful action in case these rights are threatened."[67] The AJC preferred quiet diplomacy and used one-on-one discussions with "key people" to learn about local concerns.[68] The JDC and some CRIF members welcomed the AJC's arrival in Paris since the AJC represented an alternative to the WJC. One JDC official admonished Shuster, reminding him that the AJC had "lost a lot of time and permitted the WJC to gain influence."[69] Léon Meiss, president of the CRIF and Central Consistory, reiterated that the AJC had "lost a great deal of time during the last three years when [the AJC was] not in closer touch with the Jewish organizations and leaders of France and other countries of Europe."[70] Meiss, according to Shuster, "personally is opposed to the World Jewish Congress and is of the same critical opinion of it as we are. But he could see no way of avoiding the World Jewish Congress in its many attempts to be considered as the representative of CRIF and similar organizations before the UN, for the simple reason that CRIF, which represents all the Jewish organizations in France, most of which are Zionist and leftist, cannot afford [politically] to join such a group as the AJC, the Alliance and the AJA [Anglo-Jewish Association]."[71]

Meiss was certainly referring to the Consultative Council of Jewish Organizations established by the AJC, the Alliance, and the English Anglo-Jewish Association to gain consultative status in the United Nations.[72] In this capacity, the organizations participated in discussions on Jewish civil rights, progressively being framed as human rights.[73] Meiss informed Shuster of the Alliance's lack of popularity among Jews in France, which he judged as too conservative and even tainted by the Occupation.[74] Shuster was starting to understand that the insertion of the AJC into French Jewish life would be a challenge. Writing to his superiors, he suggested the AJC would have to "convince the CRIF and the organizations represented in it that we have no particular attachment to Alliance and that their joining with us will not be contrary to their pro-Zionist or pro-leftist views."[75] In New York, the upper echelons of the AJC balked at Shuster's ignorance of its historical collaboration with the Alliance and wrote off the CRIF as an impossible ally due to its Zionist and Communist members.[76] Finding a foothold in French Jewish life from which to combat the diaspora nationalism of the WJC would prove to be a diplomatic challenge for the AJC. But what was the AJC's alternative message? Instead of embracing Jewish peoplehood, the AJC suggested that Jews settle back into their national identities, albeit with full civil rights. After the Holocaust, this message seemed somewhat naive because it ignored the common fate Jews had shared in France under the Occupation, the magnitude of their losses, and the depth of their rage.[77] Still, the AJC upheld the harmonious ideal that Jews could fully reintegrate into their respective nation states, a vision that some French Jews, especially those in native circles, embraced.

The AJC Program in France

One AJC representative's observations on French Jewish life in 1949, presented at the beginning of the chapter, shed light on what concerned the AJC about French Jews: the presence of an extreme left, disaffiliation from Judaism, conversions to Catholicism, and emigration to Israel. In advocating a "representative spokesman for French Jewry" who would "clarify for the Jew his position and relationships within the body politic and culture of the country" and at the same time "deal with the problem of Gentile ignorance or malice,"[78] the author of this text seems to have been suggesting that the Jews of France should create their own version of the AJC. In the meantime, the AJC did not hesitate to act in their place. The AJC program in France reflects this ambiguous position; the AJC tried to counter the extreme left and disaffiliation by influencing public opinion through its magazine, *Evidences*. Furthermore, it sought to stimulate the creation of a French group to work on what it called "defense," that is, the fight against antisemitism. Ever eager to fund their own initiatives, French Jews regularly solicited the AJC for funds, which it sometimes provided.[79] Finally, the AJC never abandoned its goal of representing Jews at the diplomatic level, including in French affairs, placing the AJC in direct competition with the Alliance and the CRIF.

Influencing Public Opinion

After only two weeks in Paris, Shuster was convinced of the importance of France to the general AJC program abroad. A main source of concern was the fact Jews in France, unlike American Jews, had not rejected communism. Indeed, in the immediate postwar period, the French Communist party obtained widespread support due to its significant role in the resistance, becoming the largest political party in France after the October 1945 elections.[80] Communist Jews, especially the Polish immigrants who arrived in the 1920s and 1930s, developed an extensive infrastructure in interwar Paris that flourished in the postwar political climate. While it is difficult to know exactly how many Jews in France were Communists, one journalist, writing in the early 1960s, provided the estimate of twenty thousand. In the immediate postwar period, this figure seems relatively accurate.[81] For the AJC, which was actively fighting the "Jew-Communist equation"[82] in the United States, the French situation appeared contrary to Jewish interests. Shuster felt he could remedy French Jews by educating them on life outside of their country, perhaps with the idea that exposure to American analyses would point out the dangers of and alternatives to communism. "One reason for the extremism of Jewish life in Europe," he explained, "is the fact that the sources of information are slanted in a narrow and partisan way. The lack of information is particularly obvious with regard to the Jewish community in America and the political and social trends in it. There is a great thirst for knowledge and even more for proper analysis of the Jewish situation in the world."[83]

The AJC thus committed itself to providing French Jews with a "proper analysis" of Jewish life. To do so, it drew upon its work in the United States, where it had been publishing *Commentary* magazine since November 1945. While articles involving Jews and Jewish topics held a central place in this magazine, it also covered political and cultural phenomena that extended beyond the borders of the American Jewish community.[84] By enlisting intellectuals and politicians as its writers, the magazine proved to be an effective tool in educating the American public on the AJC worldview. The AJC's Paris office quickly saw the potential in creating a French magazine modeled on *Commentary*.[85] After producing an initial brochure and sending it to a select number of individuals, the first trial issue of a new magazine, *Evidences*, appeared in France in May 1949. Edited by journalist Nicolas Baudy, *Evidences* published articles on a variety of topics linked to Jewish life and European politics over the fourteen-year period of its publication. A 1972 study of the publication shows it gave a voice to a diverse group of writers such as Raymond Aron, David Ben Gurion, Léon Blum, Albert Camus, Martin Buber, and René Cassin, among others.[86] This list shows the AJC eventually came to terms with Zionism but remained committed to creating a forum for anti-Communist politicians and intellectuals. The magazine was thus "consistently attacked in the leftist French press as an 'American war-mongering magazine.'"[87] A select group of four thousand individuals "chosen for the influence they have on general public opinion, Jewish affairs, or events affecting Jews"[88] received free subscriptions in 1950. In its first year, 70 percent of the articles covered Jewish subjects or had an appeal for a Jewish audience.[89] The very fact the AJC was aware of these statistics shows to what extent the publication was part of a conscious effort to shape public opinion. Nonetheless, it is difficult to assess the extent its mission was successful or whether French Jews chose to read *Evidences* instead of the WJC's publication, *La vie juive*.

The AJC sought to reconcile the postwar Jew with his nation-state yet doing so required addressing antisemitism. The organization therefore set out to find a partner organization in France that it could train in what it called defense work, that is, the fight against antisemitism.

The Search for a French Defense Group

As early as July 1947, AJC officials began meeting with French Jewish leaders to stimulate the creation of a French Jewish defense organization.[90] Even though the CRIF was created for this very purpose, the AJC pursued meetings with French Jewish notables—such as Baron Guy de Rothschild—Alliance board members Madame Fernand Halphen and her son Georges, the cantor Léon Algazi, and Central Consistory board member Samy Lattès.[91] In the course these conversations, the AJC learned of French efforts to fight antisemitism, including the Paris Israelite Center for Information (Centre israélite d'information de Paris, CII), a committee founded and presided by Lattès in 1945 and later by the writer and activist Edmond Fleg. In March 1945, this committee began publishing a monthly bulletin, *La quinzaine*, edited by Maurice Vanikoff and Maurice Moch. While both the Central Consistory and the CRIF helped found the CII,[92] the AJC considered the CII and the CRIF to be two distinct organizations. In addition to his work with the CII, Maurice Vanikoff ran the Center for Documentation and Vigilance. Finally, the CRIF published, from early 1948 onward, the *Bulletin intérieur d'information*, a bimonthly revue with a section on antisemitism.

Thus a loose configuration of individuals and groups sought to fight antisemitism instead of working together, as the AJC preferred, under one umbrella organization. The AJC therefore supported individual efforts with the hope this would lead to the creation of a defense organization. In December 1948, the AJC provided Maurice Vanikoff with F90,000 a month for a two-month trial period to keep it informed on relations between Jews and non-Jews in France.[93] In September 1949, AJC lay leader Fred Lazarus Jr. came to France to further this project by meeting with Jewish communal leaders and governmental officials.[94]

However, in spite of hopeful signs of interest, the AJC was still had no satisfactory results by December 1949. The main barrier, according to the AJC, was financial; a group of six to eight French Jewish leaders led by Georges Halphen and Léon Algazi were sincerely interested in defense work and willing to contribute F7 million to the project yet were unwilling to advance without a financial commitment from the AJC of F45 million.[95] According to the French Jewish leaders, a "Jewish Marshall Plan for Europe"[96] was needed, and it was up to the AJC to provide the lion's share of the funding. Why would these French Jews suggest the AJC instead of the more ubiquitous JDC? French Jews were paying attention; they knew that fighting antisemitism was the AJC's domain. In suggesting the AJC cover 85 percent of the costs, they implied the initiative was the American organization's project. To make their point, the French Jews leaders simply mobilized the American "Marshall Plan" lingo and added a Jewish twist. (Providing this book with a title, along the way.)

Initially, the AJC interpreted French Jews' lukewarm attitude as a result of the latter's philanthropic traditions, or lack thereof. In the words of one AJC employee, "French Jewry has never known the type of all-out generosity for Jewish institutions which exists in the United States. While leaders with whom we have conferred agree that such an organization should derive its main sustenance within France, they are still most pessimistic about the possibilities of raising an amount adequate to the carrying out of the program envisaged."[97] Another AJC employee was more blunt: "In no country in Europe are the rich Jews so miserly as in France, particularly on a project like ours about which they do not feel any urgency."[98] AJC employees were eventually forced to admit that French Jews were concerned with antisemitism in Germany and its possible spread to France, but in spite of "unanimity regarding the existence of tension toward Jews within the country [France], the relative absence of open manifestation or discrimination of any kind deprives this project of a sense of urgency."[99] As I will show below, this was not exactly the case.

In 1950, an AJC employee asked an seemingly obvious question: "I have wondered before why it is that with the CRIF in existence here, not tied to the WJC, representing all the responsible Jewish groups in the community and with no set program, but organized 'to represent,' something hasn't been done before this to try to activate them, stimulate them and get them to carry through a program which concerns the whole community here. I think it can be done and I think it's worth a try, and I think it will bring results. [...] Working with them means first cultivating them."[100] Though this astute employee had noticed the CRIF, he did not realize that French Jews did not want to be "cultivated" by American Jews.

In 1954, the progress French Jewish organizations had made in defense matters still dissatisfied the AJC. Its goal was therefore to make French Jews realize their current approach represented a problem and that its solution could come from the United States. In order to better assess French Jewish life, the AJC commissioned a survey in 1954.[101] This document revealed that "the community is quite smug about their present means of meeting manifestations of antisemitism."[102] However, according to this report, "The American investigative techniques of exposure of those who remain in the background and provide the large sums of money needed to put out [antisemitic] weekly newspapers and other printed material are virtually unknown here."[103] Recent research on postwar antisemitism challenges this passive view of French Jews and suggests that the AJC was looking for allies in the wrong places. The AJC archives rarely mention the International League against Antisemitsm (LICA), founded in 1927, or the more recent, yet Communist, Movement against Racism for Friendship among People (MRAP), established in 1949. Both were dedicated to fighting antisemitism in the postwar period.[104] For example, when the Nazi propaganda film *Jud Süss* was scheduled to air in a Paris cinema in October 1950, these organizations, along with the Jewish student association and other resistant organizations, coordinated a public campaign, including a demonstration, and succeeded in canceling the projection. There were Jews in France concerned with antisemitism, which was indeed present in the postwar era, yet the AJC most likely deemed these actors too radical.[105]

Instead, in 1954, the American organization proposed to organize "study voyages" to the United States for French Jewish communal leaders. Such an occasion, it was hoped, could help those who "have a feeling they are alone in France, to face a particular situation; and there is something uniquely French about their problems. This is rarely the case. What they are faced with are French versions of old problems. Problems which have been solved in America or are in the course of evolution and which relate directly to what they are going through here."[106]

Less than a decade after the Holocaust, the AJC emphasized the interchangeability of French and American Jewish life, smoothing over the distinct and very recent European past. Convinced that Americans had something to offer, the AJC still hoped for a unification of defense efforts and suggested it could cover the full-time salary of a director for such an organization for a limited period of time.[107] Until that point, French Jews had relied primarily on their lay leaders to fight antisemitism and negotiate restitution matters with governmental bodies.[108] This resulted in crucial matters taking second place to the demanding professional commitments of their leaders.[109] Perhaps the greatest difference separating the AJC from the French Jewish organizations was the importance American organizations placed on hiring professionals instead of relying on volunteers. The AJC would remain frustrated that defense work was not a greater priority for French Jews, that is, those with whom they chose to work. Indeed, the AJC's French Jewish contacts were especially concerned with reintegrating Jews within the nation-state. This locked the American organization into partnerships that left little room for criticizing France, let alone denouncing French antisemitism.

Interventions in French Diplomatic Matters

While the AJC had endeavored to create a French version of itself, it never relinquished its mission of serving as the "eyes and ears"[110] of American Jews in matters pertaining to Jews in France, Europe, and elsewhere. While the AJC was willing to share its methods with local organizations, it did not enter into formal negotiations with French Jewish institutions, such as the CRIF, to determine the scope of its activity in France, as had the WJC. The situation of Jews in North Africa, while not a central issue here, was a primary concern of the AJC. From the liberation of France throughout decolonization, the AJC worked quietly to secure Jewish rights in North Africa.[111] Though this represented a clear step into the domain of the Alliance and the CRIF, it did not prevent the AJC from making repeated trips to North Africa after setting up its Paris office. Understandably, this provoked a strong reaction from CRIF leaders in September 1947. Voicing his surprise, Léon Meiss declared that he would meet with Joel Wolfsohn of the AJC and explain that "these kind of initiatives would not be encouraged by the CRIF."[112] A second CRIF board member, Maître Kiefe, harshly criticized the AJC, explaining that when he was consulted by them on their opening a Paris office, he had "requested that they leave to the Jews of France the task of watching over their own interests and carefully refrain from all interference in French politics; if the American Jewish Committee persisted in its intentions, it would risk causing serious harm to all Jews living in France."[113] While refusing to relinquish its role in North

Africa, the AJC appears to have made efforts to respect the image (if not the missions) of French Jewish organizations. Before one trip to North Africa, Joel Wolfsohn reported having met with Léon Meiss and Jules Braunschvig of the Alliance. No conflict was reported, and all parties decided that Wolfsohn would travel as a tourist and not as a representative of the AJC.[114] This example suggests that Meiss—and perhaps other French Jewish leaders—were engaging in double-speak, whereby they privately acknowledged the AJC was best placed to negotiate on behalf of North African Jews yet publicly voiced surprise and dismay over such American interventions in French diplomacy. This may have been a strategy of organizations such as the CRIF to maintain credibility until they were actually ready to handle such matters on their own. However, the growing body of literature on Jews and North African decolonization suggests that, at least in the case of Algeria, French Jewish leaders may have been ready to intervene but consciously did not act in order to avoid aggravating an already tense situation.[115]

Protest from French Jewish leadership did not prevent the AJC from closely observing (and intervening in) French political life by meeting with French and North African political officials.[116] In this manner, the AJC voiced the concerns of American Jews to French government officials, especially in the highly publicized Finaly affair, in which two Jewish orphans were kidnapped by the woman who had cared for them during the war and subsequently hidden by members of the Catholic Church in France and Spain before being returned to surviving family members in Israel.[117] The AJC met several times with French Ambassador to the United States Henri Bonnet, who "agreed to communicate with Paris and inform his government of the concern that public opinion in the United States and especially Jewish public opinion has in the case, and to suggest intervention with the Spanish government to locate the children and deliver them to the French authorities."[118] It is unclear how French Jews responded to the AJC's role in the affair, or if they even knew about it.

The AJC also worked to influence American foreign policy from its Paris outpost. The Paris staff of the AJC developed contacts with Americans who worked in the Foreign Service and embassy in Paris, and others throughout Europe, with whom they were able to meet and socialize. American Jews working in American governmental institutions facilitated this relationship. Abraham Karlikow, for example, reported that at a certain point, there were as many as seven American ambassadors stationed Europe who were Jewish. On his trips to Poland, he would always stop at the American embassy, both as a safeguard and to informally exchange information.[119] Quiet diplomacy coexisted with official visits, such as that of honorary president of the AJC Judge Proskauer, who was received by the American ambassador C. Douglas Dillion and public affairs officer Mr. Leslie Brady in Paris in 1954.[120] Perhaps most significantly, the AJC regularly authored detailed reports that found their way onto the desks of American embassy and State Department officials.[121] It was most likely for this audience that the AJC was writing, with the intention of pointing out how Jews were affected by more general policy issues. One such report on the populist Poujadist movement that emerged in 1953 provided a detailed analysis of its rise, scope, and antisemitism. One deputy in particular struck the AJC as particularly dangerous due to his educational level and speaking skills, a young Jean-Marie Le Pen.[122]

Contradictions in its program, and to a certain extent, its worldview, hindered the success of the AJC in France, in spite of its astute observations. On one hand, it encouraged its French partners to take charge in the fight against antisemitism, on the other, it refused to relinquish its diplomacy on French Jewish matters. French Jews did not accept this situation, which for them represented a form of political interference. While they fought to maintain their place in diplomatic matters, they nonetheless accepted American Jewish funding. As one former AJC employee explained, French Jewish organizations worked with the attitude of "give us the money, leave the rest to us."[123] Finally, this analysis shows that the AJC isolated itself by stubbornly pursuing its partnership with conservative members of native leadership. The encounter between French Jews and the AJC was thus punctuated with frustrations that limited the transposition of the AJC's distinct approach to Jewish politics in France.

Thus far, I have explored two political organizations that each sought to influence French Jewish reconstruction according to their distinct ideologies, with varying degrees of success. As a welfare organization, the JDC claimed neutrality, yet as central actor in French Jewish life, it was also shaping the politics of reconstruction. In an environment as ideologically divided as postwar Paris, deciding who would receive funds for relief work was by nature a political act. In the early 1950s, an intensification in Cold War tensions finally forced the JDC to recognize this fact.

PARIS BETWEEN MOSCOW AND NEW YORK: THE JOINT DISTRIBUTION COMMITTEE AND THE COLD WAR

The JDC supported French Jewish welfare organizations regardless of their political affiliations. The ideal of political neutrality, of course, was subject to the complex realities dictating the war and postwar years. Nothing illustrates this better than the history of the relationship between French Jewish Communists and the JDC. In the early 1950s, events taking place behind the Iron Curtain opened a fiery debate on JDC policies in the French press, especially in the Yiddish dailies, which included the Zionist *Unzer wort* (*Our Word*), published by Right Poale Zion-Mapai, *Unzer stimme* (*Our Voice*), the organ of the Bund, and the Communist *Naye presse* (*New Press*).[124] After the promulgation of the state of Israel, Soviet antisemitism grew in intensity until Stalin's death in March 1953. Two incidents from this period are especially significant. In 1952, Rudolf Slansky, the general-secretary of the Czechoslovakian Communist Party, and thirteen other individuals (eleven of whom, including Slansky, were Jewish) were accused of treason.[125] After a show trial and failed suicide attempt, Slansky provided officials with a confession. Along with ten others, he was executed on December 3, 1952. Approximately one month later, another affair unfolded, which came to be known as the Doctors' Plot. On January 13, 1953, Soviet officials accused a group of nine Soviet doctors, six of whom had Jewish last names, of murdering Soviet officials A. A. Zhdanov and A. S. Shcherbakov and plotting to murder other senior party members.[126] This affair launched, in the words of historian David Brandenberger, "an explosion of undisguised antisemitism in the press that labeled Soviet Jews 'rootless cosmopolitans,' Zionists, and agents of U.S. and British imperialism."[127] In both the Slansky trial and the Doctors' Plot, the JDC had been targeted by Soviet authorities as a central culprit. It was accused of espionage, American imperialism, and spreading "Jewish bourgeois nationalism." While the historiography on these events does not focus on why the JDC was targeted, it should be noted that the JDC had a long history in the Soviet Union, where it had operated an extensive program in the 1920s and 1930s.[128] Furthermore, in 1952, an undercover Israeli operation called Lishka was launched in the Soviet Union in response to the increase in antisemitism. The goal of Lishka was to facilitate Jewish emigration to Israel and encourage Jewish life in the Soviet Union. The JDC only recently revealed that it helped fund this operation.[129]

It is interesting here to explore how debates on these events, which have been the subject of extensive study by scholars of Soviet history, resonated in France.[130] Indeed, thus far, this chapter has looked at Jewish politics in France primarily from the point of view of outside organizations. Yet in the days and months following these Soviet accusations, Jews in France, especially those on the left, engaged in passionate and often bellicose exchanges on the Slansky trial and the Doctors' Plot. Scholars Jacques Frémontier and François Lustman have closely documented the coverage of these events in the press. Frémontier compares the Communist Jewish *Naye presse* and the French

Communist daily *l'Humanité* and demonstrates that the Yiddish publication's coverage was double that of the French Communist daily. Lustman compares the coverage of the three Yiddish dailies and shows that the Zionist *Unzer wort* was the most active, followed by the Bundist *Unzer stimme* and finally *Naye presse*. Furthermore, Lustman shows that most of the articles were not about the events themselves but fell into the category of propaganda aimed to attack or defend. Together, these analyses show that Jewish Communists, referred to pejoratively in these articles as *Yewtzeks*, were more concerned by the events than the French Communist Party yet nonetheless faithfully defended the party. This is not to say that the relationship between Jews and the French Communist Party was not without tension.[131] Still, within Jewish circles, Jewish Communists positioned themselves as victims, claiming the Zionists and Bundists were using the opportunity to "drive *Yewtzeks* from the Jewish street."[132] The fact the JDC was targeted in Soviet accusations brought the events even closer to home and provided an opportunity to settle scores among the political groups in France, who were all receiving JDC funding for their welfare work. The JDC archives on this topic, which include translations of selected articles from the Yiddish and general press,[133] reveal a great deal about the political nature of the JDC's work in France. To understand the terms of the debate, it is first necessary gain an overview of the relationship between the Communist Jewish organizations and the JDC in postwar France.

The JDC and French Jewish Communists: An Unstable Relationship

At the end of World War II, French Jewish Communists expressed a certain bitterness regarding their relationship to the JDC when they wrote, "What often happened over the past four years, which was so deplorable, cannot be repeated. It is unacceptable that funds from the 'Joint' and the 'World Jewish Congress' were not made available to representative and unitarian [*unitaires*] organizations and that labor and working-class organizations were excluded from their control and their distribution."[134]

During World War II, in spite of its vast aid program to Jews in France, the JDC seems to have excluded Jewish Communist organizations from its funding.[135] As seen in chapter 1, during the 1942–1944 period, two French representatives, including Jules (Dika) Jefroykin, the son of the founder of the Socialist Zionist (Right Poale Zion) FSJF, ran the JDC. While political affinities certainly influenced where JDC aid would go, it should also be noted that the Jewish Communist resistance was organized within, and assumedly funded by, Communist resistance networks. The return of American JDC personnel to

France in December 1944 changed this, incorporating Jewish Communists into the fold.¹³⁶ JDC representative Arthur Greenleigh sought to fund as many Jewish welfare organizations as possible to reach the largest number of individuals in need, including two Jewish Communist organizations, the Union of Jewish Societies (known as the Farband), which played a central role organizing the Communist *landsmanshaftn* since its creation in 1938, and the Union of Jews for Resistance and Mutual Aid (UJRE), established in 1943. In the postwar period, the UJRE grew to include twenty-four sections of Paris and its suburbs and twenty-five throughout France, for a total of eight thousand members.¹³⁷ The JDC supported the UJRE's welfare work and that of its children's division, the Central Commission for Children (Commission centrale de l'enfance, CCE). According to the UJRE, the JDC was subsidizing at least 31 percent of its budget in early 1946.¹³⁸ By August 1946, the JDC grant was F1,125,000 a month, which corresponded to roughly 45 percent of the UJRE monthly budget. The UJRE then requested additional funding for two new children's homes, where it was hoping to transfer 360 children who had been living with non-Jewish families. The JDC respected the quality of care provided to the children in the UJRE homes, so JDC representative Laura Margolis did not hesitate to recommend the funding increase.¹³⁹ In 1946, the JDC provided the UJRE with a total of F27 million francs, not including supplies.¹⁴⁰

From the liberation until the late 1940s, the relationship between the JDC and the UJRE appears to have mirrored the relationships the JDC had with other Jewish children's organizations. These relationships were far from perfect; there were disagreements involving budgets and the right of the JDC to interfere in the daily life of the organizations. Like other French Jewish organizations, the UJRE received an important budget cut in early 1947 and responded like other French Jewish organizations by sending a delegation to the United States. As it had for other children's organizations, the JDC sought to conduct an audit of the UJRE books for 1947. It was only after "conferences, interviews and correspondence" during the last quarter of 1948 that an agreement was reached between the UJRE and the JDC to allow for the audit.¹⁴¹

As Cold War tensions began to increase after the Truman Doctrine in March 1947, the JDC began to display some concern over the UJRE. In April 1947, one JDC employee raised a flag in an internal memo, noting that UJRE was a "Communist-inspired Jewish agency" that needed "careful scrutiny as to its real financial needs, particularly in view of the fact that it solicit[ed] funds from other sources outside of France."¹⁴² Still, the wording of this document suggests that the employee was more concerned with the UJRE's financial integrity than with its ideological positions. He sought to ensure that the UJRE was not obtaining the bulk of its budget from another source (and thus benefiting from additional funds). Other JDC officials wanted to verify that the organization's funding was going directly to children, not propaganda.[143] As the witch hunt gathered momentum in the United States in the late 1940s, American Jews and their organizations sought to disprove what historian Peter Novick has called the "Jew-Communist equation."[144] Furthermore, other American philanthropic organizations were targeted during the McCarthy Era, such as the Unitarian Service Committee and the Rockefeller Foundation.[145] In this context, the JDC's continued financial support of the UJRE can actually be considered a rather progressive (and maybe even risky) stance, as well as a display of Jewish solidarity.

After 1950, however, the JDC's suspicion evolved into conflict. The rift was linked to the Soviet Union's shifting position on the State of Israel, which was felt in Paris. As seen in chapter 4, the JDC encouraged French Jews to establish a centralized fundraising organization based on the UJA model. After considerable planning and debate, French Jews established the United Jewish Social Fund (FSJU) in 1949, which attempted to combine the campaigns for domestic welfare and Israel. Even though leaders of Jewish Communist organizations had participated in the project from its earliest stages, they withdrew their support during the FSJU's National Constitutive Assembly in October 1949.[146] According to David Weinberg, who incorrectly places the date of this rupture in 1951, the URJE refused the Jewish Agency's authority but also took issue with the fact the structure was linked to the Rothschilds. The Communist refusal to participate in the FSJU contributed to the marginalization of Jewish Communists in French Jewish life. It also caused the relationship between Jewish Communists and the JDC to sour.[147] Instead of funding French Jewish welfare organizations through a single grant to the FSJU, the JDC had to provide a separate grant to the UJRE. Jewish Communists took advantage of this situation to accuse the JDC of discrimination in the Canadian Yiddish press.[148] Such negative press certainly did not improve the JDC-UJRE working relationship, but the JDC maintained its funding. Two years later, in 1952, when the Prague Trials began, the JDC was still providing the UJRE a monthly grant of roughly F1 million.[149] Soviet antisemitism would provide the ultimate test of this relationship.

Debating Soviet Antisemitism in Paris

The Slansky trial, followed by the Doctors' Plot, opened a debate in both the Communist and Jewish press at a particularly tense moment for French Jews. As if these affairs were not enough to increase tensions among Bundists, Zionists, and Communists, they occurred amid other events that deeply concerned this population. Indeed, as 1952 turned into 1953, Jews in France were able to open any newspaper and read about the impending execution of Ethel and Julius Rosenberg, American Jews sentenced for conspiracy to commit espionage for the Soviet Union. At the same time, larger questions of Jewish-Catholic relations and the role of the Church and State unfolded dramatically as the fate of two Jewish orphans, Robert and Gérald Finaly, was debated, both before and after they were kidnapped by the woman who had cared for them during the war—all with the assistance of members of the Catholic Church. Finally, both in France and Europe as a whole, the question of de-Nazification remained unresolved, as the Western democracies moved toward the rearmament of the Federal Republic of Germany. Discussions on the negotiations with the Federal Republic of Germany on reparations for Nazi crimes animated Jewish circles.[150] While historians now debate to what extent French Jews were immersed in a "strange silence,"[151] in late 1952 and early 1953, matters concerning Jews as a whole plunged them into the media spotlight, whether they were ready for the attention or not.[152] This context generated a certain level of unease that is important for understanding the media coverage of the Slansky trial and the Doctors' Plot and its implications in France.

In *Naye presse*, Jewish Communists followed the Soviet position during both the Slansky trial and the Doctor's Plot. Not only did the publication deny any antisemitism on the part of Soviet authorities but the daily actively portrayed these events as part of an American-Jewish-Zionist conspiracy. Jacques Frémontier shows to what extent French Jews responded locally to this debate: instead of debating the facts and their consequences in the Soviet context, *Naye presse* "grounded" its arguments in the French Jewish wartime experience and attacked local French Jewish leaders.[153] For example, when French Jews organized a protest against the Slansky trial at the Mutualité in Paris, *Naye presse* denounced "the local reactionary Zionist leaders, who did not protest against the 'Jew' René Mayer, who liberated Xavier Vallat, the assassin of 120,000 [sic] Jews of France, [who] now dare to call upon the working-class masses [*masses populaires*] for a 'protest meeting' against those who, in France as in Czechoslovakia, saved millions of Jews from Nazi extermination."[154]

The Zionist *Unzer wort* and the Bundist *Unzer stimme* returned *Naye presse's* attacks. Both denounced the antisemitic nature of the Slansky trial, pointing out that Jews were its main target.[155] Yet this was not only an affair between French Jewish Zionists, Bundists, and Communists. The JDC, as a target of Soviet accusations and primary benefactor of French Jews, was concretely dragged into the conflict. This can be seen in an article from *Unzer wort* on the day before Rudolf Slansky was executed in Prague. "It has only now become clear who are the Adamitches, the Kormans, the Alfred Grants [French Jewish Communist leaders] and the other members of the 'Union [UJRE] gang,'" wrote N.Z. of *Unzer Wort*, with a strong dose of sarcasm:

> It is perfectly obvious that they are American spies, paid through "Joint." It is really tragic and comic. It is tragic that we Jews are such good-hearted people, that we have no courage to refuse. The "Joint" has given many millions (about 20,000,000 fr.) to the people of the "Union," and with this money the "Rue de Paradis" [UJRE headquarters] was given the possibility of penetrating into Jewish life and later carry on its destructive work. Under the slogan, "Children of the Assassinated" they went on for years, living on the "Joint" and even paying the salaries of their "Tshinovnikes" (Russian functionaries) with this American money. When one thinks it over a little it becomes rather comical that at the same time when at Prague the "Joint" was accused of "spying" the Kormans and the Grants walk about quite freely in Paris, though they have, for a long time, been living on the funds of American Imperialism.[156]

The question that *Unzer wort* and others began to ask repeatedly was quite simple: Why did the JDC continue to support French Jewish Communists when the Soviet Union had placed the JDC at the center of its conspiracy theory?[157] The day after this article was published, the JDC's public relations department began to receive phone calls requesting comment on the JDC's funding of the UJRE.[158]

This question was still floating in the air when, on January 13, 1953, Soviet authorities announced the Doctors' Plot and yet again accused the JDC of "espionage, subversion and terrorism."[159] *Naye presse* ran with the story, ever faithful to the Soviet party line. In an editorial entitled "The Fifth Column," published on January 14, 1953, its editor Georges Kenig pointed out that the "Slanski [sic] trial as well as the uncovering of the murder-group in the Soviet Union has, however, completely torn off the hideous mask of the Zionist leaders, of the Zionist organisms and of 'Joint.'"[160] In total, the editorial made three references to the JDC, as did another the next day, "They Want to Light Anew the Crematories!," which argued that in plotting to murder high-level Soviet authorities, "a group of physicians under the leadership of the English-American spying apparatus and its agents of the international Zionist organizations and 'Joint' were attempting to organize new Auschwitzes [sic] and new crematoria."[161] However, while both editorials repeated the Soviet accusations against the JDC, their authors did not focus the brunt of their attacks on the organization nor did they discuss the JDC in France.

By exercising some restraint, Jewish Communists seem to have been attempting to maintain multiple allegiances. After all, Jewish Communists needed JDC funding in order to provide welfare services to "their" children. While they sensed a limit not to be crossed, others did not.

The French Communist Newspaper Ce soir and the Joint Distribution Committee: "A strange 'joint'"[162]

In his analysis of the Slansky trial and the Doctors' Plot, Frémontier concludes that *l'Humanité* (and indirectly, one can infer, the French Communist Party) preferred a more cautious coverage of these affairs that closely followed a "classic Cold War argument," which was critical of the United States.[163] However, the French Communist Party, at least until March 1953, financed two dailies, *l'Humanité* and *Ce soir*. Contrary to *l'Humanité*, which favored long political analyses, *Ce soir* sought a larger audience with its photographic coverage of events.[164] In the case of the Doctors' Plot, the French Communist Party appears to have used *Ce soir* to express what could not be said in *l'Humanité*. Unlike the coverage in *l'Humanité* and *Naye presse*, *Ce soir* eventually focused the brunt of its attack on the JDC.[165]

On the day the story broke, January 14, 1953, the JDC made front-page headlines of *Ce soir*, which denounced it as a "Zionist organization," created by "American secret services" for "spying activities and sabotage on a large-scale, in a series of countries, including the USSR."[166] *Ce soir* and its editor, Georges Soria, continued to cover the Doctors' Plot throughout the following weeks in the back pages and suggested that Joseph Schwartz, former head of the JDC's European operations, was an American intelligence officer.[167]

Ce soir's coverage of the Doctors' Plot may have gone unnoticed by the JDC had it not been for its decision to publish a series of ten articles in late January and early February 1953 that focused exclusively on the JDC. The series was entitled "Spying and Conspiracy under the Cover of Charity. The Role of the American Jewish Organization 'Joint'" and was written by former Communist Deputy Pierre Hervé.[168] With Hervé's series, the JDC found itself, yet again, on the front page.

The first article of the series sought to prove the political orientation of the JDC, as well as its anti-Soviet bias, by describing its activities in postwar Romania.[169] The next day, however, Hervé's series took a new turn by targeting local JDC employees and referring to events that had transpired during the Holocaust in France. The article launched a personal attack on Charles Malamuth, the head of public relations for the JDC in France, portraying him as a virulently anti-Soviet Trotsky supporter.[170] On January 30, Hervé focused his attention yet again on JDC employees in Paris, as well as French Jewish leaders, including Gaston Kahn, Raymond Geissman, Guy de Rothschild, and Marc Jarblum, by claiming that the JDC relied on former collaborators to operate its program.[171] Taking aim at Gaston Kahn, a former UGIF member who did indeed work closely with the JDC before and after World War II, Hervé claimed that during the war Kahn had known about the imminent arrest of a group of Jewish women and children and had chosen to remain silent.[172] The defamatory nature of Hervé's personal attacks hid what was perhaps even more unsettling: it was becoming increasingly clear that an "insider" was informing Hervé. Otherwise, how could Hervé have gained access to the documents, names, and events he cited?

On February 3, the antisemitic tone of Hervé's campaign was confirmed in an article entitled "Israel, Parasitic and Demagogical State." Hevré adhered to the Soviet position on Israel, which had, by this point, become outwardly hostile. Yet by labeling Israel a "parasitic" state, he went one step further, mobilizing a well-known anti-Jewish trope. While seemingly off-topic, Hervé managed to slip in a few paragraphs on the JDC in Paris:

> What is the atmosphere like in an organization like the JDC?
> While, for example, in 1947, an American employee received, in addition to his comfortable salary paid in dollars in a bank, an allowance of 100,000 francs a month, a French employee, who did the same work, received a total of 30,000 francs. What a beautiful example of fraternity!
> At the Joint, we are, in fact, far from idealism. The American functionaries of the Joint are not afraid to spread their disdain over all that is French, and even European: "We can buy anything for 'une bouchée de pain' [a small price].... We can do anything with money.... These people don't work.... They take two hours to eat lunch." What Joint employee hasn't heard these statements?
> But these charity professionals gorge themselves with "traditional French cuisine," to the extent that they fall asleep at the table. What rights don't they have, these new masters?[173]

Here, in what could be the grievances of a rather bitter JDC employee, Hervé voiced a discourse on the JDC that was certainly heard behind closed doors. In mocking American discourses on the French, it even resembles a 1945 comic sketch on life in the JDC offices.[174] Yet Hervé's critiques were published in a French daily, bypassing the Jewish circles in which the JDC's long history with French Jews could be debated in context.

In addition to personal attacks regarding individuals who worked for the JDC in Paris, Hervé extended his criticism to other American Jewish organizations, such as the American Jewish Committee and the Jewish Labor Committee, and even dedicated an article to attacking the American Jewish Yiddish daily, the *Forverts* (The Forward).[175] He also twisted a more classic antisemitic argument by blaming the banking families that played a founding role in the JDC for the rise of Hitler in an article entitled "American Jewish Finance Sponsored Hitler."[176]

In his last article, "The Question Is Asked: Where Are the Antisemites?" Hervé addressed the accusations that had been directed toward him and confirmed what many had already realized: members of *Naye presse* and the UJRE had helped him write the series. He wrote,

> According to Unser Stimme (Our Voice), the Bundist press, affiliated with the SFIO, "Red Jewish valets"—*yiddishe roïte moshkes*—have helped inform me over the course of this investigation. The perceptiveness of these racists is really extraordinary.
>
> What hatred, my friends, what hatred, that I've been happy to receive in the company of the "Red Jewish valets" of the UJRE and the New Press [*sic*, *Naye Presse*]! Here I am, called an antisemite because I dared attack warmongers from the "Joint," the "American Jewish Committee" and the "Labor Jewish Committee [*sic*]": because I noticed that certain Jews marked and registered their brothers when faced with the oncoming massacre and that they are today being honored: because I drew attention to the particular role of American Jewish finance in the Nazi rise to power.[177]

One should note Hervé's usage of Yiddish in the article, although he did not, one assumes, master the language. This rhetorical strategy was certainly aimed to disarm accusations of antisemitism by showing readers that Jews had helped him. Yet why did *Ce soir* (and indirectly the French Communist Party) focus on the JDC instead of the Doctors' Plot itself? What accounted for the series' antisemitic turn and did the imminent termination of the paper (set by the French Communist Party several months before for February 28, 1953)[178] permit for a certain loosening of tongues? Did Hervé use Jewish Communists or did the Jewish Communists use Hervé in order to heighten the impact of their critiques against the JDC? If the latter were true, why would the Jewish Communists bite the hand that was feeding them by focusing on their benefactor?

In his autobiographical works, a former member of *Ce soir*, Pierre Daix, provides some (albeit contradictory) clues. In one account, he states that Hervé had the idea for the series and suggested it to the Secretary of the French Communist Party, which then imposed it on *Ce soir*.[179] In a later account, however, Daix stated that Hervé was ordered to write the series by the French

Communist Party, which closely obeyed the Soviet party line.[180] Daix's later memoirs emphasize his inability to disobey the French Communist Party in the absence of Louis Aragon, editor of *Ce soir*, who was in the Soviet Union at the time.[181] According to Daix, once back in Paris, Aragon reprimanded him, stating that the series had dishonored the paper.[182]

It is possible that Jewish Communists, Hevré, and the French Communist Party all benefited from the series. By choosing the JDC as the focus instead of the Doctors' Plot itself, *Ce soir* helped French Jewish Communists redirect the debate away from Soviet antisemitism and onto a topic guaranteed to incite a conversation within Jewish circles: the JDC. Furthermore, Hervé was given access to information that had rarely traveled beyond French Jewish circles, providing him with a sensational scoop that fit well into Cold War discourse. The French Communist Party also benefitted from its bifurcated coverage of the Doctors' Plot: on the one hand, in *l'Humanité*, it could maintain a classic Cold War argument, appealing to the more educated sector of its electorate, while on the other, in *Ce soir*, it could—one month before terminating the paper—pander to growing populist tendencies on the eve of the Poujadist movement.

There is some evidence, however, that although an undetermined number of Jewish Communists lent their support to Hervé, *Naye presse* did not entirely support his series once published. One week after Hervé's series began, the person reviewing the Yiddish press for the JDC observed that *Naye presse* had stopped attacking them, and instead of citing Pierre Hervé verbatim, they only mentioned parts of his texts, perhaps in response to an increased number of canceled subscriptions.[183] One could also ask if Jewish Communists, like other Jews, were concerned about the antisemitic turn Hervé's articles had taken, or more generally, if the French took note of the growing antisemitism in the Soviet Union and, more locally, in the French Communist Party.

Jewish circles did not greet the attacks in *Naye presse* and *Ce soir* with indifference. A few members of the Jewish religious association of Cannes, as well as the Union of Jewish Students of France, wrote to the JDC to express their "indignation"[184] at the series and their "gratitude for the objective and disinterested aid."[185] Furthermore, as seen above, others canceled their subscriptions to *Naye presse* and even broke with the French Communist Party. The refusal of the UJRE to deviate from the Soviet party line also caused an upheaval in the CRIF, which debated a resolution to exclude Jewish Communists from the organization in February 1953. While the resolution did not pass, the CRIF elected a new board in May that did not include the UJRE, thus further marginalizing Jewish Communists.[186] The events of 1952 and 1953 had sounded the death knell of Jewish wartime unity.

While the French Communist Party officially refused any criticism of Moscow during both the Slansky trial and the Doctor's Plot, the French public showed some concern over its antisemitism during the affairs.[187] The satirical newspaper *Canard enchaîné* focused on Hervé's "anti-Zionist"[188] series to mock his article on American Jewish finance, pointing out that Hervé had plagiarized a book entitled *Nicolas III et les juifs*. According to *Canard enchaîné*, the book blamed the same Jewish banking families for starting the Russian Revolution. The *Canard enchaîné* concluded, in a play on words, "In comparing the names, one has the impression that Comrade Hervé found himself a strange 'joint' [*un drôle de 'joint'*]."[189]

The JDC: "A Convenient Club with Which to Belabor Their Opponents"[190]

The responses of the non-Communist Yiddish press were not quite as clear-cut. On one hand, the Bundist *Unzer stimme* denounced the "antisemitic incitement"[191] and the "racist propaganda" of *Ce soir*.[192] On the other, the daily maintained a critical view of the JDC, with headlines such as "Why Is the Leadership of the Paris 'Joint' Silent? Is It True That the 'Union' Still Receives Subventions? Jewish Public Opinion Will Not Tolerate Such a Moral Scandal."[193] Zionist *Unzer wort* also focused its attention on the JDC, publishing on the same day an article entitled "Is This True? We Demand an Immediate and Clear Reply of 'Joint.'"[194]

Though these editorials raised valid questions, one must also note that, yet again, instead of focusing on the Soviet Doctors' Plot, or even French Jewish Communists, the attacks were directed at the JDC. Why did French Jews care if the Communists received grants from the JDC if their own funding was not in danger? One reason, of course, was the ideological divide in French Jewish politics that far surpassed France. Both dailies were receiving funding from anti-Communist American organizations, such as the American Jewish Committee and in the case of *Unzer stimme*, the International Ladies' Garment Workers' Union.[195] It is also possible the JDC, as the target of these attacks, was serving another function among French Jews. Communist Jews, by expressing their complaints in the French Communist *Ce soir* through Pierre Hervé, not only expressed an explosive argument—that Jews had collaborated during the Holocaust—but they broadcast their grievances with the JDC to the general population. As seen above, they also indirectly broke the "strange silence" at a particularly tense moment. Behind closed doors, in their honor courts and in the Jewish press in both French and Yiddish, Jews had been discussing Jewish collaboration under Vichy since the liberation.[196] The fact such debates suddenly jumped from Jewish circles onto the pages of the national press was certainly jarring, especially since it enabled a display of French antisemitism. It is thus possible that Zionist and Bundist Jews, in asking the JDC to stop funding Jewish Communists, were in fact asking the JDC to function as an external mediator, capable of sanctioning those who did not respect the rules. In short, the JDC was being asked to maintain order.

How did the JDC respond to this situation? Moses Beckelman, who took over as head of the JDC European operations after Joseph Schwartz's departure in 1951, seems to have sensed that it was serving more than just a philanthropic role in France when he wrote to his New York colleague, Moses Leavitt, that "both the communist and anti-communist factions in the Jewish community find it [the JDC] a convenient club with which to belabor their opponents."[197] Beckelman appears to have initially chosen silence as the best means of handling what he called the "Paris Yiddish Press attacks" because "these attacks on JDC are not being made in good faith and will not therefore be stopped simply by explaining the facts."[198]

Perhaps even more acutely than the pressure they felt from non-Communist French Jews, the JDC leadership feared the scandal would migrate to the United States, where Cold War tensions in the American Jewish community, especially due to the pending Rosenberg executions, had never been higher. Jewish Labor Committee president Adolph Held, who was closely associated with the *Forverts*, followed the attacks from New York through press clippings and advised the JDC to be careful. "The protests seem to be gaining headway," he wrote to the JDC's Moses Leavitt. "Sitting on the outside, it would seem to me that this is a very opportune time to rid the JDC of all reason for criticism on this score. [. . .] If it is true that some of this money goes to support communist functionaries something ought to be done about it- and soon. As you note I am writing this in long hand, as I didn't even want to dictate on a subject like this."[199] The JDC heeded this advice and terminated its funding to the Communist UJRE in January 1953. Initially, Beckelman informed the editors of the Yiddish press of this decision, yet he chose not to publish a formal statement.[200]

This was not sufficient. "The attacks continued nevertheless," wrote Beckelman. "To them has now been added a new line of fire- namely that the JDC has communists on its staff."[201] Beckelman finally agreed to be interviewed in *Unzer wort* on February 27, 1953.[202] The interview closed with the request that the JDC conduct a purge of its employees.[203]

It remains unknown whether the JDC gave in to this pressure. Most likely, the JDC did in fact employ Communists.[204] In 1948, a diplomat at the US embassy in Paris expressed his concern about what he called the "fuzzy thinkers," Communists, at the JDC to a member of the American Jewish Committee's staff.[205] The personal archives of David Diamant, a UJRE leader, contain a list of individuals (presumably members of the French Communist party) who had worked at the JDC and in other Jewish organizations. The list shows that one individual left the JDC on February 1, 1953.[206] Before concluding that this person was fired by the JDC due to a Communist affiliation, it should be noted that on January 19, 1953, the Secretary of the French Communist Party had decided to "oblige party members working for the 'Joint' to leave this organization or risk expulsion from the Party ranks."[207]

The Soviet attack of the JDC, and more importantly, the local attack of the JDC in the French Communist press, destabilized it enough for it to attempt to correct the damage to its reputation in France. The JDC did this by publishing a booklet in French on its history in April 1953 that made clear mention of the "recent attacks."[208] In the same month, the Doctors' Plot was dismantled and the suspects released. How did *Naye presse* respond to this information? The mea culpa that Zionists and Bundists had long awaited never came. Instead, an editorial declared that "the setting free and rehabilitation of the 15 Moscow doctors- among whom 6 are Jews- proves most clearly the profound care of the Soviet government for justice."[209] Not only did *Naye presse* deny the deeper implications of the affair but in the following months, it repeatedly criticized the JDC for having cut off its funds. In May 1953 it referred to the "robbing on the part of the Joint of the subsidy of the American Jews."[210] That October, *Naye presse* wrote that "it is enough to remember that the Joint robbed the orphans of the Jews shot and deported of the small support (which has been a third of one per cent of its budget for France) which it gave a year ago. Thus: if the Joint believes that Jewish orphans may die from famine or may go naked and barefoot or may be thrown out in the street (fortunately the Jewish masses through their contributions did not allow that to happen), what are, then, the 'more important' purposes on which it spends the 600,000,000 francs?"[211]

As the above citation shows, the events of late 1952 and early 1953 created a rift in an already divided Jewish population. Jewish Communist organizations, more isolated since their refusal to participate in the FSJU in 1949, now found themselves marginalized within the CRIF and denied their JDC funding. The wartime unity that allowed for the emergence of the CRIF was officially over, yet paradoxically, the crisis also served to reinforce communal consensus.

The events of late 1952 and 1953 reveal the inherently political nature of the JDC's program in France. At the same time, they allowed Bundist and Zionist leaders to use the JDC to settle their scores with Jewish Communists. The former were keenly aware of fact that the JDC could not be perceived as supporting Communist organizations at the peak of McCarthyism. They skillfully maneuvered to push out their Communist rivals, getting the JDC to deliver the final blow in a decades-long political battle.

CONCLUSION

The mobilization of international and American Jewish organizations in France began in 1944 and intensified until 1947. Over the next decades, American and French Jews collaborated with an unequal, yet changing balance of power. As seen above, different factions of American Jewish organizational life came to France, enlarging the domain of intervention from welfare work to political action. By establishing programs in France, American Jewish organizations found new ways to assert their visions for the Jewish future, thus honing their positions on the postwar world. Helping French Jews was simultaneously an act of Jewish solidarity, a means to accomplish political goals, and a way in which American Jewish organizations attempted to gain recognition within the American Jewish community in this moment of transition.[212]

The World Jewish Congress and the American Jewish Committee had ambitious plans for Jews in France. Both sought to convince others with their respective viewpoints and both found local sources of support. Immigrant circles tended to embrace the WJC's vision of Jewish peoplehood, albeit Zionist or "diaspora nationalist," while more conservative native circles welcomed the anti-Communist AJC's symbiotic approach to the nation-state. Yet neither organization was able to fully win over the CRIF and neither gained a strong foothold in French Jewish life, at least in this period.[213] Though these political organizations were unable to shape French Jewish reconstruction to the extent they had desired, the same cannot be said for the JDC. This "apolitical" organization was engaging in welfare work in a highly politicized context and sought to avoid polemics. However, the JDC's decision to fund Jewish Communists, Bundists, Zionists, and Native French Jewish organizations did indeed shape Jewish reconstruction by maintaining the interwar diversity of French Jewish life. French Bundists and Zionists were certainly aware of this when they campaigned in the Yiddish press, urging the JDC to cease funding Jewish Communists in 1953. Their pressure heightened the JDC's fear of scandal and led to its decision to cut funding for Communist Jewish organizations. American Jewish programs were thus also shaped by French Jewish politics. Nonetheless, even though they managed to occasionally wangle their way with American Jewish organizations in Paris, French Jews' influence remained limited to France, whereas American Jews' influence was felt internationally.

Indeed, the evolution of postwar Franco-American Jewish power dynamics deserve note. In the immediate postwar period, French Jews used the pronoun *we* to describe the JDC's activities during World War II and accepted, begrudgingly, the increasing demands of the JDC to obtain its funding. Though JDC budgetary restrictions in spring 1947 led to a more vocal protest of French Jewish leadership, the reactions to Soviet antisemitism showed an even clearer shift. Jews in France openly defied their benefactor and at last had managed to influence JDC policy. French actions did not reverse the hierarchy between giver and receiver but do show that French Jews refused the role of silent partner in the reconstruction process. By taking issue with the JDC in the press, Jews in France forced the latter to take their views into account. And while money seems to have played a central role, it was never the only concern of French Jews. As seen in their reactions to Soviet antisemitism, principles also played a role. The relationship between the JDC and its beneficiaries was more complex than simple financial dependence, which raises the larger question of the function of the American Jewish presence in postwar France.

During the Slansky trial and the Doctor's Plot, the JDC played a symbolic role for both Soviet authorities and French Jews. As an American and Jewish organization financed by "capitalists," this organization was an easy target for Soviet authorities. For French Jews, the JDC served, on one hand, as an "external arbitrator" and, on the other, as "a convenient club with which to belabor [one's] opponents."[214] French Zionists and Bundists could have chosen to unequivocally support the JDC with the goal of fortifying their relationship with the JDC, but they did not. On the contrary, these groups marked their distance from the JDC and demanded explanations. Paradoxically, the JDC was described as both a bastion of American imperialism and as a "red" organization. Individuals could see what they wanted, a fact that provides as much information about the observer as it does about the JDC itself.

The JDC represented a model of reconstruction that could be contradicted, modified, or adopted by French Jews. As such, the JDC enabled French Jews and their communal organizations to hone their own positions. It is hard to imagine what the French Jewish community would have looked like without this "external arbitrator." Its presence contributed financial aid, a vision of reconstruction, and, as I will show in the final chapter, new methods for helping others.

SIX

"FROM CHARITY TO SOCIAL WORK"[1]

American Jewish Aid and the Reform of French Social Work

"YOU'RE LATE,"[2] A STUDENT WHISPERED to Shirley Hellenbrand as she arrived at the Château de la Maye in Versailles on a beautiful autumn day in 1949. The twenty-seven-year-old redhead who passed easily for a student was actually a new faculty member of the Paul Baerwald School of Social Work. The JDC had opened the school that October to train a new generation of European Jewish social workers. A graduate of the New York School of Social Work, Hellenbrand had become fluent in French while doing fieldwork for her master's thesis in the canteens established in New York during World War II for French sailors. Hellenbrand was working in a social service agency that specialized in helping Jewish families when the JDC offered her a position in France. She jumped at the opportunity and set sail on the Queen Mary in November 1949.

Shirley Hellenbrand came to France to help carry out a JDC project designed by a fellow American, Herman Stein, who had arrived in France in 1947. Born into a large, Yiddish-speaking family in the Bronx, Stein abandoned a promising career in Yiddish theater to study social work at the New York School of Social Work, where he obtained a master's degree in 1941. In 1947, Stein was working as a staff instructor of research at his institution when the JDC offered him a position to work in its budget and research department in Paris. Unable to serve in World War II due to injury, Stein accepted the JDC offer with enthusiasm. None of his mother's seven sisters in Warsaw had survived the war, and more than anything, Stein felt compelled to help Jewish survivors and refugees. Even though Stein was told by his colleagues in New York that he was "ruining a brilliant career," he left for France with his wife, Charmion.[3] The latter also worked for the JDC and, in a situation indicative of the gender dynamics of the period, completed her master's thesis while in France with her husband

178

as her advisor. The couple initially lived in a rat-infested apartment near the Luxembourg Gardens and had permission to shop in army post exchanges (PXs), where Stein was able to cash in on luxury items such as... ketchup.[4] At the JDC's European headquarters, Herman Stein first worked under the direction of Blanche Bernstein, a former State Department economist, and was soon asked to create a welfare department.

As the JDC's Office for France began to lay the groundwork for the United Jewish Social Fund (FSJU), others at the JDC's European headquarters, also in Paris, were asking how European Jewish life would fare without the JDC. As head of the JDC's European welfare department, Herman Stein had a comprehensive view of relief efforts for Jewish survivors throughout Europe and was critical of the social work practices he observed in European Jewish welfare agencies. Like many of his JDC colleagues, he felt the low standards of services and lack of professionalism would prevent European Jewish communities from becoming self-sufficient. Indeed, the social work profession evolved differently in France and the United States during the interwar years, in spite of American attempts to influence the French profession.[5] The strikingly different wartime conditions in both countries compounded deeply seated structural differences. As a result, in the postwar period, American social workers viewed French social work as outdated and unprofessional. The JDC initially sought help on this problem from an organizational ally, the National Council of Jewish Women, which set up a scholarship program in 1946 to send young European Jewish women to the United States to study social work. In March 1948, Herman Stein suggested that the JDC establish in-service training in social welfare concepts for local JDC employees and subsidized agencies throughout Europe.[6] By October 1948, Stein's idea had evolved into an initiative to establish an American social work school in Europe.

One year later, in October 1949, the JDC inaugurated the Paul Baerwald School of Social Work (PBS), in Versailles, named after the philanthropist and former JDC chairman. The school offered a one-year program in American social work methods and trained approximately one hundred Jewish students from Europe, Israel, and North Africa over a four-year period. The school's residential program closed in fall 1953 due to Cold War restrictions on travel and the growing Israeli need for social work training. Nonetheless, its faculty remained active throughout the 1950s, providing in-service trainings in Europe and North Africa. In 1958, after long negotiations, the school reopened at the Hebrew University of Jerusalem, where it operates to this day.

Stein justified the establishment of a social work school by pointing out that it fit into the JDC policy of "strengthening the resources of the Jewish communities so that they could carry on firmly as JDC's financial assistance is gradually withdrawn."[7] While this could certainly be argued, the PBS also represents an exception to the JDC policy of working only through local Jewish communities. If JDC employees sensed European Jews were at last open to receiving training in social work, the PBS was not a bottom-up enterprise, neither in the process of its creation nor in its institutional life.[8] The school's advisory boards in the United States and France did not include local European Jewish leaders.[9] Once established, the school offered courses conceptualized and taught, for the most part, by American-trained JDC employees. This was not the only one of its own policies the JDC circumvented. The JDC opposed the duplication of services but did not try to work with one of the sixty-two existing social work schools in France.[10] Furthermore, in 1946, the Jewish Scouts of France opened the Gilbert Bloch School in Orsay, whose four-year program in Jewish studies was designed to train a new generation of French Jewish communal workers.[11] The JDC did not consider involving the Orsay school in this project either. Instead, it decided to establish a separate social work school based entirely on its own resources and provided a budget of $250,000, derived from legacies, for this purpose.[12]

Such policy contradictions make the Paul Baerwald School an interesting example of the "Jewish Marshall Plan." This chapter questions the JDC's attempt to import American social welfare practices to Europe—and to France in particular. Others have focused on the outcome of these efforts, suggesting that the JDC had a contradictory mission designed to empower European Jews yet at the same time affirm the JDC's cultural agenda.[13] Still, as seen with the FSJU, I argue here the JDC's cultural transfer was the result of a negotiated process: though French Jews proved open to American methods, and at times even fully embraced them, their decision to do so reflected their own internal logic and strategies. Furthermore, Americans showed a strong awareness of imperialism at each step of their projects and took pains to address this critique. An extensive study of the life of the Paul Baerwald School, which can be divided into four phases—its establishment, its moment as a residential program, its in-service years, and its Israeli period—has never been conducted.[14] Likewise, the opening of the PBS corresponded to a particularly fertile moment in the general field of European social work; however, little has been written on the role of Jewish organizations in the evolution of European social practices after World War II. Indeed, what is particularly interesting about the social work story is that it allowed the "Jewish Marshall Plan" to travel beyond Jewish circles, inciting curiosity and enthusiasm from welfare professionals throughout Europe.

"FROM CHARITY TO SOCIAL WORK" 181

Before focusing on the PBS, it is important to look closely at why the JDC's American directors perceived a need to professionalize European Jewish social work and the steps they took to do so. The National Council of Jewish Women, which sent a representative to Paris in April 1946, provided a concrete, yet gendered, solution by sending European Jewish women to study in the United States. The JDC then sought out a more ambitious solution with the Paul Baerwald School. Based in Europe, the school was designed to export American social work practices with the goal of influencing the European and North African Jewish world. In the context of the larger American Marshall Plan, the school's educational mission quickly expanded to include non-Jewish European social welfare circles. Had the JDC caught a case of expansionist fever?

FRENCH JEWISH SOCIAL WORK, VIEWED BY AMERICANS

American JDC employees viewed French Jewish welfare through the lens of American social work, which provided solutions to the problems they perceived. During the immediate postwar period, three successive directors of the JDC's Office for France, and many, although not all, of its American employees, had degrees in social work from American universities.[15] Dr. Joseph Schwartz, head of JDC's European operations from 1940 through 1951, represents an interesting exception. Schwartz was an ordained rabbi who then studied Semitic languages at Yale, where he obtained a doctorate in 1927. With limited opportunities in academia as a result of increasing antisemitism and the Great Depression, Schwartz accepted a position as director of public information at the Brooklyn Federation of Jewish Charities in 1929, where he was promoted to executive director in 1931.[16] Like Schwartz, many American Jews had turned to the field of social work during the Depression. The profession provided young, left-leaning Jews with stable work and a greater chance of escaping the antisemitism prevalent in industry and law during this period in the United States. Furthermore, while the field of social work had feminized in the 1920s and 1930s, men still dominated key administrative positions and obtained family wages, a fact that certainly helped make the profession attractive to Jewish men.[17]

American Jewish welfare organizations, following larger trends in American welfare, underwent professionalization after World War I. While there were several attempts to create specifically Jewish social work schools, only one was established in the United States in 1925, which closed in 1940.[18] Yet even during this school's short existence, Jewish social services tended to hire the graduates of general social work master's programs, which furthered the integration of American Jews into larger social welfare circles. As graduates of American social work schools during a period of unprecedented consensus, most JDC employees were trained in the standard social work curriculum, which included methods such as casework, group work, community organization, public welfare, social administration, social research, and psychiatry.[19] Many were members of the National Conference for Jewish Charities and several had published articles in professional journals, such as the *Jewish Social Service Quarterly* and even in the more widely read magazine *Survey Graphic*.[20] They saw themselves as social work professionals, an identity bolstered by their mobility. For example, JDC representative Arthur Greenleigh was sent to Italy and then France before returning to the United States. In addition to her work in Cuba, China, Switzerland, and Spain during the war, Laura Margolis was the head of JDC operations in Belgium before taking over from Greenleigh in France, after which she continued on to Israel. Many others circulated throughout Europe on different assignments.[21] When faced with changing surroundings and the diverse conditions of European Jews, American social work training provided JDC employees with a reassuring and practical "guidebook" and a shared vocabulary to label the problems they observed.

Beginning with Arthur Greenleigh, the first postwar director of the JDC program for France, JDC employees never failed to comment on the low standards in local Jewish welfare agencies and their "unqualified" and "politically-biased" staff.[22] Such critiques were grounded in the reality of postwar welfare, in which each ideological shade of Jewish life operated its own aid network. While all forms of social aid can be analyzed in political terms, ideological affiliations were overtly stated in France. JDC observations also reflect the strikingly different conditions under which French and American Jews practiced social welfare during World War II. For French Jews, social welfare was often a clandestine enterprise, closely associated with resistance work. During the same period, American Jewish social workers exercised their profession in rational bureaucracies where they were rewarded for their neutrality.

Once in France, American-trained social workers from the JDC encountered French social work practices for the first time. Important differences in orientation and method separated social work in France and the United States, especially regarding the casework method, which became popular in the interwar period. In the words of historian Roy Lubove, casework "formed the basis of a professional identity"[23] in American social work. The casework method advocates for the individual treatment of each client while taking into account the environmental and social factors affecting the individual. The ultimate goal is to teach the client to mobilize his or her available resources and confront the sources of his or her poverty instead of simply receiving aid. Teaching the individual to help him or herself fit nicely with the larger self-help philosophy in American culture and what one scholar has referred to as the "empowerment tradition in American social work."[24] Therefore American-trained social workers easily took the ubiquity of casework in the United States for granted. In spite of the introduction of casework in 1920's France, the method was relatively unknown in French social work circles immediately after World War II.[25]

Other differences between American and French social work may have caused American social workers to look down upon their French colleagues. French social work emerged at the end of the nineteenth century during the fight against tuberculosis and infant mortality and maintained its medical orientation long after the creation of separate state diplomas for nursing and social work.[26] This made French social workers appear like nurses to their American colleagues. Furthermore, unlike the United States, where social work departments were integrated into the university system and its practice required a master's degree, in France, social work schools remained outside of universities and could be accessed with a high school diploma. These structural factors coupled with the absence of casework in France help explain why American JDC employees negatively perceived French social work.

To what extent was the American criticism of French Jewish welfare grounded in the above-mentioned factors and to what extent was it an expression of cultural bias? Answering these questions requires exploring the degree to which French Jewish agencies had adopted the latest French social welfare trends. While my research on the Committee for Israelite Charity of Paris (Comité de bienfaisance Israélite de Paris, CBIP) on the eve of World War II suggests that this French Jewish agency's methods were indeed outdated, more research is needed to properly assess the level of integration of French Jewish organizations in larger French social work circles during the interwar period.[27] Several observations can, nevertheless, be made. Before the war, there were few professionally trained social workers in the French Jewish welfare agencies— and even fewer after the ravages of the Holocaust. Social work was not considered a prestigious profession nor was it encouraged if one had the opportunity to obtain university training.[28] Many of the individuals who worked in French Jewish aid agencies after the war discovered social work through rescue and resistance activities during the Occupation.

Wartime experiences trained a new generation of Jewish social workers. During the war, Vivette Samuel volunteered as a social worker in the Rivesaltes internment camp under the auspices of the OSE; she later hid children throughout France. After liberation, she obtained a French social work degree and became the director of the OSE's social service in 1954.[29] During the Occupation, Georges-Michel Salomon had worked for the American Aid Center, established by Varian Fry in Marseilles, and later for the southern branch of the UGIF. After the hostilities, COJASOR recruited him to direct its social service department.[30] Gaby Wolff Cohen led convoys of children to safety during the war in the clandestine branch of the OSE and later worked for the JDC's Office for France. Finally she moved to the FSJU, where she remained until her retirement.[31] Franceline Bloch was a member of the French Jewish Scouting movement's clandestine branch, the Sixième, before working for its Social Service for Youth (Service social des jeunes, SSJ) and later for the CBIP.[32] Ignace Fink helped fellow Jews in Nice during the war before becoming the executive director of COJASOR.[33] Denise Caraco Siekierski, who had worked clandestinely in the Sixième and the Service André to hide Jewish children during the war, returned to Marseilles at liberation. There she helped open the first postwar Jewish aid committee in December 1944, which became COJASOR's Marseilles branch.[34]

For the generation that came of age during World War II, whose professional aspirations had been destroyed by Vichy's antisemitic legislation, helping the least fortunate Jews after the war occurred in continuity with rescue and resistance activities, out of both solidarity and necessity. Gaby Wolff Cohen had hoped to become a doctor. Georges-Michel Salomon had aspired to teach French, Latin, and Greek. Vivette Samuel had obtained a degree in philosophy before volunteering to work in Rivesaltes in 1940. After the war, she asked, "What did the idea of God in Malebranche—the subject of my last report at the Sorbonne—matter to me? It was social action that interested me."[35] The need for personnel in Jewish aid organizations simply exceeded the number of individuals with training. By 1948, according to one estimate, there were approximately fourteen hundred individuals employed in French Jewish welfare organizations.[36] The need for childcare workers led both the OSE and OPEJ, two childcare organizations, to set up training programs for the staff of children's homes in 1945 and 1946. The JDC funded these initiatives, but French Jews, consumed with protecting the next generation, were equally concerned.[37]

Jewish welfare organizations were not unique in their reliance on untrained social workers. Scholarship on France during World War II shows the Vichy state depended on social workers to accomplish the goals of the National Revolution, leading to an unprecedented number of social workers, often untrained.[38] At liberation, a greater appreciation for the profession as well as new legislation passed in April 1946 that limited the practice of social work to individuals with state diplomas, helped lead to greater legitimacy. Those who had practiced without formal qualifications for a period of five years were invited to take an equivalency exam. According to one source, ten thousand individuals sought qualifications in this manner, indicating the high number of social workers who had been practicing without formal training.[39] The growth of the profession can also be measured by the number of schools. In 1938, there were twelve social service schools in France. By 1948, this number had increased to sixty-five.[40]

The relationship between French social work and French Jewish welfare certainly deserves greater scholarly attention. Nonetheless, these initial observations suggest, at least until future research proves otherwise, that JDC employees, when viewing French Jewish welfare, observed a world that had developed its own discourse on aid but had not incorporated the most recent French or Anglo-American theories of assistance. In the immediate postwar period, French Jewish aid organizations, like their non-Jewish counterparts, relied heavily on individuals who had not obtained formal social work training. Furthermore, the profound sense of loss shared by Jews in France after the Holocaust was not conducive to a distanced approach to welfare. On the contrary, many French social workers were keenly aware of their luck at having escaped deportation and sought to help fellow Jews, especially children, out of gratitude.[41] To the American observers who viewed needy Jews as clients, French Jewish welfare smacked of unprofessionalism.

American JDC employees thus set out to reform French Jewish welfare through professional training. As early as November 1945, they established a twelve-week social work training program, most likely at COJASOR, taught by a French social worker. The two-hour-long classes were "designed to give the fundamentals of casework in an effort to stimulate and develop their approach to the client group."[42] Under the direction of Laura Margolis, who replaced Arthur Greenleigh in 1946, the JDC increased its efforts in reforming welfare practices. The JDC assigned each French organization a JDC liaison and, when possible, organized training for French staff. COJASOR, for example, received technical assistance from two JDC employees in 1949 with the goal of improving its welfare standards. The JDC also tried to involve COJASOR's board but assessed that none of its members were "sufficiently close to the everyday work of COJASOR, or well enough informed as to good social work practices to be fully aware of the low standard of social work that has existed until now."[43] In early 1949, the JDC established staff trainings for COJASOR's employees, including sessions with a psychiatrist on psychological problems and client case studies led by JDC staff.[44] In addition, the JDC encouraged partnerships with other American Jewish organizations to help professionalize French Jewish welfare.

The National Council of Jewish Women: A Partner in Social Work Reform

The JDC's attempt to reform French Jewish welfare encouraged other American Jewish organizations to get involved, in particular the National Council of Jewish Women (NCJW), which was created in the United States in 1893. While ideologically close to the JDC, this organization did not share the same structure or mission. The JDC hired a relatively small number of professionals to distribute the donations of the United Jewish Appeal (UJA), while the NCJW functioned through local chapters and a network of Jewish women volunteers across the United States who donated their time and financial support to the organization's domestic and international projects. In 1927, this network included fifty-one thousand women.[45] By the 1960's, the organization had over a hundred thousand members.[46] The members of the NCJW often affiliated with the Reform movement, and many had husbands involved in the American Jewish Committee. As primarily middle- and upper-class women who rarely worked outside the home, NCJW members had the leisure time to mobilize strong social networks among American Jews to coordinate a personalized approach to aiding European Jews. The NJCW was therefore not in competition with the JDC; the former simply sought to complement the JDC program by reinforcing aid for women and children.

In 1945, for example, the NCJW coordinated a Ship-a-Box program, sending food, clothes, and toys to Europe. Children's homes in France began receiving such packages in 1945, placing American Jewish women in direct contact with the directors of the homes, who in turn provided them with clear details on the children's needs. In exchange, American Jewish women received thank-you notes from children, showing the personalized nature of this philanthropy.[47] While this form of aid was certainly heartwarming for those donating, accounts from France suggest a more complex story. A former child in one of the homes, Patricia Finaly wrote in her 1970 memoir that such correspondence was reserved for the "best elements"[48] in the children's homes. Trying to impress her "Godmother from the other side of the Atlantic," the young teenager wrote of her love of Mozart and literature ... including Henry Miller. In return, she received, "in the middle of several 'books,' a few sweaters that had most likely belonged to the first immigrants,"[49] which she promptly tried to sell at the flea market. Other French accounts suggest that American gifts warped the power dynamic between the educators and their young wards.[50] The JDC felt, perhaps for this reason, the package program created an unhealthy dependence upon American Jewish philanthropy.[51]

Figure 6.1. Children in an OSE home receiving packages sent by the National Council of Jewish Women in 1946. OSE collection of the Mémorial de la Shoah.

In 1946, the NCJW sent Ms. Gloria Wagner to France as its representative. Attesting to the close nature of the JDC-NCJW collaboration, the JDC provided her office space at their Office for France. From Paris, the NCJW developed two new programs: a home for "unattached" Jewish women in Paris and, of particular interest here, a scholarship program, initiated in 1946.[52] The NCJW's goal was to send European Jewish women to the United States to study welfare-related subjects at American universities. Selected students would study for one or two years in the United States in exchange for a two-year commitment to work for a Jewish welfare organization in their home country.[53] An estimated two hundred individuals throughout Europe, most of them women, received training in the United States through this program.[54] While less than twenty people benefited from this program in France, several key figures in postwar welfare were trained in this capacity.[55] The participants, recognized for their work in the Jewish resistance, didn't just study American social welfare methods; they also gained fluency in American culture and the English language, becoming cross-cultural translators upon their return. Well respected for their important work in the Jewish resistance, Simone Weil Lipman, Gaby Wolff Cohen, and Edith Odenwald Kremsdorf studied respectively at Tulane University, the University of California-Berkeley, and the University of Chicago before returning to France and working for the JDC. Once her obligation was fulfilled, Simon Weil Lipman returned to the United States, where she worked in the field of early childhood education.[56] Gaby Wolff Cohen and Edith Odenwald Kremsdorf went on to direct the social service department at the FSJU, where they both worked until retirement in the 1980s. After studying social work in Seattle and Pittsburgh, Franceline Bloch returned to France in 1950 and worked for the Jewish Scouts of France's service for teens, SSJ. From 1974 until her retirement, she directed the CBIP.[57] The National Council program helped train a new generation of French Jewish communal workers and in doing so shifted the male-dominated nature of French Jewish welfare by producing female experts who lent new credibility to American social work methods and contributed to their positive reception in France. The JDC certainly approved of this program, which fit into its larger goal of reforming Jewish welfare practices.

ESTABLISHING THE PAUL BAERWALD SCHOOL

Like the NCJW scholarship program, the idea to establish the Paul Baerwald School was part of the larger American Jewish response to reform European Jewish welfare. Once the project was accepted, the process of establishing the school began. The JDC recruited one of Herman Stein's former professors from the New York School of Social Work, Philip Klein, to assist Stein in the development of the school. Klein was well-known in both Jewish and larger welfare circles in the United States. He had helped the World Jewish Congress establish a social work training course at the New School for Social Research for American Jews who had volunteered to work in Europe after the war and had served as the research director for the 1949 White House Conference on Children and Youth.[58] Upon Klein's arrival in France, both men visited existing European social work schools to familiarize themselves with European curricula and make contact with members of the European social work establishment. This informal survey confirmed their desire to establish an independent school to respond to the specific needs of European Jews.[59]

Advisory committees for the school were established in spring and summer 1949 in Paris and New York, scrutinizing each detail of the Paul Baerwald School—from the school's letterhead, which was in "French, and some English," to the recruitment of faculty and students.[60] Each decision represented a strategy to reach a maximum number of young European Jews who would then become partisans of American social work methods and return to their local communities, where they would apply what they had learned. The goal, therefore, was not to crudely impose an American-centric vision on European Jews but to facilitate the appropriation of their social work methods by local groups. As one internal document explained, "The Paul Baerwald School is planned along the lines of professional social work schools in the United States [...]. Naturally, this does not mean that American methods are to be applied *in toto*, but rather that the students will be taught methods which are applicable in the respective countries."[61]

Aware that their efforts might be perceived as imperialist, the founders attempted to create a "European environment" for the school. Courses were not to be taught in English, and American textbooks and case studies were to be replaced with case studies from Europe, provided by JDC employees.[62] Because vibrant Jewish communities had survived in Belgium, Switzerland, and France, the school adopted French as its official language. France, due to its relatively large Jewish population, proximity to the JDC headquarters, and its rich network of Jewish aid organizations in which students could fulfill their fieldwork requirements, was selected as the host country.[63] While the faculty had been recruited for their American social work training and ability to speak French, Herman Stein felt the director of the school should be a European in order to envision "a long range institution" and create "more of the atmosphere of an indigenous school."[64] Accordingly, the school appointed Dr. Henry Selver, a German Jew who had found refuge in the United States in 1938, as its director. Selver had obtained a doctorate in philosophy from the University of Leipzig. After immigrating to the United States, he attended the New York School of Social Work and later became the director of a Jewish children's home in New York.[65] With his European background and American social work training, Selver fulfilled Stein's vision.

The school's founders decided the PBS would provide a one-year course of study based on the American social work curriculum, with an emphasis on theory, especially casework and practice, through a hands-on learning method called "supervision."[66] After an initial orientation period, students would have classes two days a week in casework, psychology, Jewish life and culture, community organizing, social sciences, social work administration, social security legislation, public health, and group work. The rest of their time would be spent in social service agencies under the supervision of PBS faculty. The PBS's mission was to bring casework and supervision to France and in doing so import American social work practices to Europe.

Once the school opened its doors, the institution took on a life of its own. Those involved with the school—its faculty and students, the European social work professionals who grew interested in its programs, and the French Jewish social service agencies that hosted PBS students for their fieldwork—would put the importation and adaptation efforts of the school's founders to the test. French Jews' enthusiastic response suggested the school's mission resonated with their needs.

Inside the Château de la Maye: A Crossroads of Postwar Jewish Life

"Amid landscaped gardens in the outskirts of this Paris suburb, the Château de la Maye stands as an ideal retreat from the world and its problems," wrote Henry Giniger, in the *New York Times* in December 1949. "Since October 11th, when the Paul Baerwald School of Social Work opened here, thirty-five young men and women have been figuratively tearing down the cloistering walls to transform the former seat of luxury into a center for the study of community welfare for ordinary people in need."[67] Actually, as oral history interviews reveal, the students of the PBS rather appreciated the "cloistering walls" of the château, which had been redecorated to accommodate its new inhabitants.[68] Along with the coordinated curtains and bedspreads in their rooms, students received full scholarships from the JDC for their year of study at the PBS.[69] In exchange, they committed to returning to their countries of origin or immigrating to Israel, where they would work in the field of Jewish social work for at least a year.[70] While the school had originally been conceived to help European Jews reconstruct after the Holocaust, students from Israel and North Africa were eligible for admission. In fact, Israel sent the most students (seven) to participate in the first student body. The rest came from Italy (five), Sweden (four), Germany (three), Belgium (three), Morocco (three), Greece (two), Tunisia (two), and Holland (one). Only five students came from France in the first year. Women made up the majority of the student body (twenty-eight of thirty-five students) and the average student age was just under thirty.[71]

The students were recruited from the various countries where the JDC operated and reflected accordingly the diversity of Jewish life in the postwar period. Mara Coen, a member of the first graduating class of the school, was from Mantua, Italy. Her father, a doctor, was president of the local Jewish community. During the war, Coen and her immediate family fled to Switzerland, but ten members of her family perished in Auschwitz. All of the family's belongings were confiscated. After the war the family returned to its empty home. Twenty-four-year-old Coen was working as her father's assistant when a representative from the JDC came to deliver packages to local Jews. Coen agreed to help the

Figure 6.2. The Château de la Maye, Versailles, December 1950. Private collection of Jacqueline Houri-Vignon.

woman but voiced her disagreement on the distribution method. Several weeks later, she was surprised to learn that her father had received a phone call from the JDC's representative in Italy asking if his daughter might be interested in attending the PBS.[72]

Another student from the 1950–1951 academic year shows an altogether different profile. A member of the Tunisian Jewish bourgeoisie, Jacqueline Houri had defied class norms by working for the OSE's medical clinic in the Jewish neighborhood of Tunis, which had opened in 1947. Two years into this experience, she learned of the opportunity to study social work at the PBS. After an interview with a member of the JDC in Tunis, and against the wishes of her parents for whom "Paris represented a lost girl,"[73] she took off for Versailles.

The diverse student body encountered the school's faculty members, who had, for the most part, been recruited in the United States. With French as the official language, Klein and Stein faced the challenge of finding francophone faculty with American social work experience. Using their contacts from the New York School of Social Work, they recruited, in addition to the school's director Henry Selver, Freda Goldsmith, a social worker from Detroit who had taught at

Tulane University; Fred Ziegellaub, a German Jewish refugee who, like Selver, had found refuge in the United States; Edith Schulhofer, another German Jewish refugee who had taught at Tulane University; Janet Siebold, a social worker from Minnesota who had worked for the Central British Fund for Jewish Relief; and Shirley Hellenbrand, as seen above, the graduate of the New York School of Social Work who had been working in a Jewish social service agency. Libby Meyer, a social worker from Ohio who had been working at the JDC Office for France, was hired to direct student fieldwork. All but one of the initial full-time faculty were Jewish, half were American born, and, significantly, all but one were women. All had experience in the American social work field. While each faculty member spoke some French, only Shirley Hellenbrand had fluent command of the language. At times, this led to comic situations in the classroom, especially involving Freda Goldsmith who mastered only the infinitive and present tenses and for whom "the past and future [tenses] didn't count."[74]

Klein, Stein, Selver, Hellenbrand, Schulhofer, and Ziegellaub had all been affiliated with the New York School of Social Work. This institution, the descendant of the New York School of Philanthropy, was affiliated with Columbia University in 1940 and represented the forefront of American social welfare. With six key staff members linked to the New York School of Social Work, the PBS could almost be seen as its European satellite. In addition to its full-time faculty, a certain number of American JDC staff members and French individuals, both Jewish and non-Jewish, were recruited to teach specific courses at the school.[75] For example, the JDC asked Isaac Pougatch to teach at the school. Born in Kiev in 1897, Pougatch came to France in 1923, where he became a Jewish educator. During the war, he worked with Jewish youth in homes run by the OSE and the French Jewish scouting movement before fleeing to Switzerland. Upon his return to France in 1946, Pougatch immediately set out to work with the children of deportees. In his 1980 autobiography, the educator echoed JDC employees' observations when he bemoaned the lack of trained personnel in the Jewish children's homes. Instead of childcare experts, the homes had hired "monitors" who "played cards while the children played on the footboards of trains that were moving at full speed."[76] According to Pougatch, in the hands of untrained staff, the children "imposed the law of the jungle."[77] Working with those he had cared for during the war, now young adults, Pougatch set out to train a new generation of childcare workers for the homes. Under the auspices of the Program for the Protection of Jewish Children (Oeuvre de protection des enfants juifs, OPEJ) and funded by the JDC, his training school in the Paris suburb of Plessis-Trévise opened in 1946 and ran for four years.[78] The fact the JDC hired Pougatch to teach at the PBS is significant and shows that the JDC

Figure 6.3. The faculty of the PBS, 1950–1951, including Shirley Hellenbrand (*back row, second from left*). Private collection of Jacqueline Houri-Vignon.

Figure 6.4. Freda Goldsmith teaching at the PBS, Versailles, August 1951. Private collection of Jacqueline Houri-Vignon.

respected local expertise. At the same time, however, the JDC did cut funding for the Plessis-Trévis school, right after it opened the PBS. Pougatch's presence in the PBS was thus slightly more complex than a simple recognition of his credentials. The JDC took with one hand and gave with the other, but Pougatch remained a faithful collaborator.[79]

As complex as these dynamics may have been, the close working relationship between students and faculty, as well as shared meals, allowed for an informal and intimate atmosphere. Henry Selver did not hesitate to tease and discipline students, telling one who had cut her long, curly hair that had he been her father, he would have spanked her.[80] When students missed the last train after spending an evening in Paris, Selver was furious, asking them how he could have accounted for them had the château caught on fire.[81] Like other faculty members, Selver kept in touch with the graduates, writing to them about the life of the school after their departure. "To our great regret, the unforgettable pin-up girls of PBS have not reappeared this year," he wrote to one group in Israel. "As a result, the *hora* is no longer danced quite as well."[82] Even Philip Klein, who as a consultant had limited contact with the students of the school, wrote to Henry Selver after returning to the United States, requesting news on "the Italian judge, the Belgian commy, my Moroccan beauty and some of the Israelites."[83] Such correspondence reveals the informality that allowed for a strong bond to develop between faculty and students—and of course, the gender dynamics of the period that enabled male professors to refer to their students as "pin-up girls." In this manner, the PBS may have resembled other small boarding schools.

At the same time, the PBS also represented a unique experiment in postwar Jewish life. The school, while physically in France, never obtained official accreditation. France was home to other Jewish schools but only the PBS brought American, Israeli, North African, and European Jews together, creating an international space where they could compare their cultures, opinions, and wartime experiences. Israel and the diaspora also coexisted, at times loudly. When an Israeli student bumped into Italian Mara Coen in the hall and was asked to apologize, Coen was told that "in our country, in Israel, we don't apologize."[84] Coen was furious.

What did it mean to be a "Jewish" social work school? Students and faculty debated this question publicly, and in private quarters, PBS faculty at times clashed with other JDC employees on the subject.[85] Contrary to some of the Jewish children's homes in France, the food at the PBS was kosher, and the cook, a Romanian who traumatized at least one North African student with her Eastern European recipes, used two sets of dishes for milk and meat. On

Figure 6.5. Celebrating Purim at the PBS, April 9, 1951. Private collection of Jacqueline Houri-Vignon.

Friday nights, a special dinner was held to celebrate Shabbat. Even though students dressed up for Purim and celebrated Chanukah, religious observance seems to have been an issue of contention. The one non-Jewish faculty member, Janet Siebold, clearly did not hesitate to participate in these discussions. Taking inspiration from the Quakers, she affirmed (along with other staff members) that participation in religious activities should be voluntary.[86] While she publicly voiced her opinion on some matters, she chose to complain privately about the Yiddish diminutive "le," which was sometimes added to her name (Janet-le) by a male colleague. In her opinion, this made her name sound too close to "genital."[87] With Selver, and to a lesser extent Klein and Stein, overseeing an almost entirely female faculty, this complaint may have also indicated that the women were annoyed with the condescension of their male superiors.

Beyond these tensions lay the more recent and complex issue of the Holocaust. Indeed, the school represented a crossroads of the postwar Jewish world that brought individuals who had lived in occupied Europe together with those who had spent the war years in relative safety. In spite of the proximity of this event, according to two former students, the Holocaust was not discussed openly among students.

This did not mean, however, that its aftermath was not felt. The faculty was certainly aware of the trauma among its students yet seems to have dealt with it on an individual basis instead of opening a public dialogue. Shirley Hellenbrand recalled an anecdote shared by a Dutch student who had been in a Nazi camp and had lost her parents. Overhearing one North African student consoling another with the words, "Oh, my little *chérie*, my little *chérie*, how you're suffering, my little one," the Dutch student sensed that she was not alone in her pain and asked what was wrong. The Dutch student was taken aback when she found out that her fellow student's tears were simply due to the arrival of her period.[88] The Dutch student and others turned to their professors for solace, expressing in private what could not be voiced publicly.[89] It is no wonder, in light of such different experiences, students formed cliques according to language, social class, and nationality.

Twenty-nine students celebrated their graduation from the Paul Baerwald School in August 1950. Their graduation ceremony helped Hellenbrand and other faculty members realize the significance of the school in the context of recent Jewish history:

> These were very needy students. I'll never forget, the first year at the graduation, it had just never—even though I had just spent a year with the students—it had not hit me sufficiently that this was an extraordinary experience. They had gone through the most terrible deprivations, and to be in a place where they were cared for and where they could talk about themselves and their problems, never mind what they learned about the clients.... And they cried, and we all cried. [...] The North African students had not been through the camps, nor the Swedish students, but there were many who had, and we just didn't realize the impact or the feeling.[90]

As the first year came to an end, students set out to apply their new training, with mixed results.

Life after Graduation: Disseminating American Social Work Methods?

The legacy of the school, in France and elsewhere, depended on the capacity of its graduates to apply their training in organizations that, for the most part, had not come into contact with American social work methods. Twelve of the students from the first graduating class made their way to Israel and only two remained in France. Mara Coen returned to Italy in the fall of 1950 eager to apply her newly acquired skills. She soon confronted what many PBS graduates in Europe also had to face: JDC budget cuts had made hiring them practically impossible. Unable to find a position in her native

Figure 6.6. Students from the class of 1950–1951 with Shirley Hellenbrand (*second from left*). Private collection of Jacqueline Houri-Vignon.

Mantua, Coen went to Rome, where she accepted the directorship of the Jewish community's longstanding orphanage, located just across the river from the synagogue. After her fieldwork experience in a French Jewish children's home, Coen was appalled to learn that in Rome, the orphanage locked its doors to keep its wards from escaping. The children, many of whom had been abandoned by their parents as a result of poverty, were forced to wear uniforms to distinguish them from the other children in the community. Coen felt completely unprepared for the task before her yet set out to update the orphanage's practices. She gave adolescents the right to visit family on Sundays, and when a shipment of clothing arrived from the United States, she allowed each child to choose two outfits—one for Shabbat and the other for the rest of the week. Furious, the rabbi complained to Coen that he could no longer tell the orphans from the other children. Mara Coen thanked him for the compliment.[91] One sees from this example that the Italian children benefitted from a multifaceted cultural transfer; Coen most likely learned as much from the child-centered pedagogy in French children's homes as she did in her classes at the PBS. The fact Coen enthusiastically applied the new methods, both American and French, leads one to question the "American imperialism" of the school.

Three classes followed in the footsteps of the first graduates, and approximately one hundred students would obtain their degrees. In 1953, the JDC decided to close the residential program of the PBS. The reasons for its closure were multiple. First, the school had always been considered temporary. Second, soon after the school had opened its doors, it became obvious that Cold War tensions would limit the ability of Eastern European students to attend. These reasons led one JDC official to observe that "for Europe, the school has come two or three years too late."[92] Finally, and perhaps most importantly, Israel was providing the lion's share of the school's students and professional opportunities for its young graduates. Negotiations to transfer the school to Israel began as early as 1950, intensified from 1954 to 1957, and finally led to the reopening of the PBS under Israeli auspices in 1958 at the Hebrew University in Jerusalem.[93] The PBS faculty remained active by providing in-service trainings in Jewish welfare organizations throughout Europe, North Africa, and Israel until the late 1950s. This last chapter of the school's European life proved particularly important to its mission to change social work practices in France.

THE PAUL BAERWALD SCHOOL: A LASTING INFLUENCE?

At first glance, the Paul Baerwald School seems to have had little influence on French Jewish welfare. As seen above, only two students from the first graduating class remained in France after their schooling. Only five students from metropolitan France enrolled for the 1950–1951 school year and only three in the following school year.[94] The total number of (metropolitan) French graduates of the PBS was limited to approximately a dozen, to which one can add the North African students of the school who settled in France in the 1950s and 1960s. As seen above, JDC budget cuts and decreasing Jewish welfare needs forced agencies to downsize, making it difficult to integrate the new graduates into the existing social service network. Furthermore, postwar changes in French legislation required that individuals practicing social work hold a state-accredited diploma. Even though it was well aware of this regulation, the administration of the Paul Baerwald School had not obtained accreditation.[95] The graduates of the school were therefore unemployable outside of French Jewish social service agencies.

These difficulties, while nonetheless real, should not mask the larger influence of the school in France. Many employees of Jewish welfare organizations showed an interest in American social work methods and would have attended the school had their finances allowed it.[96] Furthermore, the school came into being at the same time as the Unified Jewish Social Fund (FSJU) and was seen by the JDC as a means of training this organization's future leaders. Laura

Margolis had managed to involve the FSJU in the selection of the French candidates for the PBS,[97] and the school was clearly well-known among French Jewish leadership. The guest list of its inauguration included over 140 individuals from French Jewish life.[98] Most importantly, French Jewish aid agencies, such as COJASOR and the OSE, were an integral part of the PBS because they provided fieldwork placements for its students. From 1949 to 1953, at least three times a week, these agencies opened their doors to the students and faculty of the PBS. Their staff thus grew familiar with the faculty and the teachings of the school. Some attended events at the Château de la Maye. In addition, faculty members took advantage of opportunities to train French Jewish communal workers. In 1951 and 1952, Freda Goldsmith taught a course for members of the Association of Jewish Social Workers,[99] while Fred Ziegellaub taught a course for future teachers at the Alliance.[100] When the PBS residential program closed in 1953, the contact between the former faculty and Jewish aid agencies actually intensified. With negotiations underway to move the school to Israel, the focus of its faculty shifted to providing social work training to Jewish organizations.

The In-Service Trainings of the Paul Baerwald School

In fall 1953, PBS faculty was sent in different directions with the hope of disseminating American social welfare concepts and practices directly to Jewish welfare agencies. Fred Ziegellaub and Libby Meyer went to Germany and Austria. Janet Siebold, Freda Goldsmith, and two more recent recruits, Debby Miller and Dorothy Beers, traveled to North Africa.[101] Shirley Hellenbrand, as the member of the PBS faculty most fluent in French, was reassigned to work closely with the organizations that assisted Jews in the Paris region. In 1953 and 1954, she conducted seventeen in-service trainings at COJASOR and thirteen at the Social Service for Youth, an agency that specialized in helping Jewish teens. In addition, she led seventeen seminars for the supervisors of the major Jewish aid agencies, which put her in contact with the CBIP, OSE, OPEJ, and the JDC's Office for France. Over the 1954–1955 period, Hellenbrand continued to work directly with agencies by conducting a seminar at the CBIP, attended by eight individuals; led a seminar on child placement for eleven staff members from the OSE and OPEJ; and continued working with nine supervisors of the major aid agencies, many of whom had attended her seminar the previous year. In addition to Hellenbrand's seminars, the JDC recruited a French psychologist, Dr. Claude Veil, to teach a seminar on "applied principles in dynamic psychology," which was attended by individuals from multiple agencies.[102] Hellenbrand continued her work with Parisian Jewish agencies until her return to the United States in 1956. While the JDC attempted to replace her, it appears that Hellebrand's departure effectively ended the PBS intervention in French Jewish aid agencies.[103]

According to Henry Selver, director of the PBS, in 1955, Parisian Jewish agencies employed approximately forty social workers, twenty-three of whom with no formal social work training.[104] The PBS, through its in-service trainings, was able to introduce American social work concepts in these organizations and encourage the emergence of a new professional identity among their employees. This fit nicely with the larger goals of the FSJU, which, by the mid-1950s, was slowly taking over the JDC's fundraising and planning role. Like the JDC, the FSJU advocated greater efficiency and coordination in welfare, aiming to establish a collective enterprise as opposed to a chaotic ensemble of individual agencies. As seen in chapter 4, this was not a coincidence but largely the fruit of a Franco-American collaboration.

The FSJU supported the PBS in-service trainings. In summer 1954, FSJU representative Tito Cohen wrote to Henry Selver, reporting that the groups that had participated in Hellenbrand's trainings had unanimously requested their continuation the following year.[105] In addition to the FSJU, members of the Association of Jewish Social Workers also expressed their enthusiasm for the trainings: "As much as for the training for Supervisors as for the work done at Cojasor and SSJ, the curiosity, interest and at times juvenile enthusiasm that most of our colleagues displayed in order to renew the spirit and methods of their work fully justified, in our opinion, the efforts undertaken; the number enrolled and strong attendance of Dr. Weil's [sic] course, so important that we were the first surprised, confirm this point of view, and at the same time, we notice a clear evolution in the level of social work."[106]

Like the FSJU, the Association of Jewish Social Workers requested that the PBS continue its seminars the following year.

After 1949, and especially from 1953 to 1956, the PBS endeavored to reform the practices of French Jewish aid agencies. There was indeed an exchange between the PBS and French Jewish social workers. Yet did contact with the PBS really influence practices inside the aid agencies?

Assessing the Influence: The Committee for Israelite Charity of Paris (CBIP) and the Paul Baerwald School

The Committee for Israelite Charity of Paris (CBIP), the oldest French Jewish welfare organization, created in 1809, provides an opportunity to analyze the changes that occurred as a result of its encounter with the JDC's Paul Baerwald

School. Indeed, this organization began its postwar reconstruction as early as October 1944,[107] resuming its previous methods of aiding the "poor *Israélite*." In the aftermath of the Holocaust, the CBIP was still referring to those it helped as "the assisted" (*assistés*) and more often as "the unfortunate" (*les malheureux*). While the CBIP had hired a social worker to coordinate aid requests, the CBIP's treasurer, a volunteer named Madame Heilbronner, was in charge of conducting investigations on those who made them. Furthermore, the CBIP still made use of the services of three investigators who assisted the CBIP on a volunteer basis to detect fraud.[108] The FSJU's Tito Cohen recalled his efforts in the early 1950s to persuade the CBIP to abandon what he considered the outdated practice of daily handouts, in which those in need queued up each morning in exchange for some money or a voucher.[109] The agency did not keep records on these individuals.

In spite of the apparent continuity between the pre and postwar period in the CBIP's methods and aid philosophy, the institution's archives show a slow shift toward professionalization at the end of the 1940s—yet without much criticism of the past. CBIP documents used the term "social service" in 1949, at which time the organization hired its first professionally trained social worker. The CBIP described the activities of its social service in 1948 in only five pages and in 1950 only three pages. However, in 1951 the organization produced a sixty-two-page report that described in detail both the activities and the methods in which aid was provided. Here as well, the professionalization of the CBIP coexisted with its traditional aid philosophy. Though home visits were now being conducted by paid staff instead of female volunteers (*dames patronesses*), the goal of these visits was still to detect fraud.[110]

The recruitment of Odette Schwob in 1953, a French Jewish social worker with a state diploma who had previously served as the director of the JDC's nursing school, seems to have opened a new chapter for the CBIP. As department head, Schwob instigated the practice of keeping individual case files on the those who sought assistance. As seen above, until this moment, aid appears to have been provided to those lining up for the daily handout, without a long-term plan. In other words, casework in its most rudimentary form, which requires keeping records on those assisted, was not being practiced until Schwob's arrival.

The CBIP was already on the road to updating its methods when it began receiving in-service trainings from the PBS, a fact that certainly facilitated the acceptance of the American methods. Schwob participated in Hellenbrand's training for supervisors in 1953 and 1954, and in 1954 and 1955, Hellenbrand conducted a weekly seminar within the agency that Schwob also attended. This training appears to have provided Schwob with the support, and perhaps the vocabulary, to look critically at the CBIP's past. A report on the CBIP's activities in 1954, most likely written by Schwob in 1955, reveals a new commitment to reforming the CBIP's methods and aid philosophy. Entitled "From Charity to Social Service,"[111] its author openly criticized the home visits of her predecessors, who used moral criteria to divide the poor into "worthy" and "unworthy" categories. In a plea for objective criteria, she affirmed that "the social worker does not investigate the morality of the client, but the facts of the situation in which he finds himself."[112] The report shows a shift in language: instead of referring to the "assisted" or "unfortunate," it used the term *client*. The influence of the PBS could also be seen in the author's decision to illustrate her report with client case studies, as did Hellenbrand in her seminars, to illustrate the CBIP's new working methods. The CBIP's modernization process even extended into the physical arrangement of its office. The report proudly mentioned a new improvement that allowed for client confidentiality: "tiny offices that we call 'boxes' or 'isolation rooms;' where social workers receive clients, who can talk to them with an open heart, without fear of being overheard by a stranger. It seems, one could say, as normal [*banal*] as it is natural. And yet, this wasn't always the case."[113]

With the CBIP's "clients" and "boxes" and a team of five social workers, including one PBS graduate, the JDC's school had clearly influenced the practices within the agency. Nonetheless, Hellenbrand expressed skepticism on how these changes were being made, noting the CBIP obtained "boxes" only because COJASOR had them—yet had found it too expensive to put doors on them.[114] Schwob, who had obtained French social work training before the war, eagerly participated in the programs offered by the PBS. However, in Hellenbrand's opinion, her French training and long experience in the profession "hampered her ability to learn new concepts." Schwob apparently distinguished herself from her colleagues, who "accept[ed] 'JDC methods as gospel truth' because they had no prior training in social work."[115] While the facts show an Americanization of practices, Hellenbrand's remarks suggest this was not a seamless, conflict-free process.

The most radical step toward reforming the social work practices at the CBIP occurred in 1963. As the agency that had developed a specialization in French Jews, and to a certain extent North African Jews, the CBIP had played an increasingly important role in the early 1960s as a result of the Algerian war.[116] This event placed heightened scrutiny on the CBIP's working methods and prompted its directors to make two unprecedented decisions. In June 1963, the CBIP dismissed Odette Schwob, who was three years away from retirement. Accused of resisting the modernization of its social service, and the casework method in particular, Schwob fought her dismissal by writing to

CBIP president Alain de Rothschild.[117] To defend herself, Schwob referred to her training by the Paul Baerwald School, specifying that she now had two PBS graduates in her department.

Despite protests, Schwob was replaced by Françoise Boudard, a non-Jewish French social worker in her thirties who had been teaching at the Ecole départementale de service social de la Préfecture de la Seine. In addition to her state diploma, Boudard had studied casework in an informal working group in Paris with Dr. Myriam David[118] and later at the University of Chicago. Not surprisingly, just as the NCJW had sponsored young European Jewish women to study social welfare in the United States, the France-Atlantic Association (Association France-Atlantique) sent Boudard and thirty-six other French social workers to study in the United States from 1948 through 1958.[119]

Before leaving for the United States in 1957, Boudard had met Vivette Samuel, a fellow member of the National Association of Social Workers (Association nationale des assistantes sociales, ANAS). As mentioned above, Samuel, had obtained formal training in social work after the war and was working as the director of the OSE's social service department. Samuel clearly saw in Boudard a colleague who could help modernize French Jewish welfare. In 1962, Samuel introduced Boudard to her husband, FSJU director Julien Samuel, and his colleague Adam Loss.[120] One year later, the FSJU leadership explored the possibility of Boudard taking over the CBIP's social service department. The CBIP decision to dismiss Odette Schwob thus originated, at least partially, with the FSJU, including two young women who had studied in the United States thanks to the National Council's exchange program, Gaby Wolff Cohen and Edith Kremsdorf.[121]

Schwob's colleagues at the CBIP were informed of her dismissal (and Boudard's arrival) in September 1963. They immediately protested and sent a petition, signed by twelve individuals, to the CBIP's directors. Schwob's long career and imminent retirement were seen by her staff as valid reasons for maintaining her in her position. These individuals also explicitly stated their dismay over the fact the CBIP had hired a non-Jew to direct its social service department. "Even though we social workers are from different origins, we all deplore the fact that we are no longer supervised by a Jewish head social worker," they wrote.[122] In spite of the protests, the CBIP maintained its position, placing professional qualifications above religious ties.

Along with its dismissal of Schwob, the CBIP underwent another major change to account for its new allegiance to the modern social service. In August 1963, it officially discarded the name it had held for over a hundred years. Thereafter, it was known as the Israelite Social Action Fund of Paris, (Caisse d'action sociale israélite de Paris, CASIP).[123]

From "charity" to "social action," the evolution of the CBIP-CASIP shows a desire for change surpassing the weight of tradition. French Jews who initiated and carried out the changes were clearly interested in reforming their own practices, providing fertile ground for the JDC's importation project. One sees a new generation of communal workers, some of whom trained in the United States, joining forces with the JDC. Still, the JDC's influence was powerful and felt on multiple levels. Its Paul Baerwald School trained social workers for the CBIP and later provided seminars to further disseminate its methods to its staff. As seen in chapter 4, the JDC was the main instigator behind the FSJU. As the latter developed under French Jewish leadership, it sought to control the quality of services in Jewish welfare agencies and exercised pressure on the CBIP. Finally, American Jewish organizations were also actively training a new generation of communal workers. The NJCW program to send young Jewish women to study in the United States produced new advocates for reform. The changes that occurred at the CBIP in 1963 are in large part a result of the JDC's multitiered influence. These changes were also taking place elsewhere. Under the direction of Vivette Samuel, the OSE hired its first trained social worker in 1950, and by 1963, its staff included nine trained social workers. In addition to seminars conducted by the PBS in 1954, it developed a training program for its staff. As of 1963, all of its social workers had training in casework and Samuel was using the terms *client* and *affective neutrality* to describe the work of her organization.[124] As I will show in the next section, one must look beyond Jewish circles to understand why French Jews were so open to these American ideas. They were not the only ones looking across the Atlantic.

The Paul Baerwald School and the larger field of European Social Work: "Good for the Jews"[125]

The establishment of the PBS corresponded to a particularly important moment in the history of French social work, considered its "golden age."[126] The period marked the institutionalization of the social work profession in France. The 1945 social security legislation made new public benefits available that provided social workers with an unprecedented role as gatekeepers. The National Association for Social Workers with State Diplomas, which would later become known as the ANAS, was established in December 1944. As seen above, a 1946 law established the requirement of a state diploma to exercise the profession and also protected client–social worker confidentiality. Finally, in 1949, the ANAS established a code of ethics that became largely accepted among social workers.

In addition to these changes on the national level, an international approach to social work emerged in Europe in the aftermath of World War II.[127] The newly created United Nations established a technical assistance program for social professions in Europe. The first cycle of courses took place in Paris from November 28 through December 10, 1949, corresponding with the first months of the PBS.[128] The United Nations organized seminars in English and French throughout Europe during the 1950s.[129] Like the PBS, these seminars were designed to disseminate the methods of casework and supervision, and members of the French ANAS—as well as members of another recently created professional association, the Federation of French Social Workers (Fédération française des travailleurs sociaux)—attended many of them.[130] Other international initiatives, such as the first International Congress of Schools of Social Work took place in Paris in the summer of 1950 and was attended by PBS faculty and members of the ANAS.[131] In addition to the United Nations' efforts, scholarships were provided to young women to study social work in the United States by the France-Atlantic Association, as seen above in the case of Françoise Boudard.[132] Upon returning to France, some of these social workers sought to apply their American experience to France and along with those who attended the UN seminars formed several small working groups, including Dr. Myriam David's, which met regularly in her home on the rue Pergolèse in Paris in the early 1950s.[133] The creation of the JDC's Paul Baerwald School therefore corresponded to a period in which French social workers were seeking professional legitimacy, inspiration, and qualifications from abroad.

Beyond the changes the PBS inspired within French Jewish agencies, it left a lasting impact on the larger field of French social work. Scholars on French social work recognize the PBS as one of several international influences that helped transform French social work practices in the postwar period.[134] The archives of the PBS, French social work publications, and oral histories allow me to explore in greater detail the conditions under which the encounter between the PBS and French social work took place.[135] Why did French social workers take an interest in the PBS? What motivated the PBS faculty members— who were paid to train a future generation of Jewish social workers—to redefine their mission to include European social work circles, often in their free time?

Interestingly, from its inception the PBS sought out European social welfare circles and did so by contacting other American institutions in France. Indeed, when the PBS founders were looking for part-time faculty who were familiar with American social welfare, they turned to John Grant of the Rockefeller Foundation and Irving Fasteau, the Welfare director of the American Embassy, for suggestions.[136] Rockefeller fellowship recipients who had studied in the

United States, such as Dr. Robert Henri Hazemann, the director of public health for the Seine Department, and the above mentioned Dr. Myriam David were interviewed by the PBS administration.[137] In addition to their search for local faculty, Stein and Klein, as we have seen, toured European social work schools in order to obtain a better understanding of how social work was being taught in Europe. This helped spread the word that an American social work school was indeed going to open in Versailles in fall 1949.

Once operational, the PBS immediately received solicitations from European social workers and their institutions, seeking greater information on American social work methods, especially casework. While the French government expressed an interest in the school as early as June 1949, requesting that several scholarships be made available for non-Jewish students, it was Belgian social work professionals who proved most enthusiastic.[138] In November 1949, Mademoiselle Racine and Madame Madison of the Institut d'études sociales de l'état, based in Brussels, visited the school. This encounter sparked a realization among the PBS faculty, who observed that "European social workers are fascinated and frightened by casework. They have considerable awareness of its potential helpfulness but at the same time are awed by what it will demand in terms of personnel, training, etc."[139] PBS faculty members were becoming aware of an exciting new possibility: in addition to helping reconstruct Jewish communities, they could also contribute to reforming European social work.

Influencing the larger field of European social work was clearly outside the established PBS mission. The question of accepting non-Jewish students was raised when a Belgian social work school asked that a member of its faculty spend six-months at the PBS. This provoked debate among JDC staff members and PBS faculty, pitting ethnic allegiances against professional identities. The PBS Paris advisory committee debated this request at the end of the school's first academic year. The issue was complicated due to the limited number of scholarships; accepting a non-Jewish social worker would have to come "at the expense of a Jewish student."[140] Furthermore, American Jews had donated their money for the reconstruction of European Jewish life, not European social work, and held the JDC accountable. Emphasizing their concern for Jewish reconstruction, JDC staff argued against accepting the non-Jewish student.[141] PBS faculty, however, unanimously supported the candidacy, arguing that the presence of a non-Jewish student would allow the school to contribute to the larger field of social work, which would in turn improve its overall reputation and opportunities for its graduates. Furthermore, they noted, a non-Jewish student could facilitate the entry of the PBS into non-Jewish social service agencies for fieldwork placements. These arguments were apparently convincing, and Jeanne Massart, the school's first Catholic student, arrived from Brussels for the 1950–1951 school year. In 1951 and 1952, a colleague from Liège, Rosy Goldsmidt, followed suit.

The school's deepening relationship with Belgian social workers and the idea of extending the influence of the PBS beyond the contours of the Jewish community clearly exhilarated PBS faculty. This inspired Henry Selver and Fred Ziegellaub to write a memorandum in November 1950 arguing for the creation of an American school of social work in Europe. Using the PBS as evidence such a school could be successfully implemented, the proposed school would gather European students of all nationalities and religions under the same roof to study American social work methods. Educated in Europe, they would adapt their training to the European context with less difficulty than if they had attended an American university. Finally, the authors noted that American social work methods "unquestionably belong to those contributions which America can usefully bring to other countries."[142] Catering to the culture of the Cold War and the Marshall Plan, the authors explained how American social work could "influence greatly the development of a democratic spirit in the communal life of other countries."[143] "To express it in political terms," they argued, "American social work methods can make in the area of social welfare as essential a contribution, particularly among the groups most distrustful of America, as material aid in the economic sphere."[144] Both the recipient and the outcome of this memorandum remain unknown. While one can assume this project did not gather the necessary support, it shows to what extent JDC employees had integrated the larger Marshall Plan language of the moment into their own vocabulary. Convinced of the power of their methods and the success of the PBS model, these American Jewish social workers had come to Europe to help their brethren: both Jews and fellow social workers.

Belgian social workers, who facilitated the access of their French colleagues to this new resource, matched the excitement of the PBS faculty. In May 1951, ANAS organized a weekend retreat in the French town of Draveil for twenty Belgian and twenty French social workers at the request of their Belgian colleague Monsieur Nihon, director of the Ecole ouvrière supérieure de Bruxelles. The weekend training, led by PBS faculty, was dedicated to the exploration of casework.[145] This weekend seems to have definitively awakened the interest of ANAS in the PBS. Several months later, the vice president of ANAS, Jeanne Thro, enrolled at the PBS for the 1951–1952 academic year. In addition to receiving a full scholarship from the school, Thro obtained a monthly loan from her colleagues to make up for the loss of her salary. A group of seventy social workers from ANAS toured the school in May 1952.[146] PBS faculty led another weekend retreat in Draveil that summer, and in the fall, ANAS requested that they teach a course on casework to forty or fifty members of the association.[147]

The course, organized under the auspices of ANAS and the Ecole nationale de la santé and attended by the heads of various Parisian social services, took place during the last year of the PBS residential program, in 1952 and 1953.[148] In addition to their teaching activities, PBS faculty supervised social workers from Belgium, France, and Italy.[149]

The encounter between PBS faculty and members of European social work circles led to a number of publications in the leading European social work journals. *Le service social*, published in Belgium, featured articles by Fred Ziegellaub and former students Vania Frydman and Jeanne Massart in 1952.[150] Jeanne Thro reported on her studies at the PBS in *Informations sociales*, published in France in 1953.[151] This journal dedicated an entire issue to the Paul Baerwald School in February 1953.[152] Concurrently, an article on the PBS written by Fred Ziegellaub appeared in *Travail social*, published by the French Federation of Social Workers.[153] These publications, in addition to further disseminating the teachings of the PBS, provided the PBS faculty with tangible evidence of their contribution to European social work, allowing them to prove to the JDC their efforts to influence the field had not been in vain. After the publication of an issue of *Informations sociales* in 1954 that referred to the PBS, Henry Selver wrote to a JDC colleague who had opposed the acceptance of non-Jewish students at the school, "I feel that the reference to the PBS by the leading French social work association makes their appreciation of the PBS much more a matter of public record than any number of letters they have written us, and there are quite a number of them and all in the same vein of asking for more of the same good thing they have received from us so far. [...] As in the past, I maintain that our cooperation with the non-Jewish social workers in France and in Belgium is 'good for the Jews.'"[154]

The closure of the residential program at the PBS in the fall of 1953 limited the interaction between its faculty and European social workers. As seen above, the school's faculty had now become responsible for conducting in-service trainings to Jewish aid organizations throughout Europe and North Africa. Thus, when the ANAS president wrote to Selver in 1953 asking that Hellenbrand's course on casework be continued, Selver was obliged to decline her request.[155] As the school slowly faded from the European scene, French social workers remained determined in their efforts to explore the casework method. In 1953, the Ecole de service social de la région du Nord in Lille hired PBS faculty member Freda Goldsmith to teach a course on casework. In 1956, she began teaching at the Ecole des surintendantes. While it is not clear at what point her affiliation with the JDC ended, Goldsmith remained in France until at least 1966, at which time Georges-Michel Salomon, the head of the service social at COJASOR, replaced her in Lille.[156]

The latent functions behind the encounter between European social work and the PBS also deserve consideration. French social workers, after seeking professional legitimacy in the immediate postwar period through new legislation, sought to update their methods by looking abroad. At the time, few individuals were aware that casework had been introduced in France during the interwar period only to be hindered by the outbreak of World War II.[157] Therefore in the late 1940s and early 1950s, those in France perceived casework as a new method. It may have inspired "passion, ambiguity and resistance"[158] among French social workers, yet from 1950 through 1968, casework nonetheless became the dominant working model in French social services. Becoming an expert in casework was therefore a means of asserting one's place in a developing profession. This created an "elite" and "internal hierarchy" within the French social work profession, offering French social workers greater status in their field.[159]

But why did the faculty of the PBS have such a strong desire to transmit their methods to European social workers? What motivated their "quasi-evangelical intent to disseminate the American principles of social work service and of casework in particular?"[160] The PBS faculty was possibly frustrated with what at times appeared to be a lack of interest in their message among European Jewish welfare organizations. Furthermore, the PBS faculty clearly had a vision of European Jewish reconstruction that differed from their JDC colleagues, as seen in the debates over the composition of the student body. A speech made by Henry Selver at a conference for JDC country directors in 1950 suggests that the PBS faculty was trying to prove something to their JDC colleagues:

> I need not describe what problems, resistances, misunderstandings and indifference a school had to face when it set out to build in France a social work training program patterned after American ideas and experiences, mobilize resources, and find cooperating agencies and people. [...] Beyond [the cooperation received from Jewish agencies], we have been able to get some French non-Jewish agencies sufficiently interested in our work to open their doors to our students. There are in France a number of progressive people in our profession who do not necessarily suspect that everyone and everything coming from the States is an out-growth of the [sic] Dollar Imperialism.[161]

Selver shows here a keen awareness of the "dollar imperialism," which would hinder the successful implementation of the PBS methods. In reaching out to European social workers, Selver and other PBS faculty seemed to be suggesting that Franco-American tensions, and Jewish and non-Jewish differences, could be overcome. Though postwar optimism kindled dreams of universalism, the PBS faculty was also probably just happy to escape the complicated relationship between the JDC and French Jewish welfare organizations.

CONCLUSION

Two visions of postwar Jewish welfare emerge here. According to American sources, after World War II, French Jewish welfare agencies were full of untrained and politically biased personnel who had no real methodology for helping Jewish survivors. French sources temper this critique, highlighting the important role of the Jewish resistance in forming a new generation of French Jewish communal workers yet confirm that professionally trained social workers were indeed a rarity in postwar French Jewish welfare organizations. For the JDC, this lack of social work expertise stood in the way of the long-term reconstruction of European Jewish life. The National Council of Jewish Women's scholarship program and the JDC's Paul Baerwald School were designed as solutions.

Internationalism and diversity characterized life at the Château de la Maye. The PBS represented a rare experiment in the postwar Jewish experience because it created a space where Jews from both sides of the Atlantic *and* the Mediterranean could exchange ideas, debate, and learn together. At the PBS, Jews from Israel bumped into (literally) Jews from the diaspora. For these reasons, the "château years" of the PBS can serve as a microcosm for the study of the issues and tensions that characterized postwar Jewish life. Indeed, the Holocaust formed a dividing line among the members of the school, for both faculty and students. Those who had suffered directly lived among those who had spent the war years in relative safety. This inequality, and perhaps the sheer pain of the events, made public discussions of the Holocaust taboo. The presence of the emerging state of Israel could also be felt; Israel sent a large number of students to the school, welcomed the school's graduates in its growing social service network, and provided a new home for the institution in 1958.

Like Maud Mandel, who wrote that "the Baerwald School, for all its organizers' good intentions, was unable to change understandings and practices of social work throughout Europe," most accounts of the PBS provide a mixed assessment of the school's impact.[162] This chapter on the American efforts to reform French Jewish social work helps explain Mandel's somewhat paradoxical observation that even though the PBS didn't deliver on its promises, postwar welfare nonetheless professionalized. As for Mandel's charge of cultural imperialism, evidence here suggests a more complex interaction between the American organization and its European hosts that facilitated a cultural transfer.

By focusing on the importation process and not only on its outcome, I am able to show the PBS's founders were aware of a central paradox: the JDC was asking European Jews to take charge of their lives and communities yet wanted them to use American methods to do so. Both in internal discussions and publicly, the school's founders used caution when describing the American orientation of their school, and when planning, they took measures to avoid an overly American environment. As seen in the establishment of the FSJU, PBS founders took pains to avoid the accusation of American imperialism. In both cases, larger tensions surrounding the American presence in postwar Europe carried over into Jewish communities.

The PBS faculty's awareness of the perils of Americanization helped the school leave a lasting impact on Jewish and non-Jewish social work. The slow evolution of the most traditional French Jewish welfare organization, the CBIP, serves as an example. The CBIP abandoned its "charity work" to become a "social service."[163] Even though the change of its name from Comité de bienfaisance (Charity Committee) to Caisse d'action sociale (Social Action Fund) occurred almost ten years after the PBS intervention, the employees of this French organization were still referring to the school and its teachings to justify this choice.

Jews in France, of course, were central to the importation process. Part of the reason for the PBS's success was that it coincided with a larger movement of professionalization within European social work. This made both French Jews and the European social work establishment receptive to the American school, providing a rare example of the JDC's influence in France breaking out of Jewish circles. For French social workers, the PBS provided new methods and a source of professional legitimacy at a crucial moment of transition. Social work historians fittingly recognize the school's influence on welfare practices in France.

The American Jewish presence allowed for interactions, analyzed here for the first time, that brought French Jewish welfare agencies closer to the larger field of French social work. Indeed, through the PBS, larger European social work circles learned more about the flourishing network of Jewish social services in France; PBS students were eventually able to fulfill their fieldwork requirements in non-Jewish agencies. Jewish social workers like Georges-Michel Salomon and Vivette Samuel, after their wartime and postwar experience in Jewish aid networks, went on to assume a leadership role in the larger social work field in France.[164] The PBS certainly had a role in their integration, lending prestige to Jewish social workers and validating their presence in the national social work arena. With its strong network of Jewish social services, attention to professionalism, and increased connection to general welfare circles, French Jewish life began to more closely resemble Jewish life in the United States.

CONCLUSION

When the hour of Liberation rang and the devastating ascent from hell began, we were witnesses to a harrowing reverse exodus. Dozens of millions of isolated Jews, dispersed in the countryside and the *maquis* made their way back towards the large cities of the provinces and Paris, towards their pillaged and confiscated homes, looking for lost relatives and friends, searching for news, for a reason to live. What would this wretched, drifting flock have become without the JDC's providential omnipresence? Indeed, this presence wouldn't only save these individuals on the verge of despair from physical downfall, but, a major fact from a historical point of view, it would return to these bewildered beings who had lost all contact with Judaism, the comforting sense of belonging to a large spiritual family which, through crises and catastrophes had maintained its cohesion and had come to help them. [...] However, when the renewal efforts will have come to fruition, the future historian of French Jewish life will not forget to emphasize the determinant part of the JDC in this metamorphosis that, in twenty years and despite many crises—created from a multitude of bewildered victims a large pilot community in Europe.[1]

THESE REFLECTIONS ON THE ROLE of the Joint Distribution Committee (JDC) in France, written two decades after the war by French Jewish communal leader Claude Kelman, suggest that this organization did much more than supply funds to help French Jews meet their material needs after the Holocaust. When one takes a closer look at Kelman's statement, the JDC's influence in France becomes even more evident—not only did this organization inspire Kelman's observations, it actually created and sponsored the journal in which he wrote them. This casts Kelman's observations in a different light

CONCLUSION 213

and points to the complex relationship that linked American and French Jews after the Holocaust. Their relationship was symbiotic yet unequal. It was an expression of solidarity yet punctuated with conflict and, at times, moments of synergy. French Jewish reconstruction was not only a French affair between its Jewish inhabitants and the Republic. It was also a transnational process shaped in large part by American Jewish organizations and individuals.

This study has sought to understand the ambiguities characterizing this Franco-American Jewish encounter. On one hand, this book demonstrates the "determinant part of the JDC" in the "metamorphosis"[2] of postwar French Jewish life and the role played by other American Jewish organizations and individuals, such as members of the American military. On the other, it has focused on the relationship between two branches of the Jewish diaspora and, in doing so, has shed light on a previously unconsidered chapter of Franco-American relations.

The study of the relationship between American and French Jews over the first half of the twentieth century reveals a shift from an equal partnership to one of dependence. In the interwar period, when American and French Jews began working closely together, their respective traditions of international philanthropy allowed them to view each other as partners. The rise of Nazi Germany and the ensuing Central European refugee crisis in France transformed their relationship, leading to a French Jewish dependence on American Jewish funding. During World War II, American Jewish funding proved crucial to saving Jewish lives in France. By the end of the war, French Jews were both expecting and demanding that American Jews continue their assistance. American Jews, endowed with a new sense of responsibility after the genocide, met this obligation on the condition that French Jews would strive for self-sufficiency. This agreement formed the basis of Franco-American Jewish cooperation, yet each group had its ideas concerning this pact. French Jews insisted on being treated as equals yet desperately needed American funds. American Jews wanted an autonomous Jewish community in France yet sought to dictate how it would be established. Tensions coexisted alongside cooperation and mutual understanding.

The first decade after the war provides an opportunity to closely study the Franco-American Jewish relationship at the peak of French dependence: almost 40 percent of the funds provided to France by the JDC from 1914 through 1973 were given during the decade after World War II.[3] During this period, both groups attempted to overcome conflict and the French dependence on American funds. Yet neither goal was altogether met. While French Jews took major steps toward self-sufficiency, they were still receiving roughly $1.5 million a year from the JDC in the early 1970s.[4] Fundamental differences continued to fuel debate.

JEWISH SOLIDARITY, FRANCO-AMERICAN DIFFERENCES

Just as the Marshall Plan enflamed Franco-American passions in the post–World War II period, the "Jewish Marshall Plan," an expression of Jewish solidarity, paradoxically brought national identities to the fore. Vastly different wartime experiences caused French and American Jews to approach reconstruction from different angles. As seen above, American Jewish welfare organizations, influenced by American philanthropic principles and financial considerations, were foremost concerned with weaning French Jews off of what they considered an unhealthy dependence on American aid. French Jews, who had experienced the destruction of the Holocaust firsthand, saw the renewal of French Jewish life as their greatest priority. In keeping with these different perspectives, the JDC promoted vocational training for Jewish orphans to render them self-sufficient as soon as possible, whereas French Jewish organizations fought for longer, more expensive studies that would lead to better opportunities for "their" children.[5] The American Jews who came to France and who had, for the most part, worked as welfare experts during the war, were shocked by the lack of professionalism of their French colleagues. War weary and at times even malnourished, the local Jews who worked in postwar aid committees had been focused on survival, not obtaining professional credentials. For the latter, postwar social work had often begun with mobilization in the Jewish resistance. The strong ideological convictions of French Jews caused American social workers, trained to exercise distance, to voice their disapproval.

Historical differences in Jewish welfare in France and the United States exacerbated these varying approaches to reconstructing Jewish life. American Jewish welfare in the United States boasted a highly centralized and professional approach to providing care. In the late nineteenth century, local federations were established to raise funds for Jewish welfare organizations in cities across the United States. After 1939, the United Jewish Appeal unified these federations to coordinate fundraising for local, national, and international philanthropy. Not only did American Jews have a sophisticated fundraising machine but they also had closely followed trends in the larger field of American social work, having embraced this profession in the interwar period. French Jewish welfare did not benefit from the same level of coordination in the period leading up to World War II, even though a diverse network of organizations did exist to help French and foreign Jews. Furthermore, while aid committees had

CONCLUSION 215

technically rationalized their approach to helping others, these efforts were usually aimed at decreasing fraud. Before World War II, trained social workers were rare in French Jewish aid organizations, which depended primarily on volunteers. These fundamental differences between American and French welfare influenced how these groups perceived each other.

RECONSTRUCTING JEWISH LIFE IN POSTWAR FRANCE: A TRANSNATIONAL PROCESS

Until now, French Jewish reconstruction after the Holocaust has primarily been considered in the historiography as a French affair, with Jews on one side and the French Republic on the other. This study has framed reconstruction in broader terms, taking into account its transnational dimension. American Jewish individuals and organizations shaped the reemergence of French Jewish life, and their role should not be underestimated. American Jewish chaplains and soldiers stationed in France organized makeshift aid programs and offered religious services in cities and towns throughout the country. They used their military status to obtain blankets, food, and other goods for the Jews they encountered, helped reopen synagogues, and reinstated Shabbat services. Beyond this material and spiritual assistance, as Jewish members of the military, they marked the beginning of a new postwar order in which Jews were no longer victims. Chaplains especially formed an important conduit between American and French Jews: they contacted survivors' family members in the United States, organized package programs, and went home with the stories of those they had helped, alerting individuals in the United States to the devastating condition of Europe's surviving Jews. The aid they provided may have been improvised and inconsistent, but it brought hope—and needed blankets—as Jews waited for a more organized response.

As the designated overseas representative of American Jews, the JDC ran the largest aid program in France and attempted to coordinate all other American Jewish aid efforts. Its assistance in the emergency period immediately following the war led to an explosion of private Jewish welfare initiatives. While this helped distribute aid to those most in need, it also provided the French state with an excuse to avoid taking responsibility for Jews. The JDC sought to correct these problems by reducing French dependence on its funds. By the early 1950s, the JDC had succeeded in downsizing, but it was still providing funds to twenty French Jewish welfare organizations and indirectly helping fifteen thousand individuals a month.[6] The cumulative effects of JDC aid are even more striking. For example, JDC funds enabled COJASOR to assist seventy-five thousand individuals from 1946–1950. The JDC also lent money to two Jewish lending organizations that provided interest-free loans to 23,500 individuals from 1945 through 1950.[7] In the long run, American Jewish aid helps explain how Jews in France were able to take steps toward economic recovery while awaiting restitution and reparation.[8] This assistance meant that Jews, even those without the benefits of French citizenship, were able to begin recovering their lives immediately after liberation. When the State of Israel was established in 1948, only 3,050 Jews from France (roughly 1% of the Jewish population) decided to emigrate.[9] While the decision to stay put or make *aliyah* was complex, the "Jewish Marshall Plan" can help explain why remaining in France was a viable option.

The American Jewish presence was not focused solely on welfare. The goal of the American Jewish Committee (AJC), for example, was overtly political. In seeking to reintegrate Jews into their respective nation-states and "defend" the Jews of France from both antisemitism and communism, it tried to serve as a model for French Jews to emulate. At the same time, by partnering with the organizations led by native French Jews, the AJC seems to have missed its rendez-vous with most Jews in France. The World Jewish Congress, an international organization closely associated with the American Jewish Congress, also had overtly political goals for French Jews. Fueled by a sense of Jewish peoplehood that embodied both diaspora nationalist and Zionist aspirations, the WJC sought to unify and represent Jews as Jews in national and international negotiations. Not all Jews in France were seduced by this vision; the WJC mobilized primarily Eastern European Jewish immigrants in France and struggled to gain the support of Native French Jewish circles. Nonetheless, these two organizations spread the American Jewish influence into new corners of French Jewish life. The CRIF, for example, had limited interactions with the JDC yet abundant contact with the AJC and the WJC. Perhaps more significantly, the study of their interactions shows that in the aftermath of the Holocaust, Jews remained as politically diverse as in previous periods. As Jews struggled to comprehend the magnitude of the destruction, pregenocidal conceptions of Jewish life remained relevant.

Even when not overtly political, other American Jewish organizations altered the shape of French Jewish reconstruction. The Hebrew Sheltering and Immigrant Aid Society (HIAS) had been helping Jews migrate since its origins in the late nineteenth century. In the post-Holocaust era, HIAS remained active in France and helped move surviving Jews off the European continent. While HIAS was perpetually frustrated with its lack of funds—the few statistics show that HIAS's global budget was similar to the JDC budget for France alone—the organization left its mark, helping those it assisted start anew, in spite of the limited migration possibilities of the time.[10] American Jewish organizations also helped protect the diversity of Jewish life. The cases of the Vaad Hatzala and the Jewish Labor Committee show these groups sought to operate small programs in France for specific populations. Overall, one sees that American Jews perceived postwar France as an important place to be. Helping European Jews was central, yet so was asserting one's own vision of the Jewish future.

The American Jewish contribution to France cannot be summed up in financial terms alone. Maud Mandel has argued that the JDC's importation of social welfare methods and structures allowed Jews to "maintain a visible presence,"[11] which furthermore granted legitimacy to nonreligious forms of Jewish identity. This study has built on these findings by closely analyzing the ways in which the JDC attempted to reform and coordinate welfare practices. However, by paying close attention to French responses to American aid, I argue that the successful importation of American Jewish structures and methods was not solely a result of American financial power. French Jews used their agency to assert their own distinct visions of reconstruction, and surprisingly, sometimes chose to adopt American ways. Jews in France had their own set of reasons for accepting American practices and did not hesitate to bend the missions of American Jewish organizations to meet their goals. The success of the JDC's importation project is also due to American Jewish efforts to train a new generation of French Jewish communal workers.

Indeed, the American Jewish critique of European Jewish welfare led to an extensive training program that had long-term implications for Jewish life in France and the larger field of European social work. The National Council of Jewish Women's program in France placed a new emphasis on helping Jewish women. By providing them with scholarships to study social work in the United States, the American organization contributed to training a new generation of experts and in doing so feminized French Jewish communal affairs. The JDC's Paul Baerwald School of Social Work in Versailles trained roughly a hundred students from Europe, Israel, and North Africa in a one-year social work program based on the American social work curriculum. French Jewish welfare organizations, which served as fieldwork sites for the school's students, benefited indirectly from its teachings. After the residential program closed, the school continued to provide trainings and seminars for staff members of Jewish welfare organizations. This not only influenced practices within the agencies, it led communal workers to progressively see themselves as members of a professional community. The Paul Baerwald School also had the unanticipated effect of extending the JDC's influence beyond Jewish circles. News of the school spread to the larger social work field, and soon after its opening, Belgian and French social workers, curious about American methods, solicited its faculty. PBS faculty members greeted their requests with enthusiasm, published in European social work journals, and participated in a larger international movement to disseminate the casework method in Europe.

It is perhaps natural that American Jews applied their notion of community to French Jewish life. From their arrival, the representatives of American Jewish organizations spoke of the "French Jewish community." When these Americans discovered (with surprise) that French Jewish life did not fit their definition of community, they subsequently made efforts to shape local realities into their own vision. The JDC did this by using its financial weight as a means of persuading individual organizations to work collectively. It established a common reimbursement scale that was applied to all Jewish welfare agencies. It merged organizations with similar activities to eliminate the duplication of services. Most significantly, it encouraged French Jewish leaders to develop an organization based on the United Jewish Appeal in the United States. The United Jewish Social Fund (FSJU), created in 1949, unified the fundraising campaigns of French Jewish welfare organizations for domestic needs and Israel, grouped these organizations under a common umbrella, and slowly replaced the JDC's coordinating role. Significantly, the FSJU maintained a tangible link among Jewish welfare organizations that proved elusive in France before the war and emerged under duress during the Holocaust through the Nazi-Vichy imposed UGIF and the structure created by French Jews, the CRIF. Over time, those active in French Jewish life abandoned the prewar definition of "community," which previously described the members of a given synagogue. The term took on a more vague, capacious meaning. French Jews began talking about "the French Jewish Community" at the end of the 1940s with the creation of the FSJU. This new language, along with the more collective approach to Jewish welfare and the emergence of the State of Israel reinforced the shift in French Jewish identity that began under the Occupation, which produced new conditions for thinking of Jews as a group. Nonetheless, it was American organizations that brought new vocabulary, structures, and practices that, once endorsed by French Jews, enabled the continuation of these profound changes. After many decades, the CRIF and the FSJU remain important institutions in French Jewish life, gathering multiple ideologies and organizations under common auspices and validating nonreligious forms of Jewish identity.

By importing American structures and practices to France, the JDC helped establish a structural bond between American and French Jews. By the early 1950s, French Jews were being schooled in American nursing and social work methods. They had their own United Jewish Appeal in the form of the FSJU and a highly developed network of Jewish welfare organizations. While the striking historical differences and wartime experiences of these two communities should not be underestimated, it can be said the JDC made the French Jewish community *look* and *function* more like the American Jewish one.

Finally, a transnational perspective helps to better understand the relationship between Jews and the French Republic, a central question in the historiography. Caught between their acute needs and the failure of French authorities to recognize their specific situation after genocide, French Jews turned to American Jewish organizations for help. American Jewish funding fueled the expansion of the private Jewish welfare sector in France and even tempted state-mandated agencies to renege on their responsibilities. Though the postwar period saw the expansion of the French welfare state, this did not mean the end of private welfare. This book thus argues that French Jews' reintegration into their nation-state after the Holocaust was highly influenced by the American Jewish presence.

AMERICAN JEWISH OVERSEAS AID AND POSTWAR AMERICAN JEWISH LIFE

Looking at American Jewish organizations in transnational perspective has also shed light on the dynamics within American Jewish life in the decade following the Holocaust. By documenting how deeply invested American Jews were in rebuilding European Jewish life in the aftermath, this book refutes the idea that American Jews were silent bystanders and argues for an active portrait of this population. It also provides a glimpse of American Jewish life from an entirely new angle. Domestically, American Jews reached new levels of integration into the United States during this period. Philanthropy, in addition to serving as a tangible expression of solidarity, helped American Jews reinforce their diverse Jewish identities in this time of transition. It is not surprising that some American Jews chose to establish programs in France, the new center of European Jewish life, in order to further their respective causes. American Jewish Bundists found their voice through the Jewish Labor Committee, for example, while Reform Jewish women asserted their vision by designing an aid program geared specifically to the needs of women and children, the National Council of Jewish Women. The American Jewish Committee represented establishment Jews, who relished their sense of belonging to both the American nation and the Jewish faith. They sought to tell the Jews of France that they, too, could resolve the problem of "double allegiances." HIAS, with its grassroots fundraising efforts and longtime exclusion from the United Jewish Appeal, still represented the so-called newcomers of the American Jewish community. Its squabbles with the JDC reflected larger tensions between "native" American Jews and the immigrants who did not yet feel entirely at home in the United States. Each of these organizations sought to influence French Jewish life according to its own ideology. Helping Jews in France was thus also a means of furthering their own causes in the United States.

As American Jews rose to a new leadership role in the diaspora, one sees that they affirmed the right of Jews to live outside of Israel. The very fact American Jewish organizations invested their resources in postwar France, especially after 1948, is significant. Immediately after the war, American Jews, largely supportive of Zionism, could have chosen *not* to help French Jews in order to increase international support for a Jewish state. After the creation of Israel, they could have abandoned their French programs to encourage emigration to the young country. This did not occur. Instead, American Jewish organizations affirmed life in the diaspora by helping French Jews reconstruct a vibrant Jewish community. For American Jews, helping French Jews remain in their country of origin validated their choice to do the same.

These findings point out new directions for historical research on American Jewish life. The presence of American Jews and their organizations in prominent areas of French Jewish life served as a sounding board on which Jews in France could compare and contrast their experiences and reformulate their identities. This question can be turned around as well: How were American Jews and their organizations affected by contact with French Jews and French society? Oral history interviews with American Jewish communal workers indicate that helping Jews in France altered their identities, as Jews, as Americans, as professionals, as men and as women, and provided them with a deeply felt means of responding to the Holocaust.[12] Yet how did this transnational encounter affect organizations and their policies? What did the JDC and other American Jewish organizations learn in France and how did this influence their work elsewhere? American conceptions of Jewish welfare and community accompanied them, yet what did they bring back to the United States? Future research should explore the stateside effects of the American Jewish organizations' overseas mobilization, especially in the domain of domestic American Jewish welfare.

A FRENCH JEWISH LIFE FORCE

Historians of Jewish life in postwar France have analyzed both the "vanishing" of the diaspora and its revitalization.[13] The case of postwar France provides arguments to support both claims. Disaffiliation with Judaism and diminished Jewish religious practice in general, name changes, and (albeit small) emigration to Israel coexisted with a burgeoning network of Jewish associations and cultural activities. Such associations and activities were stimulated by the postwar Jewish migrations from Eastern Europe and North Africa in the 1940s and 1950s.

This book, as a result of its focus on Jewish welfare, supports the idea that the Holocaust did not put an end to Jewish life in France. On the contrary, responding to the humanitarian emergency provided Jews in France with a means of remaining Jewish in a moment of crisis. Motivated by feelings of solidarity, or maybe just in need of paid work, some French Jews found meaning and a sense of belonging in Jewish welfare, a fact that turned Jewish aid organizations and children's homes into important sites for the transmission of Jewish identity. Furthermore, while some Americans viewed the French dependence on American aid as a sign of passivity, this book shows otherwise. When the JDC offered funding for the relief and reconstruction of French Jewish life, French Jews responded by creating new organizations (and expanding pre-existing ones), displaying a life force that can be seen in the sheer number of aid organizations and the lively (and at times vicious) debates that occurred among them. The Jewish social service network resulting from this Franco-American cooperation staunchly resisted the JDC's attempts to centralize and reduce its financial contribution. Savvy French Jewish leaders used their knowledge of American Jewish communal dynamics to maintain their American funding. They learned that one of the only ways to influence the decisions of the European-based JDC operations was to go directly to New York. They used the Yiddish press on several continents to shape the JDC's program in France. French Jewish leaders were clearly determined to execute their own visions of reconstruction, long before the massive immigration wave from North Africa in the 1960s.

In the years following World War II, American Jews made up the largest Jewish community in the diaspora, while French Jews quickly became the largest Jewish community in western continental Europe. French and American Jews thus continued to sit around the same table. This was the case when twenty-three Jewish organizations from the United States and the formerly occupied countries of Europe negotiated with the Federal Republic of Germany in 1952 during the Conference on Jewish Material Claims against Germany. The fruit of these negotiations was a settlement of over $110 million, which was dispersed in forty countries over the ten-year period from 1954 to 1964.[14] When French and American Jews sat down together at these negotiations, they were not strangers nor were they bound solely by the traditional philanthropic hierarchy of giver and receiver. At this point, French Jews had mastered the language of American Jewish welfare and had adopted many of its structures. They were also well acquainted with the ideological diversity of the American Jewish community and had identified their institutional allies across the Atlantic. This intimate connection allowed for French Jews to speak the same language as their more powerful American counterparts when they requested Claims Conference funding. It is perhaps not a coincidence that French Jewish organizations received the lion's share of the Claims Conference funding for Europe (over $22 million), which opened a new chapter in French Jewish reconstruction, deeply changing the face of French Jewish life in the decades to come.

NOTES

INTRODUCTION

1. Interview with Gaby Wolff Cohen, Paris, May 28, 2004. This citation and all others were translated from the French by the author.
2. Klarsfeld, *Vichy Auschwitz*, 180.
3. Interview with Gaby Wolff Cohen, May 28, 2004.
4. This is the amount spent by the JDC in Europe. Bauer, *Out of the Ashes*, xviii.
5. Complex factors explain the stark differences in survival rates. Such statistics mean little without contextualization but do help explain postwar perceptions. As Croes shows, the Jewish survival rate in France was 75 percent. In the Netherlands it was 27 percent and in Belgium it was 60 percent. Croes, "The Holocaust in the Netherlands and the Rate of Jewish Survival," 474. For French demographic estimations, see Bensimon et Della Pergola, *La population juive de France*, 35; Wieviorka, "Les Juifs en France au lendemain de la guerre," 5–6.
6. This had occurred by 1960. Grynberg, "Après la tourmente," 267.
7. The strong support of Jewish life in France, compared to other European countries, can be seen in a 1948 JDC report that showed the organization was financing twelve reception centers for immigrants in France while it funded two each in Portugal and Yugoslavia and one each in Austria, Belgium, Czechoslovakia, and Holland. At the same time, the JDC was funding fifty-four children's homes in France, compared to thirty-six in Romania, thirty-one in Hungary, fifteen in Poland, ten in Germany, eight each in Belgium and Italy, four in Czechoslovakia, and one each in Austria, Greece, Holland, and Yugoslavia. Archives départementales de Seine Saint Denis, David Diamant Collection, 335J/115, JDC, Budget and Research Department Report no. 59, JDC Assistees in Europe and North Africa, November 10, 1948.

8. This figure includes the funding from the JDC but excludes funding provided by other American Jewish organizations. JDC-NY, Uncatalogued, Loeb and Troper Financial Report, 1973.

9. The JDC received, like other US voluntary organizations, a reduction in shipping costs of certain items as a result of the Marshall Plan. JDC-I, File 5A3 43.604.4, Memo from Julian Breen to Herbert Katzki, March 2, 1951.

10. YIVO, AJC, RG 347.7.41, FAD 1, Box 18, File: France 1950–54, Letter from Zachariah Shuster to John Slawson, September 21, 1949.

11. Goldman, "The Involvement and Policies of American Jewry in Revitalizing European Jewry," 67–84.

12. The historiography on postwar American Jewish life is extensive. Glazer, *American Judaism*; Shapiro, *A Time for Healing*; Dinnerstein, *Uneasy at Home*, 178–196; Dash Moore, *To the Golden Cities*; *G.I. Jews. How World War II Changed a Generation*; Prell, *Fighting to Become Americans*, 142–176.

13. On the emergence of this concept, see Becker, *Messagers du désastre*.

14. The historiography on the role of American Jews during the Holocaust is too extensive to list here. On American responses to the Holocaust in the postwar period, see Diner, *We Remember with Reverence and Love*; Novick, *The Holocaust in American Life*; Leff, *The Archive Thief*.

15. Green, "To Give and to Receive," 197–226.

16. Ibid., 197. See also, Penslar, *Shylock's Children*; Woocher, *Sacred Survival*. On tensions surrounding the "Stuyvesant Promise," see Wenger, *New York Jews and the Great Depression*, 136–165.

17. Woocher, *Sacred Survival*, 1–21.

18. For example, by May of 1948, a total of 10,880 American children and adults were writing to Jewish children in Europe under the auspices of the World Jewish Congress. In France, between September 1945 and April 1948, a total of 1,168 children corresponded with American Jews. Kubowitzki, *Unity in Dispersion*, 307–308.

19. For example, philanthropist Simon-Joseph Scheurer visited France regularly and closely followed a group of Jewish students to whom he provided scholarships. American Jewish Archive, World Union for Progressive Judaism (collection 16), folder D11.

20. Wieviorka, *Déportation et génocide*, 334; Perego, "Pleurons-les, bénissons leurs noms," 719–720.

21. On Americanization in the post-WWII period, see, among others, Hogan, *The Marshall Plan*; Wall, *The United States and the Making of Postwar France*; Kuisel, *Seducing the French*; McKenzie, *Remaking France*; Tournès, *Sciences de l'homme et politique*. More broadly, on the global American presence, see Curti, *American Philanthropy Abroad* and more recently, De Grazia, *Irresistible Empire*; Hollinger, *Protestants Abroad*; Carruthers, *The Good Occupation*; Stahl, *Enlisting Faith*.

22. While works on the cultural, political, and economic influence in post-WWII France are abundant, there have been few analyses of the American influence on French welfare during this period. On transnational social welfare reform in the period leading up to World War II, see Rodgers, *Atlantic Crossings*; Diebolt and Fouché, "1917–1923, Les Américaines en Soissonais: leur influence sur la France," 45–63; Fouché, "Le Casework," 21–35.

23. Yehuda Bauer's three-volume history of the JDC represents a global institutional history of this organization. Bauer, *My Brother's Keeper*; *American Jewry and the Holocaust*; *Out of the Ashes*. Scholars have explored the role of the JDC throughout the world. On Germany, for example, see Webster, "American Relief and Jews in Germany, 1945–1960. Diverging Perspectives," 293–321; Patt, *Finding Home and Homeland*; Grossmann, *Jews, Germans and Allies*. For the most recent scholarship on the JDC, see Patt et al., *The JDC at 100*.

24. Lazare, *La résistance juive en France*, 282.

25. Zunz, *Philanthopy in America*, 8–43. Goldman, "The Involvement and Policies of American Jewry in Revitalizing European Jewry," 72.

26. JDC-NY, uncatalogued, JDC Primer, p. 8. Percentages are based on a Jewish population of one hundred and eighty to two hundred thousand individuals.

27. JDC-I, Laura Margolis Jarblum Collection, uncatalogued, Statistical Report, France, Country Directors Conference, October 1952.

28. I have explored elsewhere the role of American and British Reform Jews in reconstructing the French reform movement. Hobson Faure, "Renaître sous les auspices américains et britanniques," 82–99.

29. Elazar, *Community and Polity*, 1995.

30. Archives départementales de Seine Saint Denis, David Diamant Collection, 335J/133, *La presse nouvelle*, "Un message à nos frères des Etats-Unis," *La presse nouvelle*, n. 21, November 25, 1944.

31. The JDC lent money to two Jewish organizations that in turn provided interest-free loans to 23,500 individuals from 1945 through 1950. JDC-NY, France, File 244, JDC Program in France, 1951, April 15, 1951.

32. Hobson Faure, *Un "Plan Marshall juif."*

33. The historiography on the American presence in France has taken into account the specific experiences of women and African Americans but has not explored American Jews. Fabre, *From Harlem to Paris*; Stovall, *Paris Noir*, "The Color Line behind the Lines," 737–769, "The Fire This Time," 182–200. On Protestant women, see Fouché, "Des Américaines protestantes," 133–152. On American immigrants in France more generally, see Green, *The Other Americans in Paris*.

34. The first generation of scholarship on the reconstruction of European Jewish life focuses almost exclusively on life in the DP camps. See, for example, Bauer, *Out of the Ashes*. More recent work has situated France and its Jews in

the European context. See Lagrou, *The Legacy of Nazi Occupation*; Bessel and Schumann, *Life and Death*; Bankier, *The Jews Are Coming Back*; Ofer et al., *Holocaust Survivors, Resettlement, Memories, Identities*. On Jews in postwar Poland, see Kichewleski, *Les Survivants* and Cichopek-Gajraj, *Beyond Violence*.

35. The figure applies to the period between 1950–1970. Hyman, *The Jews of Modern France*, 194.

36. Mandel, *In the Aftermath of Genocide*, 9–10. Paula Hyman, for example, in her survey of French Jewish history, *The Jews of Modern France* (1998), dedicated a chapter to the war years, which was followed by a chapter entitled "A Renewed Community" on the North African immigration to France. Hyman, *The Jews of Modern France*, 161–214.

37. Research on the postwar period before the 1990s was sparse. It includes Roblin, *Les juifs de Paris* (1952); Rabinovitch, *Anatomie du judaïsme français* (1962); Berg, "De 1945 à 1972," 423–444. Scholarship picked up a little in the 1980s. One of the first articles on this period was Weinberg, "The French Jewish Community after World War II," 45–54. In 1985, the French Jewish studies journal *YOD* published a special issue on the period: "De la guerre à l'après-guerre." Several years later, Doris Bensimon published *Les Juifs de France et leurs relations avec Israël*. The new interest in postwar France continued into the 1990s in both France and the United States. In the early 1990s, Catherine Nicault and Annette Wieviorka analyzed postwar Zionism and the commemoration of the Holocaust, respectively. Nicault, *La France et le Sionisme* and Wieviorka, *Déportation et génocide*. In 1994, *Yale French Studies* published an issue dedicated to *Discourses of Jewish Identity in Twentieth-Century France*, which focused primarily on the postwar period, while in France, one year later, the Jewish history journal *Archives juives* published an issue on the immediate postwar period.

38. Wasserstein, *Vanishing Diaspora*.

39. David Weinberg has argued that "though it is true that after the Holocaust European Jewry suffered from severe structural and demographic weaknesses that are ongoing, it never lost its will to live" (see Weinberg, "Between America and Israel," 91), and more generally, Weinberg, *Recovering A Voice*. Maud Mandel in her comparative study *In the Aftermath of Genocide* has constructed a powerful argument against Wasserstein's prediction of the collapse of French Jewish life, as I do here. Daniella Doron has recently taken a middle-of-the-road stance on Wasserstein's claim, highlighting both the anxiety and pessimism in French Jewish life after the Holocaust, as well as the important mobilization among Jews to care for their children and families. Doron, *Jewish Youth and Identity in Postwar France*.

40. Mandel's book represents the first full-length study examining how French Jews reentered the nation after genocide and asks to what extent "the religious, ethnic and national affiliations among escapees shifted to reflect the recent

violent past." Mandel, *In the Aftermath of Genocide*, 2. See also Zytnicki, *Les Juifs à Toulouse*; Karen L. Adler, *Jews and Gender in Liberation France*; Lehr, *La Thora dans la cité*; Hand and Katz, *Post-Holocaust France and the Jews*; Weinberg, *Recovering a Voice*; Wieviorka, *Déportation et génocide*; Wolf, *Harnessing the Holocaust*; Azouvi, *Le Mythe du grand silence*; Clifford, *Commemorating the Holocaust*.

41. Hazan, *Les orphelins de la Shoah*; Doron, *Jewish Youth and Identity in Postwar France*. See also Poujol, *Les enfants cachés* and *L'Église de France*.

42. See recent work by Ghiles-Meilac, *Le CRIF*; Messika, *Politiques de l'accueil*; Perego, *Pleurons-les*; Paris de Bollardière, "La pérennité de notre people;" Burgard, "Une nouvelle vie dans un nouveau pays;" Fourtage, "Et après?;" and Grumberg, "Militer en minorité?".

43. The question of the American Jewish presence has been addressed in several works. See especially Mandel, "Philanthropy or Cultural Imperialism?" 53–94. Bauer briefly explores the case of France but ends his discussion in 1948. Bauer, *Out of the Ashes*, 23–33; 237–245. See also Goldsztejn, "Au secours d'une communauté." Other works have explored aspects of the American Jewish presence in Europe and have included France in their analyses, such as Grobman, *Rekindling the Flame*, *Battling for Souls*; Moore, *GI Jews*; Collomp, *Résister au Nazisme*. My book differs from these approaches in both scope and nature: I focus on multiple American Jewish aid organizations and individuals and the French responses to this aid.

44. Daniella Doron also discusses this field in relation to children and families. Doron, *Jewish Youth and Identity*.

45. French Jewish life in the interwar period has been debated by several generations of scholars. Weinberg, *A Community on Trial*; Hyman, *From Dreyfus to Vichy*; Benveniste, *Le Bosphore à la Roquette*; Caron, *Uneasy Asylum*; Malinovich, *French and Jewish*; most recently, Corber "L'Esprit du Corps" and Underwood, "Staging a New Community." On successful interwar collaborations on behalf of refugees, see Caron, *Uneasy Asylum*, 302–321.

46. The UGIF has inspired great debate in postwar Jewish circles and French historical literature. Jews questioned its role by holding honor courts in the immediate postwar period. Perego, "Honor Courts." For a balanced account and a discussion of its role in rescue and persecution, see Laffitte, *Un engrenage fatal* and *Juif dans la France allemande*.

47. Wieviorka, *Déportation et génocide*, 344–345; Mandel, *In the Aftermath of Genocide*, 136–137. On the CRIF, see Fredj, "La création du CRIF;" Ghiles-Meilhac, *Le CRIF* and "Centralizing the Political Jewish Voice in Post-Holocaust France."

48. A note on terms: Many of the actors in this study were Jewish. Their affiliation with postwar Jewish organizations supports the idea that they identified as Jews and allows me to avoid (to the extent possible) assigning this identity to those for whom it held no importance.

49. Schiller, Basch, and Szanton, "Transnationalism," 1–22; Basch, Schiller, and Szanton, *Nations Unbound*. For an overview of the historiography on transnationalism and migration studies, see Waldinger, *The Cross-Border Connection*, 11–36.

50. Kahn and Mendelsohn, *Transnational Traditions*, 1–6; Rosman and Cohen, *Rethinking European Jewish history*; Kobrin, *Jewish Bialystok and Its Diaspora*; Stein, *Plumes*. On France, see Joskowicz, *The Modernity of Others* and the special issue coordinated by Heidi Knörzer, "Juifs de France et d'Allemagne. Une histoire croisée," *Archives juives*, n. 46/2, 2013.

51. The vast scholarship on the American Jewish response to the Holocaust has largely focused on what American Jews did (or did not do) during World War II itself, primarily in the United States. This study complements Diner's *We Remember with Reverence and Love* by showing the strong investment of American Jews outside of the United States in order to respond to the Holocaust.

52. Werner and Zimmermann, *De la comparaison à l'histoire croisée*, 22–26. For a similar approach in Jewish history, see Grossmann, *Jews, Germans and Allies*. The need to address the role of reception societies in cultural transfers is theorized in Werner and Espagne, "La construction d'une référence culturelle allemande en France," 969–992.

53. In total, I conducted fifty-seven interviews with forty-five individuals. Of primary importance were individuals (of all nationalities) who worked in or closely with American Jewish organizations in postwar France. In addition to providing firsthand accounts of the period, my interviews generated a rich body of materials that included information on events not yet recorded in written form. However, there are limits to this data. This corpus of interviews cannot be considered a representative sample. Many individuals had passed away, and as other social scientists have recognized, the "snow-ball" method itself is inherently biased, as social networks influence who is interviewed. These interviews also led me to become part of the social networks I was studying. When an individual recommended someone to interview, he or she often called the person to talk about the study. Upon arrival, I was then usually asked for news about the individual who had sent me. On one occasion, I unwittingly located the former romantic interest of one of the interviewees. While this study has helped strengthen preexisting social networks, the interviewees may have decided (collectively) what could be revealed and what should remain private. My thoughts on this issue have been influenced by anthropological studies such as Myerhoff, *Number Our Days*; Kugelmass, *Between Two Worlds*. I have translated all citations from French unless otherwise noted.

54. Anteby-Yemini and Berthomière, "Avant-propos di[a]spositif: décrire et comprendre les Diasporas," 11.

55. In 1952, twenty-three Jewish organizations from the formerly Occupied countries of Europe and the United States began negotiations with the Federal

Republic of Germany in what was called the Conference on Jewish Material Claims against Germany. A settlement of over $110 million was reached, which was dispersed primarily over a ten-year period from 1954 to 1964. Conference on Jewish Material Claims against Germany, *Twenty Years Later, 1952–1972*, 9–10.

56. The JDC was well aware of this shift. In 1954, the JDC country director for France wrote "There has been some evidence of a change in attitude on the part of certain organizations and individuals in the community concerning their relationship to the JDC. The knowledge that a large part of the JDC budget has come from the Claims Conference has lead [sic] to remarks to the effect that, since these funds are no longer a gift of the American Jewish community, but funds to which the French Jewish community is entitled, the community should have full responsibility in deciding how they should be spent. Here again, the problem has not been serious, but is something to be watched closely, in the future." JDC-NY, France, Folder 151, Country Report France, 1954.

57. Telephone interview with Saul Kagan, February 10, 2006.

CHAPTER ONE: BEFORE THE "JEWISH MARSHALL PLAN"

1. JDC-NY, France 1939/45, File 596, Minutes of Meeting Held on December 19, 1944.

2. Safran, "Diasporas in Modern Societies," 83–99; Dufoix, *Les diasporas*, 7–13; Anteby-Yemini and Berthomière, "Avant-Propos di[a]spositif: décrire et comprendre les diasporas," 9–20.

3. Green, "Jewish Migrations to France," 135–153.

4. Elazar, *Community and Polity*, 23. On American Jewish exceptionality, see also Lipset, "A Unique People," in Lipset ed., *American Pluralism*, 3–30. This is not to say that antisemitism or legal forms of inequality did not exist in the American colonies or in the United States. Birnbaum, *Les deux maisons*, 9–47; more generally Dinnerstein, *Uneasy at Home*.

5. By decree on March 17, 1808, Napoleon established the Central Consistory, based in Paris, and regional Consistories in areas with over two thousand Jewish individuals for a total of thirteen Consistories. Albert, *The Modernization of French Jewry*. On the United States, see Sarna, *American Judaism*, 29.

6. On Eastern European immigration to the United States, see Sorin, *A Time for Building*, 12–68; Howe, *World of Our Fathers*. On France, Hyman, *From Dreyfus to Vichy*; Green, *The Pletzl of Paris*.

7. More professionals and skilled workers chose France. Hyman, *From Dreyfus to Vichy*, 64–65; Green, *The Pletzl of Paris*, 111–113.

8. Paula Hyman cites thirty thousand, but Nancy Green calculated thirty-five thousand in Paris alone and states that 80 percent of Russian Jews chose to settle in Paris. Hyman, *From Dreyfus to Vichy*, 63–64; Green, *The Pletzl of Paris*, 201–206.

9. Dobkowski, *Jewish American Voluntary Organizations*, annex 2; Bensimon and Della Pergola, *La population juive de France*, 25–35.

10. The Mortara Affair was an 1858 case in Bologna in which a Jewish boy was secretly baptized by his Catholic governess. Papal authorities considered the baptism binding and removed the child, aged six, from his parents. Despite an international mobilization, the parents were unable to retrieve their son until 1870, by which point he had become Catholic. See Hyman, *The Jews of Modern France*, 78–79; more generally, Kertzer, *The Kidnapping of Edgardo Mortara*.

11. In *The Jews in Nineteenth Century France*, Michael Graetz offers an extensive analysis of the center and periphery of French Jewry during the nineteenth century with a particular focus on the social networks that led to the creation of the AIU. Graetz's analysis challenges other works on the AIU, showing that the catalyst for its creation predates the Mortara Affair. This generation is also analyzed in Berkovitz, *The Shaping of Jewish Identity*, 111–126, 128–149. Lisa Moses Leff focuses on the discourse of the founders of the AIU and establishes its roots in the Republican, anticlerical movement in nineteenth century France (see Leff, *Sacred Bonds of Solidarity*, 157–199).

12. While in 1861 the AIU had 850 members, this number quickly increased to more than 30,000 by 1885. In addition, there were 349 local committees in communication with the AIU in Paris by 1880, of which 56 were in France, 113 were in Germany, and 20 were in Italy. French membership declined from 80 percent in 1861 to less than 40 percent in 1885, according to Rodrigue, *French Jews, Turkish Jews*, 23. Lisa Moses Leff provides slightly different membership numbers, stating that in 1881 only 23.6 percent of the total membership was French (Leff, *Sacred Bonds of Solidarity*, 164).

13. Rodrigue, *French Jews, Turkish Jews*, xii.

14. Diner, *A Time for Gathering*, 153–156; Karp, *To Give Life*, 3–43; Szajkowski, "Concord and Discord," 99.

15. Sorin, *A Time for Building*, 207.

16. Bauer, *My Brother's Keeper*, 6.

17. As to be expected, the AJRC contributed considerably more than the CCR and PRC to the JDC, which led to tensions over the clear dominance of "uptown Jews" at the JDC. Szajkowski, "Concord and Discord," 113.

18. Bauer, *My Brother's Keeper*, 7–8.

19. Szajkowski, "Private and Organized," 52–106.

20. President Wilson also established the Jewish War Sufferers Relief Day on January 27, 1916, on which $1 million was collected. Bauer, *My Brother's Keeper*, 8.

21. The federation structure sprang almost concurrently from Boston (1895) and Cincinnati (1896), where Jewish philanthropists decided to establish umbrella organizations that would be in charge of raising and distributing the funding for their cities' various Jewish charitable organizations. This

established the Federation of Jewish Charities, an idea that was then emulated in Jewish communities throughout the United States. By 1917, forty-five Jewish communities in the United States had Federations. Stein, "Jewish Social Work," 47. On the process in New York, see Dash Moore, "From Kehilla to Federation," 131–146.

22. Bauer, *My Brother's Keeper*, 6.

23. AIU, Etats-Unis, 1C04, Statement Showing the Appropriations Made by the Joint Distribution Committee since the Beginning of the War to March 1, 1919.

24. In February 1920, a team of 126 JDC workers was sent to Poland under the auspices of the ARA and the direction of JDC fundraising specialist and social worker Boris D. Bogen. Bauer, *My Brother's Keeper*, 9–10; Jaclyn Granick dates the arrival of JDC delegates in Poland one year earlier. Granick, "Humanitarian Responses," 119.

25. Bauer, *My Brother's Keeper*, 57–104; Karp, *To Give Life*, 61–62. More generally, see Dekel-Chen, *Farming the Red Land*. On larger political tensions in American Jewish life in this period, see Feingold, *A Time for Searching*, 155–224.

26. Karp, *To Give Life*, 59–73 (statistic from p. 71); Raphael, *United Jewish Appeal*.

27. During WWI, the JDC provided a grant of $5,000 out of the above-mentioned $16 million for families of Russian soldiers in France. From 1916 until 1933, it appears the JDC also provided limited grants in France and may have helped in the repatriation and care of refugees; AIU, Etats-Unis, 1C04, Statement Showing the Appropriations Made by the Joint Distribution Committee since the Beginning of the War to March 1, 1919. JDC-NY, uncatalogued, *JDC Primer*, New York, 1945, France-4. This document does not specify how much the JDC spent in France during this period.

28. The Zionist movement and Jewish youth groups provided a cadre for the encounter between French and immigrant Jewish circles. Hyman, *From Dreyfus to Vichy*, 153–219; Malinovich, *French and Jewish*, 120–148. These historians revise David Weinberg's portrayal of the French Jewish community in the 1930s, demonstrating greater mixing between French and immigrant circles. See Weinberg, *A Community on Trial*, 148–170.

29. Both Green and Hyman date the establishment of this organization to 1926. However, the Archives of the Préfecture de la Police (APP) date its creation in 1928 and note it regrouped eighty Jewish organizations before WWII, including forty-two mutual aid societies. APP, Folder BA2315.

30. Granick, "Humanitarian Responses," 109; AIU, France, AHI, Letter from ME Baynton to the AIU, August 26, 1921; Letter from Rosenberg to the AIU, April 8, 1922.

31. AIU, Etats-Unis, 1C04, Letters from Albert Lucas to the AIU, October 8 and 11, 1918.

32. AIU, Etats-Unis, 1C04, Internal JDC Memo, May 7, 1919; Letter from Lowenstein to Bigard, June 16, 1919. The JDC rejected further funding requests from the AIU for this institution.

33. AIU, Etats-Unis, 1C04, Letter from B. Bogen to the AIU, December 10, 1923.

34. Born in Sweden to Lithuanian parents, Kahn had spent great lengths of time in Germany, where he was educated in economics and later worked with the German Jewish welfare agency, Hilfsverein der deutschen Juden. In addition to his knowledge of the major European languages, Kahn spoke Yiddish and Hebrew and was affiliated with the Zionist movement. He was the European director of the JDC from 1924 until 1938; Bauer, *My Brother's Keeper*, 21–22, 251.

35. Dwork and Van Pelt, *Flight from the Reich*, 18; Bauer, *My Brother's Keeper*, 138; Nicault, "L'accueil des juifs d'Europe centrale," 54.

36. Historians present a range of interpretations of French Jewish leadership in the 1930s. Weinberg (*A Community on Trial*, 218) accuses native French Jews of giving up on aiding refugees after 1938; Caron convincingly refutes Weinberg's claim and challenges previous interpretations of this period in *Uneasy Asylum*, an analysis of Jewish relief efforts from 1936 to 1940. I have relied heavily on Bauer's and Caron's accounts of JDC involvement in France for my analysis here. See Bauer, *My Brother's Keeper*, 138–179; Caron, *Uneasy Asylum*, 94–116, 302–321.

37. Both the Ligue internationale contre l'antisémitisme (LICA), established in 1928 by Bernard Lacache, the son of Eastern European immigrants, and the Federation of Jewish Societies, which represented middle-class immigrant Jews and their mutual aid societies, organized rallies against Nazism and in favor of material aid for refugees; Weinberg, *A Community on Trial*, 103–147, especially 112–113. Also see Underwood, "Staging a New Community."

38. On these native-run committees, see Hyman, *From Dreyfus to Vichy*, 220–229; Nicault, "L'accueil des juifs d'Europe centrale," 53–59.

39. Hyman, *From Dreyfus to Vichy*, 221.

40. Established in czarist Russia in 1880 and 1912, respectively, ORT and Union OSE moved their headquarters to Berlin after the 1917 Russian Revolution and later to Paris in 1933. Unlike the JDC or larger international bodies that offered indirect aid, these organizations adopted local leadership and direction while maintaining branches and direct services throughout Europe. On the role of OSE in France from 1933 to 1939, see Lemalet, "Les comités d'accueil," 87–104; on the war years, see Kieval, "Legality and Resistance in Vichy France," 339–366; Zeitoun, *Histoire de l'OSE*; Hazan and Weill, "L'OSE et le sauvetage des enfants juifs," 259–276. More generally, see Hobson Faure et al., *Prévenir et guérir*.

41. Caron, *Uneasy Asylum*, 96–97.

42. Ibid., 107.

43. Attended by the AIU, the Jewish Colonization Association (ICA) and, of course, the JDC, each of these organizations allocated F1 million. Of these

funds, only a small percentage—F250,000—was allocated to support refugees in France. Local fundraising, while fruitful, did not entirely meet the needs of the various aid committees (Bauer, *My Brother's Keeper*, 139).

44. JDC statistics in Bauer, *My Brother's Keeper*, 141. Rothschild statistics in Caron, *Uneasy Asylum*, 97. The JDC estimated its participation at 44 percent "shortly after 1933;" JDC-NY, uncatalogued, *JDC Primer*, France-4.

45. Nicault, "L'accueil des juifs d'Europe centrale," 55.

46. It appears that the JDC organized French Jewish fundraising before WWII by working closely with the immigrant socialist Federation of Jewish Societies. Various "Jewish" professions were solicited, although it is unclear if the money raised was considered as part of the JDC contribution to the French Jewish refugee committees. JDC-NY, 287, Letter from Leon Shapiro to Harry Rosen, May 7, 1948.

47. Caron, *Uneasy Asylum*, 109, 439. National Committee leader Jacques Helbronner had strong ties to the state, which helps explain the JDC's demands. Among other Jewish leaders, Helbronner drew the attention of the local intelligence unit of the Préfecture de police de Paris, which registered his biographical information as an active member of Jewish leadership in a document dated March 15, 1941. APP, Série BA/2007. He was later deported to Auschwitz.

48. Letter from Bernard Kahn to Max Warburg, October 16, 1934, cited in Caron, *Uneasy Asylum*, 104.

49. Letter from Bernard Kahn to Paul Baerwald, June 18, 1936, cited in Bauer, *My Brother's Keeper*, 153, 318.

50. Caron, *Uneasy Asylum*, 117–170.

51. Ibid., 304. The leadership of the CAR included Albert Lévy and William Oualid, among others.

52. Kahn reported in 1937 that despite "the great difficulty we always had with the refugee committee in France, [the] new committee . . . today functions well." Letter from B. Kahn to James G. McDonald, June 28, 1937. Ibid., 305; 536, note 16.

53. Ibid., 305.

54. These were the Groupement de coordination, which oversaw thirty relief committees, and the Intercomité des oeuvres françaises d'assistance aux réfugiés, which handled the administrative aspects of relief work. A third nonsectarian committee, the Comité central des réfugiés, also known as the Bonnet committee, was established by French Foreign Affairs minister Georges Bonnet and Louise Weiss to mediate between the French government and the Groupement de coordination. Caron, *Uneasy Asylum*, 307–308; Bauer, *My Brother's Keeper*, 264.

55. Caron, *Uneasy Asylum*, 312–316. David Weinberg maintains that unity was never reached. Weinberg, *A Community on Trial*, vii–xi, 148–170.

56. Afoumado, *Exil impossible*.

57. Ibid., 111–155, 169. On the JDC negotiations in Cuba, see also the Oral History Division (OHD) of the Avraham Harman Institute on Contemporary Jewry, Hebrew University of Jerusalem, OHD (122) 28, Laura Margolis Jarblum Interview.

58. Dr. Kahn was not American and was unable to circulate in German territories. With growing tensions in Europe, the JDC felt it necessary to have an American citizen work as the director of European operations. Troper therefore replaced Kahn in the fall of 1938. Bauer, *My Brother's Keeper*, 252.

59. Weiss, *Souvenirs d'une enfance républicaine*, 11.

60. The date of their affair is not provided. Bertin, *Louise Weiss*, 321.

61. Caron, "Louise Weiss;" Weiss, *Mémoires d'une Européenne*, 233–254.

62. Afoumado, *Exil impossible*, 175–177.

63. This outcome can only be fully understood in the aftermath of the Holocaust: had the refugees been accepted in Cuba or the United States, it is likely that all would have survived the war. Of the 907 passengers on the St. *Louis*, 231 were sent to Nazi death camps, where they perished. Of the 250 passengers granted refuge in France, 78 perished in Auschwitz. Ibid., 220–222.

64. Klarsfeld, *Vichy Auschwitz*, 179. Klarsfeld bases this estimate on census data and the assumption that 10 percent of Jews did not declare themselves Jewish. These figures are problematic for this reason.

65. JDC-NY, uncatalogued, *JDC Primer*, France-6.

66. Caron, *Uneasy Asylum*, 316.

67. The first citation is from a memo from Joseph Schwartz to the JDC administration in New York on August 15, 1942. Bauer, *American Jewry*, 177. The second is from a report by Jules Jefroykin, who represented the JDC in France from 1942 to 1944. JDC-NY, France 1939/44, File 596, Report on the General Situation in France, November 1942–June 1944 (translated from French), August 1944.

68. Klarsfeld, *Vichy Auschwitz*, 180.

69. American ambassador to Vichy, Admiral Leahy, was recalled in May 1942 after the establishment of the Laval government (April 26, 1942). However, diplomatic relations between the United States and Vichy were tense but still officially intact; the United States maintained a Chargé d'Affaires in Vichy, H. Pinkney Tuck. It was not until the Allied invasion of North Africa (November 8, 1942) that diplomatic relations broke down. Paxton, *Vichy France*, 134, 312–313.

70. Bauer, *American Jewry*, 42.

71. OHD (1) 61, Jules Jefroykin Interview, 1. Jefroykin dates his employment with the JDC in December 1940, while Bauer places it one month later. Bauer, *American Jewry*, 163.

72. See, among others, Marrus and Paxton, *Vichy France and the Jews*; Klarsfeld, *Vichy Auschwitz*; Kaspi, *Les Juifs pendant l'Occupation*; Poznanski, *Les*

Juifs en France. On France's comparatively high survival rates, see Zuccotti, *The Holocaust*; Cohen, *Persécutions et sauvetages*.

73. On Jewish welfare during the occupation, see Grynberg, *Les camps de la honte*, 173–234; Poznanski, *Les Juifs en France*, 164–201; Kaspi, *Les Juifs pendant l'Occupation*, 323–374. The work of the UGIF demonstrates the complex relationship between welfare and politics during this period. See, for example, Adler, *The Jews of Paris*; Cohen, *The Burden of Conscience*; Laffitte, *Un engrenage fatal* and *Juif dans la France allemande*.

74. Alary, "Les Juifs et la ligne de démarcation," 13–49.

75. Emigration was initially encouraged by Vichy officials, who lent their support to HICEM. Marrus and Paxton, *Vichy France and the Jews*, 112–115.

76. Bauer, *American Jewry*, 152–177. The financial contribution of the JDC has been analyzed by contemporaries and historians, yet little has been written on the daily life of the JDC in France from 1940 to 1942. For a discussion of the 1942–1944 period, see Hobson Faure, "Guide and Motivator," 293–311.

77. The JDC collaboration with the American Friends Service Committee dated from the immediate post-WWI period. Bauer, *My Brother's Keeper*, 16; Granick, "Humanitarian Responses," 140–153.

78. Grynberg, *Les camps de la honte*, 12.

79. Ibid., 175, 181.

80. Of the twenty-five organizations, six were of Jewish affiliation, including the JDC, HICEM, OSE, ORT, CAR, and the Commission centrale des oeuvres juives d'assistance; Bauer, *American Jewry*, 160. The JDC provided funding to most, if not all, of these organizations. On the Nîmes Committee and aid efforts within the southern camps, see Zuccotti, *The Holocaust*, 72–80 and Grynberg, *Les camps de la honte*, 173–197. Katzki describes his work with the Nîmes committee in OHD (47) 12, Herbert Katzki Interview, 5–9.

81. JDC-NY, uncatalogued, *JDC Primer*, France-6.

82. The JDC also financed the Judenräte in Poland. Bauer, *American Jewry*, 76–84. Historians and contemporaries of this history remain divided on the role the UGIF played. Consequently, those who consider the UGIF as a form of French Jewish collaboration judge JDC support of this body harshly, such as Adler, *The Jews of Paris*, 142–145. Whereas others, such as historians Richard I. Cohen and Yehuda Bauer and contemporary Jules Jefroykin hold a more moderate view of the JDC funding of the UGIF. Cohen, *The Burden of Conscience*; Bauer, *American Jewry*, 168; OHD (1) 61, Jules Jefroykin Interview, 4. More generally, Michel Laffitte points to the need for the study of the UGIF in its national context while recognizing the diversity of its leadership and their ties to civil society. In outlining the rescue activities of members of the UGIF, he challenges previous binary analyses that separated UGIF leadership from Jewish resistance. Laffitte, "L'UGIF fut-elle un obstacle au sauvetage des juifs?," in Sémelin, Andrieu, and Gensburger,

La résistance aux génocides, 251–262. For a critical analysis of the differences between the UGIF and other Judenräte, see Laffitte, *Un engrenage fatal*, 19–23.

83. Schwartz met with Pinkney Tuck, US Chargé d'affairs. JDC-NY, AR33-44/614, Letter from J. Schwartz to JDC-NY, August 11, 1942, reprinted in Milton and Bogin, *American Jewish Joint Distribution Committee*, 929–930; Bauer, *American Jewry*, 174–177.

84. OHD (1) 61, Jules Jefroykin Interview, 10.

85. According to Anny Latour, Jules Jefroykin was appointed director for the JDC in France in spring 1942. Yehuda Bauer situates this in June. Brener, cousin and secretary to Raymond-Raoul Lambert, began working with Jefroykin that summer. Latour, *La résistance juive*, 120; Bauer, *American Jewry*, 241.

86. In December 1942, the JDC received authorization from the US Treasury Department to transfer limited funds into occupied Europe. Penkower does not state where this money was distributed. Penkower, "Jewish Organizations and the Creation of the U.S. War Refugee Board," 122–139.

87. JDC-NY, AR33-44/193, Letter from James Rosenberg to Joseph Hyman, September 21, 1939, reprinted in Milton and Bogin, *American Jewish Joint Distribution Committee*, 227.

88. OHD (47) 19, Joseph Schwartz Interview, 15.

89. OHD (1) 61, Jules Jefroykin Interview, 7. In 1940, two Zionist-Revisionist couples of Eastern European origin established an organization that became known in 1942 as the Armée juive (Jewish Army). Previous to this date, the organization had multiple names, including la Main forte, B'nei David, and, after 1944, the Organisation juive de combat. On the establishment of the Jewish Army, see Cohen, *Persécutions et sauvetages*, 378–384 and Lazare, *La Résistance juive en France*, 111–118.

90. Lambert, *Carnet d'un témoin*, 198. Lambert recorded this in his journal on November 29, 1942. However, the American representatives of the JDC had left France earlier that month and had limited contact with French Jewish leaders. Oral history interviews with JDC leadership and Jefroykin do not mention Lambert in this context nor any tensions between the JDC and Jefroykin before the JDC's departure. Lambert's statement remains unsubstantiated, both by its late date and archival evidence.

91. Latour, *La résistance juive*, 120.

92. OHD (1) 61, Jules Jefroykin Interview, 10–11.

93. CDJC, CCCLXVI-14, American Joint Distribution Committee; JDC-NY, France 1939/44, File 596, Minutes of Meeting Held on December 5, 1944, at the Office of the JDC.

94. OHD (1) 61, Jules Jefroykin Interview, 15. While Jefroykin specifies he cleared his unofficial activities with Schwartz, he does not say at what point in the war he did so. Bauer indicates that Schwartz didn't learn this until 1943. Bauer, *American Jewry*, 475.

95. Lazare, *La résistance juive*, 279, 284–286; Latour, *La résistance juive en France*, 119–124; Schmitt, "Six Millions [sic] Lent Jews by French"; Bauer, *American Jewry*, 159.
96. Bauer, *American Jewry*, 222.
97. OHD (27) 86, Mark Jarblum Interview, 20; Lazare, *La résistance juive*, 286. Jefroykin claims that he knew Mayer from before the war but had absolutely no contact with him during this period. OHD (1) 61, Jules Jefroykin Interview, 15.
98. Jarblum replaced Israël Jefroykin and became the second president of the FSJF, most likely during the war. Cohen, *Persécutions et sauvetages*, 381.
99. He was a personal friend of Léon Blum and active in the French socalist movement. Boukara, "L'ami parisien," 153–70.
100. Lazare, *La résistance juive*, 287. While Lazare specifies that Mayer's allocations to Weill were provided to Brener, and hence distributed through the JDC Council, Bauer notes that Weill received some direct funding from Mayer for the OSE, which was a source of conflict among the Jewish organizations (see Bauer, *American Jewry*, 244).
101. Bauer, *American Jewry*, 258.
102. OHD (47) 19, Joseph Schwartz Interview, 2–3. Lazare also states that the JDC received a license from the Treasury at the end of 1943, allowing it to contract loans in France with a $600,000 limit and noting that Schwartz had authorized the loan system one year before this. Lazare, *La résistance juive*, 280–281.
103. On the creation of the WRB, see Penkower, "Jewish Organizations and the Creation of the U.S. War Refugee Board," 122–139; Wyman, *Abandonment of the Jews*, 209–307; more recently, Erbelding, *Rescue Board*.
104. For example, in 1944, official JDC allocations for France were $1,657,223, while those for Belgium were $540,000; Holland $0; Yugoslavia $1,745; and Italy $347,534. Bauer, *American Jewry*, 292. For the most detailed analyses of these factors, see Zuccotti, *The Holocaust*; Cohen, *Persécutions et sauvetages*; Poznanski, *Les Juifs en France*.
105. Lazare, *La résistance juive*, 282.
106. The Vaad Hatzalah of the Jewish Agency should not be confused with the Orthodox organization of the same name. The former group allocated $8,800 per month to Jarblum, but it is not known how much was received (see Poznanski, "Jewish Resistance in France," 32).
107. AJA, WJC (coll. 361), D49/19, France (children), Gerhard Riegner, Note sur l'action de sauvetage d'enfants en France, 4/12/1945.

CHAPTER TWO: JEWISH ENCOUNTERS
IN LIBERATION FRANCE

1. Oral History Archive of the Hebrew University of Jerusalem (OHD), (4)13, Isaac Klein Interview, 3. See also Klein, *The Anguish and the Ecstasy*, 104–110; Grobman, *Rekindling the Flame*, 29. Klein does not date his arrival in

Chartres, but from his account, it must have been after the liberation of Chartres (August 15–19, 1944) and before Rosh Hashanah (September 17–19, 1944).

2. Historians Yehuda Bauer, Alex Grobman, and, most recently, Deborah Dash Moore have contemplated Jewish military-civilian interaction from different points of view. Bauer has studied the illegal immigration of Eastern European Jews to Palestine from 1944 through 1948 and looked at the role played by members of the American military in this endeavor. Like Bauer, Grobman has asked how members of the US Armed Forces assisted survivors of the Holocaust. His extensive study of American Jewish chaplains documents how this group provided material aid and political advocacy to surviving Jews, especially in the DP camps in Germany and Austria. Dash Moore has considered this question from a different angle, asking how participation in World War II and contact with European Jewish survivors influenced American Jewish GIs. While all of these works make reference to the interaction that occurred between American Jewish military personnel and Jewish survivors in France, their central concerns lay elsewhere and their analyses of France remain limited. Bauer, *Flight and Rescue*, 279–281 and 316–317; Grobman, *Rekindling the Flame*, 22–35; Dash Moore, *GI Jews*, 200–212. See also Stahl, *Enlisting Faith*, 138–145 and Ouzan, "American Jewish Chaplains and the Survivors' Return to Jewish Communal Life," 112–136.

3. Yehuda Bauer, for example, extensively studies the situation in Eastern Europe and in DP camps in *Out of the Ashes*; regarding France see pages 23–33 and 237–245. Avinoam Patt, Michael Berkowitz, and Atina Grossmann have analyzed this population with new methodological approaches. Patt and Berkowitz, *"We Are Here"*; Grossmann, *Jews, Germans, and Allies*; Patt, *Finding Home and Homeland*.

4. Hilary Footitt qualifies the Anglo-American and French historiographies on liberation France as "ethnocentric," with each group putting itself at the "centre of the stage" and assigning the other a "walk-on" role. Her recent book attempts to "integrate these two separate and parallel narratives of Liberation" (see Footitt, *War and Liberation*, 2). American historians have started enmeshing French and American perspectives, as can be seen in Alice Kaplan's *The Interpreter* or Mary Louise Robert's recent contributions, *What Soldiers Do* and *D-Day through French Eyes*. It should be noted, however, that French accounts of liberation have not ignored Americans. The exploits of American GIs were documented in the early 1980s in Marc Hillel's *Vie et moeurs*. Other French accounts of the liberation incorporate the American presence; see Husson, *La Marne et les marnais*; Torrent, *La France américaine*. More generally, see Carruthers, *The Good Occupation*, 111–150.

5. Roberts, *What Soldiers Do*, 76.

6. This situation can be contrasted with the DP camps in Germany, where the US Army established formal nonfraternization policies in September 1944,

which remained in effect until October 1945. Nonetheless, as Atina Grossmann has shown, such policies in occupied Germany did not prevent the intense interactions among Jews, Allies, and Germans. Grossmann, *Jews, Germans, and Allies*.

7. Nonetheless, Ronit Stahl makes the convincing argument that in the early Cold War, chaplains were serving the "military-spiritual complex" as "nation-builders, constructing the religious and moral foundations of societies, citizens and states" (Stahl, *Enlisting Faith*, 137–138). This helps nuance the rebellious image Jewish chaplains provided of their work. Stahl suggests their actions fit a larger military goal in the early Cold War period.

8. Here I use interviews from the Oral History Archive of the Hebrew University of Jerusalem (OHD) conducted by Yehuda Bauer and Alex Grobman. I was able to interview two former American Jewish GIs and correspond with the surviving spouse of another.

9. As Mary Louise Roberts notes: "Because historical narratives focus almost exclusively on the day-to-day heroics of the American GI, they slight the French and leave half the story untold. French civilians appear only at the peripheries of the scene, their roles reduced to inert bystanders or joyous celebrants of liberation. In short, they form nothing more than a landscape against which the Allies fight for freedom" (Roberts, *What Soldiers Do*, 16). In the Jewish military-civilian historiography, sources are primarily American (see Grobman, *Rekindling the Flame*, 3–5).

10. As Karen H. Adler points out, "Listening to individuals allows us to hear about personal experience which in turn provokes the analysis of factors that are difficult to grasp from written accounts" (Adler, *Jews and Gender*, 169–174).

11. In total, I located four individuals present in Reims during the postwar period. This city, whose Jewish population was devastated by the Holocaust, provides an opportunity to break from the Parisian-centric historiography. The small size of the Jewish community, coupled with the sustained presence of the US military, led to a great deal of interaction between American and French Jews. While far from representative, my sources explore the specific experiences of four families, out of the total forty-eight who returned to Reims after the war, yet address the larger situation of the community at this juncture. I complement this with interviews I conducted with former GIs, their spouses, and French Jews.

12. On this transition, see Wieviorka, "Au lendemain de la guerre;" Nataf, "Le judaïsme religieux," 71–104; Adler, *Jews and Gender*; Poznanski, "French Apprehensions," 25–57; Weil, "The Return of Jews," 58–70; Dreyfus, "Post-Liberation French Administration," 112–126; Fogg, "Everything Had Ended," 277–307. More generally, see Mandel, *Aftermath of Genocide*, and Doron, *Jewish Youth*.

13. Rousso, *The Vichy Syndrome*, 15–59. The historiography on Vichy memory has developed considerably. See Lagrou, *Nazi Occupation*; Golsan, *Vichy's Afterlife*, and "The Legacy of World War II France," 73–101; Suleiman, *Crises of Memory*. On the emergence of Holocaust memory in France, see Wolf, *Harnessing the Holocaust*; Rothberg, *Multidirectional Memory*; Azouvi, *Le mythe du grand silence* and Perego, *Pleurons-les*. For an excellent analysis of the historiography, see Perego, "La mémoire avant la mémoire?"

14. Rioux, *La quatrième république*, 31.

15. Roberts, *What Soldiers Do*, 21.

16. Lagrou, *Nazi Occupation*, 89.

17. For postwar statistics see Rioux, *La quatrième république*, 30–39.

18. Jockusch, *Collect and Record!*; Azouvi, *Le mythe du grand silence*; Doron, *Jewish Youth*; Perego, *Pleurons-les*; Fourtage, "Et après?"

19. Poznanski, "French Apprehensions," 34. She also refers to Article 3 of the law of August 8, which appears to have served the same purposes (Poznanski, "French Apprehensions," 45).

20. Mandel, *Aftermath of Genocide*, 62.

21. Fogg, *Stealing Home*, 7, 62–71.

22. JDC-NY, France, 1945/54, File 256, Letter from Henri Schinzer to his "Master," most likely the artist Mané-Katz, November 19, 1944.

23. Ibid.

24. This individual's observations are echoed in Adler, *The Jews of Paris*, 221–222.

25. The long-held statistic of 2,560 has recently been updated. Klarsfeld, *Vichy Auschwitz*, 179–180; Doulut, Klarsfeld, Labeau, *Mémorial des 3943 rescapés juifs de France*.

26. Wieviorka, "Au lendemain de la guerre," 5–6. At the time, the Jewish population of France was estimated at one hundred seventy thousand and deportation at one hundred ten thousand individuals. JDC-NY, France, 1945/54, 247, "France," not dated.

27. Wieviorka, "Au lendemain de la guerre," 5–6.

28. Weinberg, "Reconstruction," 172.

29. Poznanski, *Les Juifs en France*, 70.

30. On the antisemitic incidents involving restitution, see Poznanski, "French Apprehensions," 47–52; Mandel, *Aftermath of Genocide*, 52–85. Jean-Marc Dreyfus provides a more positive image of restitution, emphasizing the efficiency of French judicial policy and courts (see Dreyfus, "Post-Liberation French Administration," 112–126).

31. Weinberg, "Reconstruction," 171. Shannon Fogg states thirty-eight thousand Parisian apartments were emptied in the German furniture operation and twenty-five thousand Parisian families were evicted (an estimated one hundred thousand individuals). Fogg, *Stealing Home*, 43, 62–63. On Jewish reactions to such losses, see Auslander, "Coming Home? Jews in Postwar Paris."

32. Kaplan, "French Jewry under the Occupation," 109–110.
33. Weinberg, "Reconstruction," 169.
34. On the establishment of the CRIF, see Adler, *The Jews of Paris*, 230–233; Wieviorka, *Déportation et génocide*, 340–347; Kaspi, *Les Juifs pendant l'Occupation*, 377–381. See also Fredj, "La création du CRIF" and Ghiles-Meilhac, *Le CRIF*.
35. JDC-NY, France 1933/44, 596, Letter from Maurice Brener to Dr. Joseph Schwartz, September 8, 1944. We now know that this number is incorrect. Almost seventy-six thousand Jews were deported from France.
36. Ibid.
37. Wieviorka, "Au lendemain de la guerre," 17. The tripling of those in need is certainly due to the emergence of the Jewish population from hiding. It can be argued that Jews who received assistance during the Occupation faced additional risk of arrest, causing needy Jews to avoid seeking out aid. On the first moments of Jewish welfare in the Northern Zone, see Fourtage, "Et après," 167–215.
38. JDC-NY, France 1933/44, 596, Letter from Victor Bienstock to Arthur Greenleigh, September 22, 1944.
39. American Judaism can be divided into several branches, the largest of the 1940s were the Reform, Conservative and Orthodox movements. The Reform movement began in Germany in the first half of the nineteenth century to reconcile membership in the nation-state with the Jewish religion. In the United States, over the second half of the nineteenth century, the movement called for the radical reform of Jewish traditions. The Conservative movement was institutionalized in the United States in the early twentieth century but was highly influenced by the German Positive Historical movement of the nineteenth century and argued for the need to adapt Judaism to the period while conserving it. The Orthodox movement gathered multiple streams of orthodoxy and traditionalists in America at the end of the nineteenth century. On the development and debates among these movements, see Sarna, *American Judaism* and Raphael, *Profiles in American Judaism*.
40. Kaufman, *American Jews in World War II*.
41. There were roughly a thousand rabbis in the United States at the outbreak of the war, half of whom were disqualified for the chaplaincy due to health, age, or insufficient rabbinical training. Bernstein, "Jewish Chaplains in World War II," 174. Mobilization statistics from Grobman do not add up to 311; he does not explain this discrepancy (see Grobman, *Rekindling the Flame*, 9).
42. This is not to say American Jews did not respond to the Holocaust. The historiographical debate that sought for many years to assign blame for inaction has started to develop a more nuanced approach to the American response by assessing what was done instead of what should have, or could have, been done. See for example, Collomp, *Rescue, Relief and Resistance*; Erbelding, *Rescue Board*; or Hobson Faure, "Becoming Refugees."

43. Judah Nadich kept a diary of his activities, which he recorded for historian Alex Grobman. OHD (119) 84, Judah Nadich Interview. The original can be consulted at the US Holocaust Memorial Museum. See also Nadich, *Eisenhower*.
44. Ibid., September 5–12, 1944, 2–6.
45. OHD (47) 9, Edward Warburg Interview, 1967, 12–14. See also Bauer, *Out of the Ashes*, 27–28.
46. Wyman, *Abandonment of the Jews*, 19–58.
47. OHD (119) 44, Israel Joel Philips Interview, 12.
48. Dash Moore, *GI Jews*, 22–48.
49. For analyses of Jewish participation by city and by draft versus voluntary enlistment, see Kohs, "Jewish War Records," 153–172.
50. Auschwitz was liberated in January 1945 and confirmed worst fears. On the reactions of American Jewish military to the discovery of the death camps, see Dash Moore, *GI Jews*, 223–237. See also Levin, *In Search*, 171–295.
51. OHD (119) 47, Meyer Miller Interview, 1975, 17.
52. OHD (119) 44, Israel Joel Philips Interview, 1–2.
53. OHD, (119) 47, Meyer Miller Interview, 1–10. He did not specify which school.
54. OHD (119) 3, Isadore Breslau Interview, 21.
55. JDC-NY, 1945/54, file 294, Letter from Chaplain Eli Bohnen, HQ 42nd (Rainbow) Infantry Division, December 17, 1945.
56. Grobman, *Rekindling the Flame*, 22, 99–105. On the centralization of American Jewish fundraising, see chapter 1.
57. OHD (119) 14, Oscar Lipshutz Interview, 1974, 3–5. This package program was coordinated by the Vaad Hatzala, an American aid committee of Orthodox affiliation, which used the GIs' and chaplains' addresses until military authorities discovered the plan.
58. Grobman, *Rekindling the Flame*, 26–27.
59. OHD (119) 64, Abraham Haselkorn Interview, 1975, 7, 34.
60. Interview with Ralph Goldman, Jerusalem, May 2, 2005.
61. OHD (119) 64, Haselkorn Interview, 10.
62. OHD (119) 3, Isadore Breslau Interview, 4, 17.
63. Several American Jewish chaplains in Europe had tense relations with the US military and were investigated, including Herbert Friedman, threatened with court-martial for book theft, and Abraham Klausner, for his activism with DPs, although a systematic study has not been conducted. Grobman, *Rekindling the Flame*, 168–78; Leff, *The Archive Thief*, 124–128; Patt, "Go to Palestine." On court-martials and executions of African American GIs in France during this period, see Kaplan, *The Interpreter*.
64. Interview with René Lichtman, West Bloomfield, January 2008. René Lichtman's multiple trips to France with his photo album have allowed him to

reconnect with the descendants of his parent's friends. The grandson of one of the women in this photo confirms his grandfather was a POW in Germany at the moment this photo was taken. Interview, Michaël Rapaport, Paris, April 2019.

65. JDC-NY, 1933/1944, 596, Letter from Abraham Haselkorn to Philip Bernstein, September 6, 1944.

66. On the role of Haselkorn's efforts for Jewish children, I rely on Grobman, *Rekindling the Flame*, 24–29, and OHD (119) 64, Abraham Haselkorn Interview, unless otherwise noted.

67. This order was established in 1843 by recent Jewish converts to Catholicism with a distinct mission to encourage Jewish conversions to Catholicism, a fact that complicated the order's relationship with postwar Jewish organizations. In July 1946, the Central Consistory complained to the Catholic *nonce apostologique* that Père Devaux still had thirty Jewish children in his possession. This order was also implicated in the Affair Finaly. Poujol, *Les enfants cachés*, 35–36; 159–180. Interestingly, the American-based Commission on the European Jewish Cultural Reconstruction Committee, led by Salo Baron and Hannah Arendt, discovered the remaining children in Devaux's possession. JDC 1945/54, letter from Père Devaux to the Commission on the European Jewish Cultural Reconstruction Committee, January 16, 1946.

68. OHD (119) 84, Judah Nadich Interview, September 26, 1944, 12.

69. Levin, *In Search*, 186.

70. Hazan, "Récupérer les enfants cachés," 16–31. Doron, *Jewish Youth*, 74–117. More generally, on the nationalizing of children in the postwar period, see Zahra, *The Lost Children*.

71. Poujol, building on my research, concludes that in 1953, Devaux's order still had thirty Jewish children. Poujol, *L'Église de France*, 291–314.

72. Here Grobman and Haselkorn's accounts differ. According to Grobman, Haselkorn needed to raise $1,500–$2,000 a month, whereas Haselkorn reported needing $500 a month, and thus, by raising $5000 among his troops, had enough money for eight to ten months of operation. Grobman, *Rekindling the Flame*, 26, and OHD (119) 64, Abraham Haselkorn Interview, 3–4. For details on the history of the château, see Hazan, *Les enfants de l'après-guerre*, 74.

73. OHD (119) 64, Abraham Haselkorn Interview, 4, 10.

74. Ibid., 7, 11.

75. According to one source, these methods were not a typical practice in other French Jewish children's homes, where a point was made to not ask the children to remove their Christian medallions. Interview with Ted Comet, New York, July 20, 2004. This is confirmed in my interviews with Gaby Wolff Cohen, who worked with children during the war to establish their new identities, as well as in OSE homes after the liberation. Cohen accompanied the Finaly brothers

to Israel after their kidnapping, for example, and took them to church when they requested. Interviews with Gaby Wolff Cohen, May 28, 2004; June 8, 2004; and November 3, 2004.

76. The home was first run by Trachtenberg and then an OSE educator named Lotte Schwarz, whose account describes a chaotic and distrustful group of children who had been "trained to work on the black market" by the previous director. Schwarz introduced more constructive pedagogical methods and was assisted by Rémi Sternmann, a camp survivor, who earned the children's respect. Hazan, *Les enfants de l'après-guerre*, 74–76; Schwarz, *Je veux vivre*, 189–190.

77. See Bauer, *Flight and Rescue*; Zertal, *From Catastrophe to Power*, 52–92. On the evolutions of postwar French Zionism, see Poznanski, "L'heritage de la guerre," 237–273. For another example of an American Jewish Chaplain's Zionist activism, see Patt, "Go to Palestine," 240–276.

78. Nicault, "L'utopie sioniste du 'nouveau Juif,'" 132. Klüger was an agent of the Mossad le'Aliyah Bet, who operated in Romania, Egypt, and France. See her memoirs, in romanticized form, Klüger and Mann, *The Last Escape*.

79. Bauer, *Flight and Rescue*, 108–109.

80. OHD (119) 84, Judah Nadich Interview, May–June 1945, 35–50; Grobman, *Rekindling the Flame*, 71–72.

81. OHD (119) 64, Abraham Haselkorn Interview, 25–39; Grobman, *Rekindling the Flame*, 118–120.

82. OHD (119) 50, Robert Handwerger Interview, 3.

83. Stahl, *Enlisting Faith*, 137–138.

84. Grynberg and Nicault, "Le culte israélite," 72–88.

85. Grynberg, "Après la tourmente," 262–267; Nataf, "Le judaïsme religieux," 80–96; Wieviorka, *Déportation et génocide*, 340–354; Wasserstein, *Vanishing Diaspora*, 69–70.

86. OHD (119) 3, Isadore Breslau Interview, 16–17.

87. OHD (119) 84, Judah Nadich Interview, September 18–19, 1944, 8–9. Attendance figures may have been exaggerated by Nadich.

88. Dash Moore, *GI Jews*, 209–210.

89. Roberts, *What Soldiers Do*, 134–135, and more generally, 113–158.

90. Interview with Hyman Fox, West Bloomfield, Michigan, April 3, 2019.

91. OHD (119) 84, Judah Nadich Interview, September 26–27, 1944, 14.

92. Dash Moore argues that US Armed Forces policy encouraged religious practice and ecumenism. Dash Moore, *GI Jews*, 118–155, 209.

93. OHD (13) 4, Isaac Klein Interview, 23–25, and Klein, *Anguish and the Ecstasy*, 163–164.

94. OHD (119) 36, Isaiah Rackovsky Interview, 4–6.

95. OHD (119) 59, Carl Miller Interview, 21–24.

96. OHD (119) 84, Judah Nadich Interview, December 17, 1944, 29.

97. OHD (119) 59, Carl Miller Interview, 21–24.
98. For example, on December 9, 1944, Alvin S. of Worcester was married to Denise K. of Paris by Rabbi Julien Weill. Likewise, on March 4, 1945, Marcus M. of Pittsburgh married Annie Z. of Paris at the Notre Dame de Nazareth Temple. ACIP, GG 354, Ketuba 8057 and ACIP, GG 354, Ketuba 8070.
99. ACIP, GG 354, 355, 356. This number may be higher due to a missing file (357), which concerns this period. One hundred and eighty-three marriages were performed in Parisian consistorial temples in 1945. Nataf, "Le judaïsme religieux," 93.
100. Husson, *La Marne et les Marnais*, 303–313. Hilary Footitt, who also writes on Reims, states that 110,000 were permanently stationed in the Reims area. In addition, eight camps, each with 17,000 men, were opened in June 1945 (see Footitt, *War and Liberation*, 162, and more generally, 147–174).
101. Husson, *La Marne et les Marnais*, 310.
102. Interview with Hélène Lerner Ejnès, Tel Aviv, April 20, 2005; Footitt, *War and Liberation*, 147–150. See also Ouzan, "American Jewish Chaplains and the Survivors' Return to Jewish Communal Life," 125–128.
103. I would like to thank Madame Véronique Cahen, who generously introduced me to those who had been in contact with American Jewish military personnel in Reims. As seen above, five interviews were conducted with four individuals.
104. Madame Créange did not specify how long she worked at this hospital but states she returned to Reims after the full Occupation of France in November 1942.
105. Interview with Berthe (Harrari) Créange, Saint-Rémy-lès-Chevreuse, April 2, 2004.
106. Interview with Denyse Marx, Paris, October 21, 2004.
107. Ejnès, *Histoire des Juifs*, 15. Isaac Klein estimates the prewar Jewish population of Reims at 150 families and states that 75 returned to Reims after the war. Klein, *Anguish and the Ecstasy*, 126.
108. Husson, *La déportation*, 85. Statistics on survivors in Reims from email correspondence between Husson and the author, December 19, 2007.
109. Husson, *La déportation*, 192. Berthe Créange states the synagogue was used to store explosives, whereas Isaac Klein states it was airplane engines. Author interview with Berthe Créange, Saint-Rémy-lès-Chevreuse, April 2, 2004; Klein, *Anguish and the Ecstasy*, 126.
110. Klein, *Anguish and the Ecstasy*, 127.
111. Within twelve hours of his arrival, he wrote to Philip Bernstein of the Jewish Welfare Board that he had arranged for communal elections, a free-loan society, and the reinstatement of religious classes once enough children were present. He also requested money to help his efforts for French Jews. JDC-NY, France 1933/44, 596, Letter from Isaac Klein to Philip Bernstein, October 19, 1944.

112. Klein, *Anguish and the Ecstasy*, 131–132.
113. Ibid., 133.
114. Telephone interview with Berthe Créange, March 26, 2004.
115. Livazer, *The Rabbi's Blessing*, 76–77.
116. Interview with Berthe Créange, Saint-Rémy-lès-Chevreuse, April 2, 2004.
117. Interview with Denyse Marx, Paris, October 21, 2004.
118. Interview with Berthe Créange, Saint-Rémy-lès-Chevreuse, April 2, 2004.
119. On sexual violence perpetuated by American GIs in Reims, see Footitt, *War and Liberation*, 156–174.
120. Correspondence with author, June 20, 2005.
121. Interview with Hélène Lerner Ejnès, Tel Aviv, April 20, 2005.
122. These anecdotes were shared by Hélène Lerner Ejnès. Interview with Hélène Lerner Ejnès, Tel Aviv, April 20, 2005.
123. Hyman Fox private papers, Letter from Simon C. to Hyman Fox, July 7, 1946.
124. Husson, *La Marne et les Marnais*, volume 1, 309–311, and volume 2, 92.
125. Siekierski, *Midor LeDor*, 160–161.
126. Klein, *Anguish and the Ecstasy*, 129.
127. Letter from Schoem, reprinted in Ejnès, *Histoire des Juifs*, 319. According to Hilary Footitt, this was a common problem in the Reims area. Footitt, *War and Liberation*, 164.
128. Livazer, *The Rabbi's Blessing*, 79–81.
129. Denyse Marx, Berthe Harrari Créange, and Hélène and Serge Ejnès each shared versions of this event in their interviews. Françoise Ouzan, who independently studied chaplains in Reims, also discusses the role of the German POWs preparing the seder (see Ouzan, "American Jewish Chaplains and the Survivors' Return to Jewish Communal Life," 128).
130. JDC-NY, France, 1945/54, 256.
131. "French Family to Visit in Stratford in Continuing a Post-War Friendship," newspaper article from Stratford, Connecticut, [unknown title], January 21, 1974.
132. Ejnès, *Histoire des Juifs*.
133. Ejnès writes of this moment, "Therefore, on that morning of May 7th the explosion of joy in Reims was double [...]. Soon, in the French way, the streets of the city turned into a huge and unique open-air dancing hall where the popular joy explosed [sic]. No need to tell you that the jewish [sic] population of a decimated city, as in all towns, was not the last to join. All the more as thousands of jewish [sic] soldiers of all forces and all ranks that stationed in the city had quickly restored a feeling of security that even in their nicest dreams the jews [sic] had not imagined so definite and so jewish [sic]. Crowded synagogue, jewish [sic] classes, held by numerous 'Chaplains' such as rabbi Klein and rabbi Livazer, who must be cited here, huge seder with nearly a thousand guests, and so on. No,

the tiny Jewish [sic] community of Reims had never hoped for so much. The only regret was that no family was complete to fully appreciate it" (Ejnès, *Histoire des Juifs*, 305–306 in the French and 308–309 in English).
134. Klein, *Anguish and the Ecstasy*, 138.

CHAPTER THREE: EMERGING FROM CATASTROPHE

1. She attended French civilization courses at the Sorbonne for the following four-year period and in the evenings spent time with her husband and JDC employees. Interview with Lolita Goldstein, Geneva, March 9, 2006.
2. Herman Stein, telephone interview, November 30, 2004. Morris Laub, who worked at the JDC's European headquarters in Paris in 1945 recalled, "It was at night that those of us who were in Paris would meet in Dr. Schwartz's hotel room, have a drink, and talk. The conversation, though occasionally personal, dealt mainly with the problems facing the Jews of Europe whom we had come to help. Telephone calls would come in constantly from all parts of Europe asking for Schwartz so that he could hear the latest troubles and proposals for help. He would discuss these calls immediately with us, and, as we talked, we had a feeling that we were not only observers, but active participants in the making of Jewish history" (see Laub, *Last Barrier to Freedom*, 86).
3. One exception includes Bauer, *Out of the Ashes*. On historiographical trends, see Mazower, "Reconstruction: The Historiographical Issues," 17–28; Reinisch, "Introduction: Relief in the Aftermath of War," 371–404.
4. Bauer, *Out of the Ashes*, 23–33; 237–245; Goldsztejn, "Au secours d'une communauté;" Mandel, *In the Aftermath of Genocide*, 162–177 and "Philanthropy or Cultural Imperialism?," 53–94.
5. Recent scholarship has highlighted how humanitarian organizations somewhat paradoxically touted internationalism yet bolstered nation-states as they sought to reconstruct in the aftermath of the war. Reinisch, "We Shall Rebuild Anew a Powerful Nation. UNRRA, Internationalism and National Reconstruction in Poland," 451–476 and "Internationalism in Relief: The Birth (and Death) of UNRRA," 258–289; Zahra, *The Lost Children*, 198–221; more generally, Cohen, *In War's Wake*.
6. On the JDC program in Germany and Austria, see Bauer, *Out of the Ashes*, 34–103, 119–132, 193–236, and 261–299; Webster, "American Relief and Jews in Germany," 293–321; Shafir, *Ambiguous Relations*; and Grossmann, *Jews, Germans and Allies*, 131–182. On displaced persons in postwar Germany, see Cohen, *In War's Wake*, 126–149 and Patt, *Finding Home and Homeland*, 13–67.
7. The literature on the French state under Vichy is too vast to list here. Suffice to say that historians no longer consider Vichy as a monolithic block and have begun to address the different attitudes toward Jews within its

administrations. For a recent discussion of this trend, and as an example of it, see Lee, *Petain's Jewish Children*, 10–19. Renée Poznanski and Jean-Marc Dreyfus present two different points of view on the Jews' place in postwar French society: Poznanski emphasizes the problem of silence as a result of the return to republicanism and the disconnect this created between Jews and the rest of the French population, whereas Dreyfus notes the relatively straightforward restitution process for Jews in France as opposed to other countries. Poznanski, *Propagandes et persécutions*, 561–592 and "Jewish Expectations, French Apprehensions: From a Social Imaginary to a Political Practice," 25–57; Dreyfus, "The Post-Liberation French Administration and the Jews," 111–126. Maud Mandel provides a middle-of-the road approach, highlighting the need of private aid to compensate the weak public assistance from the state. Mandel, *In the Aftermath of Genocide*, 52–85. Most recently, on French policies for returning Jewish camp survivors, see Fourtage, "Et après?"

8. The argument that Jews remained a distinct group after Vichy is bolstered by recent research on immigration, demographics, children, diplomacy, and restitution. In her study of de Gaulle's Haut Comité consultatif de la population et de la famille and its secretary, Georges Mauco, K. L. Adler argues that postwar French rhetoric on immigration and assimilation was strongly informed by interwar and Vichy attitudes on Jews and a belief in immutable ethnic characteristics. Adler, *Jews and Gender in Liberation France*, 68–143. Tara Zahra confirms that adult Jews were not considered desirable immigrants by French authorities. Zahra, *The Lost Children*, 149–152. Julia Maspero shows that French authorities "did not seem eager to welcome [Jewish refugees]" but shows that the French provisional government did agree to allow in eight thousand Polish Jews in May 1946. Maspero, "French Policy on Postwar Migration of Eastern European Jews through France," 319–339. Daniella Doron analyzes the case of Jewish children in France, showing that this group escaped the negative assessments attributed to adult Jews and were seen as potential members of the nation by French authorities. She also shows how Jewish organizations fought the state to provide care for Jewish children, indicating that the notion of Jewish distinctiveness was also maintained by Jews. Doron, *Jewish Youth and Identity in Postwar France*, 74–117. Jean-Marc Dreyfus has written on French diplomats at the Quai d'Osay and Jews, demonstrating the particularly closed and even antisemitic milieu of the interwar and Vichy period but shows that in the immediate postwar period, Jews were finally able to access positions of influence. However, this did not make "Jewish problems" a priority. Dreyfus, *L'impossible reparation*, 13–35, 55–78. Shannon Fogg discusses housing restitutions, showing that the state sought to balance collective and individual needs and downplayed the specific situation of Jews. Fogg, "Everything Had Ended," 277–307 and more generally, Fogg, *Stealing Home*.

9. Emmanuel Mounier used the term in the journal *Esprit*. Poznanski, *Propagandes et persécutions*, 561 and Mandel, *In the Aftermath of Genocide*, 232.

10. As of November 1944, Brener's partner, Jules Jefroykin, had still not returned to Paris. JDC-NY, France 1939/1945, File 596, Cable from Joseph Schwartz to Arthur Greenleigh, via the War Refugee Board, November 2, 1944; JDC-NY, France 1939/45, File 596, Letter from Edward Warburg to Paul Baerwald, September 6, 1944, and Letter from Joseph Schwartz to Maurice Brener, October 11, 1944.

11. JDC-NY, France 1945/54, File 247, Report for France for Last Quarter of 1944, September 1945.

12. At the time, it received 13.3 percent of the JDC budget. JDC-NY, France 1945/54, File 247, Report for France for Last Quarter of 1944, September 1945. On the number of children in need of assistance, see JDC-NY, France 1945/54, File 249, Childcare under the Auspices of the Joint Distribution Committee, 1945.

13. AJA, World Jewish Congress (361), H 115/7, Letter from Marc Jarblum to Nahum Goldmann, November 21, 1944.

14. Maud Mandel has pointed out that aid and services provided by the French government were often inadequate for French Jews, who had lost their support networks. A one-time payment of F5,000, later raised to F8,000, along with a ration book for clothing, transportation, and medical care for nine months was provided to all returning deportees, regardless of the reason for deportation. Unnaturalized, foreign-born Jews often didn't qualify for government aid and others had difficulties accessing it. Other times, funds were simply not available for those who did qualify. Mandel, *In the Aftermath of Genocide*, 62–64.

15. Hazan, *Les orphelins de la Shoah*, 285–293 and "Récupérer les enfants cachés," 16–31; Poujol, *Les enfants cachés* and *L'Église de France*; Doron, *Jewish Youth and Identity in Postwar France*. For first-person accounts of life in the children's homes, see Hemmendigner, *Les Enfants de Buchenwald*; Wiesel, *All the Rivers Run to the Sea*, 109–158.

16. Doron, *Jewish Youth and Identity in Postwar France*.

17. JDC-I, Laura Margolis Jarblum Collection, uncatalogued, Country Directors Conference, Bulletin 22, February 3, 1947. On the instrumentalization of Jewish children in the postwar period, see Doron, *Jewish Youth and Identity in Postwar France*, 31–73.

18. The FSJF was funded by the JDC, the WJC, the Vaad Hatzalah of Palestine—not to be confused with the orthodox committee of the same name—the IGCR, and an Argentine aid committee. Its 1945 budget was F86,860,167 (about $1,737,203), of which 21 percent was dedicated to aiding children. AN, AJ/43, File 1252, Fédération des sociétés juives de France, rapport general d'activité, 1945.

19. Marc Jarblum began publishing *Unzer wort* in 1944. Joseph Fisher, and Israël and Jules Jefroykin were involved in the publication of *La terre retrouvée*, which was affiliated with the National Fund (KKL) and had been published since 1928.

20. Hazan, *Les orphelins de la Shoah*, 399. On the Communist Jewish children's homes, see Doron, *Jewish Youth and Identity*, 143–152. For a fictionalized account, see Bober, *Berg et Beck*.

21. Constance Pâris de Bollardière notes there were 680 members of the Bund at the end of 1947 and provides the estimate of 6,000 for the circulation of *Unzer stimme* between 1940 and 1950. Pâris de Bollardière, "La pérennité de notre peuple," 198, 255. In 1954, the American Jewish Committee estimated the circulation of *Naye presse* at 4,500, *Unzer wort* at 4,000 in France with 1,800 elsewhere in Europe, and *Unzer stimme* at 500 to 700. YIVO, American Jewish Committee RG-347.7.1, FAD 1, Box 20, File: France Jews 1943–1961, Nontitled report on the Jewish community in France, 1954.

22. Weinberg, *A Community on Trial*, 22–44.

23. One observes multiple discourses on individual and collective Jewish identities among highly assimilated French Jews during the nineteenth century. Cohen, "Ethnicity and Jewish Solidarity in Nineteenth Century France," 249–274; Leff, *Sacred Bonds of Solidarity*, 157–199.

24. Overwhelmed by the pressing welfare needs of French Jews, Jabrlum decided not to attend. AJA, World Jewish Congress (361), H 115/7, Letter from Marc Jarblum to Nahum Goldmann, November 21, 1944.

25. Those who had not been granted authorization included Mr. Lévine of the FSJF, Maître Spanien, and Mr. Adamitsch, secretary of the Communist-affiliated UJRE. AJA, WJC (361), H 115/7, Letter from Marc Jarblum to Nahum Goldmann, November 13, 1944.

26. ACIC, WJC-New York, uncatalogued, Orders from Headquarters European Theater of Operations, US Army, November 27, 1944.

27. Joseph (Ariel) Fisher was born in Odessa in 1893 and emigrated to Palestine in 1924. He was sent to France to represent the KKL and remained throughout the 1940s. Fisher and Nahum Hermann (deported in 1944) raised funds for wartime JDC activities in France by contracting loans from individuals and redirecting donations for Palestine to France. On the JDC's "loan après" system, see chapter 1.

28. JDC-NY, France 1939/45, File 596, Minutes of Meeting Held on December 5, 1944.

29. JDC-NY, France 1939/45, File 596, Memo, author unknown, December 6, 1944.

30. JDC-NY, France 1939/45, File 596, Minutes of Meeting Held on December 19, 1944.

31. Ibid.

32. The JDC eventually provided a grant of $100,000 to the Consistory. It was unspecified if this was to the Central Consistory or the Paris Consistory in 1945. JDC-NY, uncatalogued, JDC Primer, France-10. It also channeled religious articles to this organization.

33. JDC-NY, France 1939/45, File 596, Report by Noel Aronovici, General Notes on the Joint Distribution Committee's Activity in France, February 25, 1944.
34. Ibid.
35. Madame R. Pleven was most likely Anne Bompard Pleven, the wife of French Finance Minister René Pleven. JDC-NY, France 1939/45, File 596, Letter from Noel Aronovici to Isaac Levy, August 30, 1944.
36. JDC-NY, France 1939/45, File 596, Cable from Madame Pleven to the Ministère de santé publique, Paris, September 29, 1944.
37. The IGCR was established during the Evian Conference in 1938 and led by Sir Herbert Emerson, who was also the head of the High Commission on Refugees, established by the Society of Nations on January 1, 1939. In 1946, it became the International Refugee Organization.
38. JDC-NY, France 1939/45, File 596, Letter from Eddie (SHAEF mission, Belgium, G-5 section) to PB (Edward Warburg to Paul Baerwald), November 10, 1944.
39. Wieviorka, *Déportation et genocide*, 37–39. According to Yehuda Bauer, the French provisional government had refused UNRRA's assistance in France. Others state that France did not apply for UNRRA aid. Bauer, *Out of the Ashes*, 23; Friedlander, *International Social Welfare*, 1–40. For an institutional history of UNRRA, see Hoehler, *Europe's Homeless Millions* and more recently, Cohen, *In War's Wake*, 58–78; Reinisch, "We Shall Rebuild Anew a Powerful Nation," 451–476 and "Internationalism in Relief: The Birth (and Death) of UNRRA," 258–289.
40. An agreement was signed on November 25, 1944, placing UNRRA under the authority of the SHAEF, further limiting the role of the organization. Michael Marrus, *The Unwanted*, 317–325.
41. MacCormac, "Aid for Displaced Held Up in France."
42. JDC-NY, France 1939/45, File 596, Letter from DH Sulzberger (civilian, G5-SHAEF) to Moses Leavitt, October 12, 1944.
43. JDC-NY, France 1939/45, File 596, Message from Sir Hebert Emerson of the Intergovernmental Committee and Mr. Hoehler of UNRRA to Paul Baerwald, Chairman of JDC, November 2, 1944. Sent via the War Refugee Board, November 6, 1944.
44. AJHS, Cecilia Razovsky Papers, P-290, Box 6, Folder 1, Letter Dated April 20, 1945, Signed by 115 Jewish survivors.
45. JDC-NY, France 1939/45, File 596, Letter from Isaac Naiditch to Dr. Joseph Schwartz, September 8, 1944.
46. Ibid.
47. OHD (119) 84, Judah Nadich Interview, November 30, 1944. Yehuda Bauer reports that Greenleigh arrived in October 1944. Bauer, *Out of the Ashes*, 31. This

is disproven by a Jewish Telegraphic Agency update that reports Greenleigh's arrival. ACIC, invitations, uncatalogued, extraits de nouvelles données par le Jewish Telegraphic Agency, "Arthur Greenleigh est arrivé a Paris pour diriger les travaux en france du Joint Distribution Committee," Paris, December 19, 1944.

48. Lambert, "Arthur D. Greenleigh, 90, Expert on Welfare Issues and Refugees." The National Refugee Service was established in 1937 to help settle Jewish refugees in the United States.

49. AJHS, Cecilia Razovsky Papers, P-290, Box 6, Folder 1, Telegram from CH Cramer of UNRRA to Razovsky, September 6, 1944, and Letter from Director of UNRRA to Razovsky, January 18, 1945.

50. Zucker, *Cecilia Razovsky*; Hobson Faure, "Becoming Refugees," 220–225.

51. AJHS, Cecilia Razovsky Papers, P-290, Box 6, Folder 1, Collected Notes on Lecture #3, Cecelia [sic] Razovsky Davidson, July 26, 1945.

52. JDC-NY, France 1945/54, File 247, Letter from Arthur Greenleigh to Moses Leavitt, April 7, 1945.

53. AJHS, Cecilia Razovsky Papers, P-290, Box 6, Folder 1, Collected Notes on Lecture #3, Cecelia [sic] Razivsky Davidson, July, 26 1945.

54. Ibid.

55. AJHS, Cecilia Razovsky Papers, P-290, Box 6, Folder 1, "Scherzo Capriccioso in AJDC Major," Signed "Bon Voyage, Liselotte," June 28, 1945.

56. Green, *The Other Americans in Paris*, 170–174.

57. Arthur Greenleigh negotiated with agents from the SHAEF, recruited personnel for the DP camps, and finally managed to send a team to Buchenwald in June 1945, two months after the liberation of the camp. He regularly met with head chaplain, Judah Nadich, during this period. OHD (119) 84, Judah Nadich.

58. Lagrou, *The Legacy of Nazi Occupation*, 203. Complex factors explain the stark differences in survival rates. Such statistics mean little without contextualization but do help explain postwar perceptions.

59. AJA, WJC, (361), H 115/7, Letter from Marc Jarblum to Nahum Goldmann, November 21, 1944.

60. JDC-NY, France 1945/54, File 249, Childcare in France under the Auspices of the American Jewish Joint Distribution Committee, 1945.

61. AN, AJ 43/1252, Rôle de l'Oeuvre de secours aux enfants OSE en tant qu'agent bénévole du comité intergouvernemental pour les réfugies. Extrait du rapport general d'activité de 1945, January 1946.

62. JDC-NY, France 1945/54, File 249, Childcare in France under the Auspices of the American Jewish Joint Distribution Committee, 1945; JDC-I, 5A1 C. 43.045, Memo from Laura Margolis to Beckelman, December 18, 1948.

63. JDC-NY, France 1945/54, File 247, Letter from Arthur Greenleigh to Moses Leavitt, April 7, 1945. Also cited by Yehuda Bauer and Maud Mandel.

64. In June 1945 alone, COJASOR spent F21,037,825 (about $420,750 based on the 1945 exchange rate). It opened offices in Paris, Montpellier, Grenoble,

Limoges, Nice, Lyon, Marseille, Lille, Périgueux, Clermont-Ferrand, Toulouse, and Dijon. JDC-NY, France 1945/54, File 247, Relief Situation in France, January through June 1945, August 17, 1945. On the merger and early reconstruction work, see Fogg, *Stealing Home*, 157–171 and Fourtage, "Et après?," 190–197.

65. JDC-NY, France 1945/54, File 247, Relief Situation in France, January through June 1945, August 17, 1945.

66. JDC-I, France, 5A1 43.055, COJASOR, Dix ans d'action sociale, 1945–1955, 1956; JDC-NY, France 1945/54, File 283, Rapport moral et financier COJASOR, 1945–1948.

67. From 1945 through 1948, the IGCR (and later IRO) contributed a total of F170,073,119 to COJASOR for services rendered to former Austrian and German nationals, representing 11.5 percent of its total budget for the same period. The JDC financed 84 percent of the COJASOR budget during the same period. JDC-NY, France 1945/54, File 283, Rapport moral et financier COJASOR, 1945–1948, p. 32. Poland proved especially violent for returning Jews. Forty-one Jews were murdered in the Kielce pogrom in July of 1946, and a total of a thousand Jews were murdered from the time of liberation until mid-1947, causing another estimated hundred thousand to flee. Bauer, *Out of the Ashes*, 81–82, plate 17. From 1945 to 1948, COJASOR provided an increasing proportion of aid to Jews who had arrived in France after 1945; these individuals made up 22 percent of the assisted population in 1946, 38 percent in 1947, and 54 percent in 1948. JDC-I, France, 5A1 43.055, COJASOR, Dix ans d'action sociale, 1945–1955, 1956. On postwar antisemitism in Poland, see Gross, *Fear. Anti-Semitism in Poland after Auschwitz*, and Kichelewski, *Les survivants*.

68. JDC-NY, France 1945/54, File 283, Rapport moral et financier COJASOR, 1945–1948, 31.

69. For example, in 1948 the JDC took control of the aid to rabbinical and yeshiva groups due to the preferential service they were receiving at COJASOR. JDC-NY, France 1945/54, File 245, Welfare Report Number 3, June 1949; Grobman, *Battling for Souls*, 246.

70. The OSE and the FSJF also received significant amounts from the JDC (26.2% and 13.1% respectively) for the same period. JDC-NY, uncatalogued, JDC Primer, New York, 1945, France-8. The JDC states in its primer that it covered 73 percent of the entire cost of the French Jewish welfare organizations in 1945. Such estimates should be viewed critically since the JDC did not have a full view of the total cost of welfare; local agencies did not willingly share their accounting records.

71. JDC-NY, uncatalogued, JDC Primer, France-8.

72. YIVO, RG 245.5, Series 4, France IV, Reel 19,5, File 61, Letter from Maurice Brener to Messieurs les directeurs régionaux du "COJASOR," July 25, 1945.

73. No information on this conflict was found in the JDC archives. Brener's resignation letter was found in the HIAS papers at YIVO.

74. During World War II, the JDC did fund non-Jewish organizations, such as the Emergency Rescue committee or the American Friends Service Committee; however, in the postwar period, the JDC generally provided money to Jewish agencies only. In the words of one JDC employee: "JDC is sometimes called upon to make contributions to non-Jewish work of one kind or another and it does so only as a public relations matter or for other valid reasons existing at the time" (see JDC-NY, Herman Stein Papers, Carton 1, Paris Advisory Committee Meeting, June 28, 1950).

75. In April 1945, Greenleigh estimated that about seven thousand families being helped by the JDC (one third of all recipients) should have been helped by COSOR. JDC-NY, France 1945/54, File 247, Letter from Arthur Greenleigh to Moses Leavitt, April 7, 1945. On tensions between the JDC, COSOR, and the MPDR, see also Bauer, *Out of the Ashes*, 31–33 and Grobman, *Rekindling the Flame*, 51–52.

76. JDC-NY, France 1945/54, File 246. The following activity transpired in the JDC program in France during April, May, and June 1946, undated. COSOR eventually provided aid to non-French individuals in the Paris region yet did not systematically provide aid to non-French individuals in the provinces. Bauer, *Out of the Ashes*, 31. It should be noted that this organization ran children's homes in collaboration with the Vaad Hatzala. Telephone interview with Robert Sejwacz, January 19, 2015. COSOR records have recently been made available yet do not provide extensive details on its relationship to Jewish organizations (see AN 72AJ/2930-35). On this topic, see Poujol, *L'Église de France*, 286–288.

77. Fredj calls it the Comité de coordination des oeuvres d'assistances juives. It was created by the CRIF on November 15, 1944, and composed of members from the FSJF, the JDC, CGD, EI, UJRE, WIZO, and HICEM. Fredj, "La création du CRIF: 1943–1966," 47. Annette Wieviorka refers to this committee as the *Conseil des Israélites*. Wieviorka, *Deportation et génocide*, 41. Most recently, Laure Fourtage states that the CRIF's Comité de coordination des oeuvres d'assistances juives assigned the Comité d'unité et de défense des Juifs de France as the liaison to COSOR. Fourtage, "Et après?," 145.

78. JDC-NY, France 1945/54, File 247, Letter from Arthur Greenleigh to Moses Leavitt, April 7, 1945. Renée Poznanski makes a similar observation about state agencies and Jewish organizations. She notes that in May 1945, an agent of the Service des crimes de guerre asked for a monthly budget of F250,000 from Jewish organizations to finance personnel to fight against crimes committed against Jews. Poznanski, *Propagandes et persécutions*, 563.

79. JDC-NY, France 1945/54, File 247, Letter from Arthur Greenleigh to Moses Leavitt, April 7, 1945. In May 1946, COSOR officials solicited the JDC via COJASOR with the request that the latter assume all responsibility for Jews. JDC-NY, France 1945/54, File 246, The following activity transpired in the JDC program in France during April, May, and June 1946, nondated. COSOR

remained a thorn in the side of the JDC. In 1947, COSOR lost its government funding and solicited the JDC for money. Unsuccessful, the leader of this organization, the Père Chaillet, turned to Canadian Jews for financial support. Apparently, Chaillet had lists of hidden Jewish children and refused to share the complete list with the JDC. He did, however, reluctantly provide the JDC with letters of introduction to the various regional COSOR offices and incomplete versions of the list of hidden children. JDC-NY, France 1945/54, File 277. Laure Fourtage has confirmed and built upon my findings on the COSOR in "Et après?," 144–152.

80. Wieviorka, *Déportation et génocide*, 434 and Mandel, *In the Aftermath of Genocide*, 62–64.

81. Doulut, Klarsfeld, and Labeau, *Mémorial des 3943 rescapés juifs de France* and Fourtage, "Et après?," 85.

82. A British aid committee, the Jewish Committee for Relief Abroad, requested permission to send delegates to France on September 15, 1944. The MPDR issued a negative response to this request over five months later, stating that the Jewish Committee for Relief was not necessary due to the presence of the Joint Committee in France. AN, F9/3271, Letter from N. Bentwich (Jewish Committee for Relief Abroad) to Maurice Dejean (MPDR), September 15, 1944; Letter from M. Grammont (MPDR) to N. Bentwich, March 7, 1945; and Letter from Ministère MPDR to chargé de mission à Londres (MPDR), February 17, 1945. This was the only reference to the JDC I found in the archives of the Direction des affaires sociales and the direction des réfugiés of the MPDR. The JDC is not even listed in the archival inventory or among the multitude of voluntary aid organizations that worked with the MPDR.

83. Jewish deportees [*déportés Israélites*] seeking social services from the MPDR were requested to report to rue d'artois. AN, F9/3249, Compte rendu direction des services sociaux, réunion du 20 septembre 1944, September 21, 1944. On the various categories of MPDR, its deportees, and their repatriation, see Wieviorka, *Déportation et génocide*, 31–76; Lagrou, *The Legacy of Nazi Occupation*, 106–128, 225–241, especially 122–123 on the personnel of the MPDR; Fourtage, "Accueillir les déportés juifs en France," 71–96.

84. Fourtage, "Et après?," 89–96.

85. AJHS, Cecilia Razovsky Papers, P-290, Box 6, Folder 1, Collected Notes on Lecture, Cecelia [*sic*] Razovsky Davidson, July 25, 1945.

86. JDC-NY, France 1945/54, File 247, Letter from Cecelia [*sic*] Razovsky Davidson to the Department of Operations, Report on Work with the JDC, Paris, February 9–June 28, 1945, June 1945.

87. This is seen in the humorous sketch, "Scherzo Capriccioso in AJDC Major," signed "Bon Voyage, Liselotte," June 28, 1945. AJHS, Cecilia Razovsky papers, P-290, Box 6, Folder 1.

88. Interview with Mary Barnett, Paris, September 9, 2005.

89. Adler, *Jews and Gender*, 68–105; Doron, *Jewish Youth and Identity in Postwar France*, 74–117.

90. Archives de la Préfecture de police de Paris, BA 1681, Letter from 3ème bureau de la direction générale de la réglementation et des étrangers and direction générale de la sûreté nationale du Ministère de l'intérieur to Préfet de police, December 30, 1947.

91. Archives de la Préfecture de police de Paris, BA 1681, Colonie Américaine.

92. For example, the Comité américain des secours civils and its American branch, the American Friends of France, sent $2.3 million and $4 million in 1944–1945 and 1945–1946, respectively. Claflin, "Agent of Friendship: Anne Morgan and Private Philanthropy 1944–1947," 118.

93. See chapter 1.

94. Attendees included representatives from American Relief for France, the Young Men's Christian Association, the National Catholic Welfare Conference, War Relief Services, the Unitarian Service Committee, Friends Ambulance Unit, and the American Friends Service Committee. JDC-NY, France 1945/54, File 247, Meeting of Cooperative Committee of Foreign Voluntary Societies, Februray 26, 1945.

95. JDC-I, 543 C. 43.085, Report of the Activities of the Cooperative Committee of Volunteer agencies in France, June 1949.

96. JDC-I, 22B S-1300.1, Memo from Joffe to JDC Paris, April 2, 1948.

97. JDC-I, 22B S-1300.1, Meeting of American Voluntary Agencies in France Called by Mr. Irving Fasteau, September 23, 1948; Memo from A. Kahn to L. Margolis, October 7, 1948.

98. JDC-I, File 5A3 43.604.4, Memo from J. Breen to H. Katzki, March 2, 1951. Contrary to David Weinberg's observation that the JDC did not participate in the Marshall Plan (see Weinberg, *Recovering a Voice*, 269).

99. Dash Moore, *To the Golden Cities*, 1.

100. Writing in the 1950s, Nathan Glazer advanced the argument that pre-WWII distinctions between East European and German Jews were "wiped out," along with their class differences. Glazer, *American Judaism*, 106. Arthur Goren highlighted the "functional consensus" of postwar American Jewry, recognizing that while "pockets of animosity or indifference remained, within the Jewish community, the divisive issues of the interwar years—class differences, the intergenerational tensions between immigrant and native-born, conflicting notions of Jewish identity, the assimilationist-radical deprecation of Jewish life and the strident polemics over Zionism—were vanishing or gone altogether" (see Goren, "A Golden Decade for American Jews 1945–1955," 5–10. Hasia Diner has a different approach, describing postwar Jews as "a small, internally divided people with no single voice to speak 'for'

NOTES TO PAGES 98–99 257

them," thus painting a more divisive portrait of postwar Jewry (see Diner, *We Remember with Reverence*, 267). Riv-Ellen Prell characterizes postwar Jewish life as a "more complex story" in which "virtually every domain of Jewish life underwent changes with far-reaching consequences." This moment of dynamic transition was, according to Prell, "as much about differences and conflict among Jews as it was about a shared consensus" (see Prell, "Triumph, Accommodation, and Resistance," 115–116).

101. Dobkowski, ed., *Jewish American Voluntary Organizations*, annex 2.
102. Glazer, *American Judaism*, 106–128.
103. Herberg, "Jewish Labor Movement in the United States," 61; Green, "Blacks, Jews and the 'Natural Alliance,'" 79–104.
104. Diner, *We Remember*, 150–215.
105. In 1939, the UJA raised $16,250,000. In 1946, a total of $132 million was raised, of which 78 percent went to the UJA (see Raphael, *A History*, 7 and 136). For a renewed approach to the UJA, see Debligner, "In a World Still Trembling."
106. Bauer, *Out of the Ashes*, xviii.
107. Hobson Faure, "Un 'Plan Marshall juif,'" 261–338 and "Renaître sous les auspices américains et britanniques. Le mouvement libéral juif en France après la Shoah (1944–1970)," 82–99.
108. While the Vaad Hatzala and the JLC have received recent critical attention, published scholarship on HIAS is more limited. Monographs include Wischnitzer, *Visas to Freedom*; Grobman, *Battling for Souls*; Collomp, *Rescue, Relief and Resistance*; Pâris de Bollardière, "La pérennité de notre peuple." For a comparative study of the Bund in the postwar period, see Slucki, *The International Jewish Labor Bund after 1945*, 75–104.
109. HIAS's year of creation can be debated due to the multiple mergers of early committees: 1882, 1889, 1902, or 1909. Wischnitzer, *Visas to Freedom*, 16.
110. On the circumstances leading up to this, see Lederhendler, "Hard Times: HIAS under Pressure."
111. The JLC's membership base and leadership came from a number of different organizations, among them the International Ladies' Garment Workers' Union (ILGW), the Amalgamated Clothing Workers of America (ACWA), the Workmen's Circle, and the Jewish Daily Forward Association. In the 1930s, this organization led a boycott of German products, organized a "counter-Olympics" during the 1936 Olympic games in Berlin, and campaigned to gather public support against Nazism. Malmgreen, "Comrades and Kinsmen: the Jewish Labor Committee and Anti-Nazi Activity, 1934–1941," 4–20; Jacobs, "A Friend in Need," 391–417; Collomp, *Rescue, Relief and Resistance*.
112. The JLC withdrew from the United Jewish Appeal in 1942 but did receive UJA funds indirectly by soliciting donations directly from welfare funds of cities. Pâris de Bollardière, "La pérennité de notre peuple," 306–310.

113. While the HIAS was helping all Jews by the 1930s, regardless of their background, it was still funded by donations from those it had assisted and was run by former Eastern European Jews, who maintained its image as an Eastern European organization. Lederhendler, *American Jewry. A New History*, 226–227.

114. In 1944, JDC leadership in New York was still primarily of German-Jewish origin, but its staff was increasingly second-generation Eastern European. In France, examples of Eastern European Jews in power included Dr. Joseph Schwartz and Laura Margolis. Bauer, *Out of the Ashes*, xiv–xv.

115. He does not define this term or provide his source for this figure. Grobman, *Battling for Souls*, 23.

116. Following Jonathan Boyarin, I use the term *Haredi*, noting that this word was not used at the time. Instead, they used the term *traditionalist*. Boyarin, *Jewish Families*, 98–107.

117. The institutionalization of orthodoxy took a distinct path in France. Over the course of the nineteenth century, the Central Consistory while rejecting many of the precepts of the Reform movement did make some changes to the liturgy and adapted organs and mixed choirs, even on Shabbat. The Catholic influence on Franco-Judaism was also evident in the religious initiation ceremony for young girls, who wore white dresses for the occasion. Immigrant oratories and prayer groups remained in close contact with the Consistory, even after the 1905 Separation of Church and State, which turned the Consistory into a voluntary association. Berkowitz, *Rites and Passages*, 207 and, more generally, 191–212 and Green, *The Pletzl of Paris*, 82–85.

118. In postwar Paris, two synagogues were affiliated with this organization, rue Cadet (1893) and rue Montevideo (1936). Rabi, *Anatomie du judaïsme français*, 157; Perego, "Pleurons-les, bénissons leurs noms," 211.

119. Bunim, *A Fire in his Soul*, 77.

120. "Samuel Mayer Schmidt," https://www.jewishvirtuallibrary.org/schmidt-samuel-myer, accessed February 27, 2020. More generally, on the Vaad's work in Europe, see Zuroff, "Rescue Priority and Fundraising Issues during the Holocaust," 305–326.

121. Nathan Baruch eventually took over the direction of the Paris office, but Grobman does not specify when or for how long. Other employees included Eleanor Bohne-Hene and Maurice Ungar. Grobman also mentions a Vaad office on the rue de la Paix in Vincennes. Grobman, *Battling for Souls*, 110, 229–34.

122. Its Paris budget in January 1948 was $7,500 per month. Grobman, *Battling for Souls*, 249.

123. Schmidt was instrumental in obtaining visas for five hundred yeshiva students in France. The Vaad also negotiated with the State Department to approve US visas for those in France. Grobman, *Battling for Souls*, 79–81, 110–111.

124. Ibid., 113–114.

125. Ibid.
126. Rescue Children, Inc. funded children's homes in Strasbourg, Schirmeck, Aix-les-Bains, Fulbaines, Villejuif, and Barbizon. Ibid.
127. Martin and Zinberg, "Inventory to the Rescue Children, Inc. Collection," Yeshiva University, 1986, https://archives.yu.edu/xtf/view?docId=ead/rescue/rescue.xml;query=rescue%20children%20inc;brand=default, accessed April 7, 2020.
128. Poujol discusses this collaboration but does not provide a satisfactory response as to why the Orthodox Jewish group would collaborate with the secular French committee. Poujol, *L'Église de France*, 289–291.
129. The name of the children's homes shows the collaboration: "Protection des enfants de déportés, Vaad Hahatzala Emergency Committee." Thank you to Yoram Mouchenik for sharing his research on the Rescue Children, Inc. collection at the Yeshiva University archive. See series I in the collection for details on the sponsorship program. Martin and Zinberg, "Inventory to the Rescue Children, Inc. Collection," Yeshiva University, 1986, https://archives.yu.edu/xtf/view?docId=ead/rescue/rescue.xml;query=rescue%20children%20inc;brand=default, accessed April 7, 2020. For more on the Rescue Children, Inc. sponsorship program, see Debligner, "In a World Still Trembling," 183–231.
130. Grobman, *Battling for Souls*, 112.
131. Ibid., 235–240.
132. Yeshiva University, Rescue Children, Inc. collection, Series II. Certificate from COSOR, January 27, 1949.
133. Collomp, *Résister au nazisme*, 131–136.
134. Many such visits were recorded in letters whose rich details on the life in JLC children's homes appear to have been used for fundraising purposes in the United States. JLC Records, Part II, Letter from Marjorie Merlin Cohen to her father, August 30, 1948, sent to Emanuel Muravchik of the JLC on the same date.
135. Fajwel Schrager provides two dates for his recruitment in his autobiography. Schrager, *Un militant juif*, 64, 153, on his work with the JLC, see 153–172.
136. Ibid., 118.
137. Feingold, *Bearing Witness*, 220. Pâris de Bollardière suggests this was also due to the Communist influence on the conference. Pâris de Bollardière, "La pérennité de notre peuple," 107–108.
138. On the JLC's political alliances in France, see Pâris de Bollardière, "La pérennité de notre peuple," 181–238. In the first ten months of 1946, the JLC spent $180,000 in France, which can be compared with Poland ($115,000), where the JLC operated six homes. The JLC was financed by its affiliates (unions and individual members), a private fundraising campaign, and the UJA. The JLC managed to increase its campaign goals from $100,000 in 1939 to $1,000,000 in February 1944. JLC records, Part I, "Rescue of Democratic and Labor Leaders

from Nazi Occupation Forces," reprinted from Labor and Nation, January–February 1947.

139. In 1946, the JLC sent 15,656 packages to Europe. Pâris de Bollardière, "La politique et les actions internationales du Jewish Labor Committee, 1945 à 1953," 48–51.

140. Pâris de Bollardière, "La politique et les actions internationales" and "Mutualité, fraternité et travail social," 27–42; Collomp, *Résister au nazisme*, 182–189.

141. JDC-NY, France 1945–54, File 281, Memo from L. Meyer to L. Eisler, June 18, 1947.

142. JLC Records, Part II, Z. Lichtenstein, Report of the Childcare Department, date penciled as [1948?]; Pâris de Bollardière, "La politique et les actions internationales du Jewish Labor Committee, 1945 à 1953," 88–89.

143. Pâris de Bollardière, "La politique et les actions internationales," 80.

144. Simmons, *Hadassah and the Zionist Project*, 155–156; Pâris de Bollardière, "La politique et les actions internationales du Jewish Labor Committee, 1945 à 1953" 76.

145. Archives Nationales, AJ/43, File 1252, *Fédération des sociétés juives de France, rapport general d'activité*, 1945.

146. Pâris de Bollardière, "La pérennité de notre peuple," 241–296. In English, see Pâris de Bollardière, "The Jewish Labor Committee's Bundist Relief Network in France" and "The French Bundist Movement after the Holocaust."

147. One document suggests that the JLC may have also sought to facilitate more formal adoptions of Jewish children from France. JLC Records, Part II, Letter from David L. Ullman to Emmanuel Muravchik, August 24, 1955.

148. JLC Records, Part II, "The Jewish Labor Committee and Its Care for the Surviving Jewish Children. 10 Years of Child 'Adoption.'" No date. More generally, see Pâris de Bollardière, "La pérennité de notre peuple," 354–358.

149. Pâris de Bollardière, "La politique et les actions internationales du Jewish Labor Committee, 1945 à 1953," 79.

150. JLC Records, Part II, "Our Children," Undated brochure. In 1951, union membership in the five most Jewish American unions totaled one million. Only three hundred and eighty-five thousand of these individuals were Jewish. The membership of the JLC in this same year was two hundred and eighty thousand. Herberg, "Jewish Labor Movement in the United States: World War I to Present," 61.

151. American Jewish organizations showed concern over the proper representation of their overseas programs and avidly read the materials of other organizations. Thus the JDC request for information on the statement that the Workmen's Circle "in cooperation with the JLC" was caring for 25 percent of the Jewish orphans in France or the JLC's claim that it maintained sixteen havens for orphaned children in France. JDC-NY, France 1945/54, File 281, Brochure,

"About the Vladeck Home," Letter from Edward Phillips (JDC-NY) to JDC France, July 22, 1946 and JDC-NY, France 1945/54, File 249, Letter from R. Pilpel to J. Pat, February 28, 1949.

152. Constance Pâris de Bollardière provides multiple reasons for this in her doctoral dissertation. Pâris de Bollardière, "La pérennité de notre peuple," 245–295. It is my argument that the JLC's proximity to *Forverts* protected its program in France. For example, the president of the JLC from 1938 to 1968, Adolph Held, was an editor, business manager, and general manager of *Forverts* from 1907 to 1917 and from 1962 to 1967. Collomp, *Résister au Nazisme*, 35 and Jewish Telegraphic Agency, "Adolph Held Dies at 84."

153. JDC-NY, France 1945/54, File 281, Memo from Lena Meyer to Lena Eisler, June 18, 1947.

154. JDC-NY, France 1945/54, File 281, Letter from Joseph Schwartz to Lou Sobel, June 20, 1947.

155. JDC-NY, France 1945/54, File 281, Memo from Laura Margolis to Moses Beckelman, August 12, 1947.

156. Pâris de Bollardière, "Mutualité, fraternité et travail social," 30.

157. The Workmen's Circle summer camps continue to this day. The JLC offered to sell its Vladeck home in Brunoy to the French Jewish organization *Fonds social juif unifié* in 1962. This created some conflict, as French Jews felt the home could not be sold to them, because it rightfully belonged to them. The JDC served as intermediary between the JLC in the United States and the FSJU in France. By the summer of 1962, this home was being used for Jewish Algerian youth. JDC-NY, France 1954/64, File 168, Letters from Charles Jordan to M. Leavitt, February 16, 1962 and September 25, 1962.

158. Bazarov, "HIAS and HICEM," 71.

159. Lambert, *Diary of a Witness, 1940–43*, 94. According to Valery Bazarov, Schah was born in 1880 and worked as a lawyer, financial advisor, and journalist before working for HICEM in 1933. Bazarov, "In the Crosshairs," 24.

160. This work was made possible due to the Refugee Fund, which combined funds from the JDC, ICA, HIAS, the Central British Fund, and contributions from relatives in the United States; AN, AJ43/14, Memorandum of the activities of the HIAS-ICA Emigration Association (HICEM), No date, most likely 1943. See also Wischnitzer, *Visas to Freedom*, 166–175.

161. Of its seventy-seven employees in Marseille, twenty-five were sent overseas, fifty-two were sent to Corrèze, where thirty-six were discharged and eleven were arrested. Wischnitzer, *Visas to Freedom*, 180. Valery Bazarov provides a list of twenty-one HIAS employees who were murdered during the Holocaust and who were most likely deported from France in "In the Crosshairs," 27.

162. AN, AJ43/14, Letter from Wladimir Schah to HIAS-NY, September 10, 1944.

163. Board members included Robert Levi, René Mayer, René Cassin, Maurice Machtou, Jacques Meyer, Bernard Melamède, Elie Gozlan, Salomon Kagan, Raphael Spanien, and Julien Gozlan. AN, AJ43/14, Letter from Philippson to Sir Herbert Emerson, including copy of cable from Lisbon, July 26, 1944.

164. AN, AJ43/14, Adresses des comités affiliés et correspondants de la HICEM, April 20, 1945.

165. Wischnitzer, *Visas to Freedom*, 194. The offices in Limoges, Lyon, and Toulouse were closed in November 1947. YIVO, RG 245.5, Series 4, France IV, Records of postwar HICEM/HIAS 1945–1953, Reel 19.1, Note de service 160, November 25, 1947.

166. Louis Neikrug replaced Dr. James Bernstein in 1946. Wischnitzer, *Visas to Freedom*, 199, 214.

167. AN, AJ43/14, Memo from M. Biehle to Sir H. Emerson, RE: Attempt to move 500 children from Europe to Brazil, April 23, 1945. In this report, which transmits a report from HIAS made to the IGCR, HIAS explains the difficulty of this task: A group of two hundred children immigrating to Palestine were stopped before boarding the boat by the MPRD, which required paternal authorization (obviously impossible to obtain); another group of one-hundred children were cleared for immigration to Mexico, but the OSE and HIAS were unable to agree on who should go. A major conflict affecting these efforts was the desire of Zionists to send all orphans to Palestine. It is unclear if the five hundred children were able to immigrate to Brazil.

168. In 1945, this represented almost twenty thousand packages and $325,000 in cash. Bauer, *Out of the Ashes*, 183.

169. Wischnitzer, *Visas to Freedom*, 214. One document from September 1946 shows fifty-nine employees, excluding directors. YIVO, RG 245.5, Series 4, France IV, Records of postwar HICEM/HIAS 1945–1953, Reel 19.1, Note de service, September 24, 1946.

170. As Laura Jockusch has shown, Wladimir Schah associated with the CDJC. Jockusch, *Collect and Record!*, 55.

171. JDC-I, France, 5A1 43.055, COJASOR, Dix ans d'action sociale, 1945–1955, 1956.

172. This figure includes three thousand individuals from North Africa. Bensimon and Della Pergola, *La population juive de France*, 36. For a critical discussion of this figure, see Fourtage, "Et après?," 22–25.

173. Lederhendler, "Hard Times: HIAS under Pressure, 1925–26."

174. Only 137,450 Jews immigrated to the United States from 1945 to 1952. Dinnerstein, *America and the Survivors of the Holocaust*, 288 and more generally, 163–182. See also Ouzan, *Ces juifs dont l'Amérique ne voulait pas*.

175. I reached this figure by adding the years 1949 to 1952. Dinnerstein, *America and the Surivors of the Holocaust*, 288.

176. The statistic of twenty thousand appears to correspond to the total number assisted by HIAS in France. Wischnitzer, *Visas to Freedom*, 223.
177. Wischnitzer, *Visas to Freedom*, 243. The term *postwar era* is not explained.
178. This figure helps explain the statistic of thirty-five thousand calculated by Bensimon and Della Pergola. Wischnitzer, *Visas to Freedom*, 223–4.
179. Bauer, *Out of the Ashes*, 181–186. Bazarov, "HIAS and HICEM in the System of Jewish Relief Organizations in Europe, 1933–41," 69–78.
180. Lederhendler, *American Jewry. A New History*, 226.
181. On the UJA, see chapters 1 and 4. On the UJA decision to exclude HIAS, see Wischnitzer, *Visas to Freedom*, 174.
182. Its global budget remained modest for the following years, increasing to $1,964,309 in 1946 and $2,032,215 in 1947. Wischnitzer, *Visas to Freedom*, 203, 232.
183. Bazarov, "HIAS and HICEM," 69–78.
184. AN, AJ43/14, Letter from MW Beckelman to "Director," October 30, 1945.
185. YIVO, RG 245.5, Series 4, France IV, Reel 19.23, File 193, Letter from HIAS representative in Marseille (most likely Joseph Dubrowitch) to Wladimir Schah, July 24, 1945 or 1946 (unclear).
186. YIVO, RG 245.5, Series 4, France IV, Reel 19.23, File 193, Letter from J. Dubrowitch to W. Schah, July 17, 1945.
187. YIVO, RG 245.5, Series 4, France IV, Reel 19.6, File 79, Letter from HIAS Representative in Bordeaux to director in Paris, August 2, 1946.
188. YIVO, RG 245.5, Series 4, France IV, Reel 19.6, File 395, Letter from director of HIAS-France to Asofsky (HIAS-New York), August 6, 1946.
189. YIVO, RG 245.5, Series 4, France IV, Reel 19.43, File 395, Letter from Neikrug to Asofsky, August 6, 1946.
190. Bauer, *Out of the Ashes*, 186.
191. Wischnitzer, *Visas to Freedom*, 260–270. HIAS's French office remained active until 1987, when it closed due to a small caseload. HIAS Annual Report 1987, New York, 22.
192. Dreyfus, "The Post-Liberation French Administration and the Jews," 111–126.
193. Doron, *Jewish Youth and Identity in Postwar France*, 74–117. Shannon Fogg also points out that some Jewish organizations paradoxically praised republican egalitarianism but requested recognition of specific Jewish needs. Fogg, "Everything Had Ended and Everything Was Beginning Again," 288.
194. Bauer, *Out of the Ashes*, xviii; Goldsztejn, "L'American Jewish Joint Distribution Committee (AJDC) en France de 1933 à 1950," 63; more generally, Goldsztejn, "Au secours d'une communauté."
195. AN, AJ 43/13, Report of the Secretary to the Executive Committee Meeting of the JDC, Vol. II, No. 5, May 15, 1946.
196. JDC-NY, uncatalogued, JDC Primer, France-8-9.

197. JDC-I, Laura Margolis Jarblum archives (uncatalogued), Statistical report, France, Country directors conference, October 1952.
198. JDC-NY, France 1945/54, File 246, Monthly report for November and December 1945, by Arthur D. Greenleigh, March 5, 1946.
199. Kelman, "Un menorah d'espoir et de consolation," 40. On the decision to create two offices, see JDC-NY, France 1945/54, File 246, The following activity transpired in the JDC program in France during April, May, and June 1946, No date.
200. The JDC's Office for France moved to 19 Avenue Foch, in a former Rothschild mansion that had been occupied by the Gestapo, while the European headquarters remained on the rue de Téhéran.

CHAPTER FOUR: LONG-TERM RECONSTRUCTION

1. JDC-NY, France 1945/54, File 287, Letter from Harry Rosen to Philip Skorneck, May 21, 1948.
2. On the origins of the United Jewish Appeal, see chapter 1.
3. On the evolution of Jewish native-immigration relations after World War II, see Mandel, "The Encounter between 'Native' and 'Immigrant' Jews in the Aftermath of the Holocaust," 38–57. Mandel considers the war years transformative yet shows the importance of the postwar period in reconfiguring a new relationship between natives and immigrants. This somewhat revises her previous findings, which emphasize the war years. Mandel, *In the Aftermath of Genocide*, 204.
4. From 1948–1966, only 6,436 Jews immigrated to Israel. Mandel, *In the Aftermath of Genocide*, 104–113.
5. The figure thirty-two thousand designates Jewish migrations to France excluding North Africa. Bensimon and Della Pergola, *La population juive de France*, 36. On this migration, see Weinberg, "A Forgotten Postwar Jewish Immigration: East European Jewish Refugees and Immigrants in France, 1946–7," 137–49. For a first-person account, see Ertel, "Les fantômes du 9 rue Guy Patin. (En souvenirs)," 21–54. Researchers are also currently exploring this migration. See for example contributions by Pâris de Bollardière, Perego, and Biezunski in Lindenberg, *Premiers savoirs de la Shoah*, 275–334 and the special issue of *Archives juives* (54/1, 2021) coordinated by Pâris de Bollardière and Perego.
6. On the evolution of this notion among French Jews, see Kriegel, *Ce que j'ai cru comprendre*, 781–782.
7. This is not to say that nonreligious organizations and activities did not exist in French Jewish life before the war. However, excluding several exceptions in the late 1930s, the large network of nonreligious Jewish organizations were not linked together in a common structure or considered part of a community. On

the failed attempt to unify Jewish organizations in the 1930s, see Weinberg, *A Community on Trial*, 148–170.

8. According to the JDC, foreigners could not access French nursing schools due to nationality requirements. Seventy women applied for admission, and approximately twenty were accepted. Miss Esther Lipton, a former supervisor and instructor of nursing at Cornell University and consultant for the New York City Health Department, was recruited to set up the school. She worked with two French social workers, Odette Schwob and Marie-Thérèse Vieillot. The latter had worked closely with Chloe Ownings to import American casework to France in the interwar period. Fouché, "Le casework: circulation transatlantique et réception en France (1870–1939)," 30–33 and JDC-NY, France 1945/54, File 245, Quarterly Report on France, May 1948–September 1948.

9. Few historians have analyzed the role of the FSJU in postwar France due to the limited availability of its archives. My research is based almost exclusively on the JDC archives, oral history interviews, the private papers of one of its leaders, Claude Kelman (at the Mémorial de la Shoah), and FSJU publications. Part of the FSJU archives have recently been catalogued at the Central Archive for the History of the Jewish People in Jerusalem. On the FSJU, see Mandel, "Philanthropy or Cultural Imperialism?" 74–80 and *In the Aftermath of Genocide*, 165–172; Zytnicki, *Les Juifs à Toulouse entre 1945 et 1970. Une communauté toujours recommencée*, 107–182 and "L'accueil des Juifs d'Afrique du nord par les institutions communautaires (1961–1965)," 95–109; Elmaleh, *1950–2000. Fonds social juif unifié*.

10. Goldman, "The Involvement and Policies of American Jewry in Revitalizing European Jewry. 1945–1995," 70.

11. On the influences of American philanthropy in France, see among others, Diebolt and Fouché, "1917–1923, Les Américaines en Soissonais: leur influence sur la France," 45–63; Genet-Delacroix, Cochet, and Trocmé, eds., *Les Américains et la France (1917–1947) engagements et représentations*; Fouché, "Anne Morgan, la lecture publique et la France," 59–96 and "Le casework: circulation transatlantique et réception en France (1870–1939)," 21–35; Tournès, *Sciences de l'homme et politique*. More generally, see Curti, *American Philanthropy Abroad*, 1963.

12. Mandel, "Philanthropy or Cultural Imperialism?," 55.

13. Historians Michaël Werner and Michel Espagne argue for greater consideration of the complexities of exchanges and transfers, criticizing hegemonic analyses as oversimplified and binary. They have shown that models and/or practices are not simply imposed, even when one group is receiving large sums of money. If and when appropriated, transfers reflect a complex negotiation process in which the receiving party plays as important a role as the exterior influence. Werner and Espagne, "La construction d'une référence culturelle allemande en France: genèse et histoire (1750–1914)," 969–992. This emphasis on

interaction with the receiving society is central to the "histoire croisée" method, later theorized by Werner and Zimmermann, *De la comparison à l'histoire croisée*.

14. This citation and the following information on Margolis comes essentially from OHD (128) 56, Laura Margolis Jarblum Interview, conducted by Menachem Kaufman, April 24, 1976. Unfortunately, few primary sources on Laura Margolis exist. See also Kerssen, "Life's Work: The Accidental Career of Laura Margolis."

15. Margolis managed communications on shore while Cecilia Razovsky boarded the boat and counseled its passengers. The small world of Jewish international social work would bring both women to the JDC in Paris after the war. On the role of Margolis in Havana and Shanghai, see OHD (122) 28, Laura Margolis Jarblum Interview, conducted by Margalit Bejarano, 1987 and Glaser, "Laura Margolis and JDC Efforts in Cuba and Shanghai. Sustaining Refugees in a Time of Catastrophe," 167–203.

16. On her work in this home, see CDJC, Annie Latour collection, DLXI-41, "Laura Margolis."

17. The JDC was not spending $10 million in France per year. She may have been referring to a longer period. OHD (128) 56, Laura Margolis Jarblum interview, 33–34.

18. Laura Margolis used this phrase to discuss the JDC's relationship with French Jewish welfare organizations: "The reality is, the JDC has limited funds and it must administer those funds in terms of priorities and essential needs. This has been a long uphill struggle and has taken the most delicate kind of handling in order to bring the French program into some realistic line while, at the same time, not endangering the relationship with our agencies. I feel free to say that we have accomplished this and that as of today our agencies fully accept our point of view and realize that the JDC is not 'Santa Claus' and that they must bring their programs down to reality" (see JDC-I, 5A3 C 43.077, Letter from Laura Margolis to Joseph Schwartz, February 2, 1948).

19. Telephone interview with Herman Stein, November 30, 2004.

20. JDC-NY, France 1945/54, File 246, Report of Office for France, November–December 1946, February 1947.

21. Referring to Robert Gamzon, of the Jewish Scouting Movement, Margolis stated, "He still cannot forget the Halcyon days of 1944–1946, before this office got organized and caught up with him" (see JDC-I, 5A1 C.43.045, Memo from Laura Margolis to Moses Beckelman, December 18, 1948).

22. JDC-I, Laura Margolis Jarblum collection, uncatalogued, Country directors conference, Bulletin 22, February 3, 1947.

23. JDC-NY, France 45/54, File 249, Welfare department report #2, Report of childcare department, Office for France on developments from October 1946 to October 1948, April, 1949.

24. For 1945, Karp, *To Give Life*, 77–85; for 1946, Raphael, *A History of the United Jewish Appeal*, 21, 136.

25. Bauer, *Out of the Ashes*, xvii–xviii.
26. JDC-NY, France 45/54, File 249, Welfare department report #2, Report of childcare department, Office for France on developments from October 1946 to October 1948, April, 1949.
27. This fit with the needs of the population. The number of individuals receiving direct assistance from the organization diminished in the years following its creation, from 27,030 in 1945 to 23,703 in 1946 and 18,339 in 1947 to 10,845 in 1948. JDC-NY, France 1945/54, File 283, Rapport moral et financier de COJASOR, 1945–1948.
28. JDC-NY, France 1945/54, File 245, Quarterly Report on France, May 1948–September 1948 and JDC-NY, France 1945/54, File 245, Welfare Report Number 3, June 1949.
29. Ibid.
30. JDC-NY, France 1945/54, File 246, Report of Office for France, December 1946–February 1947 and JDC-NY, France 1945/54, File 255, Memo from Laura Margolis to Herbert Katzki, September 3, 1946. The council and postwar Polish Jewish immigrants are explored in Maspero, "Itinéraires de juifs polonais immigrés en France entre 1945 et 1951." More generally, see Weinberg, "A Forgotten Postwar Jewish Migration: East European Jewish Refugees and Immigrants, 1946–7," 137–149.
31. On reactions to the JDC budget cuts in Belgium and France comparatively, see Hobson Faure and Vanden Daelen, "Imported from the United States?," 279–313.
32. The committee was established by Meiss, E. Lévy, and J. Fisher. CDJC, CRIF collection, MDI, Box 1, Board meeting minutes, December 3, 1946.
33. CDJC, CRIF Collection, MDI, Box 1, Board Meeting Minutes, Feb. 4, 1947.
34. Ibid. It was expected to have twelve to fourteen members. He does not state which organizations, yet it is understood that they would be welfare organizations [*oeuvres*] and that the CRIF would have an advisory role.
35. Ibid., September 22, 1947. Potential members included Meiss, Adam, Fisher, Kelman or Jarblum, Braunschvig, G. de Rothschild, Racine, E. Dreyfus, A. Kahn, Katlin, Halter, F. Schrager, E. Lévy, A. Meyer, and several others.
36. Ibid.
37. OSE headquarters, Archives of the direction, 1948–1952, uncatalogued, Board meeting minutes, April 9, 1947.
38. Ibid.
39. Ibid.
40. In 1947, the four largest JDC programs were in Hungary, where it was spending $11 million; Germany and Austria ($9 million combined); France ($6 million); and Poland ($5.5 million). Bauer, *Out of the Ashes*, xviii.
41. ACIC, Letter from Georges Wormser to Léon Meiss, May 7, 1947.

42. Shapiro, *A Time for Healing*, 63–64. Shapiro does not specify the criteria on which this statement is based (per capita or actual amounts).

43. Raphael, *A History of the United Jewish Appeal*, 136 and also cited in Mandel, "Philanthropy or Cultural Imperialism?," 59.

44. Debligner, "In a World Still Trembling," 27–81.

45. JDC-NY, France 1945/1954, File 246, Robert Gamzon, "The Fight for Survival Goes On," undated. Gamzon wrote this article for the United Jewish Appeal after a two-week trip to the United States for the fundraising campaign of 1946.

46. JDC-NY, France 1945/54, File 246, Robert Gamzon, "The Fight for Survival Goes On," undated.

47. JDC-NY, France 1945/54, File 285, Letter from Herbert Katzki to JDC-NY, Paris letter n. 2357, March 4, 1947.

48. JDC-NY, France 1945/54, File 285. See also Hobson Faure, "Un 'Plan Marshall juif," PhD diss., 438–446, and "Performing a Healing Role," 147–148.

49. JDC-NY, France 1945/54, File 287, Jacques Pulver to B. Goldman, Report on my trip to the United States, November 5, 1946.

50. Ibid.

51. OHD (128) 56, Laura Margolis Jarblum interview, 34.

52. Ibid.

53. JDC-NY, France 1945/54, File 246, Letter no. 6697 from JDC Paris (Noel Aronovici) to JDC-NY, October 2, 1947.

54. According to Margolis, this meeting was attended by Léon Meiss, Baron Guy de Rothschild, Elie Cohen, Emmanuel Racine, Claude Kelman, and Maurice Brener. JDC-NY, Current files, noncatalogued, Reflections on the creation of the FSJU, Laura Margolis Jarblum, May 17, 1981. According to Raphaël Elmaleh, this meeting took place on October 12, 1947, and was attended by Léon Meiss, Marc Jarblum, Claude Kelman, and Adam Rayski. Guy de Rothschild was invited but could not attend. Elmaleh, *1950–2000. Fonds social juif unifié*, 13.

55. Elmaleh, *1950–2000. Fonds social juif unifié*, 13.

56. She wrote, in French, "Knowing you to be very busy, we would be happy to come meet you at the hour and place that would be most convenient for you" (see ACIC, File Joint 1948, Letter from Laura Margolis to Léon Meiss, May 20, 1948).

57. JDC-NY, France 1945/54, File 287, Letter from L. Shapiro to Harry Rosen, May 7, 1948.

58. The origins of community organizing can be traced to the widespread fundraising campaigns that took place in American cities during World War I, which inspired new ways of theorizing the link between local and national democracy. Community organization was considered an essential part of the curricula of American social work schools from 1932 to 1944. Lubove, *The Professional Altruist*, 49

and 223. See also Follett et al., *The New State: Group Organization and the Solution of Popular Government* and Lindeman, *The Community*.

59. JDC-NY, France 1945/54, File 287, Letter from Harry Rosen to Joseph Schwartz, July 9, 1948.

60. JDC-NY, France 1945/54, File 287, Letter from Harry Rosen to Philip Skorneck, June 22, 1948.

61. Ibid.

62. According to a poll conducted by the US State Department. Roger, *L'ennemi américain*, 418.

63. Ibid., 417–437. For a more general discussion of the French view of America in the postwar years, see Kuisel, *Seducing the French*, 15–102.

64. YIVO, AJC, RG-347.7.1, FAD-1, Box 20, File: "Unser wort" France 1947–1952, Memo from Shuster to Foreign Affairs Department, February 20, 1951.

65. Guy de Rothschild, president of the FSJU from 1950 to 1982, in an interview on his work with the organization, recalled that JDC personnel were "generous, intelligent, and had none of the faults that one could consider American, such as dominating others or giving lessons" (see Elmaleh, *1950–2000. Fonds social juif unifié*, 52). While time clearly sweetened Rothschild's memories of this period, this statement shows that non-Communist French Jews were not exempt from associating America with domination, even when concerning American Jews.

66. JDC-NY, France 1945/54, File 287, Letter from Harry Rosen to Joseph Schwartz, July 9, 1948.

67. This is confirmed in my oral history interviews with French Jews who worked with Margolis and Schwartz. Interview with Gaby Wolff Cohen, Paris, May 28, 2004; June 8, 2004; November 17, 2004; August 2, 2005; December 20, 2005; interview with Franceline Bloch, November 18, 2004; interview with Tito Cohen, August 2, 2005.

68. JDC-NY, France 1945/54, File 287, Cable from Joseph Schwartz to JDC-NY, July 19, 1948.

69. JDC-NY, France 1945/54, File 287, Letter from Harry Rosen to Philip Skorneck, September 29, 1948.

70. JDC-I, France, File 5A2 C.43.070.A FSJU, La réunion extraordinaire d'information, l'Appel unifié de 1950. This fundraising technique was used by the JDC in France before WWII. JDC-NY, France 1945/54, File 287, Letter from L. Shapiro to Harry Rosen, May 7, 1948.

71. JDC-NY, Current files, noncatalogued, Reflections on the Creation of the FSJU, Laura Margolis Jarblum, May 17, 1981.

72. CDJC, Archives CRIF, Fonds MDI, Carton 1, Procès verbal, February 4, 1947.

73. Explored in chapter 5.

74. Interview with Gaby Wolff Cohen, Paris, June 8, 2004.
75. ACIC, File FSJU, uncatalogued, Léon Meiss, Le fonds social juif unifié face à ses obligations, June 29, 1949.
76. Ibid.
77. Mandel, "Philanthropy or Cultural Imperialism?," 77. Raphaël Elmaleh states 275 organizations were identified by the FSJU as potential members. Elmaleh, *1950–2000. Fonds social juif unifié*, 15–16.
78. Elmaleh, *1950–2000. Fonds social juif unifié*, 17–19.
79. On withdrawal of Communists, see JDC-NY, France 1945/54, File 284, Letter from Laura Margolis to Henrietta Buchman, December 12, 1950; Elmaleh, *1950–2000. Fonds social juif unifié*, 22.
80. Guy de Rothschild's father, Edouard de Rothschild, was the president of the Central Consistory from 1911 to 1940. In 1943, Léon Meiss became president of the institution. Guy de Rothschild took over in 1949, when Meiss became the head of the Cour d'assises. Nataf, "Interview du Baron Guy de Rothschild en 1992," 287, 291. The first FSJU board included vice presidents Maurice Brener, Elie Cohen, and Claude Kelman; treasurer Robert Weill; and assistant treasurer Emmanuel Racine. Elmaleh, *1950–2000. Fonds social juif unifié*, 36.
81. Elmaleh, *1950–2000. Fonds social juif unifié*, 52.
82. On Julien Samuel, see Ferran, *Julien Samuel*; Samuel, *Rescuing the Children*, 74–75.
83. According to historian David Weinberg, this was the largest Jewish demonstration to date in postwar France. Weinberg, "The Reconstruction of the French Jewish Community after World War II," 182–183.
84. Rothschild, *The Whims of Fortune: The Memoirs of Guy de Rothschild*, 261.
85. Rothschild does not provide her first name, yet this was most likely Lilly Cicurel. Rothschild, *The Whims of Fortune*, 261. It should be noted that the Edmond James de Rothschild branch of the family was Zionist.
86. YIVO, AJC, RG 347.7.41, FAD 1, Box 18, File: France 1945–49, Letter from Joel Wolfsohn to John Slawson, June 21, 1948.
87. OHD (128) 56, Laura Margolis Jarblum Interview, 36.
88. Ibid., 3.
89. Kerssen, "Life's Work: The Accidental Career of Laura Margolis," 105; JDC-NY, France 1945/54, File 259, Letter from Laura Margolis to Robert Pilpel, October 16, 1947.
90. "By 1953 I felt the FSJU was on a [sic] solid footing. While it would continue to need the Joint's help for some time to come, the role of the FSJU as a permanent community structure to care for the health, welfare, cultural and educational needs of French Jewry was assured. It was then that I decided that my work was done, and I could move on to Israel" (see JDC-NY, Current files, uncatalogued, Reflections on the Creation of the FSJU, Laura Margolis Jarblum, May 17, 1981).

91. JDC-NY, France 1945/54, File 287, Letter from Harry Rosen to Joseph Schwartz, July 9, 1948.
92. Ibid.
93. Wasserstein, *Vanishing Diaspora*, 92.
94. JDC-I, France, File 5A2 C.43.070.A FSJU, Letter from Harry Rosen to Moses Beckelman, July 27, 1949.
95. Ibid.
96. After great debate within its ranks, the FSJU initially suggested a ratio of 60:40 in favor of Israel for the first $F500$ million raised and 70:30 thereafter. The Jewish Agency fought for 70:30 for the first $F500$ million and a split (two thirds for Israel, one third for France) thereafter. JDC-I, France, File 5A2 C.43.070.A FSJU, Letter from Laura Margolis to Joseph Schwartz, April 3, 1950.
97. After the establishment of Israel, the UJA, which had previously favored the JDC, provided 60 percent of its funds to Israel and 40 percent to the JDC for the first $50 million raised. Karp, *To Give Life*, 93.
98. JDC-I, France, File 5A2 C.43.070.A FSJU, "French Jews Emulate United Jewish Appeal, Launch Their First United Fundraising Drive," Jewish Telegraphic Agency, New York Bulletin, February 15, 1950. The article stipulated that pro-Communist groups were not a part of the FSJU. This may have been good news for American Jews, but it was bad for the FSJU, which had fewer participants due to the withdrawal of the Jewish Communist organizations.
99. JDC-I, France, File 5A2 C.43.070.A FSJU, Letter from Harry Rosen to Robert Pilpel, February 6, 1950.
100. JDC-I, France, File 5A2 C.43.070.A FSJU, Letter from Laura Margolis to Guy de Rothschild, April 24, 1950.
101. JDC-I, Laura Margolis Jarblum Collection, uncatalogued, Statistical Report, France, Country Directors Conference, October 1953.
102. Two figures are provided in two different documents: JDC-I, Laura Margolis Jarblum Collection, uncatalogued, JDC Program in France in 1951, April 5, 1951, Country Directors Conference, Paris, Statistical Report on France, October 1952. Elmaleh, *1950–2000. Fonds social juif unifié*, 40. The statistical report contradicts with Elmaleh, who seems to have reversed the campaign results of 1951 with those of 1950.
103. The figure of 7.5 percent is based on the contribution estimate of $F27$ million. JDC-I, Laura Margolis Jarblum Collection, uncatalogued, Country Directors Conference, Paris, Statistical Report on France, October 1952.
104. These two agencies were the CAR and the FSJF. JDC-NY, France 1945/54, File 247, Report for France for the Last Quarter of 1944, September 1945. In 1951, the JDC was still funding some twenty Jewish welfare organizations that were assisting fifteen thousand people a month, of whom sixty-four hundred were receiving cash assistance. JDC-I, Laura Margolis Files, uncatalogued, Administrative Committee Meeting Minutes, May 22, 1951.

105. The two funds were the *Fonds de démarrage économique* and the *Caisse Israélite des prêts*. JDC-I, Laura Margolis Files, uncatalogued, Administrative Committee Meeting Minutes, May 22, 1951. Rabinovitch also discusses the social mobility of French Jews after WWII, noting the growth of a middle class. Rabinovitch, *Anatomie du judaïsme français*, 153–154.

106. OHD (128) 56, Laura Margolis Jarblum Interview, 35.

107. JDC-I, France, File 5A2 C.43.070.A FSJU, Letter from Laura Margolis to H. Levy, April 11, 1950; JDC-I, France, File 5A2 C.43.070.A FSJU, Letter from Guy de Rothschild to Dr. Joseph Schwartz, March 28, 1950.

108. JDC-I, France, File 5A2 C.43.070.A FSJU, Letter from Laura Margolis to Joseph Schwartz, March 1, 1950.

109. OHD (128) 56, Laura Margolis Jarblum Interview, 34.

110. Margolis does not date this event, which most likely occurred in November 1950. Ibid.

111. The French image of American women as "energetic, efficient and independent," emerged in the aftermath of World War I (see Green, *The Other Americans in Paris*, 32–37 and 209–213).

112. Rosen's departure was discussed by his JDC colleagues and attributed to the poor FSJU campaign results and conflict with the "French Jewish community." JDC-NY, Herman Stein Papers, Box 1, Letter from Henry Selver to Herman Stein, November 21, 1950.

113. Margolis divided the JDC program in France into two sections: the care of what it called the "refugee and transient populations" and its local welfare needs. The FSJU was asked to take responsibility only for the costs of local welfare. Together, the JDC and the FSJU determined an annual budget, estimated their contributions, and drew up a five-year plan. OHD (128) 56, Laura Margolis Jarblum Interview, 34–35.

114. JDC-I, France, File 5A2 C.43.070.A FSJU, FSJU assemblé générale des 31 Mars et 1er Avril 1951, Les répartitions de fonds et l'évolution du programme social en 1950 et 1951.

115. JDC-I, France, File 5A2 C.43.070.A FSJU, Letter from Laura Margolis to Guy de Rothschild, April 3, 1950.

116. Interview with Tito Cohen, Paris, August 2, 2005.

117. JDC-I, France, File 5A2 C.43.070.A FSJU, FSJU assemblé générale des 31 Mars et 1er Avril 1951, Les répartitions de fonds et l'évolution du programme social en 1950 et 1951.

118. JDC-I, Laura Margolis Jarblum Collection, uncatalogued, Country Directors Conference, Paris, Statistical Report on France, October 1952.

119. Ibid.

120. JDC-NY, France 1945/54, File 287, Letter from Judah Shapiro to Henrietta Buchman, March 30, 1953.

121. JDC-NY, Current Files, uncatalogued, Reflections on the Creation of the FSJU, Laura Margolis Jarblum, May 17, 1981. According to Oliver Zunz, fund matching was pioneered in the early twentieth century by Julius Rosenwald to incite African Americans to support the Rosenwald schools. Zunz, *American Philanthropy*, 39.

122. JDC-NY, France 1945/54, File 287, Executive Committee Meeting Minutes, June 23, 1953. This contradicts with the lower figure of $F133.6$ million, provided in JDC-I, Laura Margolis Jarblum Collection, uncatalogued, Country Directors Conference, Paris, Statistical Report on France, October 1953; and also with a lower campaign goal of $F120$ million reported in JDC-NY, Current Files, uncatalogued, Reflections on the Creation of the FSJU, Laura Margolis Jarblum, May 17, 1981.

123. JDC-I, Laura Margolis Jarblum Collection, uncatalogued, Country Directors Conference, Paris, Statistical Report on France, October 1952.

124. JDC-NY, France 1945/54, File 287, Letter from Judah Shapiro to Henrietta Buchman, March 30, 1953.

125. JDC-NY, France 1945/54, File 287, Memo from Ester Hentges, April 13, 1953.

126. JDC-NY, France 1945/54, File 244, Executive Committee Meeting Minutes, November 17, 1953.

127. JDC-I, Laura Margolis Jarblum Collection, uncatalogued, Country Directors Conference, Paris, Statistical Report on France, October 1952.

128. The entire 1953–1956 period was reviewed for this study.

129. In 1954, the FSJU established a five-year program of "cultural action," including training programs for communal workers, the opening of meeting places and learning centers, an editorial policy, publications and the development of pedagogical materials, and assistance to small communities outside of Paris. Elmaleh, *1950–2000. Fonds social juif unifié*, 43. As Mandel points out, this corresponds with the arrival of the Conference on Jewish Material Claims against Germany, a new source of funding that transformed French Jewish life. Mandel, *In the Aftermath of Genocide*, 172.

130. Mandel, *In the Aftermath of Genocide*, 165; "Philanthropy or Cultural Imperialism?" 78.

131. Interviews with Tito Cohen and Gaby Wolff Cohen, Paris, August 2, 2005.

132. JDC-NY, uncatalogued, Laura Margolis Personnel File, Letter from L. Margolis to JDC France, August 23, 1950.

133. JDC-NY, Laura Margolis Personnel File, "Le FSJU manifeste sa reconnaissance à Madame Laura Margolis-Jarblum," *Nouvelles juives mondiales*, December 2, 1953.

134. Ibid.

135. Mandel, "Philanthropy or Cultural Imperialism?," 53–54.

136. JDC-NY, uncatalogued, Laura Margolis Personnel File, Communiqué: Laura Margolis to Serve as JDC representative in Belgium, April 12, 1945. Others soon followed, such as Bea Vulcan, Kate Mandel, Henrietta Buchman, and Blanche Bernstein.

137. CDJC, CRIF Collection, MDI, Box 1, Board Meeting Minutes, April 1, 1947.

138. David Weinberg asserts the contrary. Weinberg, *Recovering a Voice*, 118; Hobson Faure and Vanden Daelen, "Imported from the United States?," 295.

139. Hobson Faure and Vanden Daelen, "Imported from the United States?," 293–301; Vanden Daelen, *Laten we hun lied verder zingen*.

140. Rabinovitch provides estimates that for the period preceding 1956, two hundred thousand Jews lived in the Paris region, forty thousand in the eastern regions, fifty thousand in other cities, and thirty thousand in small towns in the provinces. Rabinovitch, *Anatomie du judaïsme français*, 150. Renée Poznanski also confirms the rebirth of Paris as the center of French Jewish organizational life. Poznanski, "L'Heritage de la guerre: Zionisme en France dans les années 1944–1947," 241.

141. Mandel, *In the Aftermath of Genocide*, 162–164.

142. Zytnicki, "L'accueil des Juifs d'Afrique du nord par les institutions communautaires (1961–1965)," 103. Mandel wrote, "The FSJU's arrival on the scene thus not only marked a profound shift that had been taking place among the French Jewish population over the course of several decades but also legitimized that shift by its emphasis on Jewish culture as an appropriate manifestation of French Jewish identity" (see Mandel, "Philanthropy or Cultural Imperialism?," 78).

143. Mandel, "Philanthropy or Cultural Imperialism?," 77.

144. JDC-NY, France 1955/64, File 151, AJDC Country Directors Conference, France 1956.

145. JDC-NY, France 1955/64, File 151, Executive Committee Meeting, November 26, 1963.

CHAPTER FIVE: AMERICAN JEWISH ORGANIZATIONS AND THE POSTWAR WORLD

1. YIVO, AJC, RG 347.7.41, FAD 1, Box 18, Memo from Marvin Goldfine to Foreign Affairs Department, Communal and Cultural Trends in French Jewish life, April 15, 1949.

2. As Lisa Moses Leff has analyzed, this awareness justified the transfer and sale of Jewish books, archives, and religious articles from Europe to the United States. Leff, *The Archive Thief*, 163–178.

3. Kaufman, *An Ambiguous Partnership*, 275–311.

4. I am using this term to describe Jews of all backgrounds as opposed to their organizations.

5. First theorized by Simon Dubnow, diaspora nationalism has recently been defined by Zohar Segev as a "complex condition, whereby a scattered minority that shares ethnic and economic attributes is either unable or unwilling to integrate fully with the wider society and therefore constitutes a quasi-national cultural, political and social population that lacks a sovereign territorial base" (see Segev, *The World Jewish Congress during the Holocaust*, 210–216). On Dubnow's theorization of Jewish autonomy, see Pinson, "The National Theories of Simon Dubnow," 335–358.

6. On French Jewish tensions in the postwar period, see Pâris de Bollardière, "La pérennité de notre peuple," 245–296; Perego, "Pleurons-les, bénissons leurs noms," 158–173. On the political turn toward the Democratic Party, see Wenger, *New York Jews and the Great Depression*, 103–135; Feingold, *A Time for Searching*, 189–224. On the postwar period, see Shapiro, *A Time for Healing*, 218–228; Novick, *The Holocaust in American Life*, 92–100; Dash Moore, *To the Golden Cities*, 189–226.

7. I thank Renée Poznanski for emphasizing this point in her comments on the first edition of this book, Centre Medem, Paris, January 2014. I am also indebted to Green, "To Give and to Receive," 197–226; Penslar, "The Origins of Modern Jewish Philanthropy," 197–214.

8. Catherine Collomp and Constance Pâris de Bollardière show in their respective analyses the JLC's far-reaching and complex political views, even if its aid was targeting specific elements of French Jewish life. Collomp, *Résister au nazisme*, 17–44; Pâris de Bollardière, "La pérennité de notre peuple," 69–178.

9. Cohen, *Not Free to Desist*, 10–13.

10. Remus, "Agency History," *An Inventory to the Records of the World Jewish Congress*, American Jewish Archives, accessed June 29, 2021, http://collections .americanjewisharchives.org/ms/ms0361/ms0361.html. On the origins of the WJC, see Zelmanovits, *Origin and Development of the World Jewish Congress*; Kubowitzki, *Unity in Dispersion*. On its role during the Holocaust, see Segev, *The World Jewish Congress during the Holocaust*, 1–22.

11. The AJC participated in the American Jewish Congress and the Paris Peace Conference. This was not without tensions. Fink "Louis Marshall: An American Jewish Diplomat in Paris, 1919," 21–40.

12. By 1949, the AJC had grown to include thirty-eight local chapters, and its membership had increased from four hundred individuals to eighteen thousand; Cohen, *Not Free to Desist*, 338.

13. Feingold, *A Time for Searching*, 245–246 and more generally, 225–265; Cohen, *Not Free to Desist*, 249–260. In the postwar period, the AJC came to embrace a two-state solution. Kaufman, *Ambiguous Partnership*, 275–311.

14. Even if the JDC discreetly supported illegal immigration to Palestine, its objective was to allow Jews to live with full rights in the nation of their choice. Bauer, *Out of the Ashes*, xiv–xv.

15. As seen in chapter 3, the JDC was reimbursed for shipping costs for certain goods. On French perceptions of the US Marshall Plan, see Kuisel, *Seducing the French*, 37–69.

16. Segev, *The World Jewish Congress during the Holocaust*, 210, 214.

17. Three members of the elected eight-member executive committee were from France: Marc Jarblum, Israël Jefroykin, and Isaac Naiditch. Kubowitzki, *Unity in Dispersion*, 72.

18. This most likely includes the landsmanshaftn associated with the Federation of Jewish Societies of France. Weinberg, *A Community on Trial*, 112–113, 140.

19. American Jewish Archives (AJC), WJC (361), D49/19, Gerhart Riegner, *Note sur l'action de sauvetage d'enfants en France*, April 12, 1945. On the role of the WJC during WWII, see Riegner, *Ne jamais désespérer*; Segev, *The World Jewish Congress during the Holocaust*, 124–167.

20. Wieviorka, *Déportation et génocide*, 344–347; Ghiles-Meilhac, "Centralizing the Political Jewish Voice in Post-Holocaust France," 59–70.

21. According to Segev, the fundraising campaign sought to raise $100 million. Segev, *The World Jewish Congress during the Holocaust*, 175.

22. As seen in chapter 3, this is due to the fact some delegates were denied permission to travel.

23. This contradicts the work of Jacques Fredj, who states the WJC was not very concerned with the CRIF. Fredj, "La création du CRIF: 1943–1966," 60–65. On broader functions of the CRIF in the postwar period, see Ghiles-Meilhac, "Centralizing the Political Jewish Voice in Post-Holocaust France, "59–70; Ghiles-Meilhac, *Le Crif. De la résistance juive à la tentation de lobby*, 13–46.

24. AJA, WJC (361), H113/5, Letter from Marc Jarblum to Nahum Goldmann, March 17, 1945.

25. AJA, WJC (361), H113/5, Letter from Léon Meiss to Stephen Wise, January 22, 1945.

26. AJA, WJC (361), H113/5, Letter from Marc Jarblum to Nahum Goldmann, March 17, 1945. Most likely typed on an American typewriter since there are no accents in the original French.

27. Samuel Ghiles-Meilhac nuances Maud Mandel's assertion that the CRIF was a Zionist organization. Mandel, *In the Aftermath of Genocide*, 136–137; Ghiles-Meilhac, "Centralizing the Political Jewish Voice in Post-Holocaust France," 59–70.

28. Alliance Executive Committee Minutes, July 25, 1945, in Grynberg, "Reconstruction et nouvelles orientations," 338. On the postwar relationship between the AIU and the CRIF, see Nicault, "L'Alliance au lendemain de la Seconde Guerre mondiale," 23–53.

29. After the Holocaust, the term *israélite*, typically used by French native Jews to describe themselves (often in opposition to immigrant Jews) came under criticism as Jews sought to reappropriate the pejorative term *Jew*. Soon after

the war, the CRIF, which used *israélite* in its charter after considerable debate, transformed the *I* in its name to *institutions juives*. Ghiles-Meilhac, "Centralizing the Political Jewish Voice in Post-Holocaust France," 61.

30. Fredj, "La création du CRIF: 1943–1966," 61.
31. AJA, WJC (361), H113/5, Letter from Nahum Goldmann to Léon Meiss, September 21, 1945.
32. AJA, WJC (361), H112/1, Paris Office of the World Jewish Congress, Program for the Next Six Months, October 29, 1945.
33. AJA, WJC (361), H113/5, Letter from Marc Jarblum to Nahum Goldmann, March 17, 1945.
34. AJA, WJC (361), H113/5, Letter from Claude Kelman to Leon Kubowitzki, November 30, 1945.
35. Fredj, "La création du CRIF: 1943–1966," 61.
36. AJA, WJC (361), H112/5, Letter from Sylvain Cahn-Debré to Leon Kubowitzki, January 14, 1946. While the final list of delegates is not available, the board of the delegation included Blumel, Dreyfus, Jarblum, Spanien, Grinberg, Kellman [*sic*], Fisher, Luxembourg, Raisky, Lubetski, Minkowski, and Cahn-Debré.
37. Opposition came from the UJRE, the Union des sociétés juives de France (the Farband) and the Organisation des juifs polonais. The articles appeared in *Naye presse* in Yiddish and in *Droit et liberté* in French. AJA, WJC (361), H/112/2, "Déclaration sur le congrès juif mondial," February 27, 1946.
38. AJA, WJC (361), H/112/2, Letters from Sylvain Cahn-Debré to Leon Kubowitzki, March 12, 1946; April 10, 1946.
39. Ibid., April 2, 1946.
40. Ghiles-Meilhac, "Centralizing the Political Jewish Voice in Post-Holocaust France," 64. On the postwar relationship between the AIU and the CRIF, see Nicault, "L'Alliance au lendemain de la Seconde Guerre mondiale," 23–53; Grynberg, "Reconstruction et nouvelles orientations," 331–340.
41. Kurz, "In the Shadow of Versailles: Jewish Minority Rights at the 1946 Paris Peace Conference," 198. See also Fredj, "La création du CRIF: 1943–1966," 60–65. The minutes of the CRIF board meetings also reveal continued conflict, especially after 1947. CDJC, Archives CRIF, Fonds MDI.
42. Kubowitzki, *Unity in Dispersion*, 311–334, 361–362. The WJC was not the only organization to obtain this status: The AIU, American Jewish Committee, and the Anglo-Jewish Association (England) established the Consultative Council of Jewish Organizations; the American Jewish Conference, the Board of Deputies of British Jews, and the South African Jewish Board of Deputies also created the Coordinating Board of Jewish Organizations.
43. Conference on Jewish Material Claims against Germany, *Twenty Years Later, 1952–1972*, 76. For figures by country, see Zweig, *German Reparations*

and the Jewish World, 9 and 122. Note that Israel does not appear on the list of beneficiary countries and may have received more funds than France.

44. AJA, WJC (361), H112/1, Paris Office of the World Jewish Congress, Program for the Next Six Months, October 29, 1945.

45. From May 1, 1945, through May 1, 1948, the WJC shipped a total of 110,258 pounds (50,120 kilos) of clothing and 98,683 pounds (44,856 kilos) of food to metropolitan France, in addition to sending $9,479.40 in medicine and other materials. Kubowitzki, *Unity in Dispersion*, 301.

46. Ibid., 302–305.

47. This included the Rinah home in Malmaison (OPEJ), the Anna Szenes Home in Verneil (Oeuvres Anna Szenes), the Cap d'Ail home in Marsac (FSJF), the Vésinet home in Vésinet (Mizrachi), and the Zebulon home in Marseilles (Zebulon Maritime Association), in addition to a home run by the UJRE. AJA, WJC (361), D 73/9, Foster Children in Europe, April 30, 1947.

48. Ibid.

49. Kubowitzki, *Unity in Dispersion*, 307–308; Segev, *The World Jewish Congress during the Holocaust*, 177–184.

50. The WJC had a conflictual relationship with the JDC during the war years. As Jewish children were evacuated from France to Spain by members of the Jewish resistance, both the WJC and the JDC opened children's homes to receive them. The JDC opened its home in Spain, leaving the WJC home in Portugal empty and creating a great embarrassment for the them. For more on this conflict, see Avni, "The Zionist Underground in Holland and France and the Escape to Spain," 555–590; Segev, *The World Jewish Congress*, 134–157.

51. Letter from Joseph Hyman to Nahum Goldmann, February 13, 1945, in Kaufman, *Ambiguous Partnership*, 187.

52. AJA, WJC (361), H115/9, Letter from Nachum Goldmann to Arieh Tartakower, July 31, 1946.

53. AJA, WJC (361), D 73/9, Letter from Leon Kubowitzki to Sylvain Cahn-Debré and S. Perl, March 20, 1947; JDC-NY, France 1945/54, File 249, Agreement between the World Jewish Congress and the American Joint Distribution Committee, December 26, 1947.

54. Hobson Faure, "Towards Consensus?," 79–96.

55. On the influence of these conferences on French Jewish life, see Simon-Nahum, "'Penser le judaïsme.' Retour sur les colloques des intellectuels juifs de la langue française, 1957–2000," 79–106.

56. Rabinovitch, *Anatomie du judaïsme français*, 175–176.

57. Ibid., 176.

58. Postwar figures and quote from Weiner Cohen, *Not Free to Desist*, 338.

59. Nicault, "L'Alliance au lendemain de la Seconde Guerre mondial," 27.

60. Weiner Cohen, *Not Free to Desist*, 4–5, 35, 146.

61. Perego, "Jury d'honneur," 137–164.
62. YIVO, AJC, RG 347.7.41, FAD 41, Box 10, File France FO-Eur 1945–1949, 57, Letter from Max Gottschalk to Raymond Geissman, November 7, 1946. Geissman was most likely still on the AJC payroll until the following spring (April 30, 1947). YIVO, AJC, RG 347.7.41, FAD 1, Box 18, File "AJC Correspondent Geissman," Letter from Max Gottschalk to Raymond Geissman, March 24, 1947.
63. Kurz, "In the Shadow of Versailles," 187–209. More generally, see Kurz, "A Sphere above the Nations? The Rise and Fall of International Jewish Human Rights Politics, 1945–1975."
64. Sources differ on the number of Jewish delegations; the figure eleven is from Kurz, "In the Shadow of Versailles," 197–198. See also Cohen, *Not Free to Desist*, 272–275; Kubowitzki, *Unity in Dispersion*, 248–260.
65. Telephone interview with former AJC employee, August 3, 2005. See also New York Public Library, American Jewish Committee Oral History Collection, Zachariah Shuster Interview Conducted by Mitchell Krauss, June 6, 1972.
66. Telephone interview with Abraham Karlikow, October 27, 2005. See also New York Public Library, American Jewish Committee Oral History Collection, Abraham Karlikow Interview Conducted by Mimi Harmon, October 15, 1980; Abraham Karlikow Interview Conducted by Irma Krents, April 18, 1988.
67. This is how the organization described its mission to the Paris prefecture. YIVO, AJC, RG 347.7.41, FAD 41, Box 14, France Organizations (Misc.) FO-EUR 1947–1949, 51, Association AJC, Bulletin officiel, undated.
68. YIVO, AJC, RG 347.7.41, FAD 41, Box 14, File: Key People FO-EUR 47. One list of people to meet included Justin Godart, Léon Meiss (CRIF, Consistoire), Samy Lattès (Consistoire, Alliance), Gaston Kahn (JDC, B'nai B'rith), Isaac Schneerson (Centre de documentation juive contemporaine), Herbert Katzki (JDC), Robert Kiefe (CRIF), and Fajwel [Félix] Shrager (Cercle amical).
69. YIVO, AJC, RG 347.7.41, FAD 41, Box 14, File: Key People FO-EUR 47, Re: Herbert Katzki, Secretary of JDC for Europe and with Long Experience Both in JDC Work in France and Other European Countries, April 7, 1947.
70. YIVO, AJC, RG 347.7.41, FAD 1, Box 18, File: France 1945–1949, Memo from Zachariah Shuster to Foreign Affairs Department, April 4, 1947.
71. Ibid.
72. This status was granted in Spring 1947. Ibid.
73. A growing historiography explores this issue. See Kurz, "A Sphere above the Nations?"
74. As Catherine Nicault points out, the Alliance received funding from the Vichy government's Service des oeuvres françaises à l'étranger even after 1942, when it was forced to join the UGIF. Nicault, "Dans la tourmente de la Seconde Guerre mondiale (1939–1944)," 295–330.

75. YIVO, AJC, RG 347.7.41, FAD 1, Box 18, File: France 1945–1949, Memo from Zachariah Shuster to Foreign Affairs Department, April 4, 1947.

76. YIVO, AJC, RG 347.7.41, FAD 1, Box 18, File: France 1945–1949, Letter from Max Gottschalk to John Slawson, April 15, 1947.

77. Simon Perego's recent book explores how French Jews grappled with the Holocaust through commemoration. Perego, *Pleurons-les*.

78. YIVO, AJC, RG 347.7.41, FAD 1, Box 18, File: France 1945–1949, Memo from Marvin Goldfine to Foreign Affairs Department, "Communal and Cultural Trends in French Jewish Life," April 15, 1949.

79. The AJC discreetly financed French Jewish organizations that shared its worldview. For example, in 1948, Rabbi Zaoui of the Rue Copernic Reform synagogue received funding for its magazine, *Le rayon*. Robert Gamzon of the French Jewish scouting movement also received funding to reimburse debt. In 1952, René Cassin asked the AJC to share a $6,000 fee with the JDC to prevent the seizure of archives of the Centre d'archives juives contemporaines [*sic*] (probably the CDJC). YIVO, AJC, FAD 41, Box 14, Organisations de France (misc) FO-EUR 1947–1949, 51, Memo from Marvin Goldfine to Joel Wolfsohn, November 1948; YIVO, AJC, FAD 1, Box 20, Scouting, Eclaireurs Israélites, 1946–1949, Letter from Robert Gamzon to Ohrbach, September 21, 1948; YIVO, AJC, FAD 1, Box 19, CDJC, France, AJC 1947–1952, Unsigned Letter to John Slawson, March 12, 1952.

80. The French Communist party won 27 percent percent of the vote and thus shared power with the Socialist Party (SFIO, 24%) and the Christian Democrat People's Republican Movement (MRP 25%). Stovall, *France since the Second World War*, 14–19.

81. Zoé Grumberg finds that Rabi's estimate is not unrealistic for the immediate postwar period based on the membership in the Communist Jewish organizations UJRE and the CCE (ten to eleven thousand individuals in 1948) and those who received free medical care from the Farband's clinics (twenty-six thousand in 1947). Rabinovitch, *Anatomie du judaïsme Français*, 170; Grumberg, email correspondence with author, May 20, 2020. See also Grumberg's dissertation, "Militer en minorité?"

82. Novick, *The Holocaust in American Life*, 85–102.

83. YIVO, AJC, RG 347.7.41, FAD 1, Box 18, File: France 1945–1949, Memo from Zachariah Shuster to Foreign Affairs Department, April 11, 1947.

84. By 1960, *Commentary* had a circulation of twenty thousand. Shapiro, *A Time for Healing*, 27.

85. YIVO, AJC, RG 347.7.41, FAD 1, Box 18, File: France 1945–1949, Memo from Zachariah Shuster to Foreign Affairs Department, April 11, 1947.

86. Attal, "Index de la revue 'Evidences' (1949–1963).''

87. YIVO Archives, American Jewish Committee RG-347.7.1, FAD-1, Box 18, File: Evidences-Comments 1949–1955, Letter from Edwin Lucas to Roy (no last name), April 30,1953.

88. YIVO, AJC, RG 347.7.41, FAD 1, Box 18, File: Evidences, 1947–1962, Facts about Evidences, March 2, 1950.
89. Ibid.
90. The AJC went through an American member of the Foreign Service, Donald Bloomingdale, to meet with Alain de Rothschild and discuss this question with him. YIVO, AJC, RG 347.7.41, FAD 1, Box 18, File: France 1945–1949, Letter from Joel Wolfsohn to John Slawson, October 8, 1947. Bloomingdale was in fact married to Bethsabée de Rothschild. ACIP, GG 165, Kétouba 8041.
91. Samy Lattès, whose name has also been spelled without an accent, was an Italian language specialist. YIVO, AJC, RG 347.7.41, FAD 1, Box 18, File: France 1945–1949, Letter from (unclear) to John Slawson, June 27, 1948; YIVO, AJC, RG 347.7.41, FAD 41, Box 12, File: Correspondence, Reports and Clippings, FO-Europe, Letter from M. Fernand Halphen to AJC, December 7, 1948.
92. Moch, *Conseil représentatif des juifs de France*, 8–9; AJA, WJC (coll. 361), H/115/12, French Jewish Representative Committee, 1944–1947, Centre Israélite d'information de Paris (no date).
93. YIVO, AJC, RG 347.7.41, FAD 41, Box 14, File: France Vanikoff, Maurice Correspondence, Reports FO-EUR-48-50-51, Letter from Marvin Goldfine to Maurice Vanikoff, December 17, 1948. It is unclear whether Vanikoff was hired as a consultant or as a member of the CII.
94. He met with Edgar Faure, René Cassin and Baron Guy de Rothschild; YIVO, AJC, RG 347.7.41, FAD 1, Box 18, File: France 1950–54, Letter from Zachariah Shuster to John Slawson, September 21, 1949.
95. YIVO, AJC, RG 347.7.41, FAD 1, Box 18, File: France 1945–1949, Memo from Marvin Goldfine to Zachariah Shuster, December 6, 1949. The AJC found French demands unrealistic but was willing to grant $20,000 with the condition of local participation.
96. Shuster quotes French Jews in YIVO, AJC, RG 347.7.41, FAD 1, Box 18, File: France 1950–1954, Letter from Zachariah Shuster to John Slawson, September 21, 1949.
97. YIVO, AJC, RG 347.7.41, FAD 1, Box 18, File: France 1945–1949, Memo from Marvin Goldfine to Zachariah Shuster, December 6, 1949.
98. YIVO, AJC, RG 347.7.41, FAD 1, Box 18, File: France 1945–1949, Letter from John Slawson to Fred Lazarus, December 12, 1949. Slawson is quoting Zachariah Shuster.
99. YIVO, AJC, RG 347.7.41, FAD 1, Box 18, File: France 1945–1949, Memo from Marvin Goldfine to Zachariah Shuster, December 6, 1949.
100. YIVO Archives, American Jewish Committee RG-347.7.1, FAD-1, Box 18, file France 1950–1954, Memo from J. B. Lightman to Jacob Blaustein and John Slawson, September 22, 1950.
101. YIVO, AJC, RG 347.7.41, FAD 1, Box 18, file France 1950–1954, Memo from Zachariah Shuster to John Slawson, April 1, 1954.

102. YIVO, AJC, RG 347.7.41, FAD 1, Box 20, File: French Jews 1943–1961. Report (nontitled) of French Jewish Community in 1954.
103. Ibid.
104. An exception: YIVO Archives, American Jewish Committee RG-347.7.1, FAD-1, Box 19, File: Conseil représentatif des juifs de france 45–51, Memo from Lightman (Director of Community Relations for Europe) to Shuster, Some Aspects of Present Day Civic-Defense Problems in the CRIF, Paris, June 15, 1951.
105. Debono, "Le *Juif Süss* au quartier Latin en 1950," 95–114. On postwar antisemitism, see also Grynberg, "Des signes de résurgence de l'antisémitisme dans la France de l'après-guerre (1945–1953), 171–223; Debono, *Le racisme dans le prétoire, racisme, antisémitisme et xénophobie devant la loi*; Debono, "L'antisémitisme en France au lendemain de la Seconde Guerre mondiale."
106. YIVO, AJC, RG 347.7.41, FAD 1, Box 20, File: French Jews 1943–1961. Report (nontitled) of French Jewish Community in 1954.
107. Ibid.
108. Several exceptions exist. For example, the LICA and the MRAP may have had a small number of employees at this time. However, the former's postwar archives were destroyed in the 1990s, and the archive of the latter has not yet been catalogued. Likewise, the CII requested financial aid from the WJC to finance its annual budget of F1.9 million, which included F400,000 for its director. It is unknown if the CII was able to raise these funds. AJA, WJC (coll. 361), H/115/12, French Jewish Representative Committee, 1944–1947, Centre Israélite d'information de Paris (no date); Author correspondence with Emmanuel Debono, June 10, 2020.
109. For example, after WWII, Léon Meiss served as president of the Central Consistory and the CRIF. In addition, in the period leading up to his death in 1966, he was president or honorary president of *ten* other Jewish organizations. But as one historian has pointed out, he was also vice president of the Tribunal de la Seine and judge at the Court of Cassation; Fredj, "La création du CRIF: 1943–1966," 67.
110. Telephone interview with former AJC employee, August 3, 2005.
111. Cohen, *Not Free to Desist*, 511–529; Oumansour, "Le rôle de l'American Jewish Committee pendant la guerre d'Algérie, 1954–1962," 227–245. See also, more generally, Messika, *Politiques de l'accueil*, 79–91.
112. CDJC, Archives CRIF, Collection MDI, Box 1, Board Meeting Minutes, September 22, 1947.
113. Ibid.
114. YIVO, AJC, RG 347.7.41, FAD 41, Box 10, File: France FO-Eur 1945–1949, 57, Letter from Joel Wolfsohn to John Slawson, September 25, 1947.
115. Mandel, *Muslims and Jews in France*, 35–58.
116. For example, the AJC meeting with Pierre Mendès-France in 1954. YIVO, AJC, RG 347.7.41, FAD 1, Box 19, File: Government Officials France 1957–1960,

Letters from Zachariah Shuster to John Slawson, June 29, 1954 and November 12, 1954. Meetings also took place with André Mayer, Jacques Soustelle, and others. The AJC organized a luncheon in honor of French Ambassador Henri Bonnet in January, 1955. YIVO, AJC, RG 347.7.41, FAD 1, Box 17, File: France 55–57, Invitation. On AJC meetings with Algerian Front de libération nationale leaders in New York, see Oumansour, "Le role de l'American Jewish Committee pendant la guerre d'Algérie," 239–242.

117. On this affair, see Poujol, *Les enfants cachés*; Doron, *Jewish Youth and Identity*, 68–73, 106–117.

118. YIVO, AJC, RG 347.7.41, FAD 1, Box 19, File: Finaly Affair, France, Meeting with Henri Bonnet, Ambassador of France, June 22, 1953.

119. Telephone interview with Abraham Karlikow, October 27, 2005.

120. A true American in Paris, the now elderly Judge Proskauer also went to Chartres, had a picnic under the "open sky," went to the Louvre, and "on the last evening before his departure I [Shuster] dined with him and Mrs. Proskauer on the Place du Tertre near Sacre Coeur at the restaurant La Mère Catherine, and the Judge was in such high spirits that he got up after the meal and attempted to become the Toscanini of the small orchestra" (see YIVO, AJC, RG 347.7.41, FAD 1, Box 18, File: France 1950–1954, Letter from Zachariah Shuster to John Slawson, April 15, 1954).

121. Telephone interview with Abraham Karlikow, October 27, 2005.

122. YIVO, AJC, RG 347.7.41, FAD 1, Box 17, File: France 55–57, The Poujade Movement, March 28, 1956.

123. Telephone interview with former AJC employee, August 3, 2005.

124. The coverage in the Jewish press in French was less extensive due to the fact, by this period, most French language publications were bimonthlies or monthlies. The three dailies were in Yiddish. In 1954, the AJC estimated the circulation of the *Naye Presse* at forty-five hundred; *Unzer wort* at four thousand in France and eighteen hundred elsewhere in Europe; and *Unzer stimme* at five to seven hundred. YIVO, American Jewish Committee RG-347.7.1, FAD 1, Box 20, File: France Jews 1943–1961, Nontitled Report on the Jewish Community in France, 1954. Rabinovitch estimates the circulation of these newspapers to be three thousand each in 1968; Rabinovitch, *Anatomie du judaïsme français*, 173. David Slucki qualifies *Unzer stimme* as the least circulated Yiddish daily in Paris. Slucki, *The International Jewish Labor Bund*, 81. More generally, on the postwar Yiddish press in France, see Lustman, *Entre Shoah, communisme et sionisme*, especially chapters 7–11.

125. The number of accused implicated in these trials differs in several works. The quoted figures are from Wasserstein, *Vanishing Diaspora*, 53. Pauline Peretz states that eight Czech Communist officials of Jewish origin were sentenced to death. Peretz, *Le combat pour les Juifs soviétiques*, 53.

126. Wasserstein, *Vanishing Diaspora*, 57.

127. Brandenberger, "Stalin's Last Crime?,"194.
128. On this chapter of JDC history, see Dekel-Chen, *Farming the Red Land*.
129. It was also known as Lishat Hakesher and later as Nativ. Shachtman, *I Seek My Brethren*, 105–110; Peretz, *Le combat pour les Juifs soviétiques*, 62–76.
130. On this chapter of Soviet history, see Marie, *Les derniers complots de Staline*; Brent and Naumov, *Stalin's Last Crime, The Doctors' Plot*; Brandenberger, "Stalin's Last Crime?." On postwar Soviet antisemitism, see Peretz, *Le combat pour les Juifs soviétiques*, 52–56; Wasserstein, *Vanishing Diaspora*, 36–57.
131. Cohen and Wall, "French Communism and the Jews," 81–102; Weinberg, *Recovering a Voice*, 253–254.
132. Lustman, *Entre Shoah, communisme et sionisme*, 217–227, 239. Frémontier notes that *Naye presse* published almost seven thousand lines on the Slansky trial, including fifty-three articles, and sixty-four hundred lines on the Doctors' Plot, including forty-three articles. He compares this with the less extensive coverage of these affairs in *l'Humanité*, which published twenty-five hundred lines on the Slansky trial, including twenty-one articles, and three thousand lines on the Doctors' Plot, including twenty-four articles. Frémontier thus demonstrates the specific interest these affairs held for the Jewish Communist newspaper. Frémontier, "Les Juifs communistes en France depuis 1945," 841–877.
133. My analysis of the Yiddish articles is based on these translations.
134. Archives départementales de Seine Saint Denis (ADSSD), David Diamant Collection, 335J/133, *La Presse nouvelle*, "Un message à nos frères des Etats-Unis."
135. Adler, *The Jews of Paris*, 143, 209–222; Lazare, *La résistance juive en France*, 119–129, 283–284; Renée Poznanski conversation with author, Krakow, October 10, 2008.
136. JDC-NY, France 1945/54, File 247, Report for France for Last Quarter of 1944, September 1945. This document shows that the UJRE did not obtain JDC funding at this time.
137. These figures are for the year 1948. Perego, "Pleurons-les, bénissons leurs noms," 132–133; Zoé Grumberg, email correspondence with author, May 20, 2020.
138. According to the UJRE, from the earliest phases of the postwar JDC program until December 1945, the JDC provided them with a grant of F500,000 a month for its six children's homes. After December 1945, the JDC provided the UJRE F700,000 a month for its work among children, thus contributing just under 50 percent of its total children's budget of F1.5 million in early 1946. The JDC allocated an additional F75,000 a month for the dispensaries on December 1, 1945. In addition to this monthly grant, the JDC also provided a one-time grant to the UJRE of F500,000 for repairs to its children's homes. In early 1946, the monthly budget of the UJRE was F2.5 million. JDC-NY, France 1945/54, File 297, Letter from UJRE to the American Jewish Committee, January 22, 1946.

139. JDC-NY, France 1945/54, File 249, Meeting on Proposed Budgets for Children's Organizations in France, August 2, 1946.
140. JDC-NY, France 1945/54, File 284, Memo from Research Department (Nathan Reich) to Robert Pilpel, April 2, 1947.
141. JDC-NY, France 1945/54, File 245, Welfare Report Number 3, June 1949.
142. JDC-NY, France 1945/54, File 284, Memo from Research Department (Nathan Reich) to Robert Pilpel, April 2, 1947.
143. JDC-NY, France 1945/54, File 281, Letter from Joseph Schwartz to Lou Sobel, June 20, 1947.
144. Novick, *The Holocaust in American Life*, 85–102.
145. The House of Representatives' Cox and Reece investigations (1952–1954) targeted the work of American foundations to verify the political leanings of their grant recipients. In this context, JDC funding for Communists is quite unusual. Subak, *Rescue and Flight*, 217–232.
146. This date is used in JDC sources and confirmed in the institutional history of the FSJU, which state the UJRE supported but did not participate in the FSJU. JDC-NY, France 1945/54, File 284, Letter from Laura Margolis to Henrietta Buchman, December 12, 1950; Elmaleh, *1950–2000. Fonds social juif unifié*, 27.
147. JDC-NY, France 1945/54, File 284, Letter from Laura Margolis to Henrietta Buchman, December 12, 1950.
148. JDC-NY, France 1945/54, File 284, Letter from Robert Pilpel to Editor of the Canada Jewish Weekly, October 27, 1950. *Canadian Jewish Weekly* (*Vochenblatt*) "JDC Revokes Monies Orphan Homes Require," September 28, 1950; "Evidence Confirms JDC Discrimination," undated, but after October 28, 1950. On the JDC's response to the charges, see JDC-NY, France 1945/54, File 284, Letter from Laura Margolis to Henrietta Buchman, December 12, 1950.
149. JDC-NY, France 1945/54, File 297, Letter from Richard Cohen to Moses Beckelman and Herbert Katzki, December 3, 1952.
150. On this theme, see Shafir, *Ambiguous Relations*, 159–216; Dreyfus, *L'impossible réparation*, 119–152.
151. Maud Mandel uses this term to analyze this phenomenon, which Emanuel Mounier, editor of the journal *Esprit*, used in September 1945 to describe the absence of Jews in the public discourse. Mounier, "Les juifs parlent aux nations," 458; Mandel, *In the Aftermath of Genocide*, 232. However, as Renée Poznanski points out, the observation was made by Sartre in his essay "Un portrait d'un antisémite," written in October 1944 and first published in November 1945. It would later be developed in his *Réflexions sur la question juive*. Poznanski, *Propagandes et persécutions*, 561–562.
152. The historiography has nonetheless begun to deconstruct the notion of a Jewish silence in the postwar period. For example, K. L. Alder has attributed a more active role for French Jews in her study of the post-liberation press. Adler,

Jews and Gender in Liberation France, 59–67. Renée Poznanski has argued that French Jews were not silent in the immediate postwar period, even if they learned to adapt their discourse to non-Jewish responses. Poznanski, *Propagandes et persécutions*, 561–592. Laura Jokusch has shown how early French Jewish activists sculpted Holocaust memory in order to render it palatable to the French public by downplaying French collaboration while also producing an extensive body of literature on the Holocaust in France and Europe. Jockusch, *Collect and Record!* 46–83. François Azouvi has also recently refuted the silence regarding Auschwitz in postwar French memory and has shown that Jews were, to a certain extent, engaging with the French public about the specificity of Jewish experiences during World War II in the immediate postwar period. Azouvi, *Le mythe du grand silence*, 38–52. Similar historiographical trends can be seen in the United States with the publication of Hasia Diner's *We Remember with Reverence and Love*. For a thorough analysis of the historiography, see Perego, "La mémoire avant la mémoire," 77–90.

153. Frémontier, "Les Juifs communistes en France depuis 1945," 841–877.

154. Ibid., 846.

155. Lustman, *Entre Shoah, communisme et sionisme*, 226–231, 237.

156. JDC-NY, France 1945/54, File 297, "At the Union There Are Spies: The 'Union' Has Received Million from the 'Joint,'" *Unzer Wort*, December 2, 1952.

157. *Unzer wort* continued to ask this question throughout the month of December in at least two articles: JDC-I, S-2418 "I" 18A, N. Z. "I Confess," *Unzer Wort*, December 12, 1952; JDC-I, 5A1 C.43.047, I. Jacubovitch, "What the Prague Trials Did Not Teach Us," *Unzer Wort*, December 16, 1952.

158. JDC-NY, France 1945/54, File 297, Letter from Richard Cohen to Moses Beckelman and Herbert Katzki, December 3, 1952.

159. Wasserstein, *Vanishing Diaspora*, 56.

160. JDC-I, S-2418 "I" 18A, G. Kenig, "The Fifth Column," *Naye presse*, January 14, 1953.

161. JDC-I, S-2418 "I" 18A, L. Korman, "They Want to Light Anew the Crematories!" *Naye presse*, January 15, 1953.

162. JDC-I, S-2418 "I" 18A, "Une prise de Judas," *Canard enchaîné*, February 23, 1953.

163. Frémontier, "Les Juifs communistes en France depuis 1945," 872.

164. ADSSD, Inventory, Fonds des archives départementales, 2936 Per/243J6.

165. A brief (and erroneous) analysis of *Ce soir*'s series can be found in Marie, *Les derniers complots de Staline*, 160–170. Anne Grynberg cites Marie in her analysis of postwar antisemitism in the French Communist Party. Grynberg, "Des signes de résurgence de l'antisémitisme dans la France de l'après-guerre (1945–1953)?," 192–203. David Weinberg also touches on this in Weinberg, *Recovering a Voice*, 251. More generally, see Cohen and Wall, "French Communism and the Jews," 81–102.

166. ADSSD, Fonds des archives départementales, 2936 Per/114, "L'agence soviétique Tass révèle dans un communiqué, Jdanov a été assassiné par un groupe de médecins liés aux services secrets britanniques et au 'Joint,' organisation sioniste," *Ce soir*, January 14, 1953.

167. Born in 1914 in Tunis, Georges Soria was an editorialist and head of the foreign service of *Ce soir*. He is also the author of several essays, including *La France deviendra-t-elle une colonie américaine?* Paris, Le Pavillon, 1948. Maitron and Pennetier, "Georges Soria," 360–1. ADSSD, 2936 Per/114, Soria, "Quand les racistes parlent de l'antisémitisme," *Ce soir*, January 15, 1953; Soria, "Seules, leurs blouses étaient blanches," *Ce soir*, January 16, 1953; ADSSD, Fonds des archives départementales, 2936 Per/114, "'En soutenant la politique d'agression américaine, les sionistes se conduisent comme des ennemis du peuple juif' écrit *Temps nouveaux*," *Ce soir*, January 22, 1953.

168. ADSSD, Fonds des archives départementales, 2936 Per/114, *Ce soir*, January 27, 1953. Born in 1913, Pierre Hervé was Communist Deputy of Finistère from 1945–1948. In 1952, he became a member of the Central Comittee's propaganda section, where he served until 1954. In 1958, Hervé left the PCF for the French Socialist Party. Maitron and Pennetier, "Pierre Hervé," 334–336. On Hevré's antisemitic writings, see Cohen and Wall, "French Communism and the Jews," 89.

169. ADSSD, Fonds des archives départementales, 2936 Per/114, Pierre Hervé, "'La lutte contre le régime populaire est indispensable. Dépensez les sommes nécessaires...' recommande, à propos de la Roumanie, un haut dignitaire de l'agence juive américaine au directeur de l'organisation en Israël," *Ce soir*, January 27, 1953.

170. ADSSD, Fonds des archives départementales, 2936 Per/114, Pierre Hervé, "La preuve qu'il ne s'agit pas de philanthropie. C'est qu'on voit confier les fonctions de chef du service des 'public relations' de Paris à un fidèle de Trotsky," *Ce soir*, January 28, 1953.

171. ADSSD, Fonds des archives départementales, 2936 Per/114, Pierre Hervé, "Professionnels de la charité, les 'Irving Brown' du judaïsme ont éliminé, à la libération, les vrais résistants," *Ce soir*, January 30, 1953.

172. This incident was most likely the arrest and deportation of the women and children of the UGIF's *Maison de la Verdière*, located outside of Marseille, in October 1943. According to Claude Kelman, member of the FSJF, Gaston Kahn was warned of the arrest by the head of the Gestapo in Marseille with the threat that if the home was evacuated, an additional roundup would take place in Marseille. Najman and Hayman, *Claude Kelman, une ambition pour le judaïsme*, 64–65; Laffitte, *Un engrenage fatal*, 258–264.

173. ADSSD, Fonds des archives départementales, 2936 Per/115, Pierre Hervé, "Israël, état parasitaire et démagogique," *Ce soir*, February 3, 1953.

174. See chapter 3, "Scherzo Capriccioso in AJDC Major." See also Hobson Faure, "American Jewish Mobilization in France after World War II: Crossing the Narratives."

175. ADSSD, Fonds des archives départementales, 2936 Per/114, *Ce soir*, January 29, 1953.

176. ADSSD, Fonds des archives départementales, 2936 Per/115, *Ce soir*, February 1 and 2, 1953.

177. Ibid., February 6, 1953.

178. Daix, *Tout mon temps, révisions de ma mémoire*, 329.

179. Daix, *J'ai cru au matin*, 314.

180. Daix, *Tout mon temps*, 324.

181. Ibid.

182. Ibid., 328.

183. JDC-I, S-2418 "I" 18A, Review of Press, JDC, February 3, 1953.

184. JDC-I, S-2418 "I" 18A, Letter from the Association cultuelle israélite de Cannes to Judah Shapiro, January 20, 1953.

185. JDC-I, S-2418 "I" 18A, Letter from Pierre Atal, Adam Loss, and Léon Askenasi to Laura Jarblum, February 2, 1953.

186. Ghiles-Meilhac, "Centralizing the Political Jewish Voice," 67; Fredj, "La création du CRIF: 1943–1966," 72–73; Perego, "Pleurons-les, bénissons leurs noms," 160–62; Weinberg, *Recovering a Voice*, 254–256.

187. For a discussion of the French Communist Party and some dissent during the Doctor's Plot, see Dreyfus, *L'antisémitisme à gauche*, 208–213.

188. JDC-I, S-2418 "I" 18A, "Une prise de Judas," *Canard enchainé*, February 23, 1953.

189. Ibid.

190. JDC-NY, France 1945/54, File 297, Letter from Moses Beckelman to Moe Leavitt, February 23, 1953.

191. JDC-I, S-2418 "I" 18A, Press Review, JDC, January 30, 1953.

192. Ibid., February 2, 1953.

193. JDC-I, S-2418 "I" 18A, "Why Is the Leadership of the Paris 'Joint' Silent? Is It True That the 'Union' Still Receives Subventions? Jewish Public Opinion Will Not Tolerate Such a Moral Scandal," *Unzer stimme*, January 29, 1953; Leneman, "We Too Accuse the Joint," *Zionistische bleter*, January 26, 1953.

194. JDC-I, S-2418 "I" 18A, "Is This True? We Demand an Immediate and Clear Reply of 'Joint,'" *Unzer wort*, January 29, 1953.

195. YIVO, AJC, RG-347.7.1, FAD-1, Box 20, File: "Unser wort" France 1947–1952, Memo from Shuster to Foreign Affairs Department, February 20, 1951; YIVO Archives, American Jewish Committee RG-347.7.1, FAD-1, Box 20, File: "Unser wort" France 1947–1952, Letter from Simon Segal to Zach, July 12, 1950; Pâris de Bollardière, "Pour la pérennité de notre peuple," 199–201.

196. On the issue of postwar silence, see note 151; Poznanski, "French Apprehensions, Jewish Expectations," 57; Azouvy, *Le mythe du grand silence*, 19–182; Jockush, *Collect and Record!*, 56–63. For an analysis of the of honor courts and discussions of Jewish collaboration in the Jewish press, see Perego, "Pleurons-les, bénissons leurs noms," 603–624 and "Jury d'honneur," 137–164.
197. JDC-NY, France 1945/54, File 297, Letter from Moses Beckelman to Moe Leavitt, February 23, 1953.
198. Ibid.
199. JDC-NY, France 1945/54, File 297, Letter from Adolph Held to Moe Leavitt, undated.
200. JDC-NY, France 1945/54, File 297, Letter from Moses Beckelman to Moe Leavitt, February 23, 1953; JDC-I, S-2418 "I" 18A, Statement by Moses Beckelman, Director-General, Submitted to the Editors of *Unzer stimme, Unzer wort*, and *Zionistische bleter*, undated.
201. JDC-NY, France 1945/54, File 297, Letter from Moses Beckelman to Moe Leavitt, February 23, 1953.
202. JDC-I, S-2418 "I" 18A, "Activity of 'Joint' up to Now and Plans for the Future, Interview with the Director-General, Mr. Beckelman," *Unzer wort*, February 27, 1953.
203. Ibid.
204. One former JDC employee who prefers to remain anonymous in this context was labeled a "fellow traveler" and had been fired from a secretarial position at the US embassy. Interview, Paris, September, 2005.
205. The term *fuzzy thinker* is defined in YIVO, RG 347.7.41, FAD 41, Box 10, File: France, American Embassy in Paris, FO-EUR 47–48, 50–56, Letter from Wolfsohn to Slawson, June 30, 1948.
206. ADSSD, David Diamant Collection, 335J/115, Organisations et organismes ayant reçu du secours du joint, undated.
207. ADSSD, 2 No. 4/10, Parti communiste française Collection, Minutes from the Secretary Meeting, January 19, 1953.
208. ACIC, File FSJU, uncatalogued, Brochure sur l'American Joint Distribution Committee, April 1953.
209. JDC-I, S-2418 "I" 18A, Georges Kenig, "Justice and Vigilence," *Naye presse*, April 7, 1953.
210. JDC-I, S-2418 "I" 18A, M. Vilner, "Summer Colonies for Orphans and for Needy Jewish Children," *Naye presse*, May 7, 1953.
211. JDC-I, S-2418 "I" 18A, Letter from Richard Cohen to Moses Beckelman, Herbert Katzki, and Charles Jordan, October 30, 1953, with an October 29, 1953 article from *Naye presse*.
212. These organizations also fought in the United States. In 1951, R. MacIver wrote in his report on the American Jewish organizations that made up the

National Community Relations Advisory Council: "The tendency to put organizational prestige ahead of concerted endeavor became more obvious. Instead of getting together for the sake of their common interest the agencies have been kept apart by mutual jealousies and suspicions, not merely by their differences in ideology. There has been a scrambling for membership, an insistence on the merits of independence, and, on the part of certain agencies, an exaggerated bid for exclusive credit in advancing the cause in which they are all enlisted" (see MacIver, *Report on the Jewish Community Relations Agencies*, 13). See also, Hobson Faure, "Towards Consensus?," 79–96.

213. One could argue that the WJC later managed to develop its activities through its annual Congress of Francophone Jewish Intellectuals and the creation of local chapters in the late 1950s. In this respect, the WJC was more successful than the AJC.

214. JDC-NY, France 1945/54, File 297, Letter from Moses Beckelman to Moe Leavitt, February 23, 1953. Gaby Wolff Cohen, in one of several interviews, insisted on the importance of the JDC as an "external arbitrator" that allowed for local groups to overcome their conflicts in order to coordinate their actions. Interview with Gaby Wolff Cohen, November 17, 2004.

CHAPTER SIX: "FROM CHARITY TO SOCIAL WORK"

1. This title is taken from a 1955 report of the Committee of Israelite Charity of Paris (CBIP), which traced the organization's rationalization process. Archives CASIP-COJASOR, CBIP AC1, Activité du service social du CBIP (1948–1962), *De la charité au service social: 1954, 1955*.

2. Interview with Shirley Hellenbrand, New York, July 18, 2005.

3. Telephone interview with Herman Stein, November 30, 2004.

4. Ibid., November 14, 2004.

5. On the influence of American organizations on French social work during the interwar period, see Gradvohl, "L'histoire du service social: l'influence américaine," 7–16; Fouché, "Le casework," 21–35; more broadly, on the cultural transfers that occurred between Europe, especially in the United Kingdom, and the United States, see Rodgers, *Atlantic Crossings*.

6. JDC-NY, Herman Stein Papers, Box 1, Memo from Herman Stein to Joseph Schwartz, Moses Beckelman, March 17, 1948.

7. Ibid.

8. For example, in the words of Laura Margolis, "The 'education' we have been working on for almost three years now has taken root in this community and is acting as a boomerang. By that I mean that our agencies are now not only asking for financial help, but for leadership to help them implement a good set of social service standards" (see JDC-NY, France 1945/54, File 245, Letter from Laura Margolis to Bill Pilpel, February 22, 1949).

9. An initial French advisory committee was made up of American employees of the JDC Office for France and European Headquarters, including: Herbert Katzki, Dr. Lee Janis, Moses Beckelman, Dr. Joseph Schwartz, Philip Klein, Laura Margolis, Harry Rosen, Judah Shapiro, Herman Stein. The New York committee included top JDC leadership and social work experts: Paul Baerwald, Edward Warburg, Moses Leavitt, Philip Klein, Louis Sobel, Samuel Goldsmith, Dr. Abeloff; JDC-NY, Herman Stein Papers, Box 11, Letter from Herman Stein to Moses Beckelman, February 28, 1949; Box 11, Minutes of advisory committee, April 21, 1949; June 2, 1949. Laura Margolis, did, however, establish a local advisory board among local French Jewish leaders for the selection of students from France; JDC-I, File 5A2 C. 43.070.3, Compte rendu succinct de la réunion du comité directeur provisoire, June 22, 1949.

10. JDC-NY, Herman Stein Papers, Box 1, Meeting of the Committee on Cultural-Religious Affairs of the JDC (NY), June 27, 1949.

11. On this school, see Albert, "Les origines de l'école d'Orsay," 91–100; Lehr, *La Thorah dans la cite*, 60–82.

12. JDC-NY, Herman Stein Papers, Box 1, Minutes of French Advisory Committee, June 2, 1949; Memo from Herman Stein to Moses Beckelman, November 30, 1948.

13. Maud Mandel included the Paul Baerwald School in her larger study of the JDC's impact on French Jewish life; Mandel, "Philanthropy or Cultural Imperialism?," 73–74.

14. The JDC commissioned a study on this school. While useful, this work reflects the organization's view of its accomplishment. Neipris, *The American Jewish Joint Committee and Its Contribution to Social Work Education*.

15. These included Arthur Greenleigh, Laura Margolis, Auren Kahn, Lena (Libby) Meyer, Lena Eisler, to name a few.

16. Encyclopedia Judaica, "Joseph Schwartz," 1019; Bauer, *American Jewry and the Holocaust*, 41.

17. For example, social workers and teachers represented 5 and 14 percent of the Jewish work force, respectively. Feingold, *Entering the Mainstream*, 146–152. By 1930, four out of five social workers were women. Walkowitz, "The Making of a Feminine Professional Identity," 1051–1075.

18. The Graduate School for Jewish Social Work was headed by Maurice Karpf. Stein, "Jewish Social Work in the United States, 1654–1954," 53, 87.

19. From 1932 to 1944, these subjects made up the curricula of accredited social work programs. In 1939, American social workers were required to have a master's degree in order to gain entry into the American Association of Social Work. Lubove, *The Professional Altruist*, 223.

20. Among others, see Margolis, "A Race against Time in Shanghai," 168–171; Stein, "Welfare and Childcare Needs of European Jewry," 297–307; Jordan,

"Current European Emigration Problems," 354–361; Klein, "The Paul Baerwald School of Social Work," 544–553.

21. See for example the JDC news bulletins, which document the arrivals and departures of JDC staff. AN, AJ/43/13, JDC News Bulletin (Vols. 8, 9, and 10) September 1 and 20, 1946.

22. JDC-NY, France 1945/54, 247, Letter from Arthur Greenleigh to Moses Leavitt, April 7, 1945; 249, Welfare Department Report #2, Report of Child Care Department, Office for France on Developments from October 1946 to October 1948, April 1949. Oral history interviews with former members of the PBS support these conclusions. For example Herman Stein mentioned the "paucity of competent people." Telephone interview with Herman D. Stein, August 3, 2004.

23. Lubove, *The Professional Altruist*, 49. The origins of casework can be traced to England, where social reformer Octavia Hill (1838–1912) developed an individualized method of working with the poor in the 1870s. Hill's approach was emulated in the United States through the work of the Charity Organization Society, branches of which were founded throughout the country. An employee of this organization who later became the head of the charity department of the Russell Sage Foundation, Mary Richmond, took inspiration from Hill's work and proceeded to theorize what came to be called "casework." Richmond published two widely read books, *Social Diagnosis* (1917) and *What Is Social Casework?* (1922). Fouché, "Le casework," 23–27.

24. Simon, *The Empowerment Tradition in American Social Work*.

25. Fouché, "Le casework," 21–35; Bouquet, "Réactions au case-work: passions, ambiguïté, résistances," 95–110.

26. Knibiehler, *Nous, les assistantes sociales*, 16–23. For a comparative discussion of American and French social work, see Mandel, "Philanthropy or Cultural Imperialism?," 66–69.

27. For a study of interwar social practices at the CBIP, see Hobson Faure, "Un 'Plan Marshall juif.'" PhD diss., 107–127; 385–392. See also the special issue of *Archives juives*, edited by Céline Leglaive-Perani, "Le 'moment' philanthropique de juifs de France (1800–1940)."

28. As the journal of Hélène Berr makes tragically clear, those involved in Jewish social work during the war were at high risk of deportation. Berr, *Journal, 1942–1944*. My observations on the prewar image of social work among the Jews of France are based on my interview with Franceline Bloch, Paris, November 18, 2004; Interview with Gaby Wolff Cohen, Paris, November 17, 2004. The social profession's lack of popularity among Jews was bemoaned in the newspaper *Archives Israélites* in 1902, when it reported on the Institut français des infirmières à domicile, founded by Madame Emile Alphen-Salvador. Bouquet, "A l'origine de 'Montrouge,'" 73.

29. Samuel, *Rescuing the Children*, 139–141.

30. Interview with Georges-Michel Salomon, Paris, September 26, 2005.

31. Interview with Gaby Wolff Cohen, Paris, May 28, 2004.
32. Interview with Franceline Bloch, Paris, November 18, 2004.
33. Archives CASIP-COJASOR, Témoignage de Ignace Fink, June 2, 1954. In Nice, Fink worked with the Comité d'aide aux refugiés (CAR), which was known as the Comité de Dubouchage.
34. Siekierski, *Midor ledor*, 159–165.
35. Samuel, *Rescuing the Children*, 140.
36. Mandel, "Philanthropy or Cultural Imperialism?," 67. At its peak, COJASOR employed 363 aid workers in various offices throughout France. JDC-NY, France 1945/54, File 283, Rapport moral et financier de COJASOR, 1945–1948. In 1949, the JDC Office for France employed 72 individuals, including 57 local hires. JDC-I, Laura Margolis Jarblum Collection, uncatalogued, Statistical Report, France, Country Directors Conference, October 1952.
37. Doron, *Jewish Youth and Identity in Postwar France*, 139–140; Boussion, "A la croisée des réseaux transnationaux de protection de l'enfance," 186–205.
38. Mabon-Fall, *Les assistantes sociales au temps de Vichy*; Le Tallec, *Les assistantes sociales dans la tourmente*; Le Crom, *Au secours Maréchal! L'instrumentalisation de l'humanitaire, 1940–44*.
39. Thirty-three hundred individuals received a diploma in this manner. Knibiehler, *Nous, les assistantes sociales*, 262.
40. Knibiehler, *Nous, les assistantes sociales*, 82, 378.
41. French Jewish communal workers openly discuss their solidarity and proximity to those they assisted. See for example, Tito Cohen in chapter 4; Samuel, *Rescuing the Children*; Masour-Ratner, *Mes vingt ans à l'OSE, 1941–1961*; Hemmindinger, *Les enfants de Buchenwald*; Siekierski, *Midor ledor*.
42. JDC-NY, France 1945/54, 246, Monthly Report for November and December 1945, Arthur D. Greenleigh, March 5, 1946.
43. JDC-I, 18C/19A S.3101, Welfare Department Report 3, June 30, 1949.
44. Ibid.
45. Rogow, *Gone to Another Meeting*, 167–174. More generally, on the NCJW leading up to WWII, see Klapper, *Ballots, Babies, and Banners of Peace, American Jewish Women's Activism, 1890–1940*.
46. Encyclopedia Judaica, "National Council of Jewish Women," 871.
47. AJHS, Cecilia Razovsky Davidson Papers, P-290, Letter from E. Masour to Cecilia Razovsky Davidson, January 9, 1946.
48. Finaly, *Le Gai Ghetto*, 142.
49. Ibid., 142–143.
50. Schwarz, *Je veux vivre jusqu'à ma mort*, 174–177.
51. The Ship-a-Box program in France lasted until at least 1949 and may have been extended to North African children awaiting passage to Israel in transit camps in Marseilles. JDC-I, 15B C 43.029, National Council of Jewish Women Home,

Letter from Laura Margolis to Joe Schwartz, October 17, 1949; JDC-NY, France 1945/54, File 260, Letter from Charles Passman to JDC Headquarters in New York, September 2, 1949.

52. The NCJW home opened its doors in summer 1947. See Hobson Faure, "Shaping Children's Lives: American Jewish Aid in Post-WWII France," 173–193.

53. JDC-I, 18A S2700.5, Scholarships, National Council of Jewish Women, Meeting with the NCJW at the JDC office, April 30, 1947.

54. Encyclopedia Judaica, "National Council of Jewish Women," 870.

55. An incomplete list of the scholarship recipients from France includes Simone Weil Lipman, Franceline Bloch, Gaby Wolff Cohen, Edith Odenwald Kremsdorf, Fanny Sorkine Drapkin, Adrienne Schwerner, Myriam Greilsammer Salon, Ruth Stern, and three men admitted by exception to the program, Michel Vasserberger, Henri Milstein, and Roland Musnik. For more on this program, see Hobson Faure, "Un 'Plan Marshall juif.'" PhD Diss., 286–299.

56. Telephone interview with Simone Weil Lipman, April 30, 2004.

57. Interview with Franceline Bloch, November 18, 2004.

58. The program took place in early 1945. Fifty-four completed the training and went on to work for UNRRA. AJA, World Jewish Congress Collection (361), D12/2, Courses on Jewish Social Work, Summary Report, C. Varchaver, June 25, 1945; Stein, "From Paris to Jerusalem. Origins of the Paul Baerwald School," 8. Stein felt the school would incite interest in the more general American social work field and that it would be wise to involve "the professional social work field in the United States in this endeavor" (see JDC-NY, Herman Stein Papers, Box 1, Memo from Herman Stein to Moses Beckelman, December 3, 1948).

59. JDC-NY, Herman Stein Papers, Box 1, Minutes of Advisory Committee Meeting, June 2, 1949.

60. JDC-NY, Herman Stein Papers, Box 1, Minutes of French Advisory Committee, April 21, 1949.

61. JDC-NY, Herman Stein Papers, Box 1, Meeting of the Committee on Cultural-Religious Affairs of the JDC, June 27, 1949.

62. JDC-NY, Herman Stein Papers, Box 1, Memo from Herman Stein to Moses Beckelman, November 30, 1948.

63. JDC-NY, Herman Stein Papers, Box 1, Minutes of French Advisory Committee, June 2, 1949; Telephone interview with Herman D. Stein, August 3, 2004.

64. JDC-NY, Herman Stein Papers, Box 1, Memo from Herman Stein to Moses Beckelman, November 30, 1948. According to one French social worker, the PBS offered Marie-Thérèse Vieillot, French social worker and casework advocate, the position director of the school, but she declined. Salomon, "L'Ecole Paul Baerwald," 42.

65. *New York Times*, "Dr. Henry Selver, Educator, 56, Dies," September 22, 1957, 86; Röder and Strauss, "Henry Selver," 688.

66. "Supervision" had developed in social service agencies in the United States in the late 1920s to help standardize a set of social work skills for individuals with diverse educational backgrounds and was institutionalized as part of the American social work curriculum soon after this period. Lubove, *The Professional Altruist*, 168.

67. Henry Giniger, "School Is Started in Royal Chateau."

68. Interviews were conducted with Shirley Hellenbrand, Mara Coen, and Jacqueline Houri-Vignon. Herman Stein, Georges-Michel Salomon, Françoise Boudard, Franceline Bloch, Gaby Cohen also provided insight in their interviews.

69. According to one source, the JDC spent an average of $3,300 a student per year. YIVO, AJC, RG-347.7.1, FAD-1, Memo on Committee Meeting of AJC and the Paul Baerwald School, December 20, 1950.

70. This may have been modified to two years at a later date.

71. Henry Giniger, "School Is Started in Royal Chateau."

72. Interview with Mara Coen, Rome, June 22, 2006.

73. Interview with Jacqueline Houri-Vignon, Paris, September 14, 2005.

74. Interview with Shirley Hellenbrand, New York, July 20, 2004; interview with Mara Coen, Rome, June 22, 2006.

75. Locally recruited instructors included Isaac Pougatch, a Jewish educator, and Dominique Ceccaldi, a non-Jewish civil servant from the Ministry of Public Health, who taught a course on French social legislation. JDC staff included Moses Beckelman, Dr. Lee Janis, Judah Shapiro, Herman Stein, and Harry Rosen, who had come to France to set up the FSJU.

76. Pougatch, *A l'écoute de son people*, 228.

77. Ibid.

78. On the Plessis-Trévise school and its termination, see Pougatch, *A l'écoute de son people*, 287–304. See also Boussion, "A la croisée des réseaux transnationaux de protection de l'enfance," 186–205; Doron, *Jewish Youth and Identity in Postwar France*, 139–140.

79. He went on to run the JDC's educational center. Pougatch, *A l'écoute de son people*, 305–318.

80. Interview with Jacqueline Houri-Vignon, Paris, September 14, 2005.

81. Interview with Mara Coen, Rome, June 22, 2006.

82. JDC-I, France, Dossier 189/190A, Correspondence with PBS Alumni 1949–1951, Letter from Harry Selver to Former Students in Israel, February 7, 1951.

83. JDC-NY, Herman Stein Papers, Box 1, Letter from Philip Klein to Harry Selver, December 2, 1949.

84. Interview with Mara Coen, Rome, June 22, 2006.

85. JDC-I, Folder 190B/191/192A, Paul Baerwald Department, Faculty Meeting Minutes, March 17, 1950. Henry Selver asked, "Are we training

Jewish community leaders as Jews with a missionary goal or are we training technicians, who know about Jewish content?" After a debate, it was eventually agreed that the school was to train "technical personnel, who in addition to learning methods need to acquire a Jewish knowledge, in order to sharpen their awareness of Jewish content in their professional activities" (see JDC-NY, Herman Stein Papers, Box 1, Letter from Harry Selver to Carl Urbont, November 2, 1949).

86. JDC-I, Folder 190B/191/192A, Paul Baerwald Department, Faculty Meeting Minutes, March 17, 1950.

87. Interview with Shirley Hellebrand, New York, July 18, 2005.

88. Ibid., July 20, 2004.

89. Hellenbrand explains this role: "We had these students and we did something that was partially right and partially wrong. We used sort of the American model and got into some very personal things with the students that I really don't approve of professionally now. But it was really quite appropriate. Those people really had no chance to talk to anybody about their experiences [during the Holocaust]. So not because it was professionally right, as a form of training, but because it was humanely right, and so we heard quite a lot about different.... And—I say we—certainly *I* was greatly moved" (see ibid., July 18, 2005).

90. Ibid., July 20, 2004.

91. Interview with Mara Coen, Rome, June 22, 2006.

92. JDC-NY, Herman Stein Papers, Box 1, JDC Country Directors Conference, Report on the PBS by Harry Selver, October 1950.

93. Stein, "From Paris to Jerusalem. Origins of the Paul Baerwald School"; Neipris, *The American Jewish Joint Distribution Committee and Its Contribution*, 97–145.

94. JDC-NY, Herman Stein Papers, Box 1, JDC Country Directors Conference, Report on the PBS by Harry Selver, October 1950; Letter from Harry Selver to Henrietta Buchman, November 25, 1950; JDC-I, 189/190A, Correspondence with PBS Alumni 1949–1951, Student List 1951–1952, undated.

95. JDC-NY, Herman Stein Papers, Box 1, Paris Advisory Committee Meeting, June 28, 1950.

96. The school provided scholarships to students and gave them some spending money, but this could not replace a salary. Those with families were thus, for the most part, unable to attend.

97. ACIC, FSJU, uncatalogued, Letter from the Comité Paul Baerwarld of the FSJU to the Commission de dépistage, September 1, 1949.

98. JDC-I, 73A n.313, Paul Baerwald School 1948–1950, List of People from French Jewish Community Invited to Opening of PBS, April 21, 1950.

99. Established in 1947, the JDC supported this association and at its creation provided food for members to purchase at reduced rates. Its members could also

receive medical services at JDC funded clinics and, for the first three summers of its existence, vacation in a summer home partially funded by the JDC. Kahn, "Resume of Jewish Social Work in Post-War France," 359–368.

100. JDC-I, 190B/191/192A, Faculty Meeting Minutes, November 7, 1951.

101. JDC-NY, France 1955/64, 312, Future of the Paul Baerwald School and Related Activities in Israel, North Africa, and Europe, Philip Klein, March 15, 1955; Interview with Shirley Hellenbrand, New York, July 18, 2005.

102. JDC-I, 18C/19A S.3101.1, Report on the Scope and Organization of Activities, Social Service, Paris, Winter 1953–1955.

103. She returned several times in the summers in the 1970s and 1980s to conduct trainings for the OSE. Interview with Shirley Hellenbrand, New York, July 18, 2005.

104. JDC-I, 18C/19A S.3101.1, Report on the Scope and Organization of Activities, Social Service, Paris, Winter 1953–1955.

105. JDC-I, 18C/19A S.3101.1 "F," Letter from Tito Cohen to Harry Selver, July 27, 1954.

106. JDC-I, 18C/19A S.3101.1 "F," Letter from l'Association des travailleurs sociaux juifs to Harry Selver, June 17, 1954.

107. Date provided in the 1946 general assembly. However, the "registre de deliberations" shows an interruption from 1941 until February 1945. CASIP-COJASOR Archives, CBIP Registres de délibérations de CBIP, 1938–1947.

108. CASIP-COJASOR Archives, CBIP A5.1, "Assemblés générales" 1907–1948, Assemblé générale 1946.

109. Interview with Tito Cohen, Paris, August 2, 2005.

110. CASIP-COJASOR Archives, CBIP AC1, Activité du service social du CBIP (1948–1962), Note relative à l'activité du service social exercice 1948; Note relative à l'activité du service social exercice 1950; Rapport d'activité du service social 1951.

111. CASIP-COJASOR Archives, CBIP AC1, Activité du service social du CBIP (1948–1962), De la charité au service social: 1954.

112. Ibid.

113. Ibid.

114. JDC-I, 18C/19A S.3101.1 "F," Training Program, Social Workers in Paris, Academic Year 1953–1954, Shirley Hellenbrand.

115. Ibid.

116. Interview with Franceline Bloch, Paris, November 18, 2004; interview with Françoise Boudard, August 2 and 8, 2005; interview with Jacqueline Houri-Vignon, former CBIP employee, September 14, 2005. More generally, see Messika, *Politiques de l'accueil*, 101–140.

117. CASIP-COJASOR Archives, CBIP-C1-0.0.6, Alain de Rothschild Correspondence, 1948–1965, Letter from Odette Schwob to Alain de Rothschild,

June 23, 1963. It should be noted that Schwob received F40,000 from the CBIP to compensate for the loss of her salary.

118. David obtained her medical degree in Paris in 1942 and was then arrested and deported to Auschwitz. According to one source, she obtained a scholarship with the Rockefeller Foundation to study medicine in the United States for ten months in 1948. Base de données, "Les boursiers français du programme fellowships and scholarships de la Fondation Rockefeller (1917–1970)," Ludovic Tournès, http://www.pasteur.fr/infosci/archives/f-rock.html, accessed December 1, 2015. Other sources indicate that her stay was in fact three to four years long, from 1946 to 1950. She returned to France and began working at Necker Children's Hospital. During this period, she was interviewed for part-time employment at the PBS by Herman Stein. In addition to her professional responsibilities, David started a working group in her home, on the rue Pergolèse, to help disseminate casework among French social workers. Bouquet, "Les groupes de travail: le groupe Pergolèse, le groupe de Genève, le groupement de recherche sur le case-work, le groupe des enseignantes aux méthodes de service social," 54–56; Golse, "Myriam David, pionnière de la santé mentale de la petite enfance."

119. Boudard, "L'association France-Atlantique," 31–39.

120. Interview with Françoise Boudard, Paris, August 8, 2005.

121. CASIP-COJASOR Archives, CBIP-C1-0.0.6, Alain de Rothschild Correspondence, 1948–1965, Letter from Françoise Boudard to Gaby Cohen and Edith Kremsdorf, April 10, 1963.

122. CASIP-COJASOR Archives, CBIP-C1-0.0.6, Alain de Rothschild Correspondence, 1948–1965, Letter from the CBIP Social Workers to Alain de Rothschild, September 25, 1963.

123. CASIP-COJASOR Archives, CBIP-C1-0.0.6, Alain de Rothschild Correspondence, 1948–1965, Statuts. This was not the first time the CBIP had changed its name. Before 1839, it was known as the Société israélite de secours et d'encouragement. In updating its name yet again in 1963, the CBIP maintained the term *israélite*, even though elsewhere it was increasingly being replaced by "Jew" or "Jewish."

124. OSE, Archives de direction, Vivette Samuel Collection, Box 17, "L'évolution du service sociale de l'OSE," Vivette Samuel, undated (after 1963). Similar changes in method can be seen in the case files of COJASOR. Fourtage and Hobson Faure, "Les survivants de la Shoah d'Europe centrale et orientale," 130–145.

125. JDC-I, 18C/19A S.3101.1 "F," Letter from Harry Selver to Herbert Katzki, February 5, 1954.

126. Jovelin and Bouquet, *Histoire des métiers du social en France*, 35–39.

127. On the Americanization of social work in Germany and Austria during this period, see Louis, "A Second Chance in Exile?," 211–235.

128. Racine, "Le cycle d'études sociales européen des Nations Unies à Paris," 143–154.

129. Seminars were organized by Miss Marguerite Pohek, an American, and took place in Vienna (1950), Holland (1951), Finland (1952), Italy (1953), and England (1954). French language seminars were conducted in Geneva (1952), Montrouge (1953), and Antwerp (1956). Cheminée, "Historique de l'évolution du case-work en France," 10.

130. The FFTS was established in 1950. Salomon, "La fédération Française des travailleurs sociaux et le case-work," 88; Cassegrain, "Le rôle de l'ANAS dans la diffusion du case-work," 90.

131. Cheminée, "Historique de l'évolution du case-work en France," 8; JDC-NY, Herman Stein Papers, Box 1, Memo, The Usefulness of an American School of Social Work in Europe, Harry Selver, Fred Ziegellaub, November 1950.

132. Boudard, "L'association France-Atlantique," 31–39.

133. Bouquet, "Les groupes de travail," 55.

134. See the special issue "Eléments pour une histoire du case-work en France (1945–1970)," especially Salomon, "L'Ecole Paul Baerwald"; Cheminée, "Historique de l'évolution du case-work en France." See also Knibiehler, *Nous, les assistantes sociales,* 294–306; Friedlander, *Individualism and Social Welfare,* 216.

135. Following the suggestion of historians Michaël Werner and Michel Espagne, we can question how factors in the "receiving society" influenced the transfer, as well as its latent functions for both parties. Werner and Espagne, "La construction d'une référence culturelle allemande en France: genèse et histoire (1750–1914)," 969–922.

136. Fasteau apparently became a close enough collaborator of the school to be invited to shabbat dinner to celebrate the end of his tenure at the embassy. JDC-I, 190B/191/192A, Paul Baerwald Department Minutes of Faculty Meetings, Faculty Minute Meetings, May 17, 1952.

137. JDC-I, 189/190A, Correspondence Outside Lecturers 1949–1953, Letter from Herman Stein to Harry Selver, January 1950; Letter from Harry Selver to John Grant, March 3, 1950. Hazemann was recruited to teach a course at the PBS in public health. To my knowledge, David was not hired. Other Rockefeller scholarship recipients suggested to the school were Professor Jean Weiller and François Bourricaud. JDC-I, 189/190A, Correspondence Outside Lecturers 1949–1953, Letter from Herman Stein to Harry Selver, November 8, 1949; Tournès, Database, "Les boursiers français du programme *Fellowships and Scholarships* de la Fondation Rockefeller (1917–1970)."

138. JDC-NY, Herman Stein Papers, Box 1, Meeting of the JDC Committee on Cultural-Religious Affairs, June 27, 1949.

139. JDC-I, 190B/191/192A, Paul Baerwald Department Minutes of Faculty Meetings, Faculty Minute Meetings, December 2, 1949.
140. JDC-NY, Herman Stein Papers, Box 1, Paris Advisory Committee Meeting, June 28, 1950.
141. Ibid.
142. Herman Stein Papers, Box 1, Memo, "The Usefulness of an American School of Social Work in Europe," Harry Selver, Fred Ziegellaub, November 1950.
143. Ibid.
144. Ibid.
145. Cheminée, "Historique de l'évolution du case-work en France," 10–11.
146. JDC-I, 190B/191/192A, Paul Baerwald Department, Faculty Meeting Minutes, May 17, 1952.
147. Ibid., November 7, 1952.
148. Cheminée, "Historique de l'évolution du case-work en France," 13.
149. Requests were made for the supervision of Jeanne Massart and Rosy Goldsmidt from Belgium; Jeanne Thro and Jacqueline Philbée from France; Alba Canali from Italy.
150. Ziegellaub and Frydman, "L'application des méthodes de case-work à la réadaptation d'un cas considéré comme inadaptable," 17–26; Massart, "Enseignements tirés d'un séjour d'études à l'Ecole de service social Paul Baerwald," 149–164.
151. Thro, "Essai sur le case-work," 4–19.
152. Selver, "La formation d'un travailleur social à l'Ecole de service sociale Paul Baerwald," 120–133; Siebold, "Le stage de travail social spécialisé," 134–147; Ziegellaub, "Le cours de travail social individualisé," 148–153.
153. Ziegellaub, "Contribution à l'évolution des techniques sociales en France," in Salomon, "L'Ecole Paul Baerwald (1949–1953),"47.
154. JDC-I, 18C/19A S.3101.1 "F," Letter from Harry Selver to Herbert Katzki, February 5, 1954; Lavoine, *Informations sociales*, "Rapport moral," 10–11; David, "Ouverture des travaux," 1115–1126.
155. JDC-I, 18C/19A S.3101.1 "F," Letter from Agnès de Laage to Harry Selver, December 21, 1953.
156. Salomon, "L'Ecole Paul Baerwald," 46.
157. Fouché, "Le casework," 21–35.
158. Bouquet, "Réactions au case-work: passions, ambiguïté, résistances," 95–110.
159. Ibid., 107.
160. JDC-NY, France 1955/64, 312, "Future of the Paul Baerwald School and Related Activities in Israel, North Africa, and Europe," Philip Klein, March 15, 1955.
161. JDC-NY, Herman Stein Papers, Box 1, JDC Country Directors Conference, Report on the PBS by Henry Selver, October 1950.

162. Mandel, "Philanthropy or Cultural Imperialism?," 73; Friedlander, *Individualism and Social Welfare*, 216. Shirley Hellenbrand also expressed her regret that the school had not done more to influence European social work. Interview with Shirley Hellenbrand, July 20, 2004 and July 18, 2005.

163. CASIP-COJASOR Archives, CBIP AC1, "Activité du service social du CBIP (1948–1962), De la charité au service social: 1954," 1955.

164. In addition to his teaching activities in French social work schools, Salomon became president of the Confédération française des professions sociales, a national professional association. Samuel taught at the Institut de service social de Montrouge, was a member of the Bureau d'études des questions sociales, and provided in-service trainings for various state social work schools. Interview with Georges-Michel Salomon, Paris, September 14 and 27, 2005; OSE, Archives de direction, Vivette Samuel Collection, Box 19, Curriculum Vitae of Vivette Samuel.

CONCLUSION

1. Kelman, "Une menorah d'espoir et de consolation," 39, 43.
2. Ibid.
3. From 1914–1973, $69.9 million were donated to French Jews, including $26.9 million from 1944–1954; JDC-NY, uncatalogued, Report by Loeb and Troper, October 1914 through December 31, 1973.
4. Ibid.
5. Interview with Gaby Wolff Cohen, Paris, May 28, 2004.
6. JDC-NY, France, File 244, JDC Program in France, 1951, April 15, 1951.
7. Ibid.
8. Mandel points out that "for Jewish returnees attempting to put their lives in order, the incomplete [restitution] legislation and bureaucratic slowdowns caused great difficulties" (see Mandel, *In the Aftermath of Genocide*, 64–85).
9. This statistic is based on the 1948–1951 period. Wasserstein, *Vanishing Diaspora*, 92.
10. Wischnitzer, *Visas to Freedom*, 203, 232.
11. Mandel, *In the Aftermath of Genocide*, 151.
12. I have explored this to a certain extent. Hobson Faure, "Performing a Healing Role," 139–156.
13. Wasserstein's thesis has been refuted by Maud Mandel and David Weinberg and nuanced by Daniella Doron's work on children. Wasserstein, *Vanishing Diaspora*; Mandel, *In the Aftermath of Genocide*; Weinberg, *Recovering a Voice*; Doron, *Jewish Youth and Identity in Postwar France*.
14. Claims Conference, "Twenty Years Later," 9–10. See also Zweig, *German Reparations and the Jewish World*.

BIBLIOGRAPHY

PRIMARY SOURCES

Archival Material

THE UNITED STATES

The American Jewish Joint Distribution Committee, New York (JDC-NY)
France, 1939–1944
Folder 596 General 1942–1944.

Saly Mayer Collection 1939–1950
Folders 32 France 1941–1943; 33 France 1941–1943; 35a France organizations: Éclaireurs Israélites, Union OSE, Comité teitel.

France, 1945–1954
Folders: 244 France, General; 245 France, General; 246 France, General; 247 France, General; 248 France, Children's Homes; 249 Children; 250 Education; 254 Heirless Assets; 255 Immigration; 256 Jewish Writers and Painters; 257 Kosher Kitchens and Canteens; 258 Loan Kassas; 259 Medical and Mental Health; 260 Migration; 261 Properties Offered; 262 Refugees; 277 France Organizations; 278 Association des Israélites pratiquants de France; 279 Centre de documentation juive contemporaine; 280 Centre éducatif; 281 Cercle amical; 282 COJASOR preliminary report; 283 COJASOR; 284 Comité central de l'enfance; 285 Éclaireurs Israélites; 286 Fédération des sociétés juives de France; 287 Fonds social juif unifié; 288 Relief Fund for Russians; 289 HEFUD; 291 National Council of Jewish Women; 292 Oeuvre de protection des enfants juifs (OPEJ); 293 Lubavitch; 294 Oeuvre de secours aux enfants (OSE); 295 Service social des jeunes; 296 Tombeau du martyr juif inconnu; 297 Union des juifs pour

la résistance et l'entraide (UJRE); 298 Union populaire juive; 299 Yeshivot; 300 Yeshiva Ohel Joseph.

France, 1955–1967
Folders: 151 General; 152 Aged; 153 Children; 154 Education 1962–1964; 155 Education 1957–1961; 158 Medical Mental Health; 161 Refugees 1963–1964; 162 Refugees 1955–1962; 167 Centre de documentation juive contemporaine; 168 Cercle amical; 169 COJASOR; 170 Fond social juif unifié (FSJU); 171 FSJU Publications; 173 Institut international d'études hébraïques; 174 Lubavitch; 175 Oeuvre de secours aux enfants (OSE); 176 Ozar Hatorah; 177 Tombeau du martyr juif inconnu; 178 Yeshiva Ohel Joseph.

General, 1945–1964
Folders: 3461 Proceedings of the Welfare Conference, September 1959; 4176 Jewish Children in Liberated Europe.

Israël 1955–1967
Folder 312 Paul Baerwald School.

Noncatalogued Archives
Personnel File of Laura Margolis; Herman D. Stein Collection (Boxes 1 and 11); JDC Primer, 1945; Loeb and Troper Report, October 1914–December 1973.

American Jewish Historical Society, New York (AJHS)
P-290 Cecilia Razovsky Davidson Collection
Box 6

SCA-AJHS 1–68, Synagogue Council of America
Box 13

YIVO Institute for Jewish Research, New York (YIVO)
American Jewish Committee
RG-347.7.1, FAD-1, Foreign Affairs Department, Foreign Countries, France (Boxes 17–20); RG 347.7.41, FAD-41, American Jewish Committee Paris Office (Boxes 10–14).

HICEM/HIAS
RG 245.5, Series 4, France IV, Records of Postwar HICEM/HIAS 1945–1953
Microfilms: 19.1, 19.4, 19.5, 19.6, 19.08, 19.20, 19.23, 19.24, 19.25, 19.42.

American Jewish Archives, Cincinnati (AJA)
World Jewish Congress Collection (361)
Series D: Relief and Rescue Departments 1939–1969; D12/1: Training Courses for Workers in Jewish Children's Homes in Europe, 1945; D12/2: Courses on Jewish Social Work, Reports, Notes, and Correspondence, 1944–1945; D12/5: Courses

on Jewish Social Work, Applications for Admission, 1945; D13/1: Recruitment of Social Workers / Securing Jobs with United Nations Relief and Rehabilitation Administration for Courses on Jewish Social Work Graduates, 1944–1945; D13/6: Courses on Jewish Social Work, Yiddish Class, Questionnaires, 1945; D49/1: France (Children), Report on WJC Rescue Work by M. Jarblum, 1945; D58/9: Report on Refugees by "Sylvia" (UNRRA, in French), 1946–1947; D 73/8: United Jewish Appeal and Joint Distribution Committee, 1947; D 73/9: Agreement with United Jewish Appeal and Jewish Joint Distribution Committee, 1947; D 73/10: Second Agreement with United Jewish Appeal and Jewish Joint Distribution Committee, 1947–1948.

Series H: Alphabetical Files, 1919–1981; H112/1: France, Cahn-Debre, Sylvain, 1945; H112/2: France, Cahn-Debre, Sylvain, January–April 1946; H113/5: France, Conseil représentatif des juifs de France, 1945; H113/6: France, Conseil représentatif des juifs de France, 1946–1950; H113/7: France, Conseil représentatif des juifs de France, Program, 1945, H113/9: France, Cultural Department, 1946, 1948–1952; H113/10: France, Cultural Department, 1953–1955, 1958; H113/11: France, Cultural Rehabilitation, 1946; H114/12: France, French Authorities, Jewish Leaders' Recognition of De Gaulle, Charles, 1944–1945; H115/7: France, Jarblum, Marc, 1944; H 115/9: France, Jewish Agency for Palestine, 1945–1946, 1949; H115/12: France, Jewish Representative Committee, 1944–1947; H120/11: France, Reading, Eva, Trip to France and Belgium, 1944; H121/5: France, Relief and Rescue, Croustillion, Joseph, 1944–1945.

World Union for Progressive Judaism Collection (16)
Series C: Conferences (1928–1986); C1/12: 9th Conference, Paris, France, 1955; C2/1: 13th Conference, Paris, France, 1964.
Series D: Office of the Honorable Secretary (1925–1993); D2/11: France, 1929–1950; D2/12: France, 1951–1956; D2/13: France, 1957–1959; D3/1: France, 1960–1961; D3/2: France, 1962–1970; D11/6: ABS Scheuer, Simon, Jarblum, Laura, France, 1952–1953; D11/7: ABS Scheuer, Simon, Kahn, Auren, France, 1948–1951; D11/8: ABS Scheuer, Simon-Katzki, Herbert, France, 1952; D11/10: ABS Scheuer, Simon-Margolis, Laura, France, 1947–1948; D11/15: ABS Scheuer, Simon, Paris, France, Home Correspondence. 1947–1948; D11/16: ABS Scheuer, Simon-Joseph, France 1947–1948; D11/17: ABS Scheuer, Simon-Union of Jewish Students, France, 1948–1950.

Bobst Library, New York University
Jewish Labor Committee (JLC), Series I and II (several documents).

New York Public Library, New York (NYPL)
American Jewish Committee Oral History Collection, Z. Shuster, 1972 and 1980; A. Karlikow, 1980 and 1988.

FRANCE

Les archives nationales, Paris (AN)
AJ43-Organisation internationale des réfugiés
Folders: 13 American Joint Distribution Committee 1938–1947; 14 HIAS-HICEM 1943–1946; 18 American Jewish Committee 1944–1947; 34 American Joint Distribution Committee 1947; 75 American Joint Distribution Committee, Correspondence 1945–1947; 540 Accords entre l'OIR et diverses organisations bénévoles (HIAS et AJDC) 1948–52; 1253 and 1252 Correspondance entre la délégation de l'OIR à Paris et l'ADJC, COJASOR, HIAS 1946–1952.

F9-Archives du ministère des prisonniers, déportés et réfugiés (MPDR)
Folders: 3249 Direction d'affaires sociales; 3252 (H. listes des associations des réfugiés); 3271 (mission à Londres, dossier sur le rapatriement des juifs, semaine de l'absent, correspondance avec l'UNRRA, Save the Children Fund).

Archives départementales de Seine Saint Denis (ADSSD)
French Communist Party Collection
2936 PER/114 (*Ce soir*, January 1953); 2936 PER/115 (*Ce soir*, February 1953); Réunion du secrétariat, procès verbal du January 19, 1953 (2 no. 4/10).

David Diamant Collection (335J)
335J65, Union des juifs pour la résistance et de l'entraide (UJRE), historique et fonctionnement, 1944–1949; 335J 69, UJRE bureau exécutif et secrétariat; 335J 73, Rapports d'activité et rapports moraux; 335J 79, Publications diverses de l'UJRE; 335J 106, Organisation des juifs polonais, correspondances; 335J 115, Autres organisations juives; 335J/156, Revues de presse, Congrès juif mondial, Joint, 1944–1946; 335J 133, Périodiques.

L'Association consitoriale israélite central (ACIC)
Uncatalogued Files
FSJU; Amérique du nord 1947–1948; Joint 1947–1948; Congrès juif mondial 1947–1949; Invitations, New York, 1944; Meiss and Kaplan, Congrès juif mondial, New York, 1944); American Jewish Conference; FSJU Folder on Claims 1955–1958.

L'Association consistoriale israélite de Paris (ACIP)
Series B: Correspondence: B135 (1937–1947); B136 (1946–1947).
Series GG: *Ketoubot* (Marriage Contracts, by Synagogue).
GG/165 Synagogue la Victoire (1940–1949); GG/166 La Victoire (1940–1947); GG/167 La Victoire (1949–1950); GG/168 La Victoire (1954–1959); GG/169 La Victoire (1959–1966); GG/354 La Victoire (1944–1945); GG/355 La Victoire (1945); GG/356 La Victoire (1945); GG/357 missing; GG/358 La Victoire; GG/294 Mariages des divorcées, veuves et prosélytes (1939–1949); GG/295

missing; GG/296 Mariages des divorcées, veuves et prosélytes (1955–1959); GG/297 Mariages des divorcées, veuves et prosélytes (1959–1963); GG/298 Mariages des divorcées, veuves et prosélytes (1963–1965); GG/299 missing; GG/363 Temple Chasseloup-Laubat (1949–1950); GG365 Temple Chasseloup-Laubat (1953); GG/366 Temple Enghieu (1952–1953).
Series GO2: Bulletin de mariages (by Year, All Synagogues) September 1945–December 1963.

Archives de la Préfecture de police de Paris (APP)
Série BA, Période 1869–1970: BA/1681 La colonie Américaine; BA/2229 Associations religieuses; BA/2273 Communauté juive, associations; BA/1812 Communauté juive, associations; BA/2314 Communauté juive, associations; BA/2315 Communauté juive, associations; BA/1741 Culte israélite et protestante, coupures de presse, conférences; BA/2176 États-Unis, ambassade et consulat (sur le recensement des américains); BA/2007 Helbronner, Jacques; BA/2010 Jurblum, Moidko; BA/1822 Libération (dossiers concernant l'armée américaine); BA/1834 Libération (internés, étrangers et ressortissants de pays alliés); BA/2458 Manifestations, époux Rosenberg 1953; BA/2234 Orphelinats; BA/2123 Presse (journalistes étrangers anglo-américains, 1939–1948).
Série EB, Période 19^è–20^è siècle: EB/70 Synagogues.
Série GA, Période 1930–1995: GA/br25 La presse des communautés étrangères en France, tomes 1, 2, 3.

Mémorial de la Shoah
Centre de documentation juive contemporaine (CDJC)
Conseil représentatif des israélites de France-MDI
Box 1, Folders 1–5. Board Meeting Minutes 1944–1948.

COJASOR Collection
Box 22/1505 MDV Document Cojasor 1/2; Box 8/Correspondence; Dossier: Correspondence AJDC, November 6, 1946–February 18, 1951.

Latour Collection
DLXI-40 Elisabeth Hirsch (Böszi); DLXI-41 Laura Margolis Jarblum; DLXI-42 Marc Jarblum; DLXI-54 Joseph Kruh (Croustillon).

CGQJ Collection
CCCLXVI-14 American Joint Distribution Committee.

UGIF Collection
CDXVIII-90 Lettre de L. Sokolowsky à M. Brener, September 29, 1942.

Miscellaneous
DLVI (1)-27 "Ironique et juste retour des choses."

Alliance israélite universelle (AIU)
General Files
France AHI, Relations avec le Joint (1921–22); France 9D55, Émigration HIAS-ICA (1927–1935); États Unis 1C03, American Jewish Relief Committee; États Unis 1C04, American Jewish Distribution Committee; Comités en rapport avec l'Alliance; American Joint 1918–1925.

American Friends of the Alliance
AM.F.53, Box 18, Documents comptabilité de 1948; AM.F.129, Box 41, Correspondence, 1958–1960 JD; AM.F.196, Box 54. Certificat de fondation et noms des membres des American Friends; AM.F.212.2, Box 55, 1947–1952: liste de noms de donateurs aux AMF.

Oeuvre de secours aux enfants (OSE-headquarters)
Uncatalogued
Archives of the Direction (1945–1948); Vivette Samuel Collection, Boxes 15, 17, and 19.

Fondation CASIP-COJASOR (CASIP-COJASOR)
Toît familial (1954–1970)
Thirteen applications from American students.

COJASOR Collection
Sous-fonds, réfugiés, série, Égypte, Series B: COJ.R.EGY.B2; COJ.R.EGY.B5. Series E: Correspondance entre Joint et COJASOR (1957–1962); COJ.R.EGY.E; Témoignage de Ignace Fink.

Comité de bienfaisance israélite de Paris (CBIP) Collection
CBIP-C1-0.0.6 Correspondance d'Alain de Rothschild, 1948–1965; CBIP Registres de délibérations de CBIP, 1938–1947; CBIP AC1, Activité du service social du CBIP (1948–1962); CBIP AC3, Activité des organismes de la communauté juive (1950–1963); CBIP A5.1 "Assemblés générales" 1907–1948; CBIP-P1, Dossiers du personnel A à J.

ISRAEL
American Jewish Joint Distribution Committee, Jerusalem (JDC-I)
France
Folders: 5A1 C-43.055 COJASOR; 5A1 C-43.042 Conseil représentatif des organisations juives de France; 5A1 C-43.050 HEFUD; 5A1 C-43.054I Père Chaillet et le Consistoire central des Israélites en France; 5A1 C-43.056 Rescue Children Inc., Children's Rescue Committee; 5A1 C-43.045 Service social des jeunes; 5A1 C-43.047 Union des juifs pour la résistance et l'entraide (UJRE); 5A1 C-43.060 Union of Jewish Writers and Journalists; 5A1 C- 43.062 Heirless

Jewish Property; 5A1 C- 43.064 Vaad Haatzalah Institutions, France; 5A2 C-43.071 Commission de dépistage; 5A2 FSJU Founding Essay of Laura Margolis Jarblum; 5A2 C-43.070c FSJU 2; 5A2 C-43.070d FSJU 3; 5A2 C-43.070.3 FSJU Meeting; 5A2 C-43.070a FSJU 1; 5A3 C-43.078 AJDC Headquarters; 5A3 C-43.094 Association des travailleurs sociaux juifs; 5A3 C-43.077 Budget Cuts; 5A3 C-43.074 Condensed Milk Allegedly Sold; 5A3 C-43.604.4 France Program, Marseille; 5A3 C-43.091 JDC Assistance for American Citizens; 5A3 C-43.095 North African Immigration to France; 5A3 C-43.604.2 Personnel Marseille; 5A3 C-43.086 Union nationale; 5A3 C-43.085 Voluntary Agencies France; 18C/19A S.301.2 Reception for Paul Baerwald; 18C/19A S.301.1 F Paul Baerwald Department 1954–1957; 18C/19A Paul Baerwald Budget; 18C/19A S.301.1 Paul Baerwald School in North Africa and Tunisia; 18C/19A S.3101 Welfare Activities; 189/190A Correspondence with Outside Lecturers 1949–1950, 1952–1953; 189/190A Paul Baerwald Department Correspondence with PBS Alumnae 1949–1951; 15B C-43.029 National Council of Jewish Women Home; 18A S-2418 I Public Relations; 18A S-2700.5 Scholarships, National Council of Jewish Women; 22B S-1300.1 Marshall Plan; 22B S-1803 Paris Headquarters Move to Geneva; 73A n. 313 Paul Baerwald School 1948–1950; 190B/191/192A Paul Baerwald Department Minutes of Faculty Meetings 1949–1954.

Uncatalogued
Laura Margolis Jarblum Collection; Yehuda Bauer Collection, France, 1944–1950.

Oral History Division, Avram Harmon Institute of Contemporary Jewry Hebrew University of Jerusalem (OHD)
1-The Rescue of Jews via Spain and Portugal; the Jewish Underground Movement in France during World War II: 61 (1) Jefroykin, Jules; 43 (1) Margolis Jarblum, Laura
4-Berihah (Organized Escape) and the Camps in Germany 1944–1948; Holocaust Survivors in Europe, 1944: 13 (4) Klein (Rabbi, Dr. Issac).
27-Jews in the Underground in Belgium during World War II; The Rescue of Jewish Children in Belgium during World War II; The Rescue of Children from Germany, Czechoslovakia, and Austria via Western Europe, 1933–1940: 86 (27) Jarblum, Marc.
47-The Joint (American Jewish Joint Distribution Committee): 9 (47) Warburg, Edward; 12 (47) Katzki, Herbert; 19 (47) Schwartz, Dr. Joseph.
119-The Role of American Jewish Chaplains in Rescuing Holocaust Survivors in Europe, 1944–1948: 1 (119) Dembowitz, Morris; 3 (119) Breslau, Isadore; 14 (119) Lipshutz, Oscar; 28 (119) Rock, Eli; 36 (119) Rackovsky, Issiah; 44 (119) Phillips, Israel Joel; 47 (119) Miller, Meyer; 50 (119) Handwerger, Robert; 59 (119) Miller, Carl; 64 (119) Haselkorn, Abraham; 84 (119) Nadich, Judah.

128-History of the United Jewish Appeal: 103 (128) Borenstein, Paula; 56 (128) Margolis, Laura.

Oral History Interviews Conducted by Author

Abramovitch, Stanley, Jerusalem, May 5, 2005.
Barnett, Mary, Paris, September 9, 2005.
Berkowitz, Rabbi Steven, Paris, November 28, 2004; February 17, 2005.
Bloch, Francline, Paris, November 18, 2004.
Borenstein, Pessela, Paris, November 13, 2004.
Boudard, Françoise, Paris, August 2 and 8, 2005.
Calmat, Yvette, Paris, February 3, 2005.
Coen, Lou, Fontenay-sous-Bois, May 11, 2005.
Coen, Mara, Rome, June 22, 2006.
Cohen, Tito, Paris, August 2, 2005.
Cohen, Rabbi Tom, Paris, March 4, 2004.
Cohn, Louis, Antony, November 25, 2004.
Comet, Theodore, New York, July 20, 2004.
Créange, Berthe, phone interview, March 26, 2004; Saint-Rémy-les-Chevreuse, April 6, 2004; June 16, 2004.
Elbaz, Michel, Paris, March 11, 2005.
Ejnès, Serge, Tel Aviv, April 20; 2005.
Eschborn Goldstein, Lolita, phone interview, October 27, 2005; Geneva, March 9, 2006; Paris, July 3, 2006.
Former employee of the American Jewish Committee, phone interview, August 3, 2005.
Fox, Hyman, West Bloomfield, April 3, 2019.
Goldman, Ralph, Jerusalem, May 2, 2005.
Hellenbrand, Shirley, New York, July 20, 2004; July 18, 2005.
Houri Vignon, Jacqueline, Paris, September 14, 2005.
Jerusalmi, Isaac, Cincinnati, May 5 and 6, 2006.
Kagan, Saul, phone interview, February 7, 2006.
Karlikow, Abraham, phone interview, October 27, 2005.
Kessler, Colette, Levallois-Perret, January 29, 2007.
Konvitz, Joseph, Paris, February 22, 2005.
Lerner Ejnès, Hélène, Tel Aviv, April 20, 2005.
Marx, Denyse, Paris, October 21, 2004.
Michel, Ernst, New York, July 19, 2004.
Rosenthal, Liliane, Paris, June 16, 2005.
Salamon, Claudine, Paris, December 2006.
Salomon, Georges Michel, Paris, September 14 and 27, 2005.
Senderey, Alberto, Paris, January 7, 2005.

Spingarn, Odette, Levallois-Perret, January 17, 2007.
Spokoiny, Andres, Paris, October 20, 2004.
Stein, Herman, phone interview, July 29, 2004; August 3, 2004; November 14 and 30, 2004.
Taub, Gaby, Paris, May 4, 2004.
Weil Lipmann, Simone, phone interview, April 30, 2004.
Williams, Rabbi Michael, Paris, February 2, 2005.
Wolff Cohen, Gaby, Paris, May 28, 2004; June 8, 2004; November 17, 2004; August 2, 2005; December 20, 2005.

PUBLISHED PRIMARY SOURCES

Press

Informations sociales (1949–1954)
La revue du Fonds social juif unifié (1953–1956)
Le service social (1949–1954)

Books and Articles

Aliav Klüger, Ruth, and Peggy Mann. *The Last Escape*. New York: Doubleday, 1973.
Bernstein, Philip S. "Jewish Chaplains in World War II." *American Jewish Yearbook* 47 (1945–1946): 173–200.
Berr, Hélène, and Patrick Modiano. *Journal: 1942–1944*. Points 2163. Paris: Seuil, 2009.
Bober, Robert. *Berg et Beck*. Paris: POL, 1999.
Boudard, Françoise. "L'association France-Atlantique." *Vie sociale* 1 (1999): 31–39.
Conference on Jewish Material Claims against Germany. "Twenty Years Later, 1952–1972: Activities of the Conference on Jewish Material Claims against Germany." New York, 1972.
Daix, Pierre. *J'ai cru au matin*. Paris: Laffont, 1976.
———. *Tout mon temps, révisions de ma mémoire*. Paris: Fayard, 2001.
David, Myriam. "Ouverture des travaux." *Informations sociales* 10 (1957): 1115–1126.
Ejnès, Serge. *Histoire des Juifs de Reims pendant la Seconde Guerre mondiale: témoignages, documents, déportés (avec le concours de Jocelyn Husson et Françoise Nochimowski, préface de Serge Klasfeld)*. Tel Aviv: Tinqueux, 1995.
Ertel, Rachel. "Les fantômes du 9 rue Guy Patin. (En souvenirs)." *Les temps modernes* 5, no. 686 (2015): 21–54.
Finaly, Patricia. *Le gai ghetto*. Paris: Gallimard, 1970.
Giniger, Henry. "School Is Started in Royal Chateau, American Social Work Methods Are Taught at Versailles in Baerwald Center." *New York Times*, December 4, 1949.

Hemmendinger, Judith. *Les enfants de Buchenwald*. Mémoires du XXe siècle. Paris: L'Harmattan, [1984] 2002.
Jordan, Charles. "Current European Emigration Problems." *Jewish Social Service Quarterly* 26, no. 4 (1950): 354–361.
Kahn, Auren. "Resume of Jewish Social Work in Post-War France." *Journal of Jewish Communal Service* XXXI, no. 4 (1954): 359–368.
Kaplan, Jacob. "French Jewry under the Occupation." *American Jewish Year Book* 47 (1945): 71–118.
Kaufman, Isidor. *American Jews in World War II: The Story of 550,000 Fighters for Freedom*. Vol. I and II. New York: Dial, 1947.
Kelman, Claude. "Une menorah d'espoir et de consolation." *Echanges: périodique consacré aux oeuvres juives de santé, d'assistance sociale et d'éducation* 20 (1964): 39–43.
Klein, Isaac. *The Anguish and the Ecstasy of a Jewish Chaplain*. New York: Vantage, 1974.
Klein, Philip. "The Paul Baerwald School of Social Work." *Jewish Social Service Quarterly* XXVI, no. 4 (1950): 544–553.
Lambert, Raymond-Raoul. *Carnet d'un témoin 1940–1943*. Présenté et annoté par Richard Cohen. Paris: Librairie Arthème Fayard, 1985.
Laub, Morris. *Last Barrier to Freedom. The Internment of Jewish Holocaust Survivors on Cypress*. Berkeley, CA: JL Mangus Museum, 1985.
Lavoine, Mlle. "Rapport moral." *Informations sociales* 1 (1954): 10–11.
Levin, Meyer. *In Search*. New York: Horizon, 1950.
Livazer, Hersh. *The Rabbi's Blessing: From the Memories of a Chaplain in the US Army (1943–1965)*. Jerusalem: H. Livazer, 1980.
Margolis, Laura. "Race against Time in Shanghai." *Survey Graphic* XXXIII, no. 3 (March 1944): 168–170, 190–191.
Masour-Ratner, Jenny. *Mes vingt ans à l'OSE: 1941–1961*. Collection témoignages de la Shoah. Paris: Éditions le Manuscrit, 2006.
Massart, Jeanne. "Enseignements tirés d'un séjour d'études à l'ecole de service social Paul Baerwald." *Le service social*, no. 4 (1952): 149–164.
Moch, Maurice. *Le CRIF. Vingt-cinq ans d'activités*. Paris: CRIF, 1970.
Mounier, Emmanuel. "Les juifs parlent aux nations." *Esprit* 10 (September 1945): 457–459.
Nadich, Judah. *Eisenhower and the Jews*. New York: Twayne Publishers, 1953.
Pougatch, Issac. *A l'écoute de son peuple. Un éducateur raconte*. Paris: Albin Michel, 1980.
Racine, A. "Le cycle d'études sociales Européen des nations unies à Paris." *Le service social* 3 (1950): 143–154.
Riegner, Gerhart M. *Ne jamais désespérer: soixante-années au service du peuple juif et des droits de l'homme*. Paris: Editions du cerf, 1998.

Rothschild, Guy de. *The Whims of Fortune: The Memoirs of Guy de Rothschild*. New York: Random House, 1985.
Salomon, Georges-Michel. "La fédération Française des travailleurs sociaux et le case-work." *Vie sociale* 1 (1999): 87–88.
———. "L'Ecole Paul Baerwald." *Vie sociale* 1 (1999): 41–47.
Samuel, Vivette. *Rescuing the Children: A Holocaust Memoir*. Madison: University of Wisconsin Press, 2002.
Schrager, Fajwel. *Un militant juif*. Paris: Les editions polyglotte, 1976.
Schwarz, Lotte. *Je veux vivre jusqu'à ma mort*. Traversée Du Siècle. Paris: Seuil, 1979.
Selver, Henry. "La formation d'un travailleur social à l'Ecole de service social Paul Baerwald." *Informations sociales* 3 (1953): 120–133.
Siebold, Jeanne. "Le stage de travail social spécialisé." *Informations sociales* 3 (1953): 134–147.
Siekierski, Denise. *Midor LeDor: de génération en génération*. Paris: L'Harmattan, 2004.
Stein, Herman. "From Paris to Jerusalem: Origins of the Paul Baerwald School of Social Work of the Hebrew University." In *Academic Social Work Education in Israel: Past, Present and Future*, edited by Uri Avram, 23–48. Tel Aviv, 2003.
———. "Welfare and Child Care Needs of European Jewry." *Jewish Social Service Quarterly* XXVI, no. 4 (1949).
Thro, Jeanne. "Essai sur le case-work social." *Informations sociales* 1 (1953): 4–19.
Weiss, Louise. *Mémoires d'une Européene. Tome III: 1934–1939*. Paris: Payot, 1970.
———. *Souvenirs d'une enfance republicaine*. Paris: Denoël, 1937.
Wiesel, Elie. *All Rivers Run to the Sea: Memoirs*. New York: Schocken Books, 1996.
Ziegellaub, Fred. "Contribution à l'évolution des techniques sociales en France." *Travail social de la fédération Française des travailleurs sociaux* 2ème trimestre (1953).
———. "Le cours de travail social individualisé." *Informations sociales* 3 (1953): 148–153.
Ziegellaub, Fred, and Vania Frydman. "L'application des méthodes de case-work à la réadaptation d'un cas considéré comme inadaptable." *Le service social* 1 (1952): 17–26.

SECONDARY SOURCES

Works Cited

Adler, Jacques. *The Jews of Paris and the Final Solution: Communal Response and Internal Conflicts, 1940–1944*. New York: Oxford University Press, 1987.
Adler, Karen L. *Jews and Gender in Liberation France*. Cambridge, UK: Cambridge University Press, 2003.

Afoumado, Diane. *Exil impossible: l'errance des Juifs du paquebot "St.-Louis."* Paris: L'Harmattan, 2005.
Alary, Eric. "Les Juifs et la ligne de démarcation." *Cahiers de la Shoah* 5 (2001): 13–49.
Anteby-Yemini, Lisa, and William Berthomière. "Avant-propos di[a]spositif: décrire et comprendre les diasporas." In *Les diasporas: 2000 ans d'histoire*, edited by Lisa Anteby-Yemini, William Berthomière, and Gabriel Sheffer, 9–20. Rennes: Presses universitaires de Rennes, 2005.
Attal, Robert. "Index de la revue 'Évidences' (1949–1963)." Jerusalem, 1972.
Auslander, Leora. "Coming Home? Jews in Postwar Paris." *Journal of Contemporary History* 40, no. 2 (2005): 237–259.
Avni, Haïm. "The Zionist Underground in Holland and France and the Escape to Spain." In *Rescue Attempts during the Holocaust. Proceedings of the Second Yad Vashem International Historical Conference. Jerusalem, April 8–11, 1974*, edited by Yisrael Gutman and Efraim Zuroff, 555–590. Jerusalem: Yad Vashem, 1977.
Azouvi, François. *Le mythe du grand silence: Auschwitz, les Français, la mémoire.* Paris: Fayard, 2012.
Bankier, David, ed. *The Jews Are Coming Back: The Return of the Jews to Their Countries of Origin, 1943–1947.* Jerusalem: Yad Vashem, 2005.
Basch, Linda G., Nina Glick Schiller, and Cristina Szanton Blanc. *Nations Unbound: Transnational Projects, Postcolonial Predicaments, and Deterritorialized Nation-States.* Basel: Gordon and Breach, 1994.
Bauer, Yehuda. *American Jewry and the Holocaust: The American Jewish Joint Distribution Committee, 1939–1945.* Detroit, MI: Wayne State University Press, 1981.
———. *Flight and Rescue: Brichah; The Organized Escape of the Jewish Survivors of Eastern Europe.* New York: Random House, 1970.
———. *My Brother's Keeper: A History of the American Jewish Joint Distribution Committee 1929–1939.* Philadelphia, PA: The Jewish Publication Society, 1974.
———. *Out of the Ashes: The Impact of American Jews on Post-Holocaust Jewry.* Oxford, UK: Pergamon, 1989.
Bazarov, Valery. "HIAS and HICEM and the System of Jewish Relief Organizations in Europe." *East European Jewish Affairs* 39, no. 1 (2009): 69–78.
———. "In the Crosshairs." *Passages, The Magazine of HIAS* 6, no. 2 (2007): 22–27.
Becker, Annette. *Messagers du désastre: Raphael Lemkin, Jan Karski et les génocides.* Paris: Fayard, 2018.
Bensimon, Doris. *Les Juifs de France et leurs relations avec Israël, 1945–1988.* Paris: L'Harmattan, 1989.
Bensimon, Doris, and Sergio Della Pergola. *La population juive de France: sociodémographie et identité.* Jerusalem: The Institute of Contemporary Jewry, The

Hebrew University of Jerusalem Centre national de la recherche scientifique, 1984.
Benveniste, Annie. *Le Bosphore à la Roquette: la communauté judéo-espagnole à Paris (1914–1940)*. Paris: L'Harmattan, 1989.
Berg, Roger. "De 1945 à 1972." In *Histoire des Juifs en France*, edited by Bernhard Blumenkranz, 423–444. Toulouse, France: Privat, 1972.
Berkovitz, Jay R. *The Shaping of Jewish Identity in Nineteenth-Century France*. Detroit, MI: Wayne State University Press, 1989.
Bertin, Celia. *Louise Weiss*. Paris: Albin Michel, 2015.
Bessel, Richard, and Dirk Schumann, eds. *Life and Death: Approaches to a Cultural and Social History of Europe during the 1940s and 1950s*. Cambridge, UK: Cambridge University Press, 2003.
Birnbaum, Pierre. *Les deux maisons: essai sur la citoyenneté des juifs (en France et aux Etats-Unis)*. Paris: Gallimard, 2012.
Boukara, Philippe. "L'ami parisien: les relations politiques et personnelles entre David Ben Gourion et Marc Jarblum." In *Les Juifs de France, se sionisme et l'Etat d'Israël, actes du colloque international*, edited by Doris Bensimon and Benjamin Pinkus, 153–170. Paris: Publications Langues'O, 1987.
Bouquet, Brigitte. "A l'origine de 'Montrouge': une oeuvre sociale." *Vie sociale* 5-6 (1989): 63–85.
———. "Les groupes de travail: le groupe Pergolèse, le groupe de Genève, le groupement de recherche sur le case-work, le groupe des enseignantes aux méthodes de service social." *Vie sociale* 1 (1999): 54–55.
———. "Réactions au case-work: passions, ambiguïté, résistances." *Vie sociale* 1 (1999): 95–110.
Bouquet, Brigitte, and Christine Garcette. *Assistante sociale aujourd'hui*. Paris: Maloine, 1998.
Boussion, Samuel. "À la croisée des réseaux transnationaux de protection de l'enfance: L'OSE et les communautés d'enfants de l'après-guerre." In *Prévenir et guerir dans un siècle de violences*, edited by Laura Hobson Faure, Katy Hazan, Catherine Nicault, and Mathias Gardet, 184–205. Paris: Armand Colin, 2014.
Boyarin, Jonathan. *Jewish Families*. New Brunswick, NJ: Rutgers University Press, 2013.
Brandenberger, David. "Stalin's Last Crime? Recent Scholarship on Postwar Soviet Antisemitism and the Doctor's Plot." *Kritika: Explorations in Russian and Eurasian History* 6, no. 1 (2005): 187–204.
Brent, Johnathan, and Vladimir Naumov. *Stalin's Last Crime, The Doctors' Plot*. London: John Murray, 2003.
Bunim, Amos. *A Fire in His Soul: Irving M. Bunim, 1901–1980, the Man and His Impact on American Orthodox Jewry*. Jerusalem: Feldheim, 1989.

Burgard, Antoine. "Une nouvelle vie dans un nouveau pays: Trajectoires d'orphelin de la Shoah vers le Canada (1947–52)." PhD diss., Université Lumière Lyon 2 / Université du Québec à Montréal, 2017.
Caron, Vicki. "Louise Weiss." In *Jewish Women: A Comprehensive Historical Encyclopedia*. Jewish Women's Archive, March 1, 2009. https://jwa.org/encyclopedia/article/weiss-louise.
———. *Uneasy Asylum: France and the Jewish Refugee Crisis, 1933–1942*. Stanford, CA: Stanford University Press, 1999.
Carruthers, Susan L. *The Good Occupation: American Soldiers and the Hazards of Peace*. Cambridge, MA: Harvard University Press, 2016.
Cassegrain, Denise. "Le rôle de l'ANAS dans la diffusion du case-work." *Vie sociale* 1 (1999): 89–93.
Cheminée, Lucie. "Historique de l'évolution du case-work en France." *Vie sociale* 1 ([1957] 1999): 7–18.
Cichopek-Gajraj, Anna. *Beyond Violence: Jewish Survivors in Poland and Slovakia, 1944–48*. Cambridge, UK: Cambridge University Press, 2014.
Claflin, Kyri Watson. "Agent of Friendship: Anne Morgan and Private Philanthropy 1944–1947." In *Les Américains et la France (1917–1947) engagements et représentations: colloque international, Reims, 22–23 Mai 1997*, edited by Marie-Claude Genet-Delacroix, François Cochet, and Hélène Trocmé, 109–123. Paris: Maisonneuve et Larose, 1999.
Clifford, Rebecca. *Commemorating the Holocaust: The Dilemmas of Remembrance in France and Italy*. Oxford, UK: Oxford University Press, 2013.
Cochet, F., M. C. Genet-Delacroix, and H. Trocmé. *Les Américains et la France (1917–1947) engagements et représentations: colloque international, Reims, 22–23 Mai 1997*. Paris: Maisonneuve et Larose, 1999.
Cohen Albert, Phyllis. "Ethnicity and Jewish Solidarity in Nineteenth Century France." In *Mystics, Philosophers and Politicians: Essays in Jewish Intellectual History in Honor of Alexander Altman*, edited by Jehuda Reinharz and Daniel Swetschinski, 249–274. Cambridge, UK: Cambridge University Press, 1982.
———. "Les origines de l'ecole d'Orsay." *Pardès* 23 (1997): 91–107.
———. *The Modernization of French Jewry: Consistory and Community in the Nineteenth Century*. Hanover, MA: Brandeis University Press, 1977.
Cohen, Asher. *Persécutions et sauvetages. Juifs et Français sous l'occupation et sous Vichy*. Paris: Editions du Cerf, 1993.
Cohen, Gerard Daniel. *In War's Wake: Europe's Displaced Persons in the Postwar Order*. Oxford Studies in International History. Oxford, UK: Oxford University Press, 2011.
Cohen, Jeremy, and Moshe Rosman, eds. *Rethinking European Jewish History*. Oxford, UK: Littman, 2009.

Cohen, Naomi Weiner. *Not Free to Desist. The American Jewish Committee, 1906–1966*. Introduction by Salo W. Baron. Philadelphia, PA: Jewish Publication Society of America, 1972.

Cohen, Richard I. *The Burden of Conscience: French Jewish Leadership during the Holocaust*. Bloomington: Indiana University Press, 1987.

Cohen, William B., and Irwin Wall. "French Communism and the Jews." In *The Jews in Modern France*, edited by Frances Malino and Bernard Wasserstein, 81–102. Hanover, MA: Brandeis University Press, 1985.

Collomp, Catherine. *Rescue, Relief and Resistance: The Jewish Labor Committee's Anti-Nazi Operations, 1934–1945*. Detroit, MI: Wayne University Press, 2021.

———. *Résister au nazisme: le Jewish Labor Committee, New York, 1934–1945*. Paris: CNRS Éditions, 2016.

Corber, Erin. "L'esprit du corps: Bodies, Communities, and the Reconstruction of Jewish Life in France, 1914–1940." PhD diss., Indiana University, 2013.

Croes, Marnix. "The Holocaust in the Netherlands and the Rate of Jewish Survival." *Holocaust and Genocide Studies* 20, no. 3 (2006): 474.

Curti, Merle. *American Philanthropy Abroad*, 1963.

Dash Moore, Deborah. "From Kehillah to Federation: The Communal Functions of Federated Philanthropy in N.Y. City, 1917–1933." *American Jewish History* 2 (1978): 131–46.

———. *GI Jews: How World War II Changed a Generation*. Cambridge, MA: Belknap Press of Harvard University Press, 2004.

———. *To the Golden Cities: Pursuing the American Jewish Dream in Miami and L.A*. New York: Maxwell Macmillan International, 1994.

Deblinger, Rachel. "'In a World Still Trembling,' American Jewish Philanthropy and the Shaping of Holocaust Survivor Narratives in Postwar America (1945–1953)." PhD diss., University of California Los Angeles, 2014.

Debono, Emmanuel. "Le Juif Süss au quartier Latin en 1950. Entre emballement médiatique et réalité de l'antisémitisme." *Archives juives, revue d'histoire des juifs de France* 49, no. 2 (2016): 95–114.

———. *Le racisme dans le prétoire. Racisme, antisémitisme et xénophobie devant la loi*. Paris: Presses Universitaires de France, 2019.

De Grazia, Victoria. *Irresistible Empire: America's Advance through Twentieth-Century Europe*. Cambridge, MA: Belknap Press of Harvard University Press, 2006.

Dekel-Chen, Jonathan L. *Farming the Red Land: Jewish Agricultural Colonization and Local Soviet Power, 1924–1941*. New Haven, CT: Yale University Press, 2005.

Diebolt, Evelyne, and Nicole Fouché. "1917–1923, Les Américaines en Soissonais: leur influence sur la France." *Revue française d'études américaines* 59 (1994): 45–63.

Diner, Hasia R. *A Time for Gathering: The Second Migration, 1820–1880*. Baltimore, MD: Johns Hopkins University Press, 1992.

———. *We Remember with Reverence and Love: American Jews and the Myth of Silence after the Holocaust, 1945–1962*. New York: New York University Press, 2009.

Dinnerstein, Leonard. *America and the Survivors of the Holocaust*. New York: Columbia University Press, 1982.

———. *Uneasy at Home: Antisemitism and the American Jewish Experience*. New York: Columbia University Press, 1987.

Dobkowski, Michael N., ed. *Jewish American Voluntary Organizations*. Westport, CT: Greenwood, 1986.

Doron, Daniella. *Jewish Youth and Identity in Postwar France: Rebuilding Family and Nation*. The Modern Jewish Experience. Bloomington: Indiana University Press, 2015.

Doulut, Alexandre, Serge Klarsfeld, and Sandrine Labeau. *Mémorial des 3943 rescapés juifs de France: convois 1–82 : liste & témoignages*, 2018.

Dreyfus, Jean-Marc. *L'impossible réparation. Déportés, biens spoliés, or nazi, comptes bloqués, criminels de guerre*. Au fil de l'histoire. Paris: Flammarion, 2015.

———. "The Post-Liberation French Administration and the Jews." In *Holocaust Survivors: Resettlement, Memories, Identities*, edited by Dalia Ofer, Françoise S. Ouzan, and Judy Tydor Baumel-Schwartz. New York: Berghahn Books, 2011.

Dufoix, Stéphane. *Les diasporas*. Paris: Presses Universitaires de France, 2003.

Dwork, Deborah, and Robert Jan Van Pelt. *Flight from the Reich: Refugee Jews, 1933–1946*. New York: W. W. Norton, 2012.

Elazar, Daniel J. *Community and Polity: The Organizational Dynamics of American Jewry. Revised and Updated Edition*. Philadelphia, PA: Jewish Publication Society of America, 1995.

Elmaleh, Raphaël. *1950–2000. Fonds social juif unifié. L'espoir en movement*. Paris: Fonds social juif unifié, 2000.

Encyclopaedia Judaica. Jerusalem, New York: Keter and Macmillian, 1972.

Erbelding, Rebecca. *Rescue Board: The Untold Story of America's Efforts to Save the Jews of Europe*. New York: Doubleday, 2018.

Fabre, Michel. *From Harlem to Paris: Black American Writers in France, 1840–1980*. Urbana: University of Illinois Press, 1993.

Feingold, Henry. *Bearing Witness: How America and Its Jews Responded to the Holocaust*. Syracuse, NY: Syracuse University Press, 1995.

———. *A Time for Searching: Entering the Mainstream, 1920–1945*. Baltimore, MD: Johns Hopkins University Press, 1992.

Ferran, Paule. *Julien Samuel. Un homme engagé*. Paris: Alliance israélite universelle, 1999.

Fink, Carole. "Louis Marshall: An American Jewish Diplomat in Paris, 1919." *American Jewish History* 94, no. 1/2 (2008): 21–40.

Fogg, Shannon. "'Everything Had Ended and Everything Was Beginning Again': The Public Politics of Rebuilding Private Homes in Postwar Paris." *Holocaust and Genocide Studies* 28, no. 2 (2014): 277–307.
Fogg, Shannon Lee. *Stealing Home: Looting, Restitution, and Reconstructing Jewish Lives in France, 1942–1947.* Oxford, UK: Oxford University Press, 2017.
Follett, Mary Parker. *The New State: Group Organization and the Solution of Popular Government.* University Park: Pennsylvania State University Press, [1918] 1998.
Footitt, Hilary. *War and Liberation in France: Living with the Liberators.* London: Palgrave Macmillan, 2004.
Fouché, Nicole. "Anne Morgan, la lecture publique et la France. Le lent cheminement d'une influence culturelle américaine, 1917–1969." *Cahiers de l'institut Charles-V* 28 (2000): 59–96.
———. "Des Américaines protestantes à l'origine des University Women françaises, 1919–1964." *Bulletin de la société d'histoire du protestantisme français* 146 (2000): 133–152.
———. "Le casework: circulation transatlantique et réception en France (1870–1939)." *Revue Européenne d'histoire sociale et histoire sociétés* 11 (2004): 21–35.
Fourtage, Laure. "Accueillir les déportés juifs en France (Novembre 1943–Novembre 1945)." In *Terre d'exil, terre d'asile, migrations juives en France aux XIXe et XXe siècles*, edited by Colette Zytnicki, 71–96. Paris: Editions de l'éclat, 2010.
———. "Et après? Une histoire du secours et de l'aide à la réinsertion des rescapés juifs des camps nazis (France, 1943–1948)." PhD diss., Université Sorbonne Panthéon-Paris 1, 2019.
Fourtage, Laure, and Laura Hobson Faure. "Les réfugiés juifs d'Europe centrale et orientale." *Hommes et migrations*, 4 (2015): 134–137.
Fredj, Jacques. "La création du CRIF: 1943–1966." MA thesis, Université de Paris IV, 1988.
Frémontier, Jacques. "Les Juifs communistes en France depuis 1945. Essai d'histoire orale." PhD diss., Ecole des hautes etudes en sciences sociales, 2000.
Friedlander, Walter A. *Individualism and Social Welfare: An Analysis of the System of Social Security and Social Welfare in France.* East Lansing: Board of Trustees of Michigan State University, 1962.
———. *International Social Welfare.* Englewood Cliffs, NJ: Prentice Hall, 1975.
Ghiles-Meilhac, Samuel. "Centralizing the Political Jewish Voice in Post-Holocaust France. Discretion and Development." In *Post-Holocaust France and the Jews, 1945–55*, edited by Seán Hand and Steven T. Katz, 59–70. New York: New York University Press, 2015.
———. *Le CRIF. De la résistance juive à la tentation du lobby, de 1943 à nos jours.* Paris: Robert Laffont, 2011.

Glazer, Nathan. *American Judaism*. 2nd ed., rev. Chicago: University of Chicago Press, 1972.
Glick Schiller, Nina, Linda G. Basch, and Cristina Blanc-Szanton. "Transnationalism. A New Analytic Framework for Understanding Migration." *Annals of the New York Academy of Sciences* 645 (July 1992): 1–22.
Goldman, Ralph. "The Involvement and Policies of American Jewry in Revitalizing European Jewry. 1945–1995." In *European Jewry: Between America and Israel: Jewish Centers and Peripheries 50 Years after the Holocaust*, edited by S. Ilan Troen, 67–84. New Brunswick, NJ: Transaction, 1998.
Goldsztejn, Isabelle. "Au secours d'une communauté: l'American Jewish Joint Distribution Committee en France (1933–1950)." MA thesis, Université de Paris I, 1992.
———. "L'American Jewish Joint Distribution Committee (AJDC) en France de 1933 à 1950." In *Les Américains et la France (1917–1947) engagements et représentations: colloque international, Reims, 22–23 Mai 1997*, edited by Marie-Claude Genet-Delacroix, François Cochet, Hélène Trocmé, 54–63. Paris: Maisonneuve et Larose, 1999.
Golsan, Richard J. "The Legacy of World War II France: Mapping the Discourses of Memory." In *The Politics of Memory in Postwar Europe*, edited by Richard Ned Lebow, Wulf Kansteiner, and Claudio Fogu. Durham, NC: Duke University Press, 2006.
———. *Vichy's Afterlife: History and Counterhistory in Postwar France*. Lincoln: University of Nebraska Press, 2000.
Golse, Bernard. "Myriam David, pionnière de la santé mentale de la petite enfance." *Le Monde*. January 6, 2005.
Goren, Arthur. "A Golden Decade for American Jews 1945–1955." In *A New Jewry? America since World War II*, edited by Peter Medding, 3–20. New York: Oxford University Press, 1992.
Gradvohl, Paul. "L'histoire du service social: l'influence américaine." *La revue de l'economie sociale* 16 (1989): 7–16.
Graetz, Michael. *The Jews in Nineteenth-Century France: From the French Revolution to the Alliance Israélite Universelle*. Translated by Jane Marie Todd. Stanford, CA: Stanford University Press, 1996.
Granick, Jaclyn. "Humanitarian Responses to Jewish Suffering by American Jewish Organizations." PhD diss., The Graduate Institute Geneva, 2015.
Green, Nancy L. "Blacks, Jews and the 'Natural Alliance': Labor Cohabitation and the ILGWU." *Jewish Social Studies* 4 (1997): 79–104.
———. "Jewish Migrations to France in the Nineteenth and Twentieth Centuries: Community or Communities?" *Studia Rosenthaliana. Journal for Jewish Literature and History in the Netherlands and Related Subjects*. XXIII, no. 2 (1989): 135–153.

———. *The Other Americans in Paris: Businessmen, Countesses, Wayward Youth, 1880–1941*. Chicago: University of Chicago Press, 2014.
———. *The Pletzl of Paris: Jewish Immigrant Workers in the Belle Epoque*. New York: Holmes and Meier, 1986.
———. "To Give and to Receive: Philanthropy and Collective Responsibility among Jews in Paris, 1880–1914." In *The Uses of Charity*, edited by Peter Mandler, 197–226. Philadelphia: University of Pennsylvania Press, 1990.
Grobman, Alex. *Battling for Souls: The Vaad Hatzala Rescue Committee in Post-Holocaust Europe*. Jersey City, NJ: KTAV, 2004.
———. *Rekindling the Flame: American Jewish Chaplains and the Survivors of European Jewry, 1944–1948*. Detroit, MI: Wayne State University Press, 1993.
Gross, Jan. *Fear: Anti-Semitism in Poland after Auschwitz. An Essay in Historical Interpretation*. New York: Random House, 2007.
Grossmann, Atina. *Jews, Germans, and Allies: Close Encounters in Occupied Germany*. Princeton, NJ: Princeton University Press, 2007.
Grumberg, Zoé. "Militer en minorité? Le 'secteur juif' du Parti communiste français de la Libération à la fin des années cinquante." PhD diss., Sciences Po, 2020.
Grynberg, Anne. "Après la tourmente." In *Les Juifs de France. De la révolution française à nos jours*, edited by Jean-Jacques Becker and Annette Wieviorka, 249–286. Paris: Liana Levi, 1998.
———. "Des signes de résurgence de l'antisémitisme dans la France de l'après-guerre (1945–1953)." *Les cahiers de la Shoah* 5 (2001): 171–223.
———. *Les camps de la honte. Les internés juifs des camps français, 1939–1944*. Paris: La Découverte, 1999.
———. "Reconstruction et nouvelles orientations." In *Histoire de l'Alliance israélite universelle de 1860 à nos jours*, edited by André Kaspi, 331–340. Paris: Armand Colin, 2010.
Grynberg, Anne, and Catherine Nicault. "Le culte israélite en France pendant la Seconde Guerre mondiale: droit et réalités d'exercice." *Archives juives, revue d'histoire des juifs de France* 28, no. 2 (1995): 72–88.
Hand, Seán, and Steven T. Katz, eds. *Post-Holocaust France and the Jews, 1945–1955*. New York: New York University Press, 2015.
Hazan, Katy. *Les enfants de l'après-guerre dans les maisons de l'OSE*. Paris: OSE, Oeuvres de secours aux enfants, somogy éditions d'art, 2012.
———. *Les orphelins de la Shoah: les maisons de l'espoir, 1944–1960*. Histoire, vol. 46. Paris: Belles lettres, 2000.
———. "Récupérer les enfants cachés: un impératif des oeuvres juives dans l'après-guerre." *Archives juives, revue d'histoire des juifs de France* 37, no. 2 (2004): 16–31.
Hazan, Katy, and Georges Weill. "L'OSE et le sauvetage des enfants juifs, de l'avant-guerre à l'après-guerre." In *La résistance aux génocides. De la pluralité*

des actes de sauvetage, edited by Jacques Sémelin, Claire Andrieu, and Sarah Gensburger, 259–276. Paris: Presses de sciences po, 2008.

Herberg, Will. "Jewish Labor Movement in the United States: World War I to Present." *Industrial and Labor Relations Review* 6, no. 1 (1952): 44–66.

Hillel, Marc. *Vie et moeurs des GI's en Europe, 1942–1947*. Paris: Balland, 1981.

Hobson Faure, Laura. "American Jewish Mobilization in France after World War II: Crossing the Narratives." *Transatlantica*, no. 1 (2014).

———. "Becoming Refugees: The Migrations of Central European Jewish Children through France to the United States, 1938–1942." Habilitation à diriger des recherches, Sciences Po, 2018.

———. "'Guide and Motivator' or 'Central Treasury'? The Role of the American Jewish Joint Distribution Committee in France, 1942–44." In *Rescue Practices Facing Genocides: Comparative Perspectives*, edited by Jacques Sémelin, Andrieu Claire, and Gensburger Sarah, 293–311. New York: Hurst/Columbia University Press, 2011.

———. "'Performing a Healing Role:' American Jewish Communal Workers and the American Jewish Joint Distribution Committee in Post–World War II France." *Parcours judaïques* 10 (2006): 139–156.

———. "Renaître sous les auspices américains et britanniques. Le mouvement libéral juif en France après la Shoah (1944–1970)." *Archives juives, revue d'histoire des juifs de France* 40, no. 2 (2007): 82–99.

———. "Shaping Children's Lives: American Jewish Aid in Post-World War II France (1944–1948)." In *Re-Examining the Jews of Modern France: Images and Identities*, 173–193. Leiden, The Netherlands: Brill, 2016.

———. "Towards Consensus? American Jewish Organizations in France after the Shoah." In *American Responses to the Holocaust: Transatlantic Perspectives*, edited by Derek Rubin and Hans Krabbendam, 79–96. Bern, Switzerland: Peter Lang, 2017.

———. "Un 'Plan Marshall juif': La présence juive Américaine en France après la Shoah, 1944–54." PhD diss., Ecole des hautes etudes en sciences sociales, 2009.

———. *Un "Plan Marshall juif": La présence juive Américaine en France après la Shoah, 1944–1954*. Paris: Armand Colin, 2013.

Hobson Faure, Laura, Mathias Gardet, Katy Hazan, and Catherine Nicault, eds. *L'Oeuvre de secours aux enfants et les populations juives au XXe siècle: prévenir et guérir dans un siècle de violences*. Paris: Armand Colin, 2014.

Hobson Faure, Laura, and Veerle Vanden Daelen. "Imported from the United States? The Centralization of Private Jewish Welfare after the Holocaust: The Cases of Belgium and France." In *The JDC at 100: A Century of Humanitarianism*, edited by Atina Grossmann, Linda Levi, Maud Mandel, and Avinoam Patt, 279–314. Detroit, MI: Wayne State University Press, 2019.

Hoehler, Fred K. *Europe's Homeless Millions*. New York: Foreign Policy Association, 1946.
Hogan, Michael. *The Marshall Plan: America, Britain and the Reconstruction of Western Europe*. Cambridge, UK: Cambridge University Press, 1987.
Hollinger, David A. *Protestants Abroad: How Missionaries Tried to Change the World but Changed America*. Princeton, NJ: Princeton University Press, 2017.
Howe, Irving. *World of Our Fathers: The Journey of the East European Jews to America and the Life They Found and Made*. New York: Harcourt Brace Jovanovich, 1976.
Husson, Jean-Pierre. *La Marne et les Marnais à l'épreuve de la Seconde Guerre mondiale*. 2 vols. Reims, France: Presses universitaires de Reims, 1998.
Husson, Jocelyne. *La déportation des Juifs de la marne, 1942–1944*. Reims, France: Presses universitaires de Reims, 1999.
Hyman, Paula. *From Dreyfus to Vichy: The Remaking of French Jewry, 1906–1939*. New York: Columbia University Press, 1979.
———. *The Jews of Modern France*. Berkeley: University of California Press, 1998.
Jacobs, Jack. "A Friend in Need: The Jewish Labor Committee, and Refugees from the German Speaking Lands, 1933–1945." *Yivo Annual of Jewish Science* 23 (1996): 391–417.
Jockusch, Laura. *Collect and Record! Jewish Holocaust Documentation in Early Postwar Europe*. New York: Oxford University Press, 2012.
Joskowicz, Ari. *The Modernity of Others: Jewish Anti-Catholicism in Germany and France*. Stanford Studies in Jewish History and Culture. Stanford, CA: Stanford University Press, 2014.
Jovelin, Emmanuel, and Brigitte Bouquet. *Histoire des métiers du social en France*. Paris: Editions ASH, 2005.
Kahn, Ava Fran, and Adam Mendelsohn, ed. *Transnational Traditions: New Perspectives on American Jewish History*. Detroit, MI: Wayne State University Press, 2014.
Kaplan, Alice. *The Interpreter*. Chicago: University of Chicago Press, 2005.
Karp, Abraham J. *To Give Life: The UJA in the Shaping of the American Jewish Community*. New York: Schocken, 1981.
Kaspi, André. *Les Juifs pendant l'Occupation*. Paris: Seuil, 1991.
Kaufman, Menahem. *An Ambiguous Partnership: Non-Zionists and Zionists in America, 1939–1948*. American Jewish Civilization Series. Jerusalem: Magnes, Hebrew University, 1991.
Kerssen, Julie L. "Life's Work: The Accidental Career of Laura Margolis Jarblum." MA thesis, University of Wisconsin, 2000.
Kertzer, David I. *The Kidnapping of Edgardo Mortara*. New York: Knopf, 1997.
Kichelewski, Audrey. *Les survivants: les Juifs de Pologne depuis la Shoah*. Paris: Belin, 2018.

Kieval, Hillel J. "Legality and Resistance in Vichy France: The Rescue of Jewish Children." *Proceedings of the American Philosphical Society* 124, no. 5 (1980): 339–366.

Klapper, Melissa R. *Ballots, Babies, and Banners of Peace: American Jewish Women's Activism, 1890–1940.* New York: New York University Press, 2013.

Klarsfeld, Serge. *Vichy Auschwitz. Le rôle de Vichy dans la "solution finale" de la question juive en France, 1943–1944.* Paris: Fayard, 1985.

Kobrin, Rebecca. *Jewish Bialystok and Its Diaspora.* The Modern Jewish Experience. Bloomington: Indiana University Press, 2010.

Kohs, Samuel C. "Jewish War Records of World War II." *American Jewish Yearbook* 47 (1945–1946): 153–172.

Kriegel, Annie. *Ce que j'ai cru comprendre.* Paris: Robert Laffont, 1991.

Kubowitzki, A. Leon. *Unity in Dispersion: A History of the World Jewish Congress.* New York: World Jewish Congress, 1948.

Kugelmass, Jack, ed. *Between Two Worlds. Ethnographic Essays on American Jewry.* Ithica, NY: Cornell University Press, 1988.

Kuisel, Richard. *Seducing the French: The Dilemma of Americanization.* Berkeley: University of California Press, 1993.

Kurz, Nathan. "In the Shadow of Versailles: Jewish Minority Rights at the 1946 Paris Peace Conference." *Simon Dubnow Institute Yearbook* 15 (2016): 187–209.

———. "A Sphere above the Nations? The Rise and Fall of International Jewish Human Rights Politics, 1945–1975." PhD diss., Yale University, 2015.

Laffitte, Michel. *Juif dans la France Allemande.* Paris: Editions Tallandier, 2006.

———. "L'UGIF fut-elle un obstacle au sauvetage des juifs ?" In *La résistance aux génocides. De la pluralité des actes de sauvetages,* edited by Jacques Sémelin, Claire Andrieu, and Sarah Gensburger, 251–262. Paris: Presses de Sciences Po, 2008.

———. *Un engrenage fatal: L'UGIF face aux réalités de la Shoah, 1941–1944.* Paris: Liana Levi, 2003.

Lagrou, Pieter. *The Legacy of Nazi Occupation: Patriotic Memory and National Recovery in Western Europe, 1945–1965.* Cambridge, UK: Cambridge University Press, 2000.

Lambert, Bruce. "Arthur D. Greenleigh, 90, Expert on Welfare Issues and Refugees." *New York Times,* October 31, 1993.

Latour, Anny. *La résistance juive en France (1940–1944).* Paris: Stock, 1970.

Lazare, Lucien. *La résistance juive en France.* Paris: Stock, 1987.

Le Crom, Jean-Pierre. *Au secours, Maréchal! L'instrumentalisation de l'humanitaire, 1940–1944.* 1re éd. Paris: Presses universitaires de France, 2013.

Lederhendler, Eli. *American Jewry: A New History.* Cambridge, UK: Cambridge University Press, 2017.

———. "Hard Times: HIAS under Pressure, 1925–26." *Yivo Annual of Jewish Science* 22 (1995): 105–129.

Lee, Daniel. *Petain's Jewish Children: French Jewish Youth and the Vichy Regime, 1940–1942*. Oxford, UK: Oxford University Press, 2014.
Leff, Lisa Moses. *The Archive Thief: The Man Who Salvaged French Jewish History in the Wake of the Holocaust*. Oxford, UK: Oxford University Press, 2015.
———. *Sacred Bonds of Solidarity: The Rise of Jewish Internationalism in Nineteenth-Century France*. Stanford, CA: Stanford University Press, 2006.
Lehr, Johanna. *La Thora dans la cité: l'émergence d'un nouveau judaïsme*. Lormont: Le bord de l'eau, 2013.
Lemalet, Martine. "Les comités d'accueil aux réfugiés et l'Oeuvre de secours aux enfants (1933–1939)." In *Justin Godart, un homme dans son siecle (1871–1956)*, edited by Annette Wieviorka and Jean-Jacques Becker, 87–104. Paris: CNRS Éditions, 2004.
Le Tallec, Cyril. *Les assistantes sociales dans la tourmente, 1939–1946*. Paris: L'Harmattan, 2003.
Levy Simon, Barbara. *The Empowerment Tradition in American Social Work: A History*. New York: Columbia University Press, 1994.
Lindeman, Eduard. *The Community. An Introduction to the Study of Community Leadership and Organization*. New York: Association, 1921.
Lindenberg, Judith, ed. *Premiers savoirs de la Shoah*. Paris: CNRS Éditions, 2017.
Lipset, Seymour M. *American Pluralism and the Jewish Community*. New Brunswick, NJ: Transaction, 1990.
———. "A Unique People in an Exceptional Country." In *American Pluralism and the Jewish Community*, 3–30. New Brunswick, NJ: Transaction, 1990.
Litvac Glaser, Zhava. "Laura Margolis and JDC Efforts in Cuba and Shanghai. Sustaining Refugees in a Time of Catastrophe." In *The JDC at 100. A Century of Humanitarianism*, edited by Avinoam J. Patt, Atina Grossmann, Linda Levi, and Maud S. Mandel, 167–203. Detroit, MI: Wayne State University Press, 2019.
Louis, Barbara. "A Second Chance in Exile? German-Speaking Women Refugees in American Social Work after 1933." PhD diss., University of Minnesota, 2015.
Lubove, Roy. *The Professional Altruist: The Emergence of Social Work as a Career*. Cambridge, MA: Harvard University Press, 1965.
Lustman, François. *Entre Shoah, communisme et sionisme. Les Juifs yiddish de Paris et leur presse au lendemain de la Seconde Guerre mondiale*. Paris: Honoré Champion, 2012.
Mabon-Fall, Armelle. *Les assistantes sociales au temps de Vichy: du silence à l'oubli*. Paris: L'Harmattan, 1995.
MacCormac, John. "Aid for Displaced Held Up in France, Sample of European Postwar Problem Is Made Worse by Regime's Attitude." *New York Times*, October 13, 1944.
MacIver, R. M. *Report on the Jewish Community Relations Agencies*. New York: National Community Relations Advisory Council, 1951.

Maitron, Jean, and Claude Pennetier. "Georges Soria." In *Dictionnaire bibliographique du mouvement ouvrier français, tome XLI, quatrième partie: 1914–1939 de la Première à la Seconde Guerre mondiale*, 360–361. Paris: Les éditions ouvrières, 1992.

———. "Pierre Hervé." In *Dictionnaire bibliographique du mouvement ouvrier français, tome XXXI*, 334–336. Paris: Les éditions ouvrières, 1988.

Malinovich, Nadia. *French and Jewish: Culture and the Politics of Identity in Early Twentieth Century France*. Oxford, UK: Littman Library of Jewish Civilisation, 2007.

Malmgreen, Gail. "Labor and the Holocaust: The Jewish Labor Committee and the Anti-Nazi Struggle." *Jewish Spectator* 57 (1992): 31–36.

Mandel, Maud S. "The Encounter between 'Native' and 'Immigrant' Jews in the Aftermath of the Holocaust." In *Post-Holocaust France and the Jews, 1945–1955*, edited by Seán Hand and Steven T. Katz, 38–57. New York: New York University Press, 2015.

———. *In the Aftermath of Genocide: Armenians and Jews in Twentieth Century France*. Durham, NC: Duke University Press, 2003.

———. *Muslims and Jews in France: History of a Conflict*. Princeton, NJ: Princeton University Press, 2014.

———. "Philanthropy or Cultural Imperialism? The Impact of American Jewish Aid in Post-Holocaust France." *Jewish Social Studies* 9, no. 1 (2002): 53–94.

Marie, Jean-Jacques. *Les derniers complots de Staline. L'affaire des blouses blanches*. Brussels, Belgium: Editions complexe, 1993.

Marrus, Michael R. *The Unwanted: European Refugees from the First World War through the Cold War*, with Foreword by Aristide Zolberg. Oxford, UK: Oxford University Press, 2001.

Marrus, Michael R., and Robert O. Paxton. *Vichy France and the Jews*. Stanford, CA: Stanford University Press, 1995.

Maspero, Julia. "French Policy on Postwar Migration of Eastern European Jews through France and French Occupation Zones in Germany and Austria." *Kwartalnik Historii Żydów Jewish History Quarterly* 246, no. 2 (June 2013): 319–339.

———. "Itinéraires de juifs polonais immigrés en France entre 1945 et 1951." MA thesis, Université de Paris I Panthéon-Sorbonne, 2005.

Mazower, Mark. "Reconstruction: The Historiographical Issues." *Past and Present* 210, no. 6 (2011): 17–28.

McKenzie, Brian Angus. *Remaking France: Americanization, Public Diplomacy, and the Marshall Plan*. Explorations in Culture and International History Series 2. New York: Berghahn, 2005.

Messika, Martin. *Politiques de l'accueil. États et associations face à la migration juive du Maghreb en France et au Canada des années 1950 à la fin des années 1970*. Rennes, France: PU Rennes, 2020.

Milton, Sybil, and Frederick D. Bogin, eds. *Volume 10. American Jewish Joint Distribution Committee, New York, Parts One and Two*. Archives of the Holocaust. An International Collection of Selected Documents. New York: Garland, 1995.
Myerhoff, Barbara G. *Number Our Days*. 1st Touchstone ed. A Touchstone Book. New York: Simon and Schuster, 1980.
Najman, Judith, and Emmanuel Hayman. *Claude Kelman, une ambition pour le judaïsme*. Paris: Alliance israélite universelle-Nadir, 2001.
Nataf, Claude. "Interview du Baron Guy de Rothschild en 1992." In *La synagogue de la Victoire, 150 ans du judaïsme Français*, edited by Jacques Canet and Claude Nataf, 284–288. Paris: Porte Plume, 2016.
———. "Le judaïsme religieux au lendemain de la libération: rénovation ou retour au passé?" *Les cahiers de la Shoah* 1, no. 5 (2001): 71–104.
Neipris, Joseph. *The American Joint Distribution Committee and Its Contribution to Social Work Education*. American Joint Distribution Committee, 1992.
New York Times. "Dr. Henry Selver, Educator, 56, Dies; Headed Training School in France of Joint Distribution Committee." *New York Times*, September 22, 1957.
Nicault, Catherine. "Dans la tourmente de la Seconde Guerre mondiale, 1939–1944." In *Histoire de l'Alliance israélite universelle de 1860 à nos jours*, edited by André Kaspi, 295–330. Paris: A. Colin, 2010.
———. "L'accueil des juifs d'Europe centrale par la communauté juive française." In *De l'exil à la résistance: réfugiés et immigrés d'Europe centrale en France, 1933–1945*, edited by Karel A. Bartosek, Réné Gallissot, and Denis Peschanski, 53–59. Paris: Presses universitaires de Vincennes Arcantère, 1989.
———. *La France et le sionisme 1897–1948. Une rencontre manquée?* Paris: Calmann-Lévy, 1992.
———. "L'Alliance au lendemain de la Seconde Guerre mondiale: ruptures et continuités idéologiques." *Archives juives, revue d'histoire des Juifs de France* 34, no. 1 (2001): 23–53.
———. "L'utopie sioniste du 'nouveau Juif' et la jeunesse juive dans la France de l'après-guerre: contribution à l'histoire de l'Alyah Française." *Les cahiers de la Shoah* 1, no. 5 (2001): 105–169.
Novick, Peter. *The Holocaust in American Life*. Boston: Houghton Mifflin, 1999.
Ofer, Dalia, Françoise S. Ouzan, and Judith Tydor Baumel Schwartz, eds. *Holocaust Survivors, Resettlement, Memories, Identities*. New York: Berghahn, 2011.
Oumansour, Brahim. "Le rôle de l'American Jewish Committee pendant la guerre d'Algérie, 1954–1962." *Revue française d'études américaines* 151, no. 2 (2017): 227–245.
Ouzan, Françoise. *Ces Juifs dont l'Amérique ne voulait pas*. Brussels, Belgium: Editions complexe, 1995.

Pâris de Bollardière, Constance. "The French Bundist Movement after the Holocaust: Between Self and Collective Reconstruction, 1944–1948." In *Bundist Legacy after the Second World War. "Real" Place versus "Displaced" Time*, edited by Vincenzo Pinto, 39–55. Leiden, The Netherlands: Brill, 2018.

———. "The Jewish Labor Committee's Bundist Relief Network in France, 1945–1948." *Kwartalnik Historii Żydow/Jewish History Quarterly* 246, no. 2 (2013): 293–301.

———. "'La pérennité de notre peuple': une aide socialiste juive Américaine dans la diaspora yiddish, le Jewish Labor Committee en France (1944–48)." PhD diss., Ecole des hautes etudes en sciences sociales, 2017.

———. "La politique et les actions internationales du Jewish Labor Committee, 1945 à 1953." MA thesis, Université Paris, 2008.

———. "Mutualité, fraternité et travail social chez les bundistes de France, 1944–1947." *Archives juives, revue d'histoire des juifs de France* 45, no. 1 (2012): 27–42.

Patt, Avinoam. "'The People Must Be Forced to Go to Palestine': Rabbi Abraham Klausner and the She'erit Hapletah in Germany." *Holocaust and Genocide Studies* 28, no. 2 (2014): 240–276.

Patt, Avinoam J. *Finding Home and Homeland: Jewish Youth and Zionism in the Aftermath of the Holocaust*. Detroit, MI: Wayne State University Press, 2009.

Patt, Avinoam J., and Michael Berkowitz, eds. *"We Are Here": New Approaches to Jewish Displaced Persons in Postwar Germany*. Detroit, MI: Wayne State University Press, 2010.

Patt, Avinoam J., Atina Grossmann, Linda G. Levi, and Maud Mandel, eds. *The JDC at 100: A Century of Humanitarianism*. Detroit, MI: Wayne State University Press, 2019.

Paxton, Robert O. *Vichy France: Old Guard and New Order 1940–1944*. New York: Columbia University Press, 2001.

Penkower, Monty. "Jewish Organizations and the Creation of the U.S. War Refugee Board." *The Annals* 450 (1980): 122–139.

Penslar, Derek J. "The Origins of Modern Jewish Philanthropy." In *Philanthropy in the World's Traditions*, edited by Warren F. Ilchman, Stanley N. Katz, and Edward L. Queen II, 197–214. Bloomington: Indiana University Press, 1998.

———. *Shylock's Children: Economics and Jewish Identity in Modern Europe*. Berkeley: University of California Press, 2001.

Perego, Simon. "Jury d'honneur. The States and Limits of Purges among Jews in France after Liberation." In *Jewish Honor Courts. Revenge, Retribution, and Reconciliation in Europe and Israel after the Holocaust*, edited by Gabriel Finder and Laura Jockusch, 137–164. Detroit, MI: Wayne State University Press, 2015.

———. "La mémoire avant la mémoire? Un retour sur l'historiographie du souvenir de la Shoah en France de l'après-guerre." *20 & 21. Revue d'histoire* 145 (March 2020): 77–90.

———. "'Pleurons-les, bénissons leurs noms'. Les commémorations de la Shoah et de la Seconde Guerre mondiale dans le monde juif parisien entre 1944 et 1967 : rituels, mémoires et identités." PhD diss., Sciences Po, 2016.
———. *Pleurons-les. Les juifs de Paris et la commémoration de la Shoah, 1944–1967*. Paris: Champ Vallon, 2020.
Peretz, Pauline. *Combat pour les Juifs soviétiques. Washington-Moscou-Jérusalem, 1953–1989*. Paris: Armand Colin, 2006.
Pinson, Koppel S. "The National Theories of Simon Dubnow." *Jewish Social Studies* 10, no. 4 (1948): 335–358.
Poujol, Catherine. *L'Église de France et les enfants juifs. Des missions vaticanes à l'affaire Finaly, 1944–1953*. Paris: Presses universitaires de France, 2013.
———. *Les enfants cachés, l'affaire Finaly*. Paris: Éditions Berg International, 2006.
Poznanski, Renée. "French Apprehensions, Jewish Expectations: From a Social Imaginary to a Political Practice." In *The Jews Are Coming Back: The Return of the Jews to Their Countries of Origin after WWII*, edited by David Bankier, 25–57. Jerusalem: Yad Vashem, 2005.
———. "A Methodological Approach to the Study of Jewish Resistance in France." *Yad Vashem Studies* XVIII (1987): 1–39.
———. *Les Juifs en France pendant la Seconde Guerre mondiale*. Paris: Hachette littératures, 1997.
———. "L'héritage de la guerre. Le sionisme en France dans les années 1945–1947." In *Les Juifs de France, le sionisme et l'etat d'Israël, actes du colloque international 1987, langues orientales*, edited by Doris Bensimon and Benjamin Pinkus, 237–273. Paris: Publications Langues'O, 1987.
———. *Propagandes et persécutions. La Résistance et le "problème juif," 1940–1944*. Paris: Fayard, 2008.
Prell, Riv-Ellen. *Fighting to Become Americans: Jews, Gender, and the Anxiety of Assimilation*. Boston, MA: Beacon, 1999.
———. "Triumph, Accommodation, and Resistance: American Jewish Life from the End of World War II to the Six-Day War." In *The Columbia History of Jews and Judaism in America*, edited by Marc Lee Raphael, 114–141. New York: Columbia University Press, 2009.
Rabinovitch (Rabi), W. *Anatomie du judaïsme français*. Paris: Les éditions de minuit, 1962.
Raphael, Marc Lee. *A History of the United Jewish Appeal*. Chico, CA: Scholars, 1982.
———. *Profiles in American Judaism. The Reform, Conservative, Orthodox and Reconstructionist Traditions in Historical Perspective*. San Francisco: Harper & Row, 1984.
Reinisch, Jessica. "Internationalism in Relief: The Birth (and Death) of UNRRA." *Past and Present* 210, no. 6 (2011): 258–289.

———. "Introduction: Relief in the Aftermath of War." *Journal of Contemporary History* 43, no. 3 (2008): 371–404.

———. "We Shall Rebuild Anew a Powerful Nation. UNRRA, Internationalism and National Reconstruction in Poland." *Journal of Contemporary History* 43, no. 3 (2008): 451–476.

Remus, Ina. "An Inventory to the Records of the World Jewish Congress." Finding Aid. American Jewish Archives, undated.

Richmond, Mary. *Social Diagnosis*. New York: Russel Sage Foundation, 1917.

———. *What Is Social Casework? An Introductory Description*. New York: Russel Sage Foundation, 1922.

Rioux, Jean-Pierre. *La France de la quatrième république: l'ardeur et la nécessité (1944–1952)*. Nouvelle histoire de la France contemporaine, 15.1. Paris: Seuil, 1980.

Roberts, Mary Louise. *D-Day through French Eyes: Normandy 1944*. Chicago: University of Chicago Press, 2014.

———. *What Soldiers Do: Sex and the American GI in World War II France*. Chicago: University of Chicago Press, 2013.

Roblin, Michel. *Les juifs de Paris. Démographie, economie, culture*. Paris: Editions A. et J. Picard, 1952.

Röder, Werner, and Herbert A. Strauss. "Henry Selver." In *Biographisches handbuch der deutschsprachigen emigration nach 1933*, 688. Bd. I. Munich: K. G. Saur, 1999.

Rodgers, Daniel T. *Altantic Crossings: Social Politics in a Progressive Age*. Cambridge, MA: Belknap Press of Harvard University Press, 1998.

Rodrigue, Aron. *French Jews, Turkish Jews: The Alliance Israélite Universelle and the Politics of Jewish Schooling in Turkey, 1860–1925*. Bloomington: Indiana University Press, 1990.

Roger, Philippe. *L'ennemi américain. Géneologie de l'antiaméricainisme français*. Paris: Seuil, 2002.

Rogow, Faith. *Gone to Another Meeting: The National Council of Jewish Women, 1893–1993*. Tuscaloosa: University of Alabama Press, 1993.

Rothberg, Michael. *Multidirectional Memory: Remembering the Holocaust in the Age of Decolonization*. Cultural Memory in the Present. Stanford, CA: Stanford University Press, 2009.

Rousso, Henry. *The Vichy Syndrome: History and Memory in France since 1944*. Cambridge, MA: Harvard University Press, 1991.

Safran, William. "Diasporas in Modern Societies: Myths of Homeland and Return." *Diaspora: A Journal of Transnational Studies* 1, no. 1 (Spring 1991): 83–99.

Sarna, Jonathan. *American Judaism: A History*. New Haven, CT: Yale University Press, 2004.

Schmitt, Dana Adams. "Six Millions Lent Jews by French." *New York Times*, January 11, 1945.

Segev, Zohar. *The World Jewish Congress during the Holocaust: Between Activism and Restraint*. Berlin: De Gruyter, 2017.
Sémelin, Jacques, Claire Andrieu, and Sarah Gensburger, eds. *La résistance aux génocides: De la pluralité des actes de sauvetage*. Paris: Presses de Sciences Po, 2008.
Shachtman, Tom. *I Seek My Brethren. Ralph Goldman and the "Joint." Rescue, Relief and Reconstruction—The Work of the American Jewish Joint Distribution Committee*. New York: New Market, 2001.
Shafir, Shlomo. *Ambiguous Relations: The American Jewish Community and Germany since 1945*. Detroit, MI: Wayne State University Press, 1999.
Shapiro, Edward. *A Time for Healing: American Jewry since World War II*. Baltimore, MD: American Jewish Historical Society, Johns Hopkins University Press, 1992.
Simmons, Erica. *Hadassah and the Zionist Project*. Lanham, MD: Rowman & Littlefield, 2006.
Simon-Nahum, Perrine. "'Penser le judaïsme.' Retour sur les colloques des intellectuels juifs de la langue française, 1957–2000." *Archives juives, revue d'histoire des juifs de France* 38, no. 1 (2000): 79–106.
Slucki, David. *The International Jewish Labor Bund after 1945: Toward a Global History*. New Brunswick, NJ: Rutgers University Press, 2012.
Sorin, Gerald. *A Time for Building: The Third Migration, 1880–1920*. Baltimore, MD: Johns Hopkins University Press, 1992.
Stahl, Ronit Y. *Enlisting Faith: How the Military Chaplaincy Shaped Religion and State in Modern America*. Cambridge, MA: Harvard University Press, 2017.
Stein, Herman D. "Jewish Social Work in the United States, 1654–1954." *American Jewish Yearbook* 57 (1956): 2–98.
Stein, Sarah Abrevaya. *Plumes: Ostrich Feathers, Jews, and a Lost World of Global Commerce*. New Haven, CT: Yale University Press, 2010.
Stovall, Tyler. "The Color Line behind the Lines: Racial Violence in France during the Great War." *The American Historical Review* 103, no. 3 (1998): 737–769.
———. "The Fire This Time: Black American Expatriates and the Algerian War." *Yale French Studies* 98 (2000): 182–200.
———. *France since the Second World War*. London: Pearson, 2002.
———. *Paris Noir: African Americans in the City of Light*. Boston: Houghton Mifflin, 1996.
Subak, Susan Elisabeth. *Rescue & Flight: American Relief Workers Who Defied the Nazis*. Lincoln: University of Nebraska Press, 2010.
Suleiman, Susan R. *Crises of Memory and the Second World War*. Cambridge, MA: Harvard University Press, 2006.
Szajkowski, Zosa. "Concord and Discord in American Jewish Overseas Relief." *Yivo Annual of Jewish Science* 14 (1969): 99–158.

———. "Private and Organized American Jewish Overseas Relief (1914–1938)." *American Jewish Historical Quarterly* LVII, no. 1 (1967): 52–106.

Torrent, Régine. *La France Américaine: controverses de la libération*. Brussels, Belgium: Racine, 2004.

Tournès, Ludovic. "Les boursiers Français du programme 'Fellowships and Scholarships' de la Fondation Rockefeller (1917–1970)." L'institut Pasteur, n.d. http://www.pasteur.fr/infosci/archives/f-rock.html.

———. *Sciences de l'homme et politique: les fondations philanthropiques américaines en France au XXe Siècle*. Bibliothèque des sciences sociales 1. Paris: Classiques Garnier, 2011.

Underwood, Nick. "Staging a New Community: Immigrant Yiddish Culture and Diaspora Nationalism in Interwar Paris, 1919–1940." PhD diss., University of Colorado-Boulder, 2016.

———. *Yiddish Paris. Staging Nation and Community in Interwar France*. Bloomington: Indiana University Press, 2022.

Waldinger, Roger. *The Cross-Border Connection. Immigrants, Emigrants and Their Homelands*. Cambridge, MA: Harvard University Press, 2015.

Walkowitz, Daniel J. "The Making of a Feminine Professional Identity: Social Workers in the 1920s." *American Historical Review* 95, no. 4 (1990): 1051–1075.

Wall, Irwin. *The United States and the Making of Postwar France*. New York: Cambridge University Press, 1991.

Wasserstein, Bernard. *Vanishing Diaspora: The Jews in Europe since 1945*. Cambridge, MA: Harvard University Press, 1996.

Webster, Ronald. "American Relief and Jews in Germany, 1945–1960. Diverging Perspectives." *Leo Baeck Institute Yearbook* XXXVIII (1993): 293–321.

Weil, Patrick. "The Return of Jews in the Nationality or in the Territory of France." In *The Jews Are Coming Back. The Return of the Jews to Their Countries of Origin after WWII*, edited by D. Bankier, 58–71. Jerusalem: Yad Vashem, 2005.

Weinberg, David. "Between America and Israel; the Quest for a Distinct European Jewish Identity in the Post-War Era." *Jewish Culture and History* 5, no. 1 (2002): 91–120.

———. *A Community on Trial: The Jews of Paris in the 1930s*. Chicago: University of Chicago Press, 1977.

———. "A Forgotten Postwar Jewish Migration: East European Jewish Refugees and Immigrants, 1946–7." In *Postwar Jewish Displacement and Rebirth, 1945–1967*, edited by Françoise Ouzan and Manfred Gerstenfeld, 137–149. Leiden, The Netherlands: Brill, 2014.

———. "The French Jewish Community after World War II: The Struggle for Survival and Self-Definition." *Forum* 45 (1982): 45–54.

———. "The Reconstruction of the French Jewish Community after World War II." In *She'erit Hapletah, 1944–1948; Rehabilitation and Political Struggle. Proceedings of the Sixth Yad Vashem International Historical Conference, Jerusalem,*

1985, edited by Yisrael Gutman and Avital Saf, 168–186. Jerusalem: Yad Vashem, 1990.

———. *Recovering a Voice: West European Jewish Communities after the Holocaust*. Oxford, UK: Littman Library of Jewish Civilization, 2015.

Wenger, Beth S. *New York Jews and the Great Depression: Uncertain Promise*. New Haven, CT: Yale University Press, 1996.

Werner, Michaël, and Michel Espagne. "La construction d'une référence culturelle allemande en France: genèse et histoire (1750–1914)." *Annales. Histoire, sciences sociales* 42, no. 4 (1987): 969–992.

Werner, Michaël, and Bénédicte Zimmermann, eds. *De la comparaison à l'histoire croisée*. Paris: Seuil, 2004.

Wieviorka, Annette. *Déportation et génocide: entre la mémoire et l'oubli*. Paris: Plon, 1992.

———. "Les Juifs en France au lendemain de la guerre: état des lieux." *Archives juives, revue d'histoire des juifs de France* 28, no. 1 (1995): 4–22.

Wischnitzer, Mark. *Visas to Freedom, the History of HIAS*. Cleveland, OH: World, 1956.

Wolf, Joan B. *Harnessing the Holocaust: The Politics of Memory in France*. Stanford, CA: Stanford University Press, 2004.

Woocher, Jonathan. *Sacred Survival: The Civil Religion of American Jews*. Bloomington: Indiana University Press, 1986.

Wyman, David S. *The Abandonment of the Jews: America and the Holocaust, 1941–1945*. New York: Pantheon, 1984.

Zahra, Tara. *The Lost Children: Reconstructing Europe's Families after World War II*. Cambridge, MA: Harvard University Press, 2011.

Zeitoun, Sabine. *Histoire de l'OSE: de la Russie tsariste à l'Occupation en France, 1912–1944: l'Oeuvre de secours aux enfants, du légalisme à la résistance*. Paris: L'Harmattan, 2012.

Zelmanovits, L. *Origin and Development of the World Jewish Congress, A Historical Survey*. London: British Section of the World Jewish Congress, 1943.

Zertal, Idith. *From Catastrophe to Power: Holocaust Survivors and the Emergence of Israel*. Berkeley: University of California Press, 1998.

Zuccotti, Susan. *The Holocaust, the French, and the Jews*. New York: Harper Collins, 1993.

Zucker, Bat-Ami. *Cecilia Razovsky and the American-Jewish Women's Rescue Operations in the Second World War*. London: Valentine Mitchell, 2008.

Zunz, Olivier. *Philanthropy in America: A History*. Politics and Society in Twentieth-Century America. Princeton, NJ: Princeton University Press, 2012.

Zuroff, Efraim. "Rescue Priority and Fund Raising Issues During the Holocaust: A Case Study of the Relations between the Vaad Ha-Hatzala and the Joint, 1939–1941." *American Jewish History* LXVIII, no. 3 (1979): 305–326.

Zweig, Ronald W. *German Reparations and the Jewish World. A History of the Claims Conference*. Boulder, CO: Westview, 1987.

Zytnicki, Colette. "L'accueil des Juifs d'Afrique du Nord par les institutions communautaires (1961–1965)." *Archives juives, revue d'histoire des juifs de France* 31, no. 2 (1998): 95–109.

———. *Les Juifs à Toulouse entre 1945 et 1970. Une communauté toujours recommencée*. Toulouse, France: Presses universitaires du Mirail, 1998.

INDEX

Page numbers in *italics* refer to photographs and page numbers followed by *t* indicate tables.

Aberdam, Alfred, 73–74
Adler, Karen, 95–96
Algazi, Léon, 157
Alliance israélite universelle (Universal Israelite Alliance, AIU): Central European refugee crisis and, 24; Consultative Council of Jewish Organizations and, 155; creation of, 19; CRIF and, 148–150; founding of, 230n11; French reaction to, 155; membership of, 230n12; World War I reconstruction and, 23
Alsace-Lorraine region, 18, 30
American Federation of Labor, 102
American Friends Service Committee (Quakers), 30, 36
American Jewish chaplains/GIs: aid to children and, 54, 56–58, 73; assistance of Jews in France and, 48–53, 73, 215; gender and, 70–71, 74; ketubot (marriage contracts) and, 64; knowledge of the Holocaust and, 50; quality of interaction with Jewish survivors and, 41–42, 215; religious renewal in France and, 59–62, 64, 73; search for survivors and, 40–42; threat of court martial and, 53, 242n63;

Zionism and, 58, 73. *See also* Reims case study
American Jewish Committee (AJC): Alliance and, 153–155, 156, 161; American Jewish Relief Committee (AJRC) of, 20; *Ce Soir*'s Hervé series and, 170–171; communism and, 6–7, 156–157, 216; Consultative Council of Jewish Organizations and, 154–155; CRIF and, 153–154, 156, 158–161; definition of Judaism, 153; French diplomacy and, 160–162; ideology of, 154–155; JDC and, 154; Jews in the Ottoman Empire and, 19; North Africa and, 128, 160–161; operations in Paris and, 6–7, 154; Paris Peace Conference and, 153; political agenda and, 3, 144, 156–157, 176–177, 216, 280n79; political division and, 142; Poujadist movement and, 162; program in France, 99, 155–156; quest for a French Jewish defense group and, 157–160; Research Institute on Peace and Postwar Problems, 153; United Jewish Appeal (UJA) and, 152; Women's Division, 151; World Jewish Congress (WJC) and, 154; in World War II, 145, 153; Zionism and, 157

335

American Jewish Congress, 145–146, 215.
See also World Jewish Congress (WJC)
American Jewish Joint Distribution
Committee (JDC, Joint): aid to those
interred in Nazi camps in France from, 31;
American voluntary organizations and,
96–98; attacks in *Ce Soir* and, 169–173;
attempt to import American social
organizations, 5, 115, 138, 217; Belgium
and, 139; budget cuts and, 119–122, 177,
198, 215; bypassing of CRIF postwar,
79; Central European refugees crisis
and, 23–29, 25*t*, 38; *Ce Soir*'s Hervé series
and, 169–173; children and, 85, 103–105,
111; Claims Conference and, 13, 229n56;
closing of Marseille office, 32; COJASOR
and, 92–93, 215; Cold War and, 145–146;
communist employees and, 174–175;
competing welfare organization in
postwar France, 79, 103–105; coordination
of French Jews and, 11; COSOR and,
254nn75–76, 254n79; CRIF delegation
in New York and, 83–84; deportations
of French Jews to Nazi camps and, 32;
directly after liberation of France, 76–78,
110; distance between postwar American
and French leadership and, 112; Lolita
Eschborn and, 76; establishment of, 20;
exclusion of French Jewish Communists
from World War II funding and, 164;
formation of the UJA and, 22; French
Communist Party and, 163–169, 173–175;
French leadership during the war and,
78–79; French perception of, 6, 12–13,
38–39; French Resistance and, 6; French
state welfare organizations and, 94–96,
111; funding of occupied France through
Swiss organizations and, 36; funding
records of, 111, 112*t*, 215–216; Hebrew
Sheltering and Immigrant Aid Society
(HIAS) and, 107–109; interwar years
and, 21–22, 25*t*, 233n46; Jules Jefroykin
and, 33–34; "loan après" system, 34, 36;
Marshall Plan and, 97; matching funds
for FSJU 1951 campaign, 135; and meeting
with Rabbi Kaplan, 15; Nîmes Committee
and, 31; Personal Service Department, 135;
plans for World War II departure from
France, 30; Plessis-Trévis school and, 192,
194; political nature of aid and, 144, 175;
political neutrality and, 162–163; postwar
French Jewish welfare organizations
and, 85–86, 90–92; preparations to
return to Paris after the liberation,
84–87; return to Paris of, 76–77, 88–90,
110; role of in prewar France, 6; Social
Service Exchange, 110, 121, 135; social
work training and, 6, 184–185; Soviet
antisemitism and French press, 168, 174,
177; Soviet Union and, 163, 166–169;
staffing and, 88–89, 214; *St. Louis* refugees
and, 27–29, 38; transfer of department to
FSJU, 135–136; treatment of French Jewish
population, 78; treatment of German and
Austrian Jews, 78; UGIF funding and,
32, 235n82; under French leadership
(1942–1944), 80–84; United Jewish
Appeal (UJA) and, 98, 113, 115; US Trading
with the Enemy Act and, 29, 32; Vaad
Hatzala and, 99, 101–102, 152; view of
French social work and, 181–185, 210–211;
Edward Warburg and, 50; Workmen's
Circle and, 104; World Jewish Congress
(WJC) work and, 151–152, 278n50; World
War I and, 20–21; World War II support
of French and, 29–34, 37*t*; World War
I reconstruction and, 23. See also Paul
Baerwald School of Social Work
American Jewish Relief Committee (AJRC),
20
American Jewish welfare organizations:
Central European Jewish refugee crisis
and, 38; *Ce Soir*'s Hervé series and,
170–171; Cold War and, 12; diversity in, 20,
109–110, 142–143; French perception of,
12, 16; immediately after liberation, 214;
Meiss's criticisms of, 127–128; postwar
JDC and competing, 79, 98–100; role in
the reconstruction of French Jewish life
and, 10; social work and, 181–183; view
of French social work, 181–185.
See also *individual organizations*
American Jews: Damascus Affair (1840)
and, 19; effect of philanthropy in France
on, 220; financial contributions of, 2–3,
219; focus on France in postwar recovery

INDEX

work, 2–3, 5, 16, 219; ideological divisions of, 98–100, 219–220, 241n39, 256n100; interwar years, 21–22, 213; November 9–10, 1938 pogrom and, 22; philanthropic traditions of, 16, 19; political differences and, 143; postwar life of, 3–4; as privileged members of Jewish diaspora, 16–17, 37–38, 219; records of organizations of, 5; sense of identity and welfare work of, 12; *St. Louis* refugees and, 27–28; World War I and, 18–21. *See also* United Jewish Appeal (UJA); American Jewish chaplains/GIs
antisemitism, 6–7, 157, 163–169, 172
Appelbaum, S. (chaplain), 54
Aragon, Louis, 172
l'Arche, 136
Aronovici, Noel: return of the JDC to Paris, 84–86
Association of Jewish Social Workers, 199–200
Austria, 27, 78

Baerwald, Paul, 85
Beckelman, Moses, 137, 174
Beers, Dorothy, 199
Belgium, 2, 28, 117, 139, 206–207, 218
Bernstein, Blanche, 76, 179
Bernstein, James, 105–106
Bienstock, Victor, 47–48
Blaustein, Jacob, 153
Bloch, Franceline, 123, 184
Blumel, André, 83
Blum, Léon, 26
Bohnen, Eli, 51–52
Bonnet, Georges, 28
Bonnet, Henri, 161
Boudard, Françoise, 203
Brady, Leslie, 162
Brandenberger, David, 163
Braunschvig, Jules, 161
Brener, Maurice, 32, 35, 47, 49–50, 80, 87, 89, 93
Breslau, Isadore, 51, 53
Bulletin intérieur d'information, 157
Bundist Medem Library (Paris), 103

Cahn-Debré, Sylvain, 149–150
Canard enchaîné, 173

(CAR) Comité d'Assistance aux Réfugiés, 26, 31, 80, 92
Caron, Vicki, 24, 27
CBIP. *See* Committee for Israelite Charity of Paris (CBIP)
Center for Documentation and Vigilance, 157
Central Committee for Refugees (Comité central des réfugiés), 28
Central Committee for the Relief of Jewish Suffering through the War (CCR), 20
Central Consistory: after liberation, 46; Central European refugee crisis, 24; Conseil répresentatif des israélites de France (CRIF) and, 46, 147, 149; establishment of, 17–18; JDC financial backing promised during CRIF meetings and, 84; Meiss's handover of presidency and, 129; Orthodoxy and, 99, 258n117; Paris Israelite Center for Information (CII) and, 157; religious practice in France and, 60, 67
Ce Soir, 169–173
CGD (Comité général de défense des juifs), 46
Chanin, Nahum, 102
children: American Jewish chaplains/GIs and, 54, 56–58, 73; COSOR and, 254n79; Hebrew Sheltering and Immigrant Aid Society (HIAS) and, 106; JDC and, 85, 111; Jewish Labor Committee and, 103–104; National Council of Jewish Women and, 186, 187; Notre Dame de Sion order, 56, 243n67; political indoctrination and, 81–82; Program for the Protection of Jewish Children (OPEJ), 134, 192; religious future of, 56–57, 81; social work and, 192; Vaad Hatzala and, 101–102; World Jewish Congress (WJC) and, 151, 224n18. *See also* Children's Relief Agency (OSE)
Children's Relief Agency (OSE): aid for in last days of Paris occupation, 47, 80; Central European refugees and, 24; Hellenbrand and, 199; JDC budget threats and, 122; Nîmes Committee, 31; postwar aid and, 47, 58, 81; Vichy government and, 1; Vivette Samuel and, 183–184; Workmen's Circle children's homes, 103

Claims Conference. *See* Conference on Jewish Material Claims against Germany
Coen, Mara, 190–191, 194, 196–197
Cohen, Tito, 134–135, 138, 200–201
COJASOR. *See* Jewish Committee for Social Action and Reconstruction (COJASOR)
Cold War, 5, 12, 13, 143, 145–146, 197
Collomp, Catherine, 102
Comité d'accueil et d'aide aux victims de l'antisémitisme en Allemagne, 24
Comité d'Assistance aux Réfugiés (CAR), 26, 31, 80, 92
Comité d'union et de défense des juifs (CUDJ), 46
Comité général de défense des juifs (CGD), 46
Comité National français de secours aux réfugiés allemands victimes de l'antisémitisme (National Committee), 24–26
Commentary (American Jewish Committee), 156
Committee for Israelite Charity of Paris (CBIP), 183, 188, 199–204. *See also* Israelite Social Action Fund of Paris (CASIP)
Committee of Jewish Delegations (Paris Peace Conference), 144–145
Committee on Army-Navy Religious Activities (CANRA), 49
communism, 143, 156–157. *See also* French Communist Party
Conference on Jewish Material Claims against Germany, 13, 228–229n55–56; World Jewish Congress (WJC) and, 150–151
Conseil d'État (Council of State), 26
Conseil répresentatif des israélites de France (CRIF). *See* Representative Council of Israelites in France (CRIF)
Consultative Council of Jewish Organizations, 154
Cooperative Committee of Foreign Voluntary Societies, 96–97
COSOR. *See* Social Aid Committee for Resistance Organizations (COSOR)

Council of Jewish Federations and Welfare Funds, 22
Council of State (Conseil d'État), 26
CRIF. *See* Representative Council of Israelites in France (CRIF)
Cuba, 27
CUDJ (Comité d'union et de défense des juifs), 46

Daix, Pierre, 171–172
Damascus Affair (1840), 19
Dash Moore, Deborah, 50, 61, 238n2
David, Myriam, 203, 205–206, 298n118
de Gaulle, Charles, 44
Devaux, Père (Notre Dame de Sion order), 56–57
Diamant, David, 175
diaspora, about term, 16
diaspora nationalism, 146, 152, 215, 275n5
Dijour, Ilja, 105
Dillion, C. Douglas, 162
Displaced Persons Act of 1948, 107, 109
Doctor's Plot, 163, 166, 169, 172, 175, 177
Doron, Daniella, 9, 81, 96
Dreyfus Affair, 19
Dubinsky, David, 102
Dubrowitch, Joseph, 108

Ecole de service social de la région du Nord, 208
Economic Cooperation Act of 1948, 3, 97
Eichhorn, David Max, 54
Eisenhower, Dwight, 83
Ejnès, Solomon (Serge), 66, 74
Elazar, Daniel, 7
England, 28
Eschborn, Lolita, 76, 77
Essrig, Harry, 64
Evidences (American Jewish Committee), 155–157

Fasteau, Irving, 97, 205
Federal Republic of Germany, 13, 78, 158, 167, 220–221, 228–229n55–56
Federation of Jewish Societies of France (FSJF): COJASOR and, 92; emergence of, 23; FSJU and, 131–132; Jarblum and,

INDEX 339

36, 80; JDC and, 31, 47; Jefroykin and, 33; Judah Nadich and, 49; reach of, 81–82; World Jewish Congress and, 146, 149–150; Zionism and, 82
Fernand Halphen, Madame, 157
Finaly, Patricia, 186
Finaly orphans, 167
Fink, Ignace, 184
Fisher, Joseph, 83–84, 147
Fleg, Edmond, 157
Fogg, Shannon, 44
Fonds social juif unifié, *See also* Unified Jewish Social Fund (FSJU)
Forverts, 102, 104, 171
Fox, Hyman, 61–62, 63, 71
France: antisemitism and, 158, 174; Central European refugee crisis and, 18, 23–27; Council of American Voluntary Organizations, 96; Daladier government, 26–27; deportation of Jews in World War II and, 29; entry into World War II and, 29; French state welfare organizations, 94–96; High Commission for Refugees from Germany, 26; immigration and, 2, 106–107, 131; interest in reform of social work and, 205–206; JDC influence during interwar refugee crisis, 25; JDC role in World War II, 29–34; Jewish emigration from before and during war, 18; Jewish history in, 16–18; Jewish survival rate and, 2, 41, 223n5; literature on Jews and, 8–11, 225n33; Nazi invasion of, 30; Popular Front government, 26; postliberation material conditions of, 43–44, 212; postliberation political divides, 43–44; postwar changes in religiosity, 139, 220; postwar provisional government attitude toward Jews, 78; Poujadist movement in, 162; provisional government after liberation, 84–86; reaction to creation of Israel in, 130–131, 220; reception of the Marshall Plan in, 126; Slansky trial and Doctor's Plot in press of, 163–164, 167; state ambivalence toward Jews after the war, 95–96; state view of JDC, 96; status of Jews after liberation in, 44–46, 80–81, 114; *St. Louis* refugees and, 27–29; World War I period and, 22–23. *See also* General Union of Israelites in France (UGIF); Representative Council of Israelites in France (CRIF); Unified Jewish Social Fund (FSJU)
France-Atlantic Association, 203, 205
Frémontier, Jacques, 163, 167
French Communist Party, 126, 163–167. *See also Ce Soir*; *Naye presse* (UJRE); Union of Jews for Resistance and Mutual Aid (UJRE)
French Federation of Social Workers, 208
French Jewish organizations: Central European refugee crisis and, 24–27, 38; Cold War and, 12; effect of JDC's return to Paris and, 85–86, 90–92; immediately after liberation, 80–83, 91–92, 214; JDC budget cut shocks of 1947, 120–122; Paul Baerwald School of Social Work and, 199–200, 209; political division among, 82, 113–114, 121; political division and, 142–143; postwar expansionist tendencies of, 91–92; state of after liberation, 46. *See also individual organizations*
French Jews: American chaplains' religious intervention and, 13, 41, 59–62, 64; Central European Jewish refugee crisis and, 16, 38; children after liberation, 54, 56–58, 81; Claims Conference funding and, 13; decolonization and, 9; Holocaust and, 4, 9–10, 173, 195–196; in interwar period, 10, 213; JDC role in World War II, 29–34, 213; material needs of after liberation, 47–48; Occupation and, 6, 10–11, 15, 45–46; philanthropic traditions of, 15–17, 23, 37–38; political divisions and, 142–143; postwar provisional government and, 78; religious life directly after liberation and, 46, 220; status of immediately after liberation, 10–11, 44–46, 80–81, 95, 110; terminology for, 276n29; World War I reconstruction and, 23
French Ministry of Prisoners of War, Deportees and Refugees (MPDR), 94–95
Frydman, Vania, 208
FSJU. *See* Unified Jewish Social Fund (FSJU)

Gamzon, Robert, 123–124
Geissman, Raymond, 153, 170
gender: Charmion Stein and, 178–179; JDC leadership and, 87; Laura Margolis and, 134, 137–138; Paul Baerwald School of Social Work and, 194–195; US Armed forces Jewish chaplains/GIs and, 70–71, 74
General Defense Committee (CGD), 80, 92
General Union of Israelites in France (UGIF), 10, 30, 32, 36, 47, 80, 104, 235n82
German Empire, 18
Germany (Nazi), 22, 27. *See also* Holocaust; Nazis; Vichy government
Giniger, Henry, 190
Goldmann, Nahum, 80, 148–152
Goldman, Ralph, 3, 52–53
Goldsmidt, Rosy, 207
Goldsmith, Freda, 191–192, 199, 208
Goldstein, Lolita (Eschborn), 76, 77
Goldstein, Melvin, 76
Gottschalk, Max, 153
Grant, John, 205
Grass, Paul, 65, 69, 73
Greenleigh, Arthur: American voluntary organizations and, 96–97; COSOR and, 94; departure from France, 111–112; French Communist organizations and JDC under, 165; French Jewish welfare organizations and, 91, 110; response to French staffing issues and, 89; return to Paris of JDC and, 85, 88–90; work directly after war and, 252n57
Green, Nancy, 4
Grobman, Alex, 99

Hadassah, 52
Haganah, 58
Halphen, Georges, 157
Handwerger, Robert, 59
Harrari, Berthe, 65, 67–70, 73, 74
Haselkorn, Abraham, 52, 54, 56–59
Hazak, 124
Hazan, Katy, 9
Hazemann, Robert Henri, 206
Hebrew Sheltering and Immigrant Aid Society (HIAS, formerly HICEM), 6, 20, 31, 79, 105–109, 111, 144, 216

Heilbronner, Madame, 201
Helbronner, Jacques, 24, 26, 233n47
Held, Adolph, 174
Hellenbrand, Shirley, 178, 192, 196, 199–202, 296n89
Hervé, Pierre, 169–173
HICEM. *See* Hebrew Sheltering and Immigrant Aid Society (HIAS, formerly HICEM)
Hitler, 22, 23
Holland, 28
Holocaust, 4, 9–10, 50, 173, 195–196, 210, 296n89
Houri, Jacqueline, 191
l'Humanité, 164, 169, 172
Husson, Jacqueline, 74
Hyman, Irwin, 64

ICA. *See* Jewish Colonization Association (ICA)
immigration: American Jews and, 18, 20; Central European refugee crisis, 23–27; French Jews and, 18. *See also* deportation; Israel; refugees
Informations sociales, 208
Interagency Council to Aid Jewish Migrants and Transients (Conseil
Intergovernmental Committee on Refugees (IGCR), 85–86, 107
International Ladies' Garment Workers' Union, 173
International League against Antisemitsm (LICA), 159
interoeuvres d'aide aux immigrants et transitaires juifs), 121
In the Aftermath of Genocide (Mandel), 9
Israel: American Jewish postwar aid and, 3; *Ce Soir*'s Hervé series and, 170; creation of, 114, 130, 220; fundraising for in France, 131; Lishka operation in Soviet Union, 163; Paul Baerwald School of Social Work and, 190, 197, 210; Soviet position on, 166; Unified Jewish Social Fund (FSJU) and, 130–132
Israelite Social Action Fund of Paris (CASIP), 203. *See also* Committee for Israelite Charity of Paris (CBIP)

Jarblum, Marc: *Ce Soir* and, 170; CRIF and, 83, 146–149; FSJU and, 36, 80, 131; marriage to Margolis of, 136–137; on survival of French Jewish welfare organizations, 91; World Jewish Congress (WJC) and, 80, 146–148, 150; Zionism and, 58–59
JDC. *See* American Jewish Joint Distribution Committee (JDC, Joint)
Jefroykin, Israël, 26, 38
Jefroykin, Jules (Dika), 30, 32–34, 35, 38, 87, 89, 131, 164–165, 235n82
Jewish Agency for Palestine, 36–37, 58, 132, 147, 166
Jewish Army (Armée juive), 33, 36
Jewish Colonization Association (ICA), 26, 106, 232n43
Jewish Committee for Social Action and Reconstruction (COJASOR), 92–93, 120, 184, 199
Jewish Education Committee, 124
Jewish Labor Committee, 7, 79, 102–105, 111, 144, 171, 257n111
Jewish National Fund (KKL), 83
Jewish Scouts of France (EIF), 1, 47, 81, 91, 123–124, 188
Jewish Social Service Quarterly, 182
Jewish Welfare Board, 52, 54, 61
Joint. *See* American Jewish Joint Distribution Committee (JDC, Joint)
Jud Süss, 159

Kahn, Auren, 137
Kahn, Bernard, 23–26, 232n34, 234n58
Kahn, Gaston, 170
Kaplan, Jacob, 15, 38, 51, 83–84, 147
Karlikow, Abraham, 154, 161
Katzki, Herbert, 30–31
Kelman, Claude, 112, 131, 149, 212–213
Kiefe, Maître, 160
Kielce pogrom (1946), 100
Kishinev pogrom (1903), 19
Klein, Isaac, 40, 48, 62, 66–67, 68, 72, 74–75, 245n111
Klein, Philip, 188, 191, 194
Klein, Stephen, 101
Klüger, Ruth, 58–59
Kremsdorf, Edith Odenwald, 188, 203
Kristallnacht, 22, 27

Lambert, Raymond-Raoul, 26, 33
Lattès, Samy, 157
Lazarus, Fred, Jr., 158
Leavitt, Moses, 174
Left Poale Zion, 103
Le Pen, Jean-Marie, 162
Lerner, Hélène, 66, 70–73
Lerner, Louis, 66
Levin, Meyer, 56–57
Lichtman, Hélène (Hana), 53–54, 55
Lichtman, René, 53–54, 55, 242n64
Lipman, Eugene, 58
Lipman, Simone Weil, 188
Lishka operation, 163
Livazer, Hersh, 59, 67, 69, 72, 74
Loss, Adam, 203
Lowrie, Donald, 31
Lubove, Roy, 182
Lustman, François, 163–164

Mack, Julian, 146
Malamuth, Charles, 169
Mandel, Maud, 9, 115, 136, 139, 210, 217
Margolis, Laura: background of, 116–118, 182; change in JDC focus and, 112, 266n18; creation of Israel and, 131; departure from JDC of, 137; *Exodus 1947* and, 122–123; first FSJU campaigns and, 132–134; on French Jewish welfare organizations, 118; FSJU campaigns and, 132; FSJU leaders' objection to Rosen and, 134; goal of centralized fundraising organization in France, 124–125; goals for French Jewish welfare organizations, 118–119; importation of social welfare structures from United States and, 115; JDC career and, 117; marriage to Marc Jarblum, 136–137; Paul Baerwald School of Social Work and, 199; pictured, *119*; on reconstruction in France, 117; welfare organization reform and, 184
Marshall Plan, 5, 97, 126, 207, 214
Marx, Denyse, 66, 69–70, 70, 74
Marx family, 68–69, 69, 74
Marx, Georges, 66
Marx, Nicole, 66, 68–69
Massart, Jeanne, 206–207, 208
Mayer, René, 167

Mayer, Saly, 30, 33, 36
Meiss, Léon: American Jewish Committee (AJC) and, 154–155, 160–161; CRIF delegation to New York and, 83–84; CRIF's JDC Committee and, 121–122; FSJU and, 127–129, 138; Israel and, 130; on Laura Margolis, 138; War Emergency Conference and, 147; World Jewish Congress (WJC) and, 147–148, 150
Mering, Bertha, 102
"Message to Our Brothers from the United States, A" (*La presse nouvelle*), 7
Meyer, Libby, 192, 199
Miller, Carl, 64
Miller, Debby, 199
Miller, Meyer, 50–51
Moch, Maurice, 157
Morgenthau, Henry, Sr., 19–20
Mortara Affair (1858), 19, 230n10
Mossad le'Aliyah Bet, 58–59
Movement against Racism for Friendship among People (MRAP), 159
MPDR. *See* French Ministry of Prisoners of War, Deportees and Refugees (MPDR)
Munich Agreement, 27

Nadich, Judah, 49, 52, 56, 58, 60–61, 64
Naiditch, Isaac, 87
National Association of Social Workers (ANAS), 203–204, 207
National Commitee. *See* Comité National français de secours aux réfugiés allemands victimes de l'antisémitisme (National Committee)
National Conference for Jewish Charities, 182
National Coordinating Committee Fund, formation of the United Jewish Appeal for Refugee and Overseas Needs (UJA), 22
National Council of Jewish Women: Gaby Wolff Cohen and, 8; HIAS vs., 109; home for "unattached" Jewish women of, 7, 187; postwar aid and, 99; scholarship program of, 187; Ship-a-Box program of, 186, *187*, 293n51; social work education and, 181, 210, 217; UJA and, 123; welfare organization reform and, 186–188

National Jewish Welfare Board, 49
National Refugee Service, 88, 109
Naye presse (UJRE), 82, 126, 163–164, 167–168, 171–172, 175
Nazis: deportation of Jews and, 1–2, 29–30; expulsion of Jews from Alsace-Lorraine (1940), 30; French Jewish organizations and prewar antisemitism of, 24; General Union of Israelites in France (UGIF) and, 10, 30, 32, 36, 47, 80, 104, 235n82; historiography of Jews under, 9; internment camps in France and, 29, 31; JDC and, 31
Neikrug, Lewis, 109
Netherlands, 2
Neulander, Sylvia, 58
Nîmes Committee, 31, 97
Nochimowski, Françoise, 74
Notre Dame de Sion order, 56, 243n67
November 9–10 pogrom, 22, 27
Novick, Peter, 166

Odenwald Kremsdorf, Edith, 135–136
oral histories, 5, 228n53
Orloff, Chana, 51
Ottoman Empire, 19–20

Palestine, 58–59. *See also* Israel
Pâris de Bollardière, Constance, 102
Paris Israelite Center for Information (CII), 157
Paris Peace Conference (1919), 153
Paris Peace Conference (1946), 153
Paul Baerwald School of Social Work: Belgian social workers and, 206–207, 218; Château de la Maye, 190, *191*, 210; closure of residential program, 197, 208; Committee for Israelite Charity of Paris (CBIP) and, 200–204, 211; curriculum of, 189; establishment of, 115, 179, 188–189; European environment and, 189; faculty of, 191–192, 194, 211; French welfare agencies and, 199, 209, 217–218; graduates of, 196–198; Hellenbrand and, 178; Holocaust and, 195–196, 210, 296n89; in-service trainings and, 199–200, 208; international students and, 190–191,

194, 210, 217; Klein and, 188; legacy of, 198–199, 204–209; New York School of Philanthropy and, 192; pictured, *191, 193, 195*; in practice, 190–196, 210, 217; rationale for, 179–180, 210; request to admit non-Jewish student, 206–208; Unified Jewish Social Fund (Fonds social juif unifié, FSJU) and, 198–199
Philips, Israel Joel, 50–51
Pleven, R., 85, 251n35
Pougatch, Isaac, 192, 194
Program for the Protection of Jewish Children (OPEJ), 81, 134, 192, 199
Proskauer, Judge, 162, 283n120
Pulver, Jacques, 124

Quand même! (FSJF), 82
La quinzaine, 157

Rackovsky, Isaiah, 62, 64
Razovsky Davidson, Cecilia, 88–89, 95, 266n15
refugees: Central European, 18, 23–27; during interwar period in France, 10; internment of illegal under Daladier government, 27; JDC and postwar, 6; prewar Central European, 6, 25; *St. Louis* refugees, 27–29
Reims case study: American Armed Forces presence and, 65; French hospitality and, 67–70; gender and, 70–71, 74; German prisoners of war and, 73; Jewish families of, 65–66, 74–75; lasting ties and, 74; material inequality and, 69; negative side of American presence, 72–73, 75; oral interviews and, 239n11; synagogue as center of interaction and, 66–67
Representative Council of Israelites in France (CRIF): American Jewish Committee (AJC) and, 153–154, 215; *Ce Soir*'s Hervé series and, 172; delegation in New York and, 83–84, 220; diversity of Jewish communities in France and, 10, 113–114; formation of, 46; JDC Advisory Committee of, 122, 124, 128; JDC budget cuts and, 121–122; JDC bypassing of, 79, 215; legacy of, 218; Meiss and, 122, 124,

128; Paris Israelite Center for Information (CII) and, 157; World Jewish Congress (WJC) and, 146–150, 215
Representative Council of Traditional Judaism of France (Conseil représentatif du judaïsme traditionaliste de France, CRJTF), 99, 100
la Revue du FSJU, 136
Roberts, Mary Louise, 61
Rockefeller Foundation, 166, 205
Romania, 169
Rooby, George, 88
Rosenberg, Anna M., 58
Rosenberg, Ethel and Julius, 167
Rosenberg, James, 33
Rosen, Harry, 113, 125–127, 131–132, 134
Rothschild, Alain de, 203
Rothschild, Alix de, 130
Rothschild, Guy de, 83, 125, 129–130, 134, 136–138, 147, 157, 170
Rothschild Hospital nursing school, 115
Rothschild, Robert de, 24–25

Salomon, Georges-Michel, 184, 208, 211
Samuel, Julien, 129, 134, 138, 203
Samuel, Vivette, 183–184, 203–204, 211
Schah, Wladimir, 105–106
Schinzer, Henri, 44–45
Schmidt, Samuel, 100–101
Schoem, David, 69, 70, 72, 74
Schoem, Lillian, 69
Schrager, Fajwel, 102
Schulhofer, Edith, 192
Schwartz, Joseph: *Ce Soir* attacks and, 169; departure for UJA, 137; distance between postwar American and French leadership and, 112; formation of COJASOR and, 92; goal of centralized fundraising organization in France and, 125, 138; Harry Rosen and, 127; hiring of Lolita Eschborn and, 76; Jules Jefroykin and, 33; Laura Margolis and, 117, 124; postwar efforts and, 47; return of JDC to Paris after liberation and, 77, 85, 87; social work and, 181; timing of FSJU campaign and, 132; World Jewish Congress (WJC) and, 151–152; World War II and, 30, 32–33

Schwob, Odette, 201–203
Segev, Zohar, 146
Selver, Henry, 189, 192, 194, 200, 207–209
Le service social, 208
Shaltiel, David, 58–59
Shanok, Morton, 57
Shcherbakov, A. S., 163
Shuster, Zachariah, 154
Siebold, Janet, 192, 195, 199
Siekierski, Denise (Caraco), 71–72, 184
Simone (Jewish girl in Nancy), 71
Slansky, Rudolf, 163, 166, 177
Social Aid Committee for Resistance Organizations (COSOR), 94–95, 101–103, 111, 254n79, 254nn75–76
Social Service for Youth, 199
social work: American methods, 182–183, 209–211, 214; French methods, 209–211, 214–215; international approach to, 205; origins of French, 183–184, 210
Soria, Georges, 169
Soviet Union: antisemitism in, 163; Doctor's Plot and, 163; Israeli Lishka operation, 163; JDC in prewar, 6; JDC promotion of resettlement in, 21; political targeting of JDC and, 163–164; Slansky incident, 163
Stein, Charmion, 76, 178
Stein, Harry, 70, 74
Stein, Herman, 76, 178–180, 191
Stern, Juliette, 47
St. Louis crisis, 88, 116, 234n63
Sulzberger, David H., 86
Supreme Headquarters Allied Expeditionary Force (SHAEF), 65, 86, 97
Survey Graphic, 182
Synagogue Council of America, 99

La terre retrouvée (FSJF), 82, 249n19
Thro, Jeanne, 207
Trachtenberg (Jewish French resistance member), 54, 56–57
Travail social, 208
Troper, Morris: *St. Louis* refugees and, 28; World War II and, 30
Truman Directive (1945), 107
Truman Doctrine, 165
Truman, Harry S, 58–59

Unified Jewish Social Fund (FSJU): American methods and, 127, 138, 218–219; creation of, 125, 138, 268n54; first campaigns of, 132–135; French Communist groups and, 166; Israel and, 130–132; JDC's attempt to influence French welfare organizations and, 115; JDC support of, 127; Meiss's championing of, 127–129, 138; Paul Baerwald School of Social Work and, 200; Rothschild as president of, 129; success of, 135–136; understanding of JDC monies and, 133–134; unified Jewish community of France and, 140–141, 218
Union of Jewish Societies (Farband), 165
Union of Jewish Students of France, 172
Union of Jews for Resistance and Mutual Aid (UJRE), 82; Central Commission for Children of, 82, 165; *Ce Soir*'s Hervé series and, 171, 172; JDC funding and, 165–166; termination of JDC funding for, 174
Unitarian Service Committee, 31, 166
United Jewish Appeal (UJA), 8, 22, 79, 98, 102, 109, 119–120, 120t, 123–124, 214
United Nations, 150
United Nations Relief and Rehabilitation Administration (UNRRA), 77, 84–86, 107
United Palestine Appeal (UPA), 21–22
United Service for New Americans (USNA), 109
United States: break of diplomatic ties with Vichy government, 6, 29, 38, 234n69; Displaced Persons Act of 1948, 107, 109; expansionism and, 5, 13; Jewish history in, 16–18; Jewish immigration to, 18, 20; Marshall plan, 3; McCarthy Era, 166; shifting legal requirements for US aid to Nazi-occupied territories, 33–34, 36; *St. Louis* refugees and, 27–29; Truman Doctrine, 165; War Refugee Board, 36
Unzer stimme (*Our Voice*, Workmen's Circle), 82, 104, 164, 167, 173
Unzer wort (FSJF), 82, 147, 163, 167–168, 174, 249n19
US Armed Forces: aid to children and, 54, 56–58, 73; Catholic chaplains, 53; Civil Affairs staff, 47; Jewish chaplains and GIs and assistance to French Jews,

INDEX   345

49–53, 73; Jewish religious intervention of chaplains and, 59–62, 64, 73; negative side of presence in France, 53–54; numbers of Jewish chaplains in, 48; Office of the Theatre Chaplain, 49; oral history sources and, 42–43, 73; quality of interaction with Jewish survivors, 41–42, 73–74; role in the reconstruction of French Jewish life and, 10, 40–41; role of in postwar France, 8; search for Jewish survivors and, 5, 40; Supreme Headquarters Allied Expeditionary Force (SHAEF), 65

Vaad Hatzala, 7, 79, 99, 101–102, 111, 144, 152, 217
Vaad Hatzalah of the Jewish Agency, 36, 237n106
Vallat, Xavier, 167
Vanikoff, Maurice, 157–158
Vanishing Diaspora (Wasserstein), 9
Veil, Claude, 199
Vichy government: antisemitic legislation and, 29, 31, 46, 184; break of diplomatic ties with United States, 6, 29, 38, 234n69; deportation of Jews and, 1, 29, 32; General Commissariat for Jewish Affairs, 32; General Union of Israelites in France (UGIF) and, 10, 30, 32; internment camps in France and, 29; JDC and, 31; Nîmes Committee and, 31; *numerus clausus* of, 1; Vélodrome d'Hiver arrests and, 32
La vie juive, 152, 157
Vladeck, Baruch Charney, 102

Wagner, Gloria, 187
Warburg, Edward, 50, 85–86, 92
Warburg, Felix, 50
War Refugee Board, 36
Wasserstein, Bernard, 9, 226n39
Weill, Joseph, 36
Weill, Julien, 49, 51
Weiss, Louise, 26, 38
Weizmann, Chaim, 130
Werner, Michael, 11
Wieviorka, Annette, 45, 47, 94–95

Wise, Louise Waterman, 151
Wise, Stephen, 145, 148
Wolff Cohen, Gaby, 1–2, 8, 123, 128, 135–136, 184, 188, 203
Wolfsohn, Joel, 154, 160–161
Workmen's Circle (Arbeter Ring/Cercle Amical), 82, 102–103
World Jewish Congress (WJC): Alliance israélite universelle (Universal Israelite Alliance, AIU) and, 148; and, 83, 215; children and, 151, 224n18; Claims Conference, 150–151; diaspora nationalism and, 146, 152, 215, 275n5; French aid during World War II and, 36–37; Jarblum and, 80; JDC and, 151–152, 278n50; JDC funds for occupied France and, 36; political agenda of, 144, 176–177, 215; postwar aid and, 99; in postwar France, 146–152; reestablishment of in France, 149; relationship with United States and, 7; roots of, 144–146; United Nations and, 150; War Emergency Conference, 147; in World War II, 145–146; Zionism and, 146, 152, 215
World Union for Progressive Judaism, 99

Young Men's Christian Association (YMCA), 3, 31
Youth Aliyah, 103

Zhdanov, A. A., 163
Ziegellaub, Fred, 192, 199, 207–208
Zimmermann, Bénédicte, 11
Zionism: American immigration patterns and, 98; American Jewish chaplains and GIs and, 58–60; American Jewish Committee (AJC) and, 157; American Jews and, 19, 38, 220; interwar years in America and, 21; Jules (Dika) Jefroykin and, 33; Jewish Labor Committee and, 103; Laura Margolis and, 131; political divisions welfare organizations and, 142–143; World Jewish Congress (WJC) and, 146, 148
Zionist Youth Movement, 33–34, 49
Zytnicki, Colette, 139

LAURA HOBSON FAURE is Professor at the University Paris 1 Panthéon-Sorbonne, where she holds the chair of modern Jewish history and is a member of the Centre d'histoire sociale des mondes contemporains (UMR 8058). She is coeditor of *L'Oeuvre de secours aux enfants et les populations juives au XX^{éme} siècle. Prévenir et guérir dans un siècle de violence* (Armand Colin, 2014) and *Enfants 'sans famille' dans les guerres du 20^{éme} siècle* (CNRS Éditions).

www.ingramcontent.com/pod-product-compliance
Lightning Source LLC
Chambersburg PA
CBHW020635230426
43665CB00008B/181